FOR REFERENCE

Do Not Take From This Room

Encyclopedia of American Women in Business

Encyclopedia of American Women in Business

From Colonial Times to the Present

Volume II
M–Z

CAROL H. KRISMANN

Greenwood Press
Westport, Connecticut • London

Library of Congress Cataloging-in-Publication Data

Krismann, Carol
    Encyclopedia of American women in business : from colonial times to the present /
Carol H. Krismann.
        p. cm.
    Includes bibliographical references and index.
    ISBN 0–313–32757–2 (set)—ISBN 0–313–33383–1 (vol. I : alk. paper)—ISBN
0–313–33384–X (vol. II : alk. paper)
    1. Businesswomen—United States—History—Encyclopedias. 2. Businesswomen—
United States—Biography—Dictionaries. 3. Women executives—United States—
History—Encyclopedias. 4. Women executives—United States—Biography—Dictionaries.
    5. Entrepreneurship—United States—History—Encyclopedias. I. Title.
HD6054.4.U6K753 2005 *v.3 Index*
338.092'2–dc22   2004056065

British Library Cataloguing in Publication Data is available.

Library of Congress Catalog Card Number: 2004056065
ISBN: 0–313–32757–2 (Set)
        0–313–33383–1 (Vol. I)
        0–313–33384–X (Vol. II)

First published in 2005

Greenwood Press, 88 Post Road West, Westport, CT 06881
An imprint of Greenwood Publishing Group, Inc.
www.greenwood.com

Printed in the United States of America

∞™

The paper used in this book complies with the
Permanent Paper Standard issued by the National
Information Standards Organization (Z39.48–1984).

10 9 8 7 6 5 4 3 2 1

This book is dedicated with love to my husband, Jerry Keenan: my mentor, my inspiration, my best friend and kindred spirit

Contents

M

Macaskill, Bridget (1948–), Investments Executive

Before she resigned from her positions as chairman, president, and CEO of Oppenheimer Funds in September 2001, Bridget Macaskill was the highest ranking woman in the mutual funds industry. She was on *Fortune's* list of the most powerful women in American business in 1998 and 1999.

Macaskill was born in London, England, to a British career army officer, one of five children. They were brought up to be disciplined and organized. She credits her father for teaching her his values and her mother for showing, by her own example, the importance of consensus building. Macaskill graduated from Edinburgh University in Scotland in 1970. Her first job was as personal assistant to the marketing director of a major British food company, St. Ives Ltd. When she eventually became director of marketing at St. Ives, she was told she would have to wait six months to sit on the board of directors, although the previous, male director had not had to do so. When she questioned the wait, she was told she could attend board meetings as an invited guest for the six-month period. She waited it out and then called their bluff. Her approach—then and now—has been to look for ways around obstacles. Her biggest accomplishment at St. Ives was to introduce fresh-chilled orange juice delivery with daily milk delivery.

In 1981 her banker husband was transferred to New York City. Macaskill and the couple's two sons accompanied him there, and she joined Oppenheimer in its marketing department. Although she knew nothing about finance, she learned quickly and then searched for a niche for herself. That niche was selling to women, an overlooked market segment at that time. She published a study on women and money in 1992, making Oppenheimer a pioneer in the mutual funds industry. The previous year she had become president and COO of the company. By 1993 its assets were worth $22 billion. In 1995 she was named president and CEO, keeping the COO responsibilities as well. Her goal was to reach $100 billion in five years; Oppenheimer reached it in 1999. In 2001 Macaskill was named chairman and CEO. She resigned that September.

She manages through teamwork and feels that people work best in an atmosphere that is friendly and pleasant. Macaskill believes that women are particularly well suited to teamwork because they are less likely than men to be influenced by work politics or worry about being given credit for their contribution. She has a reputation for being personable, with a high energy level. She is an advocate for women's issues, particularly education for women regarding finance and economics. Her family has always been a top priority.

Macaskill has been on the boards of the National Association of Securities Dealers and Prudential PLC. As of January 2002 she sat on the board of J. Sainsbury PLC as a non-executive director. She was named a powerful corporate officer by *Vanity Fair* and one of the Hot 100 by *Success*.

See also: Finance Industry

Further Reading
Alexander, Garth. "The Cream of Wall Street."
"Mother Oils Wheels." In Ellie Wymard, p. 190–192.

Mackenzie, Nanci (1940–), Energy Executive

Nanci Mackenzie was a co-owner and, later, the sole owner, of U.S. Gas Transportation in Dallas until 2000. She was one of its founders and has continued as a company president since the sale. The company was on *Working Woman*'s list of top woman-owned companies from 1995 through 2001.

Mackenzie was raised in Texarkana, Arkansas, where her mother ran a movie theater. Her first business experience was selling tickets and popcorn at the theater when she was five. She earned her BA from Southern State Teachers College. She has been married, had five children, and is divorced. In 1973 she began working in sales for a fuel-oil broker in Dallas, Texas, and sold gasoline and diesel fuel for another company on the side. When her employer needed cash, she gave him $25,000 in exchange for half the business.

In 1975 Mackenzie started Lucky Lady Oil with a partner, Sue Palmer. She sold her share of the company in 1982 after her son Jason was killed in an automobile accident. For two years she worked at several jobs in Colorado. In 1984 she moved back to Dallas and became an independent oil and gas investment agent. Three years later, she founded U.S. Gas Transportation with two partners. The company filled orders from large natural gas customers by finding available gas and arranging to transport it, serving as a link between natural gas wells and utility companies. She bought out her partners in 1991, when annual revenues were $35 million. By 2000, when she sold the company to Aquila Energy Corporation, revenues were $360 million. She stayed on as president of the Dallas office.

Mackenzie succeeded in her business by emphasizing customer service. She guaranteed short turnaround times and round-the-clock attention to client needs.

She has belonged to the Committee of 200 and was a Southwest Area winner of the Texas Entrepreneur of the Year award in 1997 and a finalist for the state title. In 1998 *Success* named her to its Hot 100. The following year she received an honorable mention for the first Working Woman Entrepreneurial Excellence Award.

See also: Energy Industry

Further Reading

MacKenzie, Len, and Nanci MacKenzie. "The Real Fuel in the Gas Industry."

Schmuckler, Eric. "Cookin' with Gas: Nanci Mackenzie."

Suggs, Welch. "Gas Trader Fits Service to Customers' Needs."

Magazine Publishing, *see* Publishing Industry

Magerko, Maggie (1966–), Building Supplies Executive

Maggie Magerko is president and chief operating officer of 84 Lumber, the company her father founded in 1956. Since she became president in 1994, the company has been on the *Working Woman* list of top woman-owned companies in the United States eight times.

The fourth of five children, Magerko is the closest to her father in spirit and the child he chose to run the company. While he remains chairman and CEO, she is in charge of day-to-day management. When she was five, her father began taking her along to work with him, and a photo in her office shows them together; she is holding a shovel. Magerko spent two years at West Virginia University before dropping out in 1987 to work for the company. Her first assignment was to turn their ramshackle lodge into a first-class resort.

In June 1994 at age twenty-seven, she became president. As CEO her father scouts sites for new stores; she manages the company. Magerko has brought a new, service-based approach to the company's customers and has offered her employees more flexible work schedules and salary increases tied to sales goals. Her focus is on contractors as well as do-it-yourselfers; the contractor business now accounts for 70 percent of revenues. The company stopped selling wood from endangered forests in 2000. By March 2002, 434 stores in thirty-four states were employing 55,000 sales consultants. That December 84 Lumber's sales broke the $2 billion mark for the first time in its history.

Magerko has a reputation for being as tough as her father, with a brash personality and salty language. She has softened the once-harsh working conditions at the company, however, and has widened the customer focus to compete with Home Depot. She describes her leadership philosophy as "a combination of things: firm goals and objectives, a shared vision, and a work environment where associates feel a vested interest in the company's success" (Aeppel, "Nail-Tough Daughter Mirrors Dad").

Magerko has been on the *Forbes* list of the 400 richest Americans for several years and was dubbed one of the Hot 100 by *Success* in May 1998. The company donates building materials to Habitat for Humanity.

See also: Retailing Industry

Further Reading

Aeppel, Timothy. "Nail-Tough Daughter Mirrors Dad; She Runs 84 Lumber with an Iron Touch."

Moreno, Katarzyna. "Underestimated."

Sharp-Zickerman, Nancy. "Billion-Dollar Club," p. 55.

Magner, Marjorie (1949–), Banker

Marge Magner is chief operating officer of Citigroup's Consumer Global Group, one of the world's most profitable consumer businesses. *Fortune* ranked her number 38 in its 2000 list of the most powerful women in American business. By 2003, because of her clout at Citigroup, she was number 5. She is also a member of Citigroup's executive management team.

With an education in psychology, Magner joined Primerica as an executive vice president in 1987, before it merged with Citibank. After the merger, she became president and chief administrative officer of commercial credit in 1993. In 1999 she was named head of Citigroup's Consumer Global Risk Management Group and a member of the Global Planning Group. That December, she became senior vice president and chief administrative officer of Primerica Financial Services and Citibanking, North America. She was Citigroup's highest-ranking woman, responsible for more than $1 billion in sales. Her goal was to build Citigroup into a strong consumer brand, reaching out to low- and middle-income consumers. By 2001 sales had grown to $6 billion. In 2002 she was promoted to chief operating officer.

Magner has a reputation for strong people skills and good judgment. She believes strongly that banks need to be a part of their communities, and for that reason, she hosts Women's Health Issues Luncheon symposiums. She accepted, on behalf of Citigroup, the Helen Keller Achievement Award in Accessibility from the American Foundation for the Blind. The award recognized Citibank's talking ATMs, the first of their type in New York City.

See also: Banking

Further Reading

"Citigroup Names Marge Magner to Oversee Primerica Financial Services and Citi-banking, North America."

Sanger, Elizabeth, Tania Padgett, and James Bernstein. "Long Island Inc."

Mail Order Industry, *see* Saleswomen

Malone, Annie Turnbo (1869–1957), Hair Care Products Manufacturer

Annie Malone vies with Madame C. J. (Sarah) Walker for being the first to manufacture hair care products for African American women. Although Sarah Walker is better known, she was one of Malone's saleswomen; also, Malone's company did not survive the test of rapid expansion and other problems while Walker's company did.

Malone was born in 1869 in Metropolis, Illinois, the tenth of eleven children. Her father was a farmer; family legend says that he fought in the Civil War on the Union side. Since both her parents died when she was very young, she was brought up by her older sisters. She went to high school, but only sporadically because of illnesses. She did manage to take chemistry.

During that time she invented her first hair care product to enhance the sheen and texture of hair. She had always been fascinated by the way her sisters did their hair. At the time African American women were using goose fat, other oils, or strong chemical products that damaged hair rather than enhancing it. While Malone's formula used chemicals, it straightened but did not destroy the hair. She called it "Wonderful Hair Grower" and began to sell it door-to-door.

By 1902 the business was growing. Malone moved to Saint Louis, hired three assistants, and continued selling door-to-door. She gave free hair and scalp treatments to potential customers. She married, briefly, in 1903 but divorced when her husband wanted too much say in running the business. In 1904 the World's Fair came to Saint Louis, and she sold so many products there that she decided to advertise after it closed. She put ads in the African American press and toured the southern states talking about her hair care products while recruiting women for sales and as administrators. Walker was one of her Saint Louis sales agents. Malone trained these women to operate salons that also sold her products. In 1906 she copyrighted the trade name Poro for all of her products, which by now included a pressing iron and comb, hair growers, tetter reliefs, and special hair oils. She said copyrighting her trade name was important because there were too many "counterfeit" products on the market. (*Poro* is a West African term for an organization whose aim is to discipline and enhance the body physically and spiritually). Her business was now successful nationally.

In 1914 she married Aaron Malone, a former teacher and traveling Bible salesman. She later made him chief managing officer, a decision she would have cause to regret. Four years later she built a five-story factory and beauty training school in the heart of Saint Louis's upper-middle-class African American neighborhood. She named it Poro College and intended it for use by the community. It was, in fact, like a campus, with an auditorium, a cafeteria, a roof garden, an ice cream parlor, a bakery, classrooms, and, of course, the factory. By this time she employed 175 people directly. In addition, Poro franchise salons in the United States, South America, Africa, and the Philippines employed 75,000 saleswomen. The college was also used for religious, fraternal, civic, and social functions, and the National Negro Business League was headquartered there.

By 1927 Malone's income tax was reported at $40,000, the highest in the state. She lived modestly but gave away thousands of dollars to a variety of causes including the support of two students at every African American land-grant college in the United States. She also gave to the African American YMCA and Howard Medical School. She not only bought a site for the Saint Louis Colored Orphans' Home, but also paid its construction costs.

In 1927 Malone's husband filed for divorce. He demanded half of the business because he claimed to have helped build it through his contacts. He was very active socially and politically, and the case divided the community. With the help of prominent people including Mary McLeod Bethune, she won the settlement and agreed to pay him $200,000. She remained bitter, however, and in 1930 moved to Chicago, where she bought an entire city block. The business never really recovered, though, due to lawsuits by a disgruntled employee and the federal government, the latter for failure to pay required excise taxes. These depredations forced her to sell the Saint Louis property. When she died in 1957, she was worth only $100,000, very little in comparison to her worth in 1927.

Malone was an astute businesswoman, particularly at marketing, and she had a feel for popular culture. However, she trusted unworthy managers, failed to be aware of tax matters, and indulged her overly generous nature.

See also: African American Businesswomen; Beauty Industry; Walker, Sarah Breedlove (Madame C.J.)

Further Reading

Collier-Thomas, Bettye. "Annie Turnbo-Malone." In Jessie Smith, *Epic Lives*, p. 363–367.

Mongold, Jeanne Conway. "Turnbo-Malone, Annie Minerva." In Barbara Sicherman and Carol Hurd Green, p. 700–702.

Porter, Gladys. *Three Negro Pioneers in Beauty Culture.*

Management

"Management is a process that is used to accomplish organizational goals" (Luft, in Kaliski, p. 553). Managers have four key functions: planning, organizing, directing, and controlling. These functions are applied on every level of an organization. A variety of skills are necessary in a good manager, including good communication skills, personnel relationship skills, technological and technical savvy, and time-management skills.

Management theory emerged during the Industrial Revolution of the 1850s, beginning with the ideas of Adam Smith, Robert Owen, and Charles Babbage. Frederick Taylor, an engineer, introduced scientific management, which was later refined by Frank Gilbreth and Lillian Gilbreth. In the late 1800s, behavioral management was introduced, focusing on the concerns of workers. More comprehensive studies of the managerial process, called the "management process school of thought," were developed by Henri Fayol and James D. Mooney. Contemporary management process thought includes socio-technical systems and contingency theories. Management is all encompassing in an organization; it is more comprehensive than leadership, although most successful managers are also successful leaders.

Management, particularly women in management, has been subjected to many scholarly research studies since women began to assume significant management positions beginning in the 1970s. Early researchers usually took one of two positions: (1) men and women manage differently, and (2) men and women are similar to each other in management styles and business behavior. The first position hypothesizes that women adopt participative management styles and are more socially oriented, equality-based, and nurturing than men. This view also supposes that male managers tend to manage from the top down, in either an autocratic or paternalistic manner. Other gender stereotypes are also studied in this research.

The second position holds that both men and women use situational management and that their styles change depending on the situation and have little to do with gender. Later studies focus on the idea that managers tend to blend both so-called feminine and masculine management styles. These studies point out that women in top management use both nurturing and employee participation while focusing on high achievement and risk taking. Researchers continue to be fascinated by this topic.

Women in Management (WIM; www.wimonline.org) is an organization that provides a support network for women managers to exchange experiences and ideas. It also sponsors workshops and seminars.

See also: Leadership

Further Reading

Buttner, E. Holly. "Examining Female Entrepreneurs' Management Style: An Application of a Relational Frame."

Lee, Chris. "The Feminization of Management."

Luft, Roger L. "Management" and "Management: Historical Perspectives." In Kaliski, p. 553–557, 560–564.

Wajcman, Judy. *Managing Like a Man: Women and Men in Corporate Management.*

Manuel, Patti, *see* Hart, Patti S.

Manufacturing

Manufacturing, traditionally a male-dominated business, is one of the fastest-growing industries for woman-owned companies. This growth began in 1991, along with an increase in the number of women studying engineering, technology, and business.

Historically, women have been in the manufacturing workforce since before the Industrial Revolution of the 1850s. American women held low-wage jobs in the Massachusetts textile mills after 1809. In 1833, 51.5 percent of mill workers were women. As manufacturing grew into a large industry just prior to the Civil War and, particularly, once the war began, women became more prevalent in it. Most immigrants, both men and women, began their life in the United States working in manufacturing plants.

Although there were many women workers, this did not translate into management positions, except for a very few. That too has changed even though manufacturing has one of the lowest proportions of women in management. In 1990, 26 percent of all executive and administrative jobs were held by women; nine years later, that figure had risen to 33 percent. In the 1990s and early 2000s, manufacturing underwent a change, particularly in the need for computer scientists, engineers, and design professionals. People with vision who are good at multitasking and communicating are also needed. A knowledgeable and skilled woman is the equal of a man in these kinds of jobs. Physical strength is no longer a requirement.

Women owners of manufacturing firms have problems with financing and with obtaining contracts for bids. Heavy machinery can be prohibitively expensive. It is still difficult for women in manufacturing to find role models, but many of them say male mentors can be valuable. The number of woman-owned manufacturing firms is climbing.

See also: Rosie the Riveter

Further Reading
Caudron, Shari. "The Concrete Ceiling."
"Women Move Up in Manufacturing: Forget Those Images of U.S. Factories as Male-Dominated and Meet Some Unsung Women behind a Lot of the Surging Productivity."

Mark, Rebecca (1954–), Petroleum Executive

Rebecca Mark was chair and CEO of Enron International until August 2000, when she was asked to resign. In 1998 she was number 14 on *Fortune*'s list of the most powerful women in American business and in 1999, number 29. Once known as the "empress of energy," with projects all over the world, she now lives on fifteen acres in New Mexico with her new husband and twin sons by her previous marriage.

Raised on a farm in Missouri, Mark had her own livestock, was required to do chores from the age of eight, and belonged to 4-H and Future Farmers of America. She attended William Jewell College in Liberty, Missouri, for two years and graduated from Baylor University with a BA in psychology in 1976. She went on to earn an MA in international management with a concentration in finance from Baylor in 1977.

After graduation Mark entered the training program at First City National Bank in Houston, Texas. She became a commercial lending officer specializing in funding riskier projects. In 1982 she joined Continental Resources, a natural gas company, as treasurer. Four years later, Enron Power Corporation, a subsidiary of Enron Corporation, absorbed Houston Natural Gas, which had by then absorbed Continental Resources. Mark helped develop the company's first cogeneration project in Texas City and became part of Enron's executive management team. She gave birth to twin boys in 1985 and in 1987 took time off from the company to go to Harvard Business School for an MBA. She worked on Enron assignments while she was there and became known for her extraordinary ambition and energy, earning the nickname "Mark the Shark." She graduated in 1990 with distinction.

In 1991 she returned to Enron as CFO and continued on the executive management team. She became involved in emerging markets and persuaded CEO Kenneth Lay to establish a new subsidiary, Enron Development Corporation. Mark was its chairman and CEO. Concentrating on finding and developing new international marketing, she was initially successful; securing contracts to build power plants in Central America, South America, and Asia. In 1998 she became the vice chair of Enron Corporation while remaining head of Enron Development Corporation. Also in 1998 she made herself head of a subsidiary water business, Azurix. In March 1999 Azurix went public; however, there were many problems with contract fulfillment and Enron executives believed that she spent too much money on her projects. In August 2000 she resigned. The company went on to become a part of one of the biggest Wall Street scandals of the time, and later went bankrupt amid myriad lawsuits. Mark was named in some of the lawsuits, but charges against her of insider trading and stock fraud were dropped.

Mark is a tough, self-confident woman. She has worked with governments worldwide and is known as a hard negotiator. Her management style is based on setting goals and accomplishing them. She calls herself pushy and aggressive but has also taught herself to charm. During her time at Enron she traveled as much as nine months per year. Her sons accompanied her on some trips. Since she left Enron, she has served on the advisory boards of the business schools at both Yale and Harvard.

See also: Energy Industry

Further Reading

Forest, Stephanie Anderson. "Paddling as Fast as She Can."

Mack, Toni. "High Finance with a Touch of Theater."

"Mark, Rebecca." In *Current Biography*, May 1999, p. 30–32.

Swartz, Mimi, with Sherron Watkins. *Power Failure: The Inside Story of the Collapse of Enron.*

Marram, Ellen R. (1947–), Beverage Executive

In 1998 Ellen Marram was ranked number 50 on *Fortune*'s list of the most powerful women in American business. At that time she was president of the Seagram Beverage Group and an executive vice president of Seagram Company. She was the first woman to become president of a billion-dollar corporate division.

Marram grew up in Boston, the elder of two sisters. Her father was a retired postal worker who owned a suburban hat store; her mother was a stay-at-home mom and former social worker. Marram and her father were very close, and she credits him with teaching her that there are many sides to every issue, as well as many solutions. She graduated from Wellesley College with a degree in economics in 1968. She went on to Harvard Business School for her MBA, where she was one of three women in a class of one hundred. She is married with two grown stepchildren.

Her first job was as a library clerk in high school. After earning her MBA Marram went to work at Lever Brothers as a marketing assistant. In 1972 she moved to Johnson & Johnson as a group product manager and then, in 1977, she joined Standard Brands, also as a group product manager. In 1987 RJR Nabisco bought Standard Brands, and Marram became vice president of its Grocery Products Division. She began several successful new product lines and improved market share for mature products, focusing on health issues. She was promoted to president of the Seagram Beverage Group, a Nabisco subsidiary, and executive vice president of the Seagram Company in 1993 and was also a member of the office of the president of the Seagram Company. She was responsible for expanding nonalcoholic beverages and low-alcohol brands. Again, her focus was on health and food. Tropicana sales grew by 10 percent while she was in charge.

In August 1998 Seagram sold Tropicana to Pepsico and Marram decided to look for another job. The following year, she became president and CEO of efdex, a business-to-business electronic food and drink online trading exchange. She led the business through its market launch then left the company nine months later. It failed in September 2000, as many small Internet-based companies were doing at the time. Marram then became a general partner at

North Castle Partners LLC, a private equity company focused on investing in the healthy living and aging sectors. Her responsibility has been to analyze companies once they've been acquired, particularly beverage companies. In February 2002, she became a managing director.

Marram is known as a hard worker with the ability to focus and never get sidetracked. She is a persistent innovator with an intuitive grasp of consumer vagaries. She firmly believes that a team effort is what brings success to an endeavor and doesn't think that being a woman has either helped or hindered her career. In 1973 she persuaded the Harvard Club of New York City to accept women as members.

Marram sits on the boards of the Ford Motor Company, the New York Times and its audit committee, Eli Lilly, New York Presbyterian Hospital, Lincoln Center Theater, and the Conference Board. She is also on the board of associates of the Harvard Business School. In 1991 she was number 8 on *Working Woman*'s list of best-paid women, and in 1996 *Fortune* named her as one of ten women who were CEO material. *Business Week* has listed her as one of the fifty top women in business, a likely CEO, one of the best managers, and an executive to watch. Other lists to which she has been named include the AFL-CIO's top ten directors and *Working Woman*'s next CEOs.

See also: Food Industry

Further Reading
Brady, Diane. "From Nabisco to Tropicana to . . . efdex?"
Gray, P. B. "Juiced Up."
Green, Leslie. "NorthCastle Ropes in New Partner."

Martinez, Maria Montoya (1881–1980), Potter

"Maria Martinez turned the traditional art of Native American pottery into a profitable enterprise" (Drachman, *Enterprising Women*, p. 111). Maria Montoya Martinez was the mother of the black-on-black pottery industry at the San Ildefonso Pueblo in New Mexico. Her business has thrived for more than seventy years. She and her husband, Julian, who died in 1943, are credited with leading a rebirth of artistic pottery as a profitable American Indian business.

Maria Montoya was born in San Ildefonso Pueblo in 1881 and made her first pottery at age seven under the guidance of her aunt, a respected potter. She went to the pueblo's government school and then to Saint Catherine's Indian School in Santa Fe. She married Julian Martinez in 1904. They spent their honeymoon at the Saint Louis World's Fair demonstrating pueblo pottery-making and dancing.

In 1907 archeologist Dr. Edgar Hewitt, found some pieces of black Tewa pottery while excavating an ancient pueblo and wanted to find a potter to recreate the designs. Martinez was recommended to him, and by 1915 she had developed the contemporary black-on-black San Ildefonso pottery. Julian kept a notebook of historical designs and decorative drawings. In 1923 Maria began signing her pots and had taught others in the pueblo. The Rockefellers and several museums were early purchasers, and public demand grew.

Maria and Julian had four children. After Julian died, their son, Popovi Da, became her partner. Following Maria's death, the family carried on the tradition. There have been five generations of potters in the family.

In 1934 Martinez was the first American Indian woman to win the Indian Achievement Award from the Indian Council Fire. That year, she exhibited at the Chicago World's Fair. In 1954 she won the Craftsmanship Medal, the highest national honor for craftsmanship in the United States, and was awarded the Palmes Académique by France for her outstanding contribution to arts and crafts. She was also awarded two honorary doctorates. At a 1979 Smithsonian exhibition of her pottery, items were sold for prices ranging from $1,500 to $15,000. Maria Martinez died in 1980. She was not only a famous potter but was also responsible for transforming the San Ildefonso Pueblo from a poor farming community into an American Indian arts and crafts center.

See also: American Indian Businesswomen

Further Reading
"Maria Martinez (1881–1980)." In Jeanette M. Oppedisano, p. 165–167.
Marriott, Alice. *Maria, the Potter of San Ildefonso.*
Peterson, Susan. *The Living Tradition of Maria Martinez.*
Spivey, Richard L. *Maria.*

Mason, Biddy (1818–1891), Real Estate Investor

Biddy Mason was the first African American woman to own real estate in Los Angeles. Her property was on the outskirts of the city when she bought it, in an area that would eventually be in the heart of the city's commercial section.

Mason was born a slave in Georgia. She was sold to Robert Smith and his wife when she was a child. She had three daughters, probably Smith's. In 1847 Smith converted to Mormonism and eventually decided to move his family to Utah. Mason organized the move, of fifty-six white people, thirty-four slaves, two yoke of oxen, seven milk cows, eight mules, and a caravan of 300 wagons. She was responsible for getting everything and everybody to the West, a journey of 2,000 miles. She was thirty-two years old. Not only was Utah hostile territory to African Americans because of a Mormon belief that the African American race was inferior, but Smith did not find what he was looking for either. So once again the family moved, this time to San Bernardino, a new Mormon colony in California.

The date was 1851, and California had become a free state the previous year. By law, a person could keep his slaves if he was in transit but not if he was settling in California. When Smith realized the law's implications, he planned to move to Texas. Mason, with the aid of Charles Owens, a young man who had fallen in love with her eldest daughter, Ellen, tried to stay in California as a free person. Owens's father, an important African American businessman in Los Angeles, informed the sheriff of Smith's plans. The sheriff issued a writ of habeas corpus, and Mason went to court to obtain her freedom. Smith did not appear in court, and the judge ruled not only for Mason but also for her entire family, including her daughters and a grandson. This was a landmark case because it was the first time a judge had ruled that slavery could not exist in California.

The family was free. Charles and Ellen were married, and Biddy Mason and the rest of the family went to live temporarily with the elder Owens family in Los Angeles. Mason began her own business, working as a midwife and nurse and using natural remedies and herbs in her work. She also obtained a job as a confinement nurse for a doctor at $2.50 per week. Being very frugal, she saved her money and in ten years had $250, enough to buy two lots on Spring Street. With the burgeoning growth of the era, the lots soon became prime property in commercial Los Angeles, worth far more than she had paid. She was the first African American woman to own land in the city.

She rented a house and continued to save so that she could build a commercial building on part of her site. In 1884 she moved onto her land. She sold a piece of it for $1,500 to finance her building. Its rental spaces were soon full. Mason believed that owning land provided security for her family as well as a foundation for the family finances. She continued to buy lots over the years. She taught her family to respect the worth of land and how important it was to keep the first parcel. Today, the "Owens block" is in the center of downtown Los Angeles. Her real estate investments were shrewd; she saw the future of the city and profited by her foresight. At the time of her death, she had built a fortune.

> She taught her family to respect the worth of land and how important it was to keep the first parcel.

Mason's philanthropic efforts were many. She opened the first day care nursery for homeless community children; she regularly visited the inhabitants of the local jail; and following a flood in the early 1880s, she provided food for all the flood-devastated families through a local grocery. With Charles Owens, she organized the First African Methodist Episcopal Church, in 1872. Although her grave was unmarked for many years, in 1988 Mayor Tom Bradley erected a memorial tombstone. In 1989 the Broadway Spring Center was built on the site of her house, and two murals funded by the National Endowment for the Humanities were painted in her honor.

See also: African American Businesswomen; Real Estate

Further Reading
Ferris, Jeri, and Ralph L. Ramstad. *With Open Hands: The Story of Biddy Mason.*

Sims, Oscar L. "Biddy Mason." In Jessie Carney Smith, ed., *Notable Black American Women*, p. 732–734.

Taha, Kelle S. "Mason, Biddy." In Dorothy C. Salem, ed., p. 351–352.

Masters, Sybilla (circa 1675–1720), Inventor, Merchant

Sybilla Masters was quite possibly the first American woman to obtain a patent for an invention. Although her husband, Thomas Masters, was the owner of the patent, she is the inventor of record.

No one is sure when or where Sybilla was born, but she was the second daughter of seven children in a Quaker family. Her father, a planter, emigrated from Bermuda in 1687, and Sybilla appears in New Jersey court records in 1692 as a witness for her father. She probably spent her early life on her father's Delaware River plantation. Again, no records exist to date her marriage, but it was between 1693 and 1696 to Thomas Masters, a well-to-do Quaker merchant. He had also emigrated from Bermuda and would later become mayor of Philadelphia (1707–1708) and a provincial counselor (1707–1708). Sybilla and Thomas Masters had four children, two sons and two daughters. At least three other children died at an early age. The family lived in a large house on the Philadelphia riverfront and also owned a summerhouse, named Green Spring.

Sybilla Masters had a flair for mechanical invention and in 1712 announced her intention in a Quaker meeting of going to London to obtain a patent. She was given a certificate of good standing. Sources are not clear on whether Thomas accompanied her or even joined her there later. At any rate, on November 25, 1715, letters patent (no. 401) was granted under the Privy Seal to Thomas Masters for "the sole use and benefit of 'a new invention found out by Sybilla, his wife, for cleaning and curing the Indian corn growing in the several colonies in America.'" (Tolles in James, p. 508). Her invention made it possible to pulverize maize using a stamping process of mortars and pestles rather than the usual grinding done of that day. It could be powered by horses or water, and the device included several trays for drying or curing the grain.

Thomas had bought a mill near their summerhouse in 1714, probably to produce ground corn, which Sybilla named "Tuscorara Rice," claiming it cured consumption (tuberculosis). Some sources claim this was the first patent medicine sold in the Americas, but in reality it had no medicinal powers at all, but was a food product. Sales were not good, and the mill soon was used for other purposes.

Sybilla, however, was still in England, trying to get another patent. On February 18, 1716, she was granted a patent in Thomas's name for a new way of working and staining palmetto plats and leaves to cover and adorn hats. Either she or Thomas was granted a monopoly on the importation of palmetto leaf from the West Indies. She opened West India Hat and Bonnet, a shop that sold hats and other products made using palmetto leaves and her inventive method. A notice in the March 18, 1716, *London Gazette* announced that the shop sold hats as well as "dressing and childbed baskets, and matting" (Tolles in James, p. 508), for chairs and other furniture. In May 1716 she was back in Philadelphia, and on July 15, 1717, the provincial council granted permission for the recording and publishing of her patents in Pennsylvania.

Although information about Masters and her inventions is sketchy, there is a drawing of her first invention, the corn pulverizer. She went to England to obtain her patents because it was the first country to formalize the concept. By law, a woman was not able to obtain a patent, but the document clearly states the inventor's name. *Notable American Women* states that her "ingenuity and enterprise in devising and patenting her two inventions and marketing their products entitle her to a place in American industrial and economic history" (Tolles in James, p. 509).

See also: Colonial Businesswomen; Inventors

Further Reading

Tolles, Frederick B. "Masters, Sybilla." In Edward T. James, p. 508–509.

Vare, Ethlie Ann, and Greg Ptacek. *Patently Female*, p. 31–34.

Masters in Business Administration (MBA), *see* Education

McCabe, Jewell Jackson (1945–), Management Consultant

Jewell Jackson McCabe founded and has been chair of the National Coalition of 100 Black Women, a leadership forum devoted to empowering professional African American women. She is a sought-after public speaker and role model for contemporary African American women. She also owns her own consulting company, Jewell Jackson McCabe Associates.

McCabe was born in Washington, D.C., to an upper-middle-class family. Her father was a broadcast pioneer and her aunt was the first African American graduate of the Boston Conservatory of Music. McCabe graduated from Bard College in 1966. She has been married and divorced twice and has no children.

From 1970 through 1977 she worked in public affairs and public relations positions for the New York Urban Coalition, Special Service for Children in New York City, and the Women's Division of the Office of the Governor of New York. In 1977 she became director of the government and community affairs department of WNET-TV, New York City's public broadcasting station. She was instrumental in attaining millions of dollars in federal, state, and city assistance for the station. In 1981 she founded the National Coalition of 100 Black Women, an outgrowth of the New York City Coalition of 100 Black

Women. She was its first president and has been chair and president of the fund-raising arm of the organization, which counts more than 7,500 members in its sixty-two chapters in twenty-five states. The coalition presents ten Candace Awards annually to honor African American women in the arts, science, technology and business.

Jewell Jackson McCabe Associates, her consulting company, specializes in strategic communications. Its clients include American Express, Panasonic, Seagram, Matsushita Electric Corporation of America, IBM, the NAACP Legal Defense and Educational Fund, the Metropolitan Museum of Art, and the Solomon R. Guggenheim Museum.

McCabe has held several New York City, New York State, and national appointments. She was chair of the New York State Jobs Training Partnership and a member of the New York State Council on Fiscal and Economic Priorities and the New York State Council on Families. She was appointed by President Bill Clinton to serve on the U.S. Holocaust Memorial Council. McCabe has been on the boards of Reliance Group Holdings, Alight.com, the New York City Investment Fund, the Wharton School, Bard College, the National Alliance of Business, the Alvin Ailey Dance Theater, and the Children's Advocacy Center of Manhattan and has been a member of the Deloitte & Touche Diversity Advisory Board. She holds honorary doctorates from Iona College and Tougaloo College. Awards she has received include the national YWCA's Women's Equity Action League Annual Award, for her work on behalf of women in business; the Outstanding Community Leadership Award from Malcolm/King College; and the Blackbook Award. David Rockefeller has described her as "exceptionally energetic, creative and sensitive," and James D. Robinson of American Express has said that "her contribution to the advancement of women and minorities is impressive and much to be admired" (Smith, *Notable Black American Women*, p. 694).

> "Her contribution to the advancement of women and minorities is impressive and much to be admired."

See also: African American Businesswomen; Consulting; National Coalition of 100 Black Women

Further Reading

MacFarlane, Fenella. "McCabe, Jewell Jackson (1945)." In Darlene Clark Hine, ed., *Black Women in America*, p. 762–763.

Smith, Jessie Carney. "Jewell Jackson McCabe." In Jessie Carney Smith, ed., *Notable Black American Women*, p. 693–694.

www.ncbw.org/aboutus/biojewell2.html

McGovern, Gail J. (1952–), Finance Executive

When Gail McGovern was ranked thirty-sixth on *Fortune*'s 2001 list of the most powerful women in American business, she was president of distribution and services at Fidelity Personal Investments Group. In that position, she helped to build Fidelity Personal Investments' brokerage business into a major success.

McGovern was born in Brooklyn, New York, and raised in Springfield, New Jersey. She earned a BS in theoretical mathematics from Johns Hopkins and an MBA from Columbia University, where she won the Jack Popper Award for Academic Achievement. Her husband runs a software development laboratory for Hewlett-Packard. They have one daughter.

Her first job in 1974 was as a computer programmer for Bell Telephone of Pennsylvania. She advanced to be director of organizing of the yellow pages. In 1980 McGovern moved to AT&T, where she held a variety of positions in sales, marketing, product management, and operations. By 1993 she was vice president of the communications group, and two years later she was promoted to executive vice president of the Business Markets Division, which earned half of the company's revenue. McGovern was the company's highest ranking woman and sat on the executive policy council. Her idea was to offer the business customer "value bundles," and she obtained large contracts from IBM and Merrill Lynch. Based on her success in the business arena, in December 1996 she was made executive vice president of the Consumer and Small Business Division, with the expectation that she turn that division around too. This job was called "the toughest job in the phone business" (Collingwood, "The Toughest Job," p. 23).

In August 1998, wanting to learn a new business and feeling that there was no room for advancement at AT&T, McGovern joined Fidelity Investments as senior operations officer of its Personal Investments and Brokerage Group. She launched Fidelity's online service, Power Street, and was responsible for global telemarketing. Two years later, as president of Fidelity Personal Investments, she was third in Fidelity Investment's hierarchy, behind the chairman and the president. She was in charge of retail fund sales and brokerage operations on its Operating Committee and was responsible for Fidelity's rise into a leadership role in broad financial services. Then, in 2002, she accepted a position as professor of marketing at Harvard Business School. A friend described the move as a "lifestyle decision" (Healy, "Fidelity Executive Quits").

As a manager, McGovern has been characterized as approachable and responsive. She was open to suggestions from younger managers and appreciative of their input. She believed in her own ideas and pushed projects ahead when other managers hesitated. She also had a reputation for taking on jobs that no one else wanted. Family is very important to her; family time is as important as an appointment with a CEO.

McGovern sat on the boards of Conrail and the Teach for America Foundation. In 1988, she won the Catherine B. Cleary Award at AT&T's Woman of the Year celebration. *Network World* called her one of the twenty-five most powerful people in computer networking in 1995, and *Success* named her one of its fifty smartest women for 2000.

See also: Finance Industry

Further Reading
Collingwood, Harris. "The Toughest Job in the Phone Business."
Healy, Beth. "Fidelity Executive Quits to Teach at Harvard."
Smith, Geoffrey. "A Quick Scramble up Fidelity's Ladder."

McGrath, Judy (1956–), Television Executive

Judy McGrath is responsible for today's MTV. After joining the cable channel soon after it began, she expanded it from a music video channel into original programming and documentaries. She has been on *Fortune*'s list of most powerful women in American business since the list's inception in 1998. Her rank in 2003 was number 15.

McGrath was born in Scranton, Pennsylvania, to parents who were social workers. Her father loved jazz and influenced her love of music. She graduated from Cedar Crest College with a BA in English. She is married and has one daughter. In 1997, her husband left his job at the Federal Reserve Bank to be a stay-at-home father.

After her college graduation, McGrath joined a radio station in Scranton. In 1974 she moved to New York City, where she worked as a copy chief at Condé Nast magazines for seven years. In 1981 she joined MTV. She began as an on-air prompt writer at the new cable channel, then became editorial director, and later, creative director. In 1990, she was responsible for the "Rock the Vote" initiative, credited by some for Bill Clinton's victory. The following year McGrath was promoted to co–executive director. She was in charge of the creative side—programming, music, production, and promotion—while Sara Levinson directed the business side. She expanded network offerings into original programs such as *Beavis and Butthead* and *The Real World* as well as game shows and documentaries. In 1994 McGrath became president of MTV. Since then, she has spun off two channels—M2, a music channel that includes regional music; and MTVi, an online music company with over $628 million in advertising. She has launched two social campaigns since "Rock the Vote": an antiviolence campaign and an antidiscrimination campaign. In 2000 she became president of MTV Group and chairman, Interactive Music. The following year she was promoted to president of MTV Networks Music Group, responsible for all the company's digital music services. *The Osbournes*, *Beavis and Butthead*, and *The Real* World were among her first big hits.

> She expanded network offerings into original programs such as *Beavis and Butthead* and *The Real World* as well as game shows and documentaries.

McGrath has said that her job is "translating the fleeting whims of teens and young adults into cable programming" ("MTV President Hitting All the Right Notes," p. 1). The challenge is to set styles and stay popular. She accomplishes this by constant study of the network's customer age group through ratings, polls, focus groups, and online chats. She also hires sixty eighteen-to-twenty-two-year-old interns each year.

In 1999 McGrath was named to *Multichannel News*'s Wonder Woman Hall of Fame. She was number 6 on *Hollywood Reporter's* Power 50 list in 2001. That year she also received the Rock the Vote Founders Award for her eleven-year commitment to the program. She sits on the boards of Rock the Vote, LifeBeat, People for the American Way, and the New York City Ballet. She was an integral part of President Clinton's national campaign to reduce teen pregnancy, promoting spots on MTV.

See also: Broadcasting Industry

Further Reading

McConville, Jim. "McGrath Mandate: Pick Up the Tempo at VH1."

"McGrath, Judy." *Celebrity Biographies*. (Retrieved April 26, 1999.)

"MTV President Hitting All the Right Notes; Judy McGrath Has Tripled Revenue at the Cable Channel."

Meeker, Mary G. (1960–), Investment Analyst

Fortune has called Mary Meeker "Diva of the Internet Age," saying that she was "by far the most important voice for the Internet during the dot-com craze" (Elkind, "Where Mary Went Wrong," p. 70). She was also one of the investment analysts blamed by angry stock investors when the Internet stock bubble burst in 2000. She was listed by *Fortune* as one of the most powerful women in American business in both 1999 (number 3) and 2000 (number 6). By 2001, however, she was no longer on the list.

Meeker was born in Portland, Indiana, a small farming community. Her father was second to the president at Portland Forge, and when that business was sold he bought stocks, explaining his strategy to his fascinated daughter. In high school Meeker won a stock-picking contest. She majored in business and psychology at DePauw University and, after working for two years at Merrill Lynch in Chicago, received her MBA from Cornell University in 1986.

She then went to work at Cowen and Company, researching computer manufacturers. Meeker moved to Salomon Brothers as an analyst trainee and began covering Internet stocks. In 1991 she was recruited by the investment company Morgan Stanley, which was interested in building an Internet investment department. Her first notable recommendation was for America Online in 1991, and then in 1994 she put together a partnership for investing in Mosaic, now called Netscape. That initial public offering (IPO) marked the beginning of the Internet stock craze. Many other Meeker picks followed: Amazon.com, @Home, CNET, Intuit, Cisco Systems, Ascend Communications, and Broadcast.com. Meeker's research methods differed from the prevailing wisdom of the market: because the companies had no profits as yet, she based her recommendations on the future and her perceived worth of the idea. She firmly believed in the possibilities of the Internet. She also stated many times that, most likely, only 30 percent of these companies would survive. Morgan Stanley invested hugely in many of the companies and worked with them on their IPOs. Later, this would have repercussions for Meeker. In January 1999, when a few analysts warned that most Internet stocks were overpriced, she recommended Priceline.com. That June, she began touting business-to-business Internet companies. *Barron's* did an interview with her, calling her "Queen of the Net." The Internet craze, despite a few skeptics, was in full swing.

By March 2000, however, the stock market bubble had begun to burst. By the end of that year, many Internet companies had declared bankruptcy and many more were in trouble. Stock prices plummeted and investors lost money. Meeker was involved in Lastminute.com, Morgan Stanley's first European IPO, and it was a disaster. She and several other analysts were sued by disgruntled investors who blamed them for the fiasco. Although she had repeatedly warned that all the Internet stocks would not last, she did not downgrade the ratings for the stocks for which she was responsible, and she remained optimistic after other analysts had warned stockholders. It was not until 2001 that she changed her analyst reports on the companies that she covered, and in March 2002 she was saying that the worst was over, and the stock market would recover. Many investor suits were eventually either settled or dismissed by the judge. In April 2003 the Securities and Exchange Commission decided not to cite either Meeker or Morgan Stanley for securities fraud. The company was assessed fines as part of the settlement.

Meeker is a workaholic who puts in eighteen-hour days. She is known for her charm and wit. She once had a reputation for offering sound advice but moved quickly from being the heroine of the Internet craze to being blamed for its woes.

She received many awards at the height of her career. She was named a top analyst by *Institutional Investor* in 1997 and 2000, one of the twenty-five most powerful people in networking by *Network World* in 1999, and the most influential Internet analyst by *The Industry Standard* in 1999 and 2000; *Business Week* called her one of the E.Biz 25 visionaries. By 1998 she had written four books about the business of the Internet.

See also: Finance Industry

Further Reading
Cassidy, John. "The Woman in the Bubble: Internet Analyst M. Meeker."
Elkind, Peter. "Where Mary Went Wrong."
"Meeker, Mary." *Current Biography*, August 1999, p. 17–19.
Meeker, Mary, with Chris DuPuy. *The Internet Report.*

Mentors

According to Schneider and Schneider, "Mentoring is a process by which a senior or influential worker teaches, helps, and protects a junior" (*ABC-CLIO Companion*, p. 167). The word *mentor* comes from a character in Homer's *Odyssey* who acted as a guardian and adviser to Odysseus's son. Mentors are invaluable in all kinds of work and arenas, and particularly for women in business. They may give guidance in career development, act as inspirational role models, help in problem solving by listening and offering feedback, or help in orienting a newcomer to an industry or corporation. For an entrepreneur, a mentor can fill in knowledge gaps, such as developing a business plan, or can provide contacts for financing. Some have been professors or are experienced entrepreneurs who know the intricacies of starting a business or the pitfalls of legal regulations.

In 1998 an Avon Mentoring Matters Survey found that both men and women saw mentoring as a career asset. Ninety-four percent of women entrepreneurs who had mentors said that the experience was critical to their success, and that mentoring of women was rising (68 percent of women aged eighteen through twenty-nine had mentors, as opposed to 56 percent of women over fifty). Other studies have found that having a mentor alleviated stress and the sense of isolation and powerlessness in a male-dominated company. A mentor is also a safe person with whom to discuss ideas.

There are many benefits for mentors, mentees, and their business or corporation. The mentor, who can gain knowledge about workplace issues from a different perspective, has a chance to reflect on life and work experiences and is able to encourage and promote talent. A successful mentor is not a problem solver, but helps the mentee clarify goals, think through problems, strategize, and evaluate feedback from others in the organization. The mentor shares knowledge and wisdom from his or her own experience and may act as a devil's advocate. Mentors listen carefully and can identify role models and suggest contacts. The mentee receives insight into the corporate culture, professional advice, management training, performance feedback, and encouragement to discuss her fears and concerns. A successful mentee contributes openness to new ideas, initiative, and consideration for the mentor's time. She comes to meetings prepared, follows up on ideas generated, and keeps her mentor informed about her progress. The company benefits from raised skill levels, the grooming of future leaders, cross-trained individuals, better communication, lower turnover, and a stronger corporate culture.

Many corporations have formal mentoring programs. These can sidestep possible litigious problems that can arise with informal mentoring, such as sexual harassment lawsuits and charges of favoritism. Mentors and mentees do develop personal relationships, however, and these can be risky. Formal programs legitimize the relationships, particularly if programs are visibly sponsored by top management and have clear goals and objectives. Catalyst suggests integrating mentoring into a comprehensive career development program and providing training focused on the roles of both mentors and mentees (*Cracking the Glass Ceiling*, p. 53). Other necessities include having clear criteria for eligibility, a fair matching process, an established commitment time, and a process for terminating the relationship.

A good mentor can be crucial to success in a woman's career or business. Women have traditionally been few in management and professional roles and have felt isolated and without support. Mentors can offer them relief from these feelings.

See also: Networking

Further Reading

Creating Successful Mentoring Programs: A Catalyst Guide.

Duff, Carolyn. *Learning from Other Women.*

Landsberg, Max. "Mentoring." In *Business: The Ultimate Resource*, p. 326–327, 368–369, 780–781, 1925–1927.

Merchants, *see* Retailing Industry

Miller, Heidi G. (1953–), Finance Industry

Fortune listed Heidi Miller as the third most powerful woman in American business in 1998, the second most powerful in 1999, and the twentieth most powerful in 2000. The drop in 2000 was due to her move from Citigroup, where she had been chief financial officer, to a vice presidency at Priceline.com. In 2002 she was back again as number 50 because of her new job as executive vice president and chief financial officer (CFO) of Bank One.

Miller was born in New York City and grew up in Flushing, Queens, where she attended public schools. She was the youngest of three daughters of a dentist. She was in one of the first classes at Princeton University to admit women; there, she received a BA in history. Her father offered to pay her way through law school, but she chose to pay her own way and received a PhD from Yale University, in Latin American history. Later she completed studies in international finance at New York University's Stern School of Business. After earning her doctorate, she looked around for teaching jobs, but there were few. Chemical Bank was looking for Spanish-speaking people with a knowledge of Latin America, and she began working there in 1979.

At that time the Latin American countries were in economic trouble. Miller spent the next few years in a variety of places as the bank's representative in debt-restructuring negotiations. She held a number of increasingly responsible positions over her thirteen-year stint at Chemical Bank, including managing director of emerging markets. Because of an impending merger with Manufacturers Hanover Trust, she left there in 1992 to join Primerica, later Travelers Group, as vice president and assistant to the president, Sandy Weill. Miller had met Weill earlier and had been impressed with Primerica's lack of bureaucracy and emphasis on learning and teamwork. One of her achievements was to establish an effective risk-management function at Smith Barney, a subsidiary. She was promoted to CFO and senior vice president in 1995, adding corporate accounting, financial planning, and analysis to her responsibilities. Her greatest achievements in that position were to arrange financing for Travelers' purchase of Aetna Insurance and to improve Travelers' credit rating, from Baa1 in 1992 to Aa3 in 1998.

In 1998 Travelers merged with Citicorp to become Citigroup. Miller remained CFO and negotiated all regulatory requirements with the Federal Reserve Board and other regulatory agencies, a very complicated process as the two companies were forming one of the largest mergers thus far in banking history. She was also responsible for handling a smooth transition and, once it was done, for all accounting and treasury for Citigroup, which had one of the most complicated balance sheets in the United States. She sat on the senior management committee and senior planning groups for corporate banking and consumer banking.

In 2000 Miller decided to join Priceline.com, a move that stunned the financial community. Her position there was CFO and senior executive vice president in charge of business development, but Priceline.com's CEO said publicly that she would be his partner. Miller's reasons for the move were many: she wanted Internet experience, she wanted more power and a line operating job (something she had failed to get at Citigroup), she thought that Priceline.com would be a better place for a woman executive, and she sought to influence major decisions. Nine months later she resigned "to pursue opportunities and apply her talents in a more established business environment" (*American Banker*, p. 24). She learned about electronic commerce and building a consumer brand but discovered that the volatility of a new company was uncomfortable for her. She also found that Priceline.com was not more hospitable to women executives. In January 2001 she took a job as vice chairman of management for Marsh Inc., a company that provides risk management, consulting, and insurance brokering services to clients in one hundred countries. Miller was responsible for its strategy, communication, e-commerce, human resources, and technology. In March 2002 she joined Bank One and its executive planning group as executive vice president of strategy and development. Two months later she was promoted to Chief Financial Officer.

Miller's management style is authoritative but approachable, tough but disarming. She says that she is ambitious and wants to make a difference; she believes that power is about how much change a person can effect and how much influence one has. Her mottos for herself are to learn from every situation, to ask questions and pay attention to what's going on, and to work for someone you respect.

Miller is married with two sons and says that one of her biggest challenges is balancing time efficiently among her career, her spouse, and her children. Her long-time fantasy career goal is to be the president of Princeton University. She sits on several corporate boards: Merck & Co., General Mills, Mead Corporation, and Enterprise Risk Solutions. She is also on nonprofit boards including the Academy of Finance Advisory Board and the Greenwich Emergency Medical Service Board, and she serves as a trustee of Princeton and of the New York University Medical School.

See also: Banking; Insurance Industry

Further Reading
Caminiti, Susan. "Writing Her Own Ticket."
Hoffman, Jan. "Executive Names Her Own Price and Style."
Talley, Karen. "Hidden Asset: Citigroup's Little-Known CFO."

Ming, Jenny J. (1955–), Retail Executive

Jenny Ming, the president of Old Navy, was one of the team responsible for the creation of the Old Navy chain, the budget store of Gap Inc. She turned the company into a roaring success, an accomplishment that earned her the number 42 spot on *Fortune*'s 2003 list of the most powerful women in American business.

Ming was born in Canton, China, the daughter of a printer and a homemaker. When she was three months old, the communists took everything they owned and the family fled to Macao on foot and by boat. They moved to San Francisco when Jenny was in the fourth grade; only her oldest sibling spoke English at the time. Ming is the middle child of five children. Weekend jobs she took to help out included bank clerk and salesclerk, but her favorite job was working as a seamstress at home. She graduated with a degree in home economics from San José State University in 1978.

Ming's first job after college was as a management trainee for Mervyn's department store. She later became a buyer in linens and junior wear. In 1986 she joined Gap Inc. as a buyer and was later promoted to vice president and division merchandise manager for the Gap brand activewear. In 1994 she became a member of the team that created Old Navy. It was one of the fastest-growing apparel retail start-ups in history in the United States, earning $1 billion annually in sales by its fourth year. Ming was senior vice president of merchandising, responsible for production, planning, and distribution. In 1996 she was promoted to executive vice president, taking on responsibility for store planning, and in 1999 she became president. In this position she is also on

Gap Inc.'s senior operating committee. By 2001 there were 700 Old Navy stores in the United States and Canada. Ming has an eighty-five-member design staff who spot big consumer trends.

Ming is known for her knack for spotting which hip-looking clothes will appeal to Old Navy customers. Her management style is to set expectations and meet them. She also has Old Navy contribute to charitable activities, such as Hope for the Holidays, a program supporting the Elizabeth Glaser Pediatric AIDS Foundation. Ming is married with three children and never works on weekends.

Business Week named Ming one of twenty-five top managers of 1999. She belongs to the Committee of 100, a national, nonpartisan organization of U.S. citizens of Chinese and Asian descent. She sits on the board of directors of E.piphany Inc.

See also: Asian American Businesswomen; Immigrant Businesswomen; Retailing Industry

Further Reading
Lee, Louise. "A Savvy Captain for Old Navy."
Ming, Jenny J., with Amy Zipkin. "Executive Life: The Boss; Tying the Two Strands."

Minimum-Wage Legislation, *see* Compensation

Mining Industry

During the Western gold and silver rushes, several women were bitten by the precious metals bug and rushed off to the mining camps in search of gold or silver. They found that they liked their independence and the excitement. To finance their prospecting endeavors, they often provided room and board or provisions for the male miners. For some women mining was a hobby, but for many it was a career. Earning a living was just a sideline. According to Zanjani, there are a number of female names in the old mining records (*A Mine of Her Own*, p. 16). Some miners used women's names to stake their claims, but Zanjani found seventy-seven women "whose [mining] activities could be dated with reasonable certainty" during the period 1898–1910 (p. 103). Mining in the West diminished during and after World War I, but the Great Depression of the 1930s brought more women to the West. Most were subsistence miners.

Underground miners always strongly resisted women in the mines, mostly for superstitious reasons but also because of the danger involved and the need for physical strength. Women owners—and there were a few—would go underground to supervise, but it was not until the late 1970s that women mining engineers appeared. In 2001 the U.S. Department of Labor counted 87,000 women out of a total of 567,000 workers in the mining industry.

Women in Mining (www.womenmining.org) is a national organization that provides technical education and scientific programs about mining. It was founded in Denver in 1972. In 2003 it had 500 members.

Further Reading
Alberts, Laurie. "Petticoats and Pickaxes."
Woyski, Margaret S. "Women and Mining in the Old West."
Zanjani, Sally. *A Mine of Her Own.*

Minority Businesswomen

Many women of color feel that Title VII of the Civil Rights Act of 1964 and the executive orders following it were the beginning of the possibility of equal opportunity in both the workplace and business ownership. Prior to that, most minority women were relegated to low-paying support positions or jobs that no one else wanted, such as janitorial and waste management services or office staffing. They could not amass enough money to start their own business and could not obtain loans. There were exceptions, of course, but the majority were stuck behind a wall of discrimination and negative stereotypes.

In 1969 President Richard Nixon enforced Section 8a of the Small Business Act of 1953, a hitherto unused rule guaranteeing loans to disadvantaged people who wished to start their own business. The program was a result of the 1960s race riots and was aimed at minorities, but not women. It aided in expanding businesses and provided preparation and training for beginning business-people. Banks began to approve loans, but they were reluctant to do so in crime-ridden neighborhoods.

In 1978 the U.S. Congress passed the Minority Business Development Program, with the goal of creating business opportunities in the inner cities. Also in 1978 President Jimmy Carter issued his Urban Policy Statement, which recognized women as disadvantaged. It also guaranteed that 10 percent of funds for any project using federal government funding must go to minority-owned businesses. During the 1970s and the early 1980s research studies found that government help was necessary for minority businesses because their risk of failure was higher and chance of success lower than for Caucasian-owned businesses. Minority trade groups and chambers of commerce formed in this period to address community issues. In 1994, 36 percent of loans from the Minority Business Development Program were used by African Americans, 29 percent by Hispanics, and 25 percent by Asian Americans. In 1995 there were 175 minority-owned banks. From 1987 through 1999, minority businesses grew 168 percent and their revenues grew 343 percent, to $500 billion. That year, minority people, who made up 26 percent of the population, owned 12 percent of businesses and earned 6 percent of corporate revenues (U.S. Bureau of the Census, Survey of Minority-Owned Business Enterprises).

In the 1997 Economic Census there were 1,067,000 businesses owned by women of color. In the ten years from 1987 through 1996 the number grew 153 percent. They employed 1,694,300 people and had annual sales of $184.2 billion. Minority women-owned companies grew at triple the rate of small businesses overall. The top five industries were business services, health services, eating and drinking establishments, personal services, and wholesale trade. Growth rates were highest in trucking and warehousing, building and construction contracting, and printing and publishing. This growth had come about due to increased contracting and subcontracting opportunities; improved access to capital, especially by banks; and a strong motivation by minority women to improve their personal life. The major barrier is still difficulty in obtaining loans and bank credit.

In the corporate world growth on the management level, however, has been glacial. In 1998, of 2.9 million women managers and administrators, 7 percent were African American, 4 percent were Hispanic, and 3 percent were Asian Americans. In 1999, 11.9 percent of all corporate officers were women of color. Of them, 67 percent were African American, 17 percent were Hispanic, and 21 were Asian American. Catalyst counted corporate officers in the *Fortune* 500 in 2000: 1.3 percent were women of color.

Companies are beginning to see the importance of recruiting, retraining, and promoting minority women and that having a diverse workforce makes good business sense, but there is still much to be done. Barriers for these women include a sense of isolation without mentors, sometimes feeling invisible and unheard. Mandates from the board level on down through the ranks are helpful, but individual resistance and negative attitudes are difficult to overcome. Minority women feel that they have to change their personal styles in order to succeed and that they must work twice as hard. Overcoming stereotypes and uncomfortable co-workers can also be a problem. A *Fortune* 2000 survey reported that 45 percent of minority respondents had personally been the target of racial or cultural jokes (Mehta, "What Minority Employees Really Want," p. 184). Women, of course, may be subjected to both sexism and racism. Many leave corporations to begin their own businesses, where they have more control over their milieu and can be themselves.

In July 2003 *Working Mother* published an article about the best companies for women of color. Its criteria included advancement opportunities, availability, tracking of diversity programs, and accountability of managers for their oversight of diversity. In an accompanying article, Erin Texeira states: "[It is a] delicate dance: knowing that the workplace can be a foreign land; becoming fluent in its language and customs but never forgetting that she is something of a stranger" ("A Delicate Balance," p. 62).

See also: African American Businesswomen; American Indian Businesswomen; Asian American Businesswomen; Diversity; Latina Businesswomen

Further Reading

Giscombe, Katherine, and Mary C. Mattis. "Leveling the Playing Field for Women of Color in Corporate Management."

Mehta, Stephanie. "What Minority Employees Really Want."

National Foundation for Women Business Owners. *Women Business Owners of Color: Challenges and Accomplishments.*

Texeira, Erin. "A Delicate Balance."

Women of Color Executives: Their Voices, Their Journeys.

Women of Color in Corporate Management: Opportunities and Barriers.

Zinn, Maxine Baca, and Bonnie Thornton Dill. *Women of Color in U.S. Society.*

Minyard, Liz (1954–), Grocery Chain Co-Owner
Williams, Gretchen (1956–), Grocery Chain Co-Owner

Liz Minyard and Gretchen Williams are co-CEOs of Minyard Food Stores, a Texas grocery store chain that has been one of the top woman-owned companies, according to *Working Woman,* since 1993. They are sisters, daughters of the younger brother of the chain's founder. Minyard and Williams each owns 33.3 percent of the company, and a cousin owns the other third.

The Minyard grocery chain was started in 1932 during the Great Depression, when A.W. Minyard, a postal worker, bought a store so that his younger brothers, H.C. and M.T., might have jobs. Minyard was one of the first stores to offer one-stop shopping, selling dry goods, produce, and meat under one roof. A.W. never married, and when he died, his younger brothers inherited the store. M.T. was the father of Liz and Gretchen and is in the Grocers Hall of Fame.

Both women have worked at Minyard all their lives. Their mother died from leukemia when the girls were ten and twelve. They were raised by an aunt, who worked at the company as secretary/treasurer. They began as paid workers while they were in high school. One memorable job was counting coupons to be sent to the redemption center. Both women graduated from Texas Christian University with degrees in business administration. After graduation each of them worked in many different positions in the company. Liz eventually became director of consumer affairs, while Gretchen became director of employee relations. In 1980 Liz became vice president of consumer affairs and Gretchen was made vice president of corporate relations. In 1985 they were appointed vice chairs of the board of directors and then, in 1988, co-chairs of the board.

The supermarket business is famous as a male-dominated industry. Most of its executives rise from the ranks, and experience is more important than education. The ability to lift heavy objects is key in entry-level positions.

M.T. Minyard was ahead of his time leaving the company to his daughters. He always told them that they would have an opportunity there, and their aunt, who worked there until she was in her eighties, served as their role model. They, in turn, have seen to it that women have had opportunities; there are now several women store managers as well as women at headquarters. A training program actively targets women and minorities for managerial positions. The company has a multicultural relations coordinator and holds in-house career fairs. Liz was a co-chair of the Food Marketing Institute's task force on managing diversity, probably as a result of Minyard's activities in that area.

They now own three Dallas-area grocery store chains: Minyard, the flagship chain; Carnival stores, which are situated in Latino, Asian American, and, African American neighborhoods and carry foods central to those communities; and Sack 'n Save, a warehouse store. In 1996 they opened a 62,000-square-foot store that includes a dry cleaner, a postal center, and a food counter. They also opened gas stations in some of their store parking lots in 1997 called Minyard on the Go. They use major in-store promotions to compete with other chains and they offer in-store nutrition programs. In 1998 Liz and Gretchen became co-CEOs while retaining their positions as co-chairs of the board. Gretchen's husband, Sonny Williams, is president and also became chief operating officer at that time. Minyard is married to an attorney.

The company has donated over $100,000 to leukemia research. Both women are heavily involved in their profession and the community. Minyard has chaired the United Way for Dallas and Tarrant Counties; she is also a board member of Goodwill Industries of Dallas and of Michaels Stores. She has served in many capacities for the Dallas Urban League as well as the Greater Dallas Chamber of Commerce and the Anti-Defamation League. She is on the board of the Baylor Hospital Foundation. In May 2002 she was elected vice chair of the board of the Food Marketing Institute. Williams is on the boards of Cullen/Frost Bank NA in Dallas, Home Interiors & Gifts, AGAPE Social Services Inc., and Baylor Health Care Systems and is on the advisory boards of the Dallas Independent School District and Dallas Baptist University. She has chaired the Dallas/Fort Worth Retail Grocers Association and is cochair of the Leukemia Association of North Central Texas and a member of the Committee of 200.

Both women have won awards. Minyard was named Advocate of the Year by the Dallas/Fort Worth District Women in Business in 1995 and received the Business Award for Community Involvement from the Martin Luther King Jr. Community Center. She also received the Contributors Award from the Black State Employees Association of Texas and the Art of Achievement Award from the National Federation of Women Business Owners. She has won the Texas Family Business of the Year—Community Involvement Award from the Texas Institute of Family Businesses. Williams has won the Art of

Achievement Award two times, in 1995 and 1997, for the Top 50 Women Business Owners.

See also: Food Industry

Further Reading

Bamford and McHenry. "The *Working Woman* 50 Top Women Business Owners."

Lueck, Guada. *50 Years of Good Taste: A Delicious History of Minyard Food Stores.*

Sansolo, Michael. "In One Woman's Opinion: Should There Be More Female Executives in the Industry? Liz Minyard Makes It Clear Why the Answer Must Be Yes!"

Mommy Track

In the January/February 1989 issue of *Harvard Business Review*, Felice Schwartz published an article advocating an alternative track for women that allowed maternity and childcare leave, flextime, and a reduced workload that would not put their career aspirations in jeopardy ("Management Women"). She observed that there were two kinds of women in the workforce: career-primary and career-and-family oriented. She proposed that the latter have a variety of options so that they do not have to choose between their career and their family. The media quickly noticed the article and coined the phrase "mommy track" to describe her idea.

Feminists at the time heavily criticized the concept, saying that it reflected a 1950s male mentality and would destroy all the advances women had made in the workplace. They also feared that it would stop corporations from hiring women, or that women would have to settle for lower pay and lower-status jobs. Worse yet, they worried that women with children would automatically be overlooked for promotions. They also resented the perceived implication that career women give second priority to their children. Schwartz's supporters said that her statements reflected the realities of contemporary corporate culture. They also suggested, and she agreed, that these options should be available to men as well. A few progressive companies had family-friendly policies that enabled all employees to balance work and family obligations, but very few.

Schwartz hit a nerve, as evidenced by the media storm. She hated the term "mommy track" and felt it implied an inflexible solution that was demeaning to women. Her suggestions were intended as ways to enable women to have careers, but not at the cost of family life. She also believed that companies, her intended audience, would benefit because they could retain trained women who could advance in their careers later, when their family obligations had diminished. At a 1990 conference she stated that the article was intended to encourage employers to change their policies and practices to meet the needs of employees who chose to combine work and family. She was surprised at the storm of criticism but later stated that there was a need for discussion of these issues.

See also: Childcare; Flexible Work Arrangements; Husbands/Fathers; Work-Life Balance

Further Reading
Hall, Douglas T. "Promoting Work/Family Balance: An Organizational Change Approach."
Moore, Martha T., and David Proctor. "Special 4-Day Report: The Mommy Track."
Schwartz, Felice N. "Management Women and the New Facts of Life."

Moody, Lady Deborah (1586–1659), Builder, Landowner

Lady Deborah Moody was the first female English settlement leader and town planner in the American colonies. Her settlement, Gravesend, was the first colonial enterprise led by a woman.

Moody was born in Avebury, England, to radical Protestant parents, the eldest of four daughters. She grew up believing strongly in independent rights and civil liberties for everyone. Around 1605 she married Henry Moody. He was later knighted, made a baronet, and served intermittently in Parliament during the 1620s. He and Deborah had one son, Henry. When Sir Henry died in 1629, Lady Deborah moved to London, but the Court of the Star Chamber ordered her to return to the manor of Garesdon, the family estate. Her religious views were as nonconformist as her political views, so she decided to leave England, even though she was in her mid-fifties. Her son and some of the estate families accompanied her.

In 1639 she sailed to Massachusetts, where she settled in Lynn and was granted 400 acres of land. In 1641 she bought a large farm called Swampscott and joined the church in Salem. Unfortunately, she could not keep to their rules, and she was chastised for her unorthodox views in 1643. That year she moved to the Dutch colony of New Netherlands, taking a group of friends and sympathizers with her. The Dutch suggested she move her group to Gravesend, the southwest corner of Long Island. Although there was an Indian uprising shortly after the group moved, the thought of returning to Massachusetts was not feasible and they decided to stay.

On December 10, 1645, Moody received a Dutch patent for the Gravesend settlement that granted freedom of worship and self-government. Her son was one of the signers. She proceeded to plan the town and set up a democratic government. The town was planned on a grid system, with safe snug houses built to withstand the Atlantic winter. She paid the Canarsie Indians for their land, installed rules forbidding the sale of liquor to the Canarsies, and ruled that inhabitants must build habitable houses. She established an orderly English settlement, with town meetings to discuss all settlement affairs. There was some dissension with the Dutch, particularly Peter Stuyvesant, which was resolved in peaceful meetings. All differences were settled in this way. Because

Moody was a landowner she was entitled to vote; she was the first woman to vote in the colonies, in 1655.

In 1657 three Quaker missionaries visited Gravesend and were invited to meet in Moody's home. It is not known whether she converted to the Quaker religion, but several of the colonists did and Gravesend became a center of Quakerism.

After her death Henry, who never married, became the New Netherlands ambassador to Virginia. He died there two years later. The baronetcy died with him. Lady Deborah is said to be buried in the Gravesend cemetery. Her house is still standing at 27 Gravesend Road. Her substantial holdings included land in what is now Brooklyn, Coney Island, Bensonhurst, Sheepshead Bay, and Midwood.

See also: Colonial Businesswomen; Real Estate

Further Reading

Cooper, Victor H. *A Dangerous Woman: New York's First Lady Liberty; The Life and Times of Lady Deborah Moody; Her Search for Freedom of Religion in Colonial America.*

McDonald, Gerald D. "Moody, Lady Deborah." In Edward T. James, *Notable American Women 1607–1950*, p. 569–570.

Moore, Ann S. (1950–), Magazine Publisher

Ann Moore, chairman and CEO of Time Inc., has been on *Fortune*'s list of the most powerful women in American business since 1998. Her 2003 ranking was number 13. She is the first woman to lead the company and has the responsibility for more than 140 magazines, including *People, Sports Illustrated, Time,* and *Fortune.* Time Inc. is the largest magazine publisher in the world.

Moore was born in Biloxi, Mississippi, on an Air Force base, and before she was twelve had lived on eight other bases. After graduating from high school she went on to earn a degree from Vanderbilt University and embarked on a publishing career in Boston. A few years later she returned to school and received her MBA from Harvard Business School in 1978. Women MBAs in 1978 were swamped with job offers. She decided to take the lowest-paying job, as a corporate financial analyst for Time Inc., because she was a self-described magazine junkie (Zuber, p. 70).

She quickly worked her way up the ladder, first as a media manager for *Sports Illustrated,* then as assistant circulation director for *Fortune,* circulation director for *Money* and *Discover,* and as general manager and associate publisher of *Sports Illustrated.* One of her accomplishments was to change *Sports Illustrated*'s photography from black-and-white to color. In 1989 she founded *Sports Illustrated for Kids.*

Moore was the publisher of *People Weekly* from 1991 to 1994 and changed its format to color as well. A reorganization within Time Inc., the parent company, made her president of the *People* Group. In her time there, she increased both circulation and advertising revenues and launched three related magazines, with several more on hold, awaiting the right moment. Her vision was to use *People* as the parent of several related magazines and special issues. *People* is sold as a supermarket-checkout magazine, and one of the first things Moore did was to change its distribution day from Monday to Friday so that weekend shoppers, the majority, would get it hot off the press. The readership is 70 percent female, and Moore has had an excellent understanding of both her audience and her magazine. There was a high fluctuation in supermarket sales, but the spin-off magazines and several special issues have generated high revenues. Four new magazines have been launched while she was in charge: *Teen People, People en Español, InStyle,* and *Real Simple.* In June 2001 the Parenting Group was added to her responsibilities, and that year she also became executive vice president of Time Inc., with control over *People* and *Time.* On October 1, 2002, she was named chairman and CEO of Time Inc. She heads a $4.5 billion enterprise, the publisher of the world's most widely read magazines.

In 1994 Moore founded PeopleFirst, the magazine's charity foundation. She chooses charities based on the magazine's readership surveys; recently these have been related to AIDS and cancer research. She firmly believes that a business should pay back the community it relies on; in this case, celebrities. For example, the charity funds Gilda's Club, a cancer support group named for the late Gilda Radnor of *Saturday Night Live* fame.

Moore's business strategy is firmly in place. She started by increasing both circulation and advertising, which increased revenues, which increased profits. Now her mission is to keep the company growing though launching new magazines while watching the bottom line. She has been called a marketing wizard (Granatstein, p. 50), honing in on the interests of the average person on the street. She takes risks to keep a step ahead of the crowd and is an extroverted leader. She has built a talented and expert team of managers and has brought more women and Latinos into Time Inc.'s management. An astute reader with sharp editorial instincts, she seems to be universally respected and liked and treats her employees well.

Moore has been married for twenty-five years and has one son. When asked how she manages a high-powered job and a family, Moore has quipped that she moved her mother-in-law next door so that she has a firm support group (Granatstein p. 51). She is one of four women on the board of directors at Avon, where she was a member of the CEO search team. She received the Women in Communications Matrix Award from the National Association of Female Executives (NAFE) in 1994 and was named one of three Advertising Women of the Year by the Advertising Women of New York in 1997.

See also: Publishing Industry

Further Reading
Granatstein, Lisa. "*People* Person."
Seglin, Jeffrey L. "Her Hopes, Her Dreams."
Zuber, Amy. "Time Inc.'s *People* Person."

Moore, Darla D. (1955–), Banker, Investment Advisor

Named by *Fortune* in 1998 as the nineteenth most powerful woman in American business, Darla D. Moore has excelled in two arenas, banking and investment advising. In the banking world, she was known as "Queen of the DIPs" (debtors-in-possession). In her position as executive vice president of Rainwater Inc., a private investment firm, she has been a feared board of directors activist.

Moore was born and grew up on a small tobacco farm near Lake City, South Carolina. Her father taught her to excel at all sports, while her mother pushed excellence in music and school. Moore has said (Sellers and Rao, p. 64) that she was not particularly popular at school because she focused on academics and was not particularly interested in being a beauty queen or a cheerleader. She graduated from the University of South Carolina with a BA in political science and then interned with U.S. Senator Strom Thurmond. However, she found that politics did not suit her, so she went to George Washington University and studied for an MBA, graduating in 1981.

Her first job was as one of thirty-one management trainees at Chemical Bank in New York City in 1982. The following year, Moore moved into handling loans for midsize companies. She pioneered DIP financing, by which banks loan companies the money to win back the confidence of their suppliers and to try to work their way out of bankruptcy. The risk for banks is low because they are paid first, and many companies have stabilized themselves using this method of financing. In 1987 she moved into the corporate finance division, and by 1990 she was the head of Chemical Bank's bankruptcy lending unit, the fastest-growing business of the bank. In 1991 she moved to Manufacturers Hanover as managing director in charge of DIP loans. The following year Manufacturers Hanover and Chemical Bank merged, and she was in charge of the restructuring and reorganizing division. In 1993 she was chosen to be head of a new retail industrial group.

In December 1991 Moore married financier Richard Rainwater. She left Chemical Bank in 1994 to manage the investments of Rainwater Inc., her husband's corporation. Within three years she had tripled his $700 million portfolio through streamlining the business and redirecting the money into publicly held companies. She sits on the companies' boards and encourages them to change their policies. She is in charge of screening and executing all deals for the company; Rainwater forecasts the future.

Moore is known for her Southern charm, persistence, self-confidence, and assurance. She loves dealing with chaos and has a reputation for moving quickly and efficiently. She is also tough. She was the first woman to be profiled in a cover story in *Fortune,* in its September 8, 1997, issue. She sees being a woman as a competitive advantage. Her method of being a businesswoman is to become the best in the field, as she did with bankruptcy rules and regulations and, later, investment strategies.

She sits on the boards of Chase Manhattan, MPS Group, Columbia/HCA Healthcare, and Martha Stewart Living Omnimedia, as well as on several civic boards. She is on the University of South Carolina board of trustees of the South Carolina Governor's Commission for Teacher Quality and the South Carolina Chamber of Commerce Educational Excellence Commission. In 1992 Moore was on *Working Woman's* list of the highest-paid women in business and one of the top forty bankers under forty. In 1998 she pledged $25 million to the University of South Carolina for the Darla Moore College of Business Administration, the first business school named for a woman. In 2002 she co-founded the Palmetto Institute to research development and economic change in South Carolina.

See also: Banking; Finance Industry

Further Reading
Daniel, Jere. "The Loan Ranger: Banker Darla Moore Rescues Collapsing Corporations and Their Honchos from the Terrors of Bankruptcy."
Jordan, Jacob. "Financier, Darla Moore, Has All the Right Connections,"
Sellers, Patricia, and Rajiv Rao. "Don't Mess with Darla."

Moran, Pat (1945–), Automobile Retailer

Pat Moran is the chairman and CEO of JM Family Enterprises, the largest woman-owned company in the United States. It is also the world's largest Toyota and Lexus dealership. It was named in *Working Woman's* list of the top fifty American companies to work for in 1999 and 2000 and was eighteenth on *Forbes's* 2000 list of the top privately held companies in the United States. The company has been one of *Working Woman's* top five woman-owned companies since 1993.

Moran was born in Chicago, the middle child of three children. Sandwiched between two brothers, she grew up shy and introverted. Her father, Jim Moran, started an automobile dealership empire in 1955 in Chicago and was the first car dealer to advertise on television. He also sponsored a variety show featuring himself. Later, he moved the business to Florida.

Pat Moran attended Marquette University but left after one year because she was miserable. She married and divorced twice, had three children, worked as a nurse's assistant, and began her own travel agency. In 1983 her father was hospitalized and he asked her to join his company. She agreed, with the proviso that she would not work in the main office. She began as a clerk-typist and worked in a variety of departments and positions in order to learn the business. She has said that she had to work twice as hard because as a family member and a woman, it was difficult to gain respect from the "car guys." (Wells, p. F-1) Nevertheless, she managed, with perseverance and patience, to do just that.

In 1988 the company was in legal trouble, facing twelve lawsuits filed by disgruntled dealers. In 1989 she became president and CEO; her father remained as chairman of the board. One of her first changes was to repair relations with the dealers. She removed several fees and started a program encouraging sales representatives to stay. Her program reduced turnover to an acceptable 10 percent. That year she also signed a Toyota distributorship, a contract that would eventually make the company the world's largest Toyota distributorship. Her ambition was to expand the company into a nationwide chain of dealerships. She also signed Lexus and Pontiac dealerships and set up a car-import processor in Jacksonville, Florida, and a car-financing subsidiary. All of the dealer lawsuits had been settled by 1999. A subsidiary, PetroChem, was cited for spilling toxic waste, and the Florida Department of Environmental Protection later cited the cleanup as a model effort. By 1996 sales had doubled from the time she took over in 1989. In 1997 she instituted the Toyota Quality Experience Program, a push for improving customer satisfaction and quality. In 2000 Jim Moran became honorary chairman of the board, and Pat became chairman of the company.

Moran has been very successful in a male-dominated industry. She changed the culture of the company to make it a quality- and family-oriented business. One of her top priorities is to find and keep the best people. She is known as a thoughtful, detailed, and organized person who deals in a no-nonsense but fair way. She expects organization and thoroughness of her employees and in return is very loyal to them. Moran built the business against great odds that included the male culture of the industry and the Japanese business culture. She gained the trust of both through her handling of the Toyota contract. Her leadership philosophy is, "Don't fear change and innovation. Some decisions will work out well and others won't" (Sharp-Zickerman, "Billion-Dollar Club," p. 54).

> "Don't fear change and innovation. Some decisions will work out well and others won't."

In 2000 Moran received the Spirit of Leadership Award from the Women's Automotive Association, was named one of one hundred leading women in the North American automobile industry, was awarded the Distinguished Service Citation from the Automotive Hall of Fame, and was named one of the fifty smartest women in corporate America by *Money* magazine. She was number 2 in *Working Woman's* billion-dollar club in 2001. JM Family

Enterprises was on *Fortune*'s list of the best companies to work for from 1998 through 2003.

Moran sits on the board of American Heritage Life Insurance. She is also very active in philanthropic activities. She sponsors Youth Conservation Camps, supports the American Cancer Society, and sponsors African American achiever awards. She provided funding for the Jim and Jan Moran Theatre at the Times-Union Center for the Performing Arts and has donated $1 million to the Florida Philharmonic Orchestra as a challenge grant. She has also cochaired a benefit for Take Stock of Children, with Governor Jeb Bush. In 2001 she founded a nonprofit agency, Deliver the Dream, to provide a mountain retreat for people coping with life-threatening illnesses or other crises.

See also: Automobile Industry

Further Reading

Chappell, Lindsay. "Daughter Keeps Dynasty Going: Pat Moran Answered Dad's Call."
O'Donnell, Jayne. "#1: Pat Moran, CEO, JM Family Enterprises."
Wells, Judy. "Experience Still Does the Talking: EVE Awards Speaker Has Been There, Done That."

Morgan, Cristina (1953–), Investment Banker

Cristina Morgan was named the thirty-fourth most powerful woman in American business in the October 2000 issue of *Fortune*. She is the managing director and codirector of investment banking for Chase H&Q; her expertise is in technology companies. She has nurtured many high-tech companies through the equity financing process, including Marimba, Amazon.com, Adobe Systems, Siebel Systems, Inktomi, Crossworlds Software, and Websense.

Morgan was born in Florence, Italy, to a career Air Force family and has lived all over the world. She earned a BA in finance and an MBA from the University of Arizona. Her first job was in 1977, as a manager at Memorex. In 1982 she accepted a position as a junior research analyst at Hambrecht & Quist. Later that year she replaced her boss, who left suddenly.

In 1984 Morgan moved into investment banking, and by 1990 she had become managing director of the company. The firm experienced unprecedented growth under her leadership. In 1994 Hambrecht & Quist guided 37 deals worth $1.2 billion through the equity-financing process, and by 1996, 128 deals had which raised $8.7 billion. This was the heyday of high tech, and Hambrecht & Quist concentrated on this kind of company. After Chase Manhattan bought Hambrecht & Quist in December 1999, Morgan became managing director and codirector of investment banking at the new company. In these roles she is responsible for investment banking activities and serves on the company's Operating Committee and Commitment Committee.

Morgan's reputation is for hands-on nurturing of the companies she is shepherding through the process. Her distinguishing characteristic is said to be accessibility. Her take on being a lone woman is that womanhood offers her an unfair advantage because she is the easiest person to remember in a sea of men. Morgan was called "the Wonder Woman of Silicon Valley" by *Town & Country* (Powell, p. 38), and in 1997 *Working Woman* named her one of the ten most important women in technology. In May 2002 she was named Financial Woman of the Year by the Financial Woman's Association. She has been on the corporate boards of directors of Frame Technology, Visigenic Software, and Evoke Software. She is married; her husband retired at age fifty-one.

See also: Banking; Finance Industry

Further Reading
Powell, Bonnie Azab. "H&Q's Dynamic Duo Leads the Bank Merge Lane."
"The Ten Most Important Women in Tech."
www.girlgeeks.com/innergeek/inspiringwomen/morgan.html.

Morgan, Rose (1913–), Beauty Industry Pioneer

Rose Morgan founded Rose Meta House of Beauty, later Rose Morgan House of Beauty, the most successful African American beauty salon business in the United States during the late 1940s, the 1950s, and the 1960s. She was a trendsetter in the field of beauty for African American women. She was also one of the group of people who founded the Freedom National Bank in Harlem, the largest African American–owned bank in the United States.

Born in Shelby, Mississippi, to an African American sharecropper, Morgan was one of eleven children. Her father moved the family to Chicago when Rose was six. She has credited her father for teaching her methods for succeeding in business and encouraging her to try for the best that life has to offer. With his help, she began her entrepreneurial career at age ten with an artificial flower business. She organized the neighborhood children to sell flowers door-to-door. Her first beauty business was in high school, where she styled hair for her friends. After high school she graduated from the Morris School of Beauty in Chicago and leased a booth in a neighborhood beauty salon. Her first break came when she styled singer Ethel Waters's hair for a concert in Chicago in 1938. Waters loved her work and asked Morgan to come to New York City.

Morgan joined a salon in New York, and four months later she and a friend opened a hair styling business in their kitchen. In 1939 or 1947 (sources vary as to the date) she opened her first real salon, Rose Meta House of Beauty. With $10,000 in cash and $40,000 in credit, she and her partner bought an old mansion, which was known as a haunted house, and set up their salon. During the first year they served 70,000 customers with earnings of $180,000 and net profits of $45,000. By 1948 they had 68 operators and a payroll of $90,000, and by 1950 three shops in New York City were employing 300 people. Morgan developed and marketed Rose Meta Cosmetics, including hair care products, lipsticks, powder, and facial creams. These were sold in stores in more than forty cities as well as through mail order. By this time gross receipts were over $3 million. Rose Meta House of Beauty was the largest African American beauty salon in the United States and offered wig care, hair weaving, manicures, cosmetics, facials, and other beauty treatments. After ten years Morgan bought out her partner.

In 1955 Morgan opened Rose Morgan House of Beauty, a chain of beauty shops in major U.S. cities and in eight other countries, mostly Caribbean. The shops were elaborate and flamboyant. Supposedly, more than 10,000 women lined up opening day in New York, even though the weather was cold and drizzly. It grossed $200,000 its first year. She also went to Europe, particularly Paris, to promote her beauty products. She was met with enthusiasm because it was the first time that cosmetics developed just for African American women were available in Europe. By 1970 Morgan and her salons were known internationally. She continued to travel extensively, speaking and putting on fashion shows and beauty clinics. In 1972 she started developing and franchising Trim-Away Figure Contouring.

Morgan married three times, the most celebrated marriage being her second, to the heavyweight prizefighter Joe Louis. The marriage lasted only two years. She and Louis developed and marketed a cologne for men called My Man, but the product failed. She later married Louis Saunders, but they separated after two years. Morgan firmly believed in giving back to the community. She was a life member of the NAACP, a vice president of the National Council of Negro Women, and a member of the board of directors of Kilimanjaro African Coffee, the Interracial Council for Business Opportunities, the Uptown Chamber of Commerce of New York City, and the Freedom Bank of New York. She was awarded the Outstanding Achievement Award by the New York State Beauty Culturists Association.

See also: African American Businesswomen; Beauty Industry

Further Reading
Dandridge, Vonita White. "Rose Morgan (19??): Entrepreneur." In Jessie Carney Smith, ed., *Notable Black American Women*, p. 769.
Moon, Mike. "Rose Morgan: Success in Grand Style."
Morgan, Rose. "An Interview with Rose Morgan."
Walker, Juliet E. K. "Rose Meta House of Beauty—Rose Morgan." In Juliet E. K. Walker, ed., p. 473–474.

Mulcahy, Anne (1953–), Office Equipment Industry Executive

Anne Mulcahy is chairman and CEO of Xerox Corporation. She has been on the *Fortune* list of the most powerful women in American business since 2000. In 2003, she was ranked fourth.

Mulcahy was born in Rockville Centre, New York. Her father was an English professor and then an editor, and her mother, a homemaker who handles all the household finances. Anne grew up with four brothers and remembers dinner-table conversations full of ideas, with everyone expected to participate. She chose an all-girls college, Marymount, but left after her junior year to join VISTA (Volunteers in Service to America). After spending a year in poor areas of Kentucky working with preschool children, prisoners, and juvenile delinquents, she returned to Marymount and graduated with a double degree in mathematics and journalism.

Her first job was a brief stint writing for *Cosmopolitan*, and she then spent two years in a management training program at Chase Manhattan Bank. In 1976 she married Charles Roy, moved to Boston, and joined Xerox as a sales representative. They divorced three years later. As Xerox's first woman salesperson, she held several in the Northeast. In 1980 she met Joe Mulcahy on a company ski trip, and they later married. They moved to New York, where their two sons were born, in 1983 and 1987.

> Her task was huge: to remotivate the sales force . . . halt the slide of the company's stock, lower costs, and merge Xerox's traditional values. . . with entrepreneurism.

By 1988 she was a vice president and regional general sales manager. Three years later she became vice president of worldwide marketing operations planning with responsibility for South and Central America, Europe, Asia, Africa, and China. In 1992 she made a lateral move and became vice president of human resources in order to learn about the people side of the company. In this position she was responsible for compensation, benefits, human resources strategy, labor relations, management development, and employee training. Three years later she became chief staff officer for customer operations and assumed responsibility for quality, advertising, integrated marketing, communications, and public relations. In 1998 she supervised the acquisition of the color printing and image division of Tektronix Inc. She became head of General Markets Operations, a new division that she had proposed.

The acquisition of the Tektronix division was part of an effort by Xerox to change its image. In May 2000 the CEO resigned at the urging of the board of directors. Mulcahy was made president and chief operating officer, an indication that she was next in line for the CEO job, and she was promoted effective January 2002. Her task was huge: to remotivate the sales force, which was in disarray; speed digital products and services to the market; halt the slide of the company's stock; lower costs; and merge Xerox's traditional values of customer service and quality with speed, risk-taking, and entrepreneurism. By March 2003 Xerox was showing a profit after several quarters of losses.

Mulcahy is known for her persistence, her toughness, and her ability to inspire, motivate, and lead. She has a reputation for being demanding but personable, able to build strong relationships with all kinds of people. She is also considered low-key and honest. Mulcahy did not take long maternity leaves, but she has always been concerned about balancing family and career. Her family is her first priority. Her husband retired in 1997, which has helped with this balancing act.

She sits on the boards of Axel Johnson Inc., Fannie Mae, Target, and Catalyst. She has been the highest-ranking woman officer in Xerox since 1998. When Carly Fiorina, then the new CEO of Hewlett-Packard, was quoted as saying that the glass ceiling is a thing of the past, Mulcahy disagreed, replying to her in a letter. She thinks it important that there be more women in high positions like theirs. In 2001 she won a Women Elevating Science and Technology Award from TECHXNY/PC EXPO and *Working Woman*. The following year she received Office Depot's Visionary Award.

See also: Manufacturing

Further Reading
Deutsch, Claudia. "At Xerox, the Chief Earns (Grudging) Respect."
Lawlor, Julia. "Is There a Balm after the Storm?"
"Mulcahy, Anne M." In *November 2002 Current Biography*, p. 49–53.
Stirpe, Amanda. "Mulcahy's Message: Persistence Pays."

Muller, Gertrude Agnes (1887–1957), Childcare Products Inventor and Executive

---

Gertrude Muller developed and manufactured childcare products that made the life of a mother easier and the life of her child more pleasant. Her first invention was a child-size toilet seat that was portable, safe, and easy to use. She eventually manufactured these in the company she founded, Juvenile Wood Products Company.

Muller was born in 1887 in Leo, Indiana, to one of the founders of the town. Her father was prosperous, but he died in 1893 and her mother moved back to her home in Fort Wayne, Indiana. To help support the family, her mother took in boarders and made and sold doughnuts. She must have done well, for later she bought some property. Gertrude attended public schools and went to the International Business College in Fort Wayne, Indiana, for a year to learn secretarial skills. She also read voraciously, particularly about health, nutrition, and human development.

Her first job was with General Electric, where she worked for six years. Next she was employed by Van Arnam Manufacturing Company, a manufacturer of toilet seats. While she was there, her sister commented on the embarrassment of the cover's falling off her small daughter's portable toilet seat in an expensive hotel lobby. Gertrude and her sister decided to invent a better product. They designed the Toidey Seat, a collapsible small seat for children to use either on an adult-size toilet seat or on its own base. The first seats were made by Van Arnam, and Gertrude attempted to sell them through the company's clients, plumbers. This effort was not a success.

In 1924 Gertrude Muller founded Juvenile Wood Products Company to market the toilet seats to department stores and baby shops. The company grew steadily, and her older sister, who had a degree in child psychology from Columbia University, joined as vice president and assistant for educational promotion and research. They developed many more products designed to help small children and their mothers, including Toidey Two-Steps, the Comfy-Safe Auto Seat, and a folding booster seat. All the products were designed to foster growing independence as well as safety. Extensive literature accompanied each toilet seat, including a pamphlet, "Training the Baby." Gertrude wrote the literature, which was widely distributed by pediatricians and home economics teachers. With their increasing use of plastics during World War II, she decided to change the name of the company to Toidey Company to better reflect the product.

Safety was always a primary concern. The company even studied automobile crashes so it could make the car seat safer. The National Safety Council made Muller a member of the National Veterans of Safety, and she was invited to the 1954 White House Conference on Highway Safety. Muller remained president of the company until her death.

See also: Inventors

Further Reading

Carey, Charles W. Jr. "Muller, Gertrude Agnes." In John A. Garraty and Mark C. Carnes, eds., p. 273–274.

Rockefeller, Terry Kay. "Muller, Gertrude Agnes." In Barbara Sicherman and Carol Hurd Green, eds., p. 504–506.

Vare, Ethlie Ann, and Greg Ptacek. *Mothers of Invention*, p. 47.

Musham, Bettye Martin (1932–), Furniture Industry Executive

Bettye Musham's company, Gear Holdings Inc., has been included on the *Working Woman* list of top woman-owned companies in six of the years between 1992 and 2001. It was number 36 in 2000, with sales of $400 million. Musham founded her innovative furniture design, licensing, and marketing company in 1978, pioneering mix-and-match furniture and accessory patterns and designs.

Born in 1932, Musham holds a four-year degree from Duke University. After brief excursions into nursing and working as a manager for Louis Vuitton luggage, she went into business for herself. By 1992 sales were $280 million, and she employed thirty people. Her specialty is selling "environments," furniture and accessories that contribute to the whole design of a room. She licenses fabrics, coordinated posters and pictures, furniture, and even looks for the entire home. The company's "lifestyle" themes change the color of the wood, the overall color schemes, and the kinds of design and accessories to create a room or several rooms. Musham began with her own retail stores but now concentrates on selling through department stores. In 1999 she culminated four years of negotiations to bring her collections to the China-based Friendship Store Group.

Musham sits on the boards of two companies: Brunswick Corporation and Wallace Computer Services. She was chosen for the latter because of her strong background in entrepreneurship, her creative marketing skills, and her broad operating experience. She is married and has one daughter.

See also: Manufacturing

Further Reading
Lappen, Alyssa, ed. "The *Working Woman* 25," p. 66.

Music Industry, *see* Entertainment Industry

N

NAFE, *see* National Association for Female Executives

National Association for Female Executives (NAFE)

PO Box 469031, Escondido, CA 92046-9925
www.nafe.com

The National Association for Female Executives (NAFE) was founded in 1972. Its mission is to provide resources and services to empower its members to achieve career success and financial security. It promotes networking and relationships with other female executives through regional network coordinators as well as local networks in each state. The association also provides a variety of services including national conferences and leadership seminars, résumé evaluation and writing, legal assistance, and financial planning. It also offers savings on travel, rental cars, health and medical insurance, prescription plans, copying, and shipping. Membership includes a subscription to the journal *Executive Female*.

National Association of Bank Women (NABW), *see* Financial Women International

National Association of Women Business Owners (NAWBO)

1100 Wayne Ave., Suite 830, Silver Springs, MD 20910
www.nawbo.org

The National Association of Women Business Owners (NAWBO), founded in 1974, is an association of women who own and operate businesses. Its purpose is to identify these women and provide mutual support, communication, and a sharing of experience and talent. Its members also try to use their collective influence to broaden opportunities for women in business. The association offers workshops and seminars, leadership training, an information clearinghouse, a referral service, representation before governmental bodies, and liaison with other similar groups.

It is affiliated with the World Association of Women Entrepreneurs and was formerly known, until 1976, as the Association of Women Business Owners. The organization publishes a monthly newsletter, *NAWBO Time*, which includes a calendar of events. A membership directory is available to members. There is an Economic Conference Winter Meeting each year and a July annual meeting. Dues are $75 per person, plus local chapter dues. There are three state groups and sixty local groups and over 8,000 members.

National Business Hall of Fame, *see* Junior Achievement's Global Business Hall of Fame

National Coalition of 100 Black Women (NCBW)

38 W. 32nd Street, Suite 1610, New York, New York 10001-3816

Founded by Jewell Jackson McCabe in 1981, the National Coalition of 100 Black Women (NCBW) is a nonprofit organization providing programs and networking and mentoring opportunities to empower African American women. "The purpose of the Coalition is: to foster principles of equal rights and opportunities; to promote the awareness of black culture; to develop the potential of the membership for effective leadership, and to cooperate with other persons and organizations to achieve mutual goals" ("National Coalition of 100 Black Women Hosts"). Emphasis is on leadership training, economic development, career opportunities, women's health issues, and African American history with a focus on female role models. As of 2002 there were 7,000 members and sixty-five state chapters. Many of its programs are jointly sponsored by other community groups or corporations. One such program was a financial literacy campaign co-sponsored with Household International. The coalition gives Candace Awards each year to outstanding African American men or women in several categories, including business.

See also: African American Businesswomen

Further Reading
"National Coalition of 100 Black Women Hosts First Awards Luncheon."
"National Coalition of 100 Black Women (NCBW)." In *Associations Unlimited.*
   (Retrieved July 17, 2002.)

National Federation of Business and Professional Women's Clubs, Inc.

2012 Massachusetts Ave., NW, Washington DC 20036
www.bpwwusa.org

Founded by Lena Madesin Phillips in 1919, the National Federation of Business and Professional Women's Clubs, Inc. is aimed at men and women of every age, religion, political party, and socioeconomic background. Its purpose is to achieve equity for all women in the workplace through advocacy, education, and information. In 1930 Phillips also founded the International Federation of Business and Professionals Women's Clubs, with the same mission.

See also: Phillips, Lena Madesin

National Foundation for Women Business Owners, *see* Center for Women's Business Research

National Organization for Women (NOW)

Founded in 1966, the National Organization for Women (NOW) is the largest organization of feminist activists in the United States. One of its goals is to eliminate discrimination in the workplace. The organization's activities began in the 1960s in support of the Equal Rights Amendment, the election of women to Congress and other political posts, and the successful elimination of sex-segregated help-wanted advertisements. NOW's official priorities are winning economic equality for women; championing abortion rights, reproductive freedom, and other women's health issues; opposing racism and fighting bigotry; and ending violence against women.

Further Reading
www.now.org

Native American Businesswomen, *see* American Indian Businesswomen

Natori, Josie (1947–), Fashion Designer

Josie Natori founded her intimate apparel company, the Natori Company, in 1977. She is the importer, designer, manufacturer, and merchandiser of expensive fashions and she pioneered lingerie as outerwear.

Natori was born in the Philippines, the eldest daughter of six children. Her father owned a construction company, and her mother was a pharmacist as well as her father's business partner. Her grandmother, also a businesswoman, had a great influence on Natori, teaching her that women should earn their own money. Josie was a child prodigy pianist and gave her first solo performance at age nine. She was brought up a strict Catholic, educated by nuns. In 1964 she came to the United States, attending Manhattanville College, from which she graduated with honors in economics and business. She later met and married Ken Natori, a Wall Street executive. They have one son.

Her first job was with Bache Securities, in its corporate finance department. She opened a branch in the Philippines but had to close it in 1970 because of disagreements with the Philippine government. Natori then joined Merrill Lynch and switched to investment banking. Within five years she had been promoted to vice president, the company's first woman in that position; however, she really wanted to own her own business. In 1977 a friend in the Philippines sent her an embroidered blouse that Natori thought might sell in the U.S. market. She took the blouse to a buyer in Bloomingdale's, who suggested lengthening it into a nightshirt. Natori liked the idea of lingerie that could be worn as outerwear as well.

> With $150,000 in personal savings . . . she hired a freelance designer and began the Natori Company in her living room.

With $150,000 in personal savings and no design training, manufacturing background, or garment industry experience, she hired a freelance designer and began the Natori Company in her living room. Within the first three months orders totaled $150,000. Over the next three years she built a factory in Philadelphia and received orders from Saks Fifth Avenue, Neiman-Marcus, and Lord & Taylor. Her husband joined the company in 1985 to take charge of its financial side. By 1989 they were employing 900 Filipino craftsmen, whose embroidery was a focal part of her designs. She added accessories, shoes, jewelry, and perfume to her fashions. By 2002 wholesale sales had exceeded $50 million.

Natori combines craftsmanship and luxury in her designs, and she revolutionized the intimate apparel market. She learned about the industry from the ground up. She feels that her biggest assets are being a woman and being Filipina (Bush in Zia, *Notable Asian Americans*, p. 284) and uses her cultural heritage for inspiration. Her company combines business with art, and she motivates her employees with pride and workmanship.

The Natori Company holds charity fashion shows for the Philippine-American Foundation. In 1993 President Bill Clinton appointed Natori to the White House Commission for Small Business. Her awards include the Golden Shell Award for Excellent Companies, from the Philippine government; the Galleon Award, from Philippine president Corazon Aquino; and the Harriet Alger Award for Entrepreneurship, from *Working Woman*. In 1987 *Fortune* called her a woman to watch, as did *Working Woman* in 1991. Natori has chaired the Fashion & Design Council of the Philippines, which she helped to found, and is a member of the Committee of 200. She is an active philanthropist. In 1990 she helped raise relief funds for victims of an earthquake in the Philippines.

See also: Asian American Businesswomen; Fashion Industry; Immigrant Businesswomen

Further Reading
Bush, Valerie Chow. "Josie Natori." In Helen Zia, p. 282–284.
"Natori's 25 Year Mystique." Oppedisano, Jeannette M. *Historical Encyclopedia of American Women Entrepreneurs: 1776 to the Present*, p. 182–185.
Schiro, Anne-Marie. "Natori Planning to Cast a Wider Net."

NAWBO, *see* National Association of Women Business Owners

Nelson, Marilyn Carlson (1939–), Travel Industry Executive

Marilyn Carlson Nelson inherited her position as CEO of Carlson Companies, her father's $20 billion travel conglomerate, in what the *Star Tribune* called "Minneapolis's longest-running generational transfer" (Merrill, "Bridging the Generations"). She has turned the company into a worldwide behemoth. Among its holdings are Radisson Hotels, TGI Friday's, Carlson Wagonlit Travel, and a $1 billion business advising companies on employee incentives. Carlson Companies has been high on *Working Woman*'s list of top woman-owned companies since she took over. She has been on *Fortune*'s list of most powerful corporate women for several years.

Nelson was born and raised in Minneapolis. A childhood memory is of her father bringing business problems to the dinner table, asking her and her sister what they would do. She was active in extracurricular activities in high school and was a member of the student council. Her higher education was at the Sorbonne and Smith College, with a junior year abroad in Switzerland. In 1961 she graduated with honors from Smith and married Glen Nelson, a surgeon. They had a son and three daughters. Until her first child was born, she worked at Paine Webber as a securities analyst. She then stopped working because her father told her to, but she became very involved in volunteer work.

In 1971 Nelson and her sister bought Citizens State Bank of Waterville, Minnesota; they are still on its board of directors. In 1975 she became the first woman on the board of directors of First Trust Company. Her fund-raising and persuasion efforts culminated in her luring the Super Bowl of 1992 to Minneapolis, an effort that took several years.

In 1989 her father asked Nelson to join the company he had started as the Gold Bond Stamp Company in 1938. It had grown into a conglomerate of hotels, restaurant chains, travel agencies, cruise ship lines, real estate holdings, marketing agencies, and investment companies employing more than 70,000 people. Reluctant at first, she began as a vice president along with her brother-in-law Skip Gage. Power was divided between them, with Nelson in the holding company and Gage on the operating side. In 1991 Gage left the company and Nelson took over the travel unit and chaired the audit committee. She advised her father to bring in an outside chief financial officer, which he did in 1993. She also oversaw the investment committee. By 1994 her father thought that Nelson was ready to run the company. He stayed on as chair of the executive committee. Following his death in 1999 Nelson became chairman of the board in addition to her positions of CEO and president. That year she also started Carlson Travel Academies, with a plan for expansion through franchises. The following year the company developed a unique customer-tracking technology that transformed the travel business.

Nelson had several challenges: to keep the support of family members, to maintain a 15 percent growth rate, to upgrade technology, to keep the company private and train her son Curtis to take over, and to convince nonfamily executives that there was room for them too. She began a series of changes, acquisitions, and joint ventures. The acquisition of Thomas Cook in England in 1999 increased the travel business by 200 percent. She sold it in 2000. Another major change was expanding employee benefit programs. She developed the first employee attitude survey, initiated stock-sharing plans, increased the number of woman officers from fifteen to forty-two in five years, instituted leadership seminars and brought in speakers from outside the company, emphasized mentoring, and introduced flextime and a day care center. Nelson's style is consensus building, but she knows every detail at every level. She has made her style, very different from her father's, the corporate culture of the company.

Nelson believes in making grand entrances. She has arrived in a horse-drawn Cinderella coach, on Rollerblades, and in a flying suit after performing an air stunt. She celebrated her promotion to CEO by flying in an F-16 fighter jet over the Nevada desert. She is tenacious, aggressive, and a risk-taker, with abundant charm. She is also known for her vision and diplomacy and is a people person. Nelson has four grandchildren.

> She has arrived in a horse-drawn Cinderella coach, on Rollerblades, and in a flying suit after performing an air stunt.

She has sat on the boards of Exxon, Citizens State Bank, the World Travel and Tourism Council, and the U.S. National Tourism Office. She has also served on the boards of First Bank Systems, from 1978 to 1997, and Qwest. Nelson was named a top executive of 1998 by *Business Week*; executive of the year by *Corporate Report-Minnesota*; and, along with her sister, one of the *Forbes* 400. From 1995 to 2000 she was named one of the hundred most powerful women in travel by *Travel Agent*. The king of Sweden presented her with the Royal Order of the North Star, and she was awarded the Order of the White Rose by Finland. In 1999 she won the Larry King Heart Award. The College of Saint Benedict awarded her its Renaissance Award in 2001. She holds three honorary doctorates. After her daughter Juliet died in an automobile accident in 1985, Nelson decided to improve life for others. Five percent of company profits go to charitable causes each year, and she is active in community organizations. In 2002 Carlson Companies was named one of the hundred best companies for working mothers by *Working Mother*. That October she was appointed to head the National Women's Business Council by President George W. Bush. Nelson was inducted into the Enterprising Women Hall of Fame in March 2003.

See also: Travel Industry

Further Reading

Merrill, Ann. "Bridging the Generations: Consensus-Building, People Skills Are Key Tools in Nelson's Style."

Nelson, Marilyn Carlson. "Faith in Yourself: Never, Ever, Ever Give Up."

Papa, Mary Bader. "A Son Named Marilyn."

Tait, Nikki. "Matriarch of Good Relations: Profile Marilyn Carlson Nelson."

Netnokwa (circa 1745–1815), Fur Trader

Netnokwa, a member of the Ottowa tribe, was the leader, or captain, of a group of fur trappers in the Great Lakes region during the late eighteenth century. Her band of trappers consisted of her sons and sons-in-law as well as a white captive, John Tanner. She traded at Mackinac and was an important part of Algonquian society, making all the decisions for the band.

Netnokwa was born circa 1740 to 1750 in the central Great Lakes area. She wielded much authority within her family: All family property belonged to her, and she made all decisions for the family. She also was the person who asked the spirits to intervene in times of crisis, such as poor weather or scarcity of wild game. She married Tawgaweninne, who later died in a drunken brawl in the Red River area in the late 1790s. It was then that Netnokwa began her trapping career. She bought John Tanner for whiskey and other valuable gifts and treated him like a son, teaching him to hunt and set traps for beaver. Tanner wrote a book describing life with Netnokwa and her family that is said to be one of the best accounts of what life among the Indians was like in that period (A Narrative). Unfortunately, Netnokwa had a problem with liquor, and she was hungry most winters because she sold her pelts for rum. She never remarried after Tawgaweninne's death, and trapped and sold her goods for the rest of her life.

See also: American Indian Businesswomen

Further Reading
Peers, Laura. "Netnokwa." In Gretchen M. Bataille and Laurie Lisa, p. 223.
Tanner, John. A Narrative of the Captivity and Adventures of John Tanner during Thirty Years' Residence among the Indians in the Interior of North America.

Networking

According to The Human Resources Glossary, networking is "the process of acquiring, cultivating, and using a community of professionals to get advice, information, assistance, contacts, and referrals" (Tracey, p. 78). There are all kinds of networks: social networks, religious networks, organizational networks, or special purpose networks. They can be international, national, local, or just in-company. Over the past thirty years, networks for businesswomen have helped them in dealing with the old boys' network, serving as a way to become informed about careers, jobs, problem solving, business start-ups, and financing. Many entrepreneurs have credited networks for their business success. Ethnic groups have found their networks to be an enormous help. George Fraser, in Juliet K. Walker's Encyclopedia of African American Business History, points out that African American networks go back to Harriet Tubman and her underground railroad and are "based on African principles of community and tribalism" (p. 431). Building a strong personal network is a primary way to deal with isolation, land a better job, or obtain advice and help.

Many companies have their own women's networks. These grew out of the need to learn more about women's issues at work and to retain valuable women employees. They have been used to advise senior management, hold networking events, set up mentoring programs, and sponsor speakers. The most successful of these groups have support from management, a budget, a well-articulated mission statement with goals and objectives, effective leaders, and well-managed communications. Such groups are useful for support, career development, gaining leadership experience, and advising management in order to effect organizational change. "Women's networks have had an enormous impact on company culture and policy as well as the experiences of women employees" (*Cracking the Glass Ceiling*, p. 57).

See also: Mentors; Small Business Administration (SBA)

Further Reading

Cracking the Glass Ceiling: Catalyst's Research on Women in Corporate Management 1995–2000, p. 51–57.

Nierenberg, Andrea R. *Nonstop Networking.*

Whiteley, Sharon, Kathy Elliott, and Connie Duckworth. *The Old Girls' Network: Insider Advice for Women Building Businesses.*

www.nafe.com

www.onlinewbc.gov

Newspaper Publishing, *see* Publishing Industry

Nicholson, Eliza Jane Poitevent Holbrook (1849–1896), Newspaper Publisher

---

Eliza Nicholson was the first woman publisher of a daily newspaper, the New Orleans Picayune, in the Deep South. She was a particularly innovative and persevering publisher.

Nicholson was born in 1849 in her family's home in Mississippi on the Pearl River, the fifth of eight children. Because her mother was ill much of the time, Eliza was raised by a childless aunt and uncle on their plantation. While living there, she began writing poetry. She graduated from the Female Seminary in Amite, Louisiana, in 1867. By 1869 she had had poems published in an anthology. While visiting her grandfather in New Orleans, she met Alva Morris Holbrook, owner of the *New Orleans Picayune*. He admired her poetry and asked her to become the literary editor of the newspaper, for $25 a week. Although her family opposed this move, mostly because New Orleans was filled with Union soldiers involved in Reconstruction following the Civil War, she accepted his offer. She was responsible for choosing verse and editing the Sunday literary section.

Holbrook sold the paper soon afterward, and he and Eliza were married in 1872. He was forty-one years older than she. The syndicate that bought the paper failed, however, and ownership reverted to Holbrook. Following his death in 1876, Eliza inherited not only the paper but also debts amounting to $80,000. She decided to keep publishing and pay off the debts. Backed by Jose Quintero as editor and George Nicholson as business manager, she took over. She told the staff to leave if they preferred not to work for a woman, and set about changing the newspaper. In her first editorial she outlined her policy: The paper would remain neutral politically although not on principles, it would be anti-Reconstruction, and the content would be focused toward the family.

She added special departments for women and children; columns on fashion, and features on household advice, theater and culture, health and medicine; humor; and comic drawings. In 1878 she married Nicholson, who continued as business manager while she performed all the editorial supervision. In 1879 she added a society page, an innovation for the time, when people considered it an invasion of privacy. The Sunday edition included fiction by noted authors such as Rudyard Kipling, Frank Stockton, and Mark Twain.

The newspaper grew in size and coverage under her leadership, quickly erasing the debt and increasing in circulation from 6,000 daily in 1878 to more than 49,000 daily and Sunday in 1891. Eliza Nicholson was firmly committed to sound journalistic principles and covered issues of the day, including the development of the New Orleans harbor, draining the swamps, and Sunday closing laws for saloons. She refused to report on scandals, affairs, divorces, or sensational topics. She hired stable and trustworthy staff, including women. While not a supporter of woman suffrage, she believed that women should be able to support themselves.

In 1885 Nicholson founded and was the first president of the National Women's Press Association, and in 1889 she was elected the first honorary member of the New York Women's Press Club. She died from influenza in 1896, ten days after her husband. Legend says that she called her staff to her deathbed and asked them to keep the paper going until her two sons were old enough to take over. Apparently they did, for the *New Orleans Picayune* remained in Nicholson hands for the next generation. Eventually it merged with another newspaper to become the *Times-Picayune*. (As an aside, a "picayune" was a coin in New Orleans, the price of the paper.)

See also: Publishing Industry

Further Reading

Bird, Caroline. *Enterprising Women*, p. 136–138.

Dabney, Thomas E. *One Hundred Great Years: The Story of the* Times-Picayune *from Its Founding to 1940.*

Harrison, James Henry. *Pearl Rivers, Publisher of the Picayune.*

McKerns, Joseph P., ed. *Biographical Dictionary of American Journalism*, p. 513–514.

9 to 5, National Association of Working Women

1430 Peachtree Street, Suite 610, Atlanta, GA 30309
800-522-0925

In 1973, 9 to 5, National Association of Working Women, was founded by a group of Boston office workers who gathered to talk about women's issues in the workplace: sexual harassment, work/family challenges, and pay equity. Membership as of 2003 was 13,000. The association's goal is to eliminate workplace discrimination through educating women about their legal rights, monitoring enforcement agencies, expanding antidiscrimination laws, and working to pass key legislation at both the federal and the state level. It also publishes research studies on automation's effect on workers, how visual display terminals cause hazards to reproduction, family and medical leaves, and stress.

Further Reading
www.9to5.org

Nontraditional Occupations

Nontraditional occupations for women are those that are viewed as male-dominated for reasons of strength, danger, appropriateness, or skills. They include heavy labor, mining, construction, truck driving, the automobile industry, and engineering. Usually these occupations have been better paid than traditional, pink-collar women's occupations such as nursing, librarianship, dental assistance, social work, and teaching. There are several theories as to why women have been excluded from these jobs. Male resistance has been strong, and labor unions have made it difficult for women to move into these occupations. And, of course, societal values stigmatized women in men's jobs. During World Wars I and II, however, women responded to the need for workers in factories and other nontraditional positions.

A few women throughout history have excelled in business and trade and in nontraditional occupations, but it wasn't until the women's movement of the 1960s that the status quo was seriously challenged. Since then many women working in these areas have proved successful; for instance, Rebecca Lukens in iron manufacturing, Linda Alvarado and Barbara Grogan in construction, Anne Stevens and Cynthia Trudell in automobile manufacturing, Olive Beech in the aircraft industry, Louise Francesconi in defense, and Kathy Lehne and Patricia Woertz in the oil industry. In 2002 Women in the Economy released a report showing that women's participation in nontraditional occupations is increasing because women are attracted to the higher wages, better employee benefits, and better opportunities. Balancing these positives, there are fewer opportunities for flexible work arrangements (www.womenintheeconomy.org).

Further Reading
Schneider, Dorothy, and Carl J. Schneider. *ABC-CLIO Companion to Women in the Workplace.* p. 189–190, 194–195.
www.womenintheeconomy.org

Nooyi, Indra K. (1955–), Beverage Industry Executive

Indra Nooyi first appeared on *Fortune*'s list of most powerful women in American business in 2000, in the number 43 spot. With her promotion to the position of president and CFO of PepsiCo. she rose to number 10 in 2001, and in 2003 she was number 8. She is the highest-ranking Indian-born woman in the U.S. corporate world.

Nooyi was born and educated in India, receiving an MBA from the Indian Institute of Management in Calcutta. Her parents were always supportive; in fact her mother wanted her to become president of India and taught her conversational skills in preparation. Her first job was for Johnson & Johnson in India, where she introduced sanitary napkins, a difficult feat because advertising such products was not allowed. She came to the United States in 1978 and earned a master's degree in public and private management from Yale. She is married; her husband is a partner in a management consulting firm. They have two daughters and keep a traditional Hindu home. Nooyi is a baseball fan.

She began her U.S. career directing international group strategy for a Boston consulting group. After six years she became vice president and director of corporate strategy and development at Motorola. In 1990 she moved to Asea Brown Bovari as senior vice president of strategy, planning, and strategic marketing. In 1994 she joined PepsiCo as senior vice president of strategic planning. She then became senior vice president of corporate strategy and development and, in February 2000, senior vice president and chief financial officer. In this role she was instrumental in the spin-off of the restaurant and bottling business and the acquisition of Tropicana and Quaker Oats. In May 2001 Nooyi was named president and CFO of Pepsi Company and, as such, shared responsibility for running the giant company; that October she was made a director. In 2003 she also acquired responsibility for cross-divisional portfolio innovation and product initiatives.

She believes strongly in expanding her skills, and one of her goals is to read a book every day. She is considered a steady leader, careful and pragmatic. She has said that women striving for the top have to perform at a higher level than men, and that a key way to do that is to have the right people around to provide feedback. She is coolly logical and knows when to take action and when to hold back.

Nooyi sits on the board of directors of Timberland Company and Phoenix Home Life Mutual Insurance Company in addition to PepsiCo. She was named in a *Fortune* article as an executive "on the rise." She won the Hunt-Scanlon Advisors Human Capital Advantage Award that recognizes an executive who has shown excellence in human capital management while also adding to shareholder value.

See also: Asian American Businesswomen; Food Industry; Immigrant Businesswomen

Further Reading

"Hunt-Scanlon to Name Indra K. Nooyi of PepsiCo as Human Capital Award Recipient at February Conference."

"A Potent Ingredient in Pepsi's Formula."

Sellers, Patricia. "The 50 Most Powerful Women in Business: Secrets of the Fastest-Rising Stars."

NOW, *see* National Organization for Women

O

O'Dell, Jane (1940–), Truck Dealership Owner

Jane O'Dell's company, Westfall Investment Associates, has been on *Working Woman*'s list of the top fifty woman-owned businesses since 1996. In 2001 it was listed as having $590 million in sales and 600 employees. O'Dell has consistently declined interviews, saying that she'd rather be selling trucks (Schmuckler and Collingwood. "The Top 50 Women Business Owners," p. 42).

O'Dell and her husband, Ervin O'Dell, began the business as partners with the Westfalls in the 1960s under the name Westfall-O'Dell Transportation Services. Today O'Dell's daughter and son are company vice presidents. The business has expanded over the years into a major parts business, Rapidways Truck Leasing, Freightliner franchises in four Missouri cities, a truck-terminal operation, and an auto dealership. In 1995 it was the second-largest GMC truck dealership in the United States. As of 2000 the company employed more than 1,000 people nationally, and its revenues were over $445 million. O'Dell's associates say that she runs the business and is aggressive, hard working, and a natural leader (Schmuckler and Collingwood, p. 42).

See also: Automobile Industry

Further Reading
Bamford, Janet, and Jennifer Pendleton. "The Top 50 Women-Owned Businesses," p. 44.
Schmuckler, Eric, and Harris Collingwood. "The Top 50 Women Business Owners," p. 42.

Odom, Judy C. (1953–), Software Executive

Judy Odom is CEO and chairman of the board of Software Spectrum, a high-tech software retailer that has appeared on *Working Woman*'s list of the top woman-owned businesses since 1992. In 2000, with sales of $930 million and 2,400 employees, it ranked number 20, and in 2001 ranked 17.

Odom was born in Fort Worth, Texas, and received a BA in accounting from Texas Institute of Technology in 1974. She is a certified public accountant. From 1974 to 1976 Odom was a staff accountant at Coopers & Lybrand in Dallas. She then joined Grant Thornton as an auditor in 1976 and had just been made a partner in 1985 when she, her husband Richard Sims, and Frank Tindle founded Software Spectrum. Tindle retired soon thereafter; Sims became president and handled all sales; while Odom, as chief operating officer, handled the finances. The company had grown 300 percent by 1992. In 1993 it developed a program that distributed and installed software by modem, but it was best known for excellent service. Software Spectrum established its reputation by obtaining hard-to-find software for clients; most clients today are large corporations. In 1996 the company expanded into the global market and by 1998 was the largest worldwide supplier of software and technology services. Also in 1998, Odom became chairman and CEO. In 2002 Level 3 acquired Software Spectrum. The transaction was valued at approximately $109 million. Odom agreed to serve as CEO of what was now a subsidiary.

She serves on the board of directors of Leggett & Platt Inc. In 2000 she won the Dallas Richardson YWCA's award for achievement in the high-tech industry. That year her name appeared as Judy Sims in the company's annual report; the following year it was Judy C. Odom and no mention was made of Richard Sims.

See also: Information Technology Industry

Further Reading
Darrow, Barbara. "Software Spectrum: Moving to Services at Net Speed."
Forest, Stephanie A. "Software Spectrum: Have They Got a Program for You."
"Software Spectrum: Retail Entrepreneurs of the Year; Company Profile."

Office Romance

"It is basic that opposite sexes attract naturally and they've been doing this since history was first recorded. The office romance is here to stay and businesses must accept this fact in a positive way" (Powers, *The Office Romance*, p. 31). Twenty years ago, each party in an office romance ran the risk of getting fired, but particularly the subordinate, who was usually a woman. As more and more women entered the workforce beginning in the 1970s, more and more office flirting and romances occurred. Members of both sexes worked long hours, often in teams, and work became their social context as well.

The Civil Rights Act of 1991 changed the office atmosphere by forcing everyone to deal with the issues of sexual harassment and to clearly differentiate sexual harassment from romance. During the 1990s many researchers studied aspects of these issues, ranging from a fear of lowered employee morale to problems resulting from a breakup to the potential for sexual harassment suits. Other problems included supervisor–subordinate relationships, issues of favoritism, illegal evaluations, and conflicts of interest. On the positive side, those relationships that ended in marriage engendered loyalty from the couple, working conditions became more enjoyable, and both partners exhibited better teamwork, better communication, and greater productivity.

There are risks in office romances for both the company and the partners involved. Co-workers may fear a loss of power, and their productivity may diminish as their morale does. They may suspect favoritism, and the careers of one or both partners could be destroyed or their reputations damaged. If they break up and the separation is not amicable, there are risks running from allegations of sexual harassment to, at the least, distraction and turmoil within the office.

All the research points to the advantages of having a very clearly worded, written sexual harassment policy and a more lenient office romance policy. In a 1998 survey of 2,800 human resource professionals, 13 percent of companies had written policies, 14 percent had unwritten policies, and 72 percent had no policy at all (Symonds et al., "Sex on the Job," p. 31). Since then, with an increase in the number of sexual harassment suits, more companies have been putting co-worker personal relationship policies into writing. The trend is to view office romances favorably; however, if the partners are in a supervisory or evaluative relationship, a comparable position generally needs to be found. Some companies favor discreet disclosure of the relationship to a supervisor so that possible conflicts of interest or chain-of-command issues can be addressed. Above all, the office romance policy should be reasonable and well communicated, and it should emphasize mediation as a conflict-resolution technique.

See also: Sexual Harassment

Further Reading

Florence, Mari. *Sex at Work: Attraction, Orientation, Harassment, Flirtation and Discrimination.*

Powers, Dennis M. *The Office Romance: Playing with Fire without Getting Burned.*

Symonds, William C. "Sex on the Job."

Old Boys Network

According to *The Dictionary of Cultural Literacy*, the old boys network is "a set of relationships based on past friendship or acquaintance that sometimes replaces or undermines official organizations" (Hirsch, p. 405). In the business world it can show up as favoritism in recruitment and hiring practices, promotions, and corporate boards. The *Human Resources Glossary* goes on to point out that this is an "informal and exclusive club" in which successful persons, usually men, have considerable power to influence business outcomes. "Typically, the old boys are white, Anglo-Saxon, protestant males" (Tracey, p. 364).

Organizational Communication, *see* Communication

Organizational Culture, *see* Corporate Culture

Ortenberg, Elisabeth Claiborne, *see* Claiborne, Liz

Ottendorfer, Anna Sartorius Uhl (1815–1884), Newspaper Publisher

According to the *National Cyclopedia of American Biography*, Anna Ottendorfer "possessed eminent executive abilities and business skill, and by perseverance, energy and pluck succeeded in making her newspaper not only remunerative but a power in the land" (p. 194). The newspaper she published was an important part of German American life.

Ottendorfer was born in Würzburg, Germany, to a small shopkeeper and his wife. There is confusion about her last name as well as to whether she married Jacob Uhl before or after emigrating to the United States in 1836. There, she either joined a brother in Niagara County, or moved directly to New York City. In 1844, after a long struggle to make ends meet during the depression of that era, Anna and Jacob began making payments on a printing shop in the city. One of their clients was a German weekly newspaper, *New-Yorker Staats-Zeitung*. The next year they bought the paper from its founder. Its circulation grew steadily as they made it, first, into a triweekly and then, in 1849, a daily. Anna worked as a full partner in this endeavor while caring for six children. She shared in editorial planning and business management and, when necessary, helped with the typesetting and printing.

In 1852 Jacob Uhl died suddenly and Anna became the sole publisher. Despite many offers to buy the company, she did not sell it. During this period, there was a large influx of German immigrants to the United States. They needed a German-language newspaper, and Anna's became one of the foremost foreign-language papers in the country. Oswald Ottendorfer, a lawyer and liberal who had fled Germany after taking part in the Revolution of 1848, was her assistant editor. In 1858 Anna made him editor, and one year later they married. She remained general manager. Oswald's editorial policies were both liberal and political. He supported the Union during the Civil War and opposed slavery and, later, prohibition. He also fought New York City's political machine, Tammany Hall.

By 1872 the newspaper's circulation was 55,000, and the Ottendorfers began to publish books by German-American authors. They were doing so well that Anna began to give away her money, focusing on hospitals, the elderly, and the promotion of German traditions and culture. She founded the Isabella Home, named for a daughter who had died, which provided $50,000 to build a home for elderly German women. The Hermann Uhl Memorial Fund, named for a son who had died, focused on the study of German in American schools. Grants from it went primarily to the German-American Teachers College of Milwaukee. Ottendorfer also endowed the woman's pavilion at the New York German Hospital. In 1883 she was awarded a gold medal by Empress Augusta of Germany, in recognition of her philanthropy on behalf of German culture in the United States. It is estimated that she donated $750,000 during her lifetime.

New-Yorker Staats-Zeitung blended general and political news with coverage of the personalities and activities of the German-speaking community. It was successful primarily because of Anna Ottendorfer's management and business acumen.

See also: Immigrant Businesswomen; Publishing Industry

Further Reading

Bergquist, James M. "Ottendorfer, Anna Behr Uhl." In John A. Garraty and Mark C. Carnes, p. 841–842.

Langsam, Miriam Z. "Ottendorfer, Anna Sartorius." In Edward T. James, p. 656–657.

Neidle, Cecyle. *America's Immigrant Women*, p. 48–50.

Owen, Dian Graves (1940–), Health Management Company Founder

Dian Graves Owen's company, Owen Healthcare Inc., made *Working Woman*'s list of the top woman-owned companies from 1972 to 1997. When she sold the company in 1997, it was number 15, with sales of $384 million.

Owen was born in 1940 and grew up in Abilene, Texas. She attended Texas Institute of Technology and McMurray College. She married Jean Owen, a hospital pharmacist. The couple had two sons. In 1969 they founded Owen Healthcare, a hospital pharmacy management company. After Jean was killed in an airplane crash in 1976, Dian took charge of the company, despite family advice to sell it. The company was in trouble. It had contracts with twenty-five hospitals and sales of $10 million, but the largest hospital chain had not renewed its contract. Owen fought back through an aggressive sales effort, and the company signed up twenty-two new hospitals within the year.

Since 1982 the company averaged 23 percent growth per year between 1982 and 1996 and was the largest hospital pharmacy management company in the United States. Owen expanded the business through the introduction of HMS Supplyline, a purchasing database that compares drug and equipment products. She acquired Meditrol, a company that manufactures and distributes automated dispensing systems. The medical industry's need to keep down costs was good business for Owen Healthcare.

In August 1996 Owen took the company public, raising $80 million. The opening price was $12 per share, and by the end of the year it had reached $24. In March 1997 the shareholders voted to merge with Cardinal Health, a drug distributor. The agreement made Owen Healthcare a subsidiary of Cardinal. Owen had given up the presidency in 1996.

Owen has been active in her Texas hometown, sitting on the board of directors of the First National Bank of Abilene, the Abilene Chamber of Commerce, and the Hospice of Abilene. She was director of the Texas Department of Commerce from 1987 through 1991 and has been a trustee of McMurray College. She was inducted into the Texas Women's Hall of Fame in 1997.

Further Reading

Mintz, Bill. "Prescription for Growth: Owen to Merge with Cardinal Health."

Schmuckler, Eric, and Harris Collingwood. "The Top 50 Woman Business Owners," p. 34, 36.

P

Pascal, Amy (1958–), Film Executive

Amy Pascal, chairman of Columbia Tristar Motion Picture Group, is one of the top women in Hollywood. She was new to *Fortune*'s list of the most powerful women in business in 2002 and continued on it in 2003, when she was ranked number 38.

Pascal was raised in Los Angeles, California. Her first job was in junior high school, wrapping books at a local bookstore. After receiving a degree in international relations from UCLA, she spent three weeks as a secretary at Creative Artists Agency. She had always wanted to work in the film business, however, so she took a job as a secretary at Kestral Films, where she worked for the next six years. She then went to Warner Brothers as assistant to producer Tony Garnett, who became one of her mentors.

After a brief stint as vice president of production for 20th Century Fox, in 1987 Pascal joined Columbia Pictures as executive vice president of production. Initially she produced women-oriented movies, such as *Little Women* and *A League of Her Own*, but she was also responsible for *Groundhog Day*. In September 1994 she moved to Turner Pictures Worldwide, then a fledgling film company, as president of production. Her goal was to produce six to eight films per year, including developing *You've Got Mail*, *Scooby Doo*, *Michael*, and *City of Angels*. Two years later Turner merged with Time Warner, and Pascal left the company.

Later that year she became president of Columbia Pictures. One of her accomplishments was to merge Columbia and Tristar under the Columbia Pictures name, but owned by Sony Pictures Entertainment. Her goal was to make twenty-four films per year. Her first hit movie was *Big Daddy* in 1999. In December 1999 she was promoted to chairman of Columbia Pictures. In

2000 she was responsible for *Charlie's Angels*; in 2001, *Ali*; and in 2002 *Spider-Man* became the first movie to earn more than $100 million in its opening weekend. Despite three bombs in 2003, Columbia remained in second place at the box office.

Pascal credits her mentors, Dawn Steel and Tony Garnett, for her success. She is an unpretentious, natural leader who fosters open communication and teamwork. She looks for projects with stories about human behavior and character growth. She is also a perfectionist who works very hard, leading by example. She is passionate about projects she believes in and has strong relationships with screenwriters. Anne Thompson calls her "very gifted, endlessly energetic, extremely bright, and eccentric in the best way" ("A League of Her Own," p. 2).

Pascal has been on *Hollywood Reporter*'s Women in Entertainment list, and won the Crystal Award from Women in Film. In 2002 *Variety* named her Showman of the Year, she made *Vanity Fair*'s media mogul list, and she was one of *Glamour*'s Women of the Year. She has been very active in Big Sisters and won its Sterling Award in 2002. She sits on the Rand Corporation's board of trustees and has been national chair of the American Film Institute's Third Decade Council.

See also: Entertainment Industry

Further Reading

Cagle, Jess. "The Women Who Run Hollywood: The 'Boys Club' That Dominates the Film Industry Is Making Way for Three Women with Attitude—and a String of Hits."

Cohen, David. "Hands-on Leader Brings Out Best in Sony's Team."

Thompson, Anne. "A League of Her Own: Columbia Hits 'Panic Room,' 'Spider-Man' and 'MIB II' Indicate Savvy Topper's Smart Choices."

Patterson, Eleanor Medill (1881–1948), Newspaper Publisher

Eleanor "Cissy" Patterson came to newspapering late in her life and was one of the best. She was the only woman newspaper publisher in the United States in the 1930s and 1940s, and the first woman to publish a large metropolitan daily newspaper.

Patterson was born to one of the great newspaper families. Her grandfather founded the *Chicago Tribune*, and her father published it after him. Her brother, her only sibling, later founded the *New York Daily News*. Eleanor was educated by her mother at home, then became a debutante and joined her uncle, the U.S. envoy to Vienna and Saint Petersburg. She was courted in Europe by a Polish count, who she married in 1904. He turned out to be a fortune hunter and philanderer, however. They had a daughter, Felicia, but in 1908 Patterson left the count and started for London with their baby. The count's agents followed, kidnapped the baby, and put Felicia in a convent. It took pressure from Patterson's father, President William Howard Taft, and Tzar Nicholas II to retrieve her. After eight years Patterson and the count were finally divorced; the cost was rumored to be $500,000. All of this personal information was widely reported in newspapers at the time.

Patterson's life was fairly aimless for a while, although she did become the first woman to make the dangerous 163-mile boat trip through the Idaho Salmon River rapids. She traveled extensively in her private railroad car and bought a ranch in Jackson Hole, Wyoming. She wrote two novels as well as some features for the Hearst press on big game hunting and the 1920 Republican National Convention. In 1925 she married a lawyer, Elmer Schlesinger, whom she had met while campaigning for Theodore Roosevelt. Schlesinger died in 1929, and Eleanor officially changed her name to Mrs. Eleanor Patterson. Her annual income from her father's estate at this time ranged from $600,000 to $800,000.

In 1930 Patterson began her newspaper career. She persuaded William Randolph Hearst to let her be editor and publisher of his near-dead newspaper the *Washington Herald*. She was forty-nine and had no real experience running a newspaper, but her instincts were sound, and perhaps for the first time in her life she was serious about doing a good job. She lured one of the best circulation managers from Boston; hired the best reporters, many of them women; and did some reporting herself. In six years circulation doubled. For a story on the jobless during the Great Depression, she disguised herself as "Maude Martin," a destitute woman. Other stories focused on her campaign for hot lunches for Washington, D.C., children, which

> She also walked uninvited into mobster Al Capone's headquarters for an interview—and got one.

she subsidized herself until Congress took over; a cleaner Potomac; Appalachian poverty; and home rule for the District of Columbia. She also walked uninvited into mobster Al Capone's headquarters for an interview—and got one. The paper, reflecting her own personality and interest in personalities, was mercurial, witty, and fascinating. Where others printed columns of society news, she printed pages. She was a capricious and impulsive manager who would fire people and then hire them back. She thrived on controversy.

In 1937 Patterson leased the *Washington Herald* and the *Washington Times* from Hearst with an option to buy them within five years. In 1939 she exercised that option and merged them into one daily with six editions per day, the *Times-Herald*. Her first editorial was boxed and printed on the front page. Still famous in newspaper circles, it was an attack on Alice Longworth Roosevelt, daughter of former president Theodore Roosevelt. By 1943 the paper had the largest circulation in Washington, a city known for the short life of its newspapers. By 1945 net sales topped $1 million.

In 1946 her brother died. Patterson was devastated and never really recovered. She quarreled with the family about the estate and seemed to lose interest in the newspaper, leaving the staff to run it. She died suddenly in 1948, leaving an estate worth $16 million. She willed the paper to seven of its executives, who soon sold it. Patterson's obituary in *Time* describes her as "vain, shrewd, lonely and lavishly spoiled." Yet her staff cried when they heard the news of her death, and *Times-Herald* executive managing editor Michael Flynn said, "She was a hell of a sight better newspaperman than I am" (quoted in "Cissie," p. 36). An article by Dickson Hartwell in *Collier's* stated that everyone who knew Cissy agreed that "she is never dull, never happy, and one of the greatest newspaper editors this country has ever produced" ("No Prissy Is Cissy," p. 78).

See also: Late Bloomers; Publishing Industry

Further Reading
Hartwell, Dickson. "No Prissy Is Cissy."
Healy, Paul F. *Cissy: The Biography of Eleanor M. "Cissy" Patterson.*
Hoge, Alice A. *Cissy Patterson.*

Pay Equity, *see* Compensation

Payson, Joan Whitney (1903–1975), Sports Team Owner

Joan Whitney Payson, "Mother of the Mets," was born to one of the wealthiest families in the United States. It was said of her that "few people of great inherited wealth dispensed their largesse with as much conspicuous relish and as little pretentiousness" (*Current Biography Yearbook*, 1973, p. 338). She was a partner in an investment firm, founded a bookstore, co-owned a horse racing and breeding stable with her brother, and was largely responsible for the New York Mets baseball team.

Payson was born in New York City in 1903. Her paternal grandfather was W. C. Whitney, a streetcar magnate and secretary of the navy under President Grover Cleveland. Her maternal grandfather was John Hay, an assistant secretary to President Abraham Lincoln and secretary of state for Presidents William McKinley and Theodore Roosevelt. Her father, also W. C., invested in lumber, real estate, and banking and left an estate worth almost $200 million. Her father began the family tradition of breeding racehorses and helped found the Saratoga Racetrack. Joan began riding almost as soon as she began to walk. Her mother was an avid baseball fan and began taking her to New York Giants games at age six.

Joan graduated from Miss Chapin's School in New York City, and then spent a year attending both Barnard College and a business school. In 1924 she married Charles Shipman Payson, who came from a wealthy Maine family. They had five children, three girls and two boys, one of whom would be killed in the Battle of the Bulge. In 1929 she founded a children's bookstore. During the 1940s and 1950s she and her brother Jock backed many Broadway plays and movies, most notably *Streetcar Named Desire* and *Gone with the Wind*. In 1944 their mother left Greentrees Stables to the two siblings. Greentrees produced the Horse of the Year in 1949 and 1953.

Joan Whitney Payson is best remembered for the Mets, however. In 1957 the New York Giants threatened to move to California. Payson was a 10 percent owner of the team and begged majority owner Horace Stoneham not to move. She even offered to buy the team, but he moved it in 1958. New York City mayor Robert Wagner appointed William A. Shea the New York commissioner of baseball, and Shea and Payson attempted to form a third league, the Continental League. That threat forced the two major leagues to expand and to provide a new baseball team for the city, the New York Metropolitans in 1962. Payson provided $3.7 million and as 85 percent owner had a great deal of influence. She sat on the board of directors until her death and was both a vice president and president. She left policy decisions to a representative on the board, but she was responsible for persuading Casey Stengel out of retirement to manage the team. She also lured some of her other favorite Giants players away from that team. Payson had a box next to the dugout and she attended every game she could, using her own byzantine scoring system. The only woman owner in baseball, she has been described as the last of the great sportsmen who gave not only money but also loving attention to the team (Durso, p. 189). Cleveland Amory, in an article published in *Vogue*, said of Payson: "We . . . have, in the person of the owner of the Mets, one of the most remarkable ladies who ever graced the ownership of any team." He described her as a people lover with a wonderful sense of humor and fun, a thoroughly good person filled with kindness and generosity ("Mrs. Payson's Ball Park," p. 144).

Payson's philanthropic projects were many. She gave $50,000 to the Emergency Unemployment Relief Committee during the Great Depression, funded the Children's World Center at the 1939–1940 New York World's Fair, and founded the North Shore Hospital in Manhasset, Long Island. She was a governor of New York Hospital, a trustee of the Metropolitan Museum of Art and the Museum of Modern Art, president of the Helen Hay Whitney Foundation, and the donor of a large portion of the financing for the Payne Whitney Gymnasium at Yale. She founded two art galleries and was an avid collector of old masters and an encourager of young artists. Payson died in 1975, and her heirs sold the Mets to Nelson Doubleday in 1980.

Further Reading

Amory, Cleveland. "Mrs. Payson's Ball Park." *Current Biography Yearbook*, 1973, p. 338–340.

Durso, Joseph. "Joan Whitney Payson: America's Sublime Amateur—of Baseball, Racing, Art; Saint Joan of the Mets."

Pearson, Donna Sutherland (1920–), Lumber Executive

In 1998 Donna Sutherland Pearson was listed as CEO of Sutherland Lumber Company and was number 16 on the *Working Woman* list of the top thirty woman-owned businesses in the United States. The following year the company was no longer on the list.

Sutherland Lumber Company is a family-owned retail lumber company operating in several Midwestern states including Colorado, Iowa, Kansas, Nebraska, and Ohio. It was founded by Robert Sutherland in Hugo, Oklahoma, in 1917. Its headquarters is in Kansas City, and its focus is on small markets. The Sutherland family is extremely private so little information is available about Pearson.

See also: Retailing Industry

Further Reading
Fuller, Jennifer Mann. "Sutherland Lumber Often Takes the Quiet Way."
"Sutherland Lumber Company L.P." In *Business & Company Resource Center.*
www.sutherlandlumber.com

Pelham, Mary Singleton Copley (1710–1789), Shopkeeper

Mary Singleton Copley Pelham is known chiefly as the mother of John Singleton Copley, one of the American colonies' foremost portrait painters. However, she was an early colonial businesswomen as well, with a tobacco shop on the Boston wharf.

Born in Ireland, Mary Singleton came to the United States after her marriage to Richard Copley, the proprietor of a tobacco shop. After his death in 1748 she continued the business. She sold what she called "the best Virginia tobacco, cut, pigtail, and spun of all sorts, either wholesale or retail, at the cheapest price" (Dexter, p. 20). Later she married Peter Pelham, a mezzotint engraver and portrait painter, and they had a son named Henry. She continued the business and moved to a better location. Her second husband helped raise John Singleton Copley and taught him how to paint. Pelham stayed in Boston and continued her business during and after the Revolutionary War even though both her sons moved to England.

See also: Colonial Businesswomen; Retailing Industry

Further Reading
Amory, Martha Babcock. *The Domestic and Artistic Life of John Singleton Copley*, R.A.
Prown, Jules David. "Pelham, Mary Singleton Copley." In Edward T. James, ed., p. 43.

Peretsman, Nancy (1954–), Investment Banker

Nancy Peretsman, the media mergers and acquisitions specialist at investment bank Allen & Company, has been on the *Fortune* list of the most powerful women in American business since 1999. That year she was the company's star dealmaker, brokering agreements between MediaOne and AT&T, King World and CBS, and CDnow and a partnership of Time Warner and Sony. She is an adviser to some of the world's most powerful executives, including Bill Gates of Microsoft, and also put together financing for Priceline.com and Oxygen Media.

Peretsman grew up in Worcester, Massachusetts. Her mother was a social worker and therapist. She dropped out of high school because she was bored, and then scored so high on the SATs that she was admitted to Princeton before it officially admitted women. During the summer of 1976 she babysat and watched the house for Herbert Allen, CEO of Allen & Co. Later, while she was in business school at Yale, she worked as a summer intern at Allen & Co. doing risk arbitrage. It was then that her fascination with the world of business began.

Peretsman's first job was at Blythe Eastman Dillon from 1979 to 1983. In 1983 she joined Salomon Brothers, where she was one of only a few women. She built its media group; her specialty was publishing and large media companies. She experienced discrimination there: one project was taken away from her by senior members of the firm when it became clear that the client would be very important to Saloman Brothers. She stuck it out, however, and in 1990 became managing director. In 1995 she moved to Allen & Co. as managing director and executive vice president, again specializing in media and communications business. Her expertise has led to many large deals between very large companies.

Peretsman is a highly intelligent, honest, and trusted person who thrives on difficult and complex challenges Because strong long-term relationships are critical to her business, her skill in working with people is essential. She is also able to forecast trends in her specialty, staying ahead of the market. Unlike those of many other analysts, her reputation remained intact throughout the early twenty-first century stock market fluctuations.

> She once flew from California to New York and back for her daughter's school bake sale.

Peretsman is married to another investment banker and has one daughter. She believes that balancing family and work takes some juggling. She once flew from California to New York and back for her daughter's school bake sale. She has sat on the boards of Priceline.com, Charter Communications, and the New School. She was on the board of trustees at Princeton for fourteen years and is now an emerita trustee. *Crain's New York Business* called her one of the seventy-five most influential women in New York in 1996, and *Success* named her one of the fifty smartest women in the United States in 1999. In 2001 she was named Woman of the Year in the private sector by the Financial Women's Association, which said that she "has not only pursued an extraordinary career on Wall Street but also maintains a healthy value system . . . [and] has a deep understanding of serious issues, a concern for others and a strong commitment to family and community" ("Allen & Co.'s Nancy Peretsman").

See also: Finance Industry

Further Reading

"Allen & Co.'s Nancy Peretsman and New York Stock Exchange's Catherine R. Kinney Named Financial Women's Association's 'Women of the Year'."

Machan, Dyan. "Smarter Than Herbert's Dog."

Mermigas, Diane. "Art of the Media Deal: Nancy Peretsman Brings Credibility and Carefully Crafted Vision to World of Mergers and Acquisitions."

Personnel Management, *see* Human Resources Management

Philipse, Margaret Hardenbrook (c.1650–1690), Merchant, Shipowner

Margaret Philipse is believed to have been the first woman business agent in the American colonies. She lived in New Amsterdam, later known as New York City, and was known as an astute and enterprising businesswoman. Philipse was born in a small town in the Netherlands to a merchant trader and his wife. She immigrated to New Amsterdam in the late 1650s. She was in New Netherland when the banns were read for her marriage in October 1659 to Peter De Vries, a wealthy man. The next year their daughter, Marie, was born. During this marriage, Margaret was an active merchant and the business agent for a number of Dutch merchants trading with New Netherland. De Vries died in 1661, and she took over his business, shipping furs to Holland in exchange for goods that she sold in the colonies. She was probably a shipowner at this time too.

There are records of lawsuits during the next two years. One was in the Court of Orphan Masters, asking her for an accounting of her child's paternal inheritance. She did not provide it, but the court accepted an antenuptial agreement with Frederick Philipse instead. They had married in 1662. As part of the agreement with the court, he adopted Marie and renamed her Eva.

Frederick Philipse, a former carpenter for Peter Stuyvesant who was making his way up in the world, used Margaret's inheritance to build his own mercantile business. She continued her activities as well, with records showing many trips to and from Holland. The two together became one of the wealthiest couples in what was by this time New York. To show that she was a married woman doing business, depositions used her maiden name (Hardenbrook), followed by "who is now married to." Her travels were always on her own ships, the last one on the *King Charles* in 1679. Two missionaries on one of her voyages described her as incredibly "avaricious and covetous," telling a story of circling in harbor waters looking for a mop that had fallen overboard (Schneider and Schneider, p. 61).

Nothing is known of any voyages or mercantile activity after that. Although the wives of New Amsterdam were known for their business acumen, Philipse's activities were unusual because they involved international trade.

See also: Colonial Businesswomen

Further Reading

Gherke, Michael. "Philipse, Margaret Hardenbrook." In John A. Garraty and Mark C. Carnes, eds., p. 440–441.

Judd, Jacob. "Philipse, Margaret Hardenbrook." In Edward T. James, ed., p. 61–62.

McKerns, Joseph P., ed. *Biographical Dictionary of American Journalism*, p. 175–176.

Neidle, Cecyle. *America's Immigrant Women*, p. 9, 269.

Phillips, Lena Madesin (1881–1955), Business Women's Club Founder

Lena Madesin Phillips spent most of her life working for the equality of women, particularly in the workplace. She founded both the National Federation of Business and Professional Women's Clubs Inc. (NFBPWC) and the International Federation of Business and Professional Women's Clubs (IFBPWC). Born Anna Lena Phillips in Kentucky in 1881, she changed her name when she was eleven. After high school graduation she attended college determined to become a concert pianist. A fall damaged nerves in her right arm and put an end to that hope. She came home and taught music until she had a nervous breakdown in 1915. Later, Phillips became the first woman to receive a law degree from the University of Kentucky.

Her first job was at the YWCA, as secretary-treasurer for the Kentucky War Fund Committee. In 1918, as executive secretary of the YWCA National Business Women's Committee, she supervised a survey of business and professional women in the United States. The NFBPWC eventually grew out of this survey and a women's conference she had organized where the attendees suggested forming a permanent organization apart from the YWCA. In 1919 200 women met in St. Louis and officially formed the National Federation of Business and Professional Women (NFBPW), naming Lena as its first executive secretary.

In 1922 she resigned to finish law school, but she continued as a member and was president from 1926 through 1929. In 1930 she founded the IFBPWC and was its president until 1947. She also opened a very successful law practice in New York and became involved with the National Council of Women, where she organized the International Congress of Women. At the Chicago Century of Progress Exposition in 1933 Phillips gave the keynote speech to women representing thirty-one countries.

During World War II she stayed in touch with the European chapters. She traveled to Europe in 1945 to help rebuild branches, stressing the need for women to actively participate in reconstruction and work for peace. The IFBPWC's goal was to advance women's issues for all business and professional women, regardless of rank. It is still active today.

See also: National Federation of Business and Professional Women's Clubs, Inc.

Further Reading

"Phillips, Lena Madesin." In *Current Biography*, 1946, p. 477–479.

Sergio, Lisa. *A Measure Filled: The Life of Lena Madesin Phillips Drawn from Her Autobiography.*

Pickford, Mary (1893–1979), Movie Producer

Mary Pickford was the first Hollywood movie mogul. She was not only the first real movie star, but also the first woman to form her own production company and the first to co-found a film distribution company, United Artists Corporation. She was the financial brains behind United Artists.

Mary Pickford was born Gladys Smith, in Toronto, Canada. Her father died when she was five. Her formal schooling lasted only about six months. Her mother took in boarders to support the family; one of them was a theatrical melodrama producer. Mary talked him into letting her perform, billed as "Baby Gladys Smith," and she and her family traveled the stage circuit for the next nine years. She was the family's chief wage earner, though they had barely enough to live on. In 1908 Broadway theater impresario David Belasco, at her urging, cast her in *The Warrens of Virginia*. He changed her name to Mary Pickford.

After the play closed she decided to try working in Hollywood, where the film industry was just beginning. Films were a step down from the Broadway theater, but the pay was better and the work was steady. D. W. Griffith offered her a job with his American Mutoscope and Biograph Company. Actors did not get billing in those days, but audiences remembered Pickford, calling her "the girl with the curls." She soon realized the power of her popularity. She told Griffith that she had been recognized by several people on the street, and perhaps she should be paid more since she was attracting audiences. For two very prolific years she bounced back and forth between studios, obtaining more and more power over her films and higher and higher pay. By 1911 her salary was $150 a week, and she was firmly established as one of the first movie stars. In 1913 she returned to the stage and then came back to Hollywood after Adolph Zukor bought the movie rights to the play. Her salary rose to $500 a week and, five years later, $1,000 a week with budgetary and creative control. Finally, with 50 percent of profits included, her income was guaranteed to be no less than $1.04 million per picture. Pickford had pioneered the star system.

In 1918 she founded her own production company, the Mary Pickford Film Corporation. It made three films that were financed and distributed by First National. She was paid $250,000 per film and had complete artistic control. In early 1919 she, Douglas Fairbanks, D. W. Griffith, and Charlie Chaplin founded United Artists Corporation. Pickford reasoned that since distribution was an important aspect of film production United Artists should exert both creative control and control over dissemination and promotion. Her business acumen was crucial to the company; Charlie Chaplin, in his autobiography, complimented her knowledge of both business and legal terminology and maneuvers (Fenster, p. 98). The stock was initially split four ways, but Griffith soon sold his shares to the other three. After Fairbanks died Pickford and Chaplin each owned 50 percent until she sold her shares in 1956 for $3 million. It was not a happy partnership. The two fought bitterly over the financial details of the company. Its first film was *Pollyanna*, a highly successful debut, followed by *Little Lord Fauntleroy* and *Little Annie Rooney*. Pickford was tiring of her little girl image, however, and in 1928 she cut off her curls. That year she also made her first talking film, *Coquette*, which was not only a box office success but also won her an Academy Award. She made three more talkies, but her popularity waned and she retired in 1933. She was the first performer to become a millionaire from acting.

> Charlie Chaplin ... complimented her knowledge of both business and legal terminology and maneuvers.

Pickford was married three times. Her first marriage was to Owen Moore, a young, alcoholic actor, when she was eighteen. In 1920 she married Douglas Fairbanks Jr. and in 1937, Buddy Rogers, an actor and bandleader who was nine years younger than she. This marriage lasted until her death in 1979. The Fairbanks marriage was billed as the perfect union between Hollywood's favorite actress and actor; their home, Pickfair, was the social hub of the town. She kept the house when they divorced, and it remained a social center throughout her life. She and Rogers adopted two children. After she retired from acting, Pickford wrote three books. Her health was not good, and she had become an alcoholic. In 1971, after an eye operation, she rarely left her bedroom. Her last public appearance was a taped video thanking the Academy of Motion Picture Arts and Sciences for an Oscar honoring her services to the film industry. Pickford and Rogers were heavily involved in philanthropic activities. They founded the Motion Picture and Television Fund, helped fund the

Motion Picture Home, and established the Mary Pickford Foundation. All of her films are in the Library of Congress; she paid for their preservation. In 1999 Milestone Film and Video remastered six of her classic films and also released a documentary, *Mary Pickford: A Life on Film*.

See also: Entertainment Industry

Further Reading

Eyman, Scott. *Mary Pickford, America's Sweetheart*.

Pickford, Mary. *Sunshine and Shadow*.

Whitfield, Eileen. *Mary Pickford: The Woman Who Made the Movies*.

Pinckney, Eliza Lucas (1722–1793), Plantation Manager

Eliza Pinckney was, perhaps, the first woman planter in colonial America. She is certainly the most renowned. She was responsible for developing indigo as an exportable crop. This crop sustained the economy in the entire state for thirty years.

Pinckney was born in 1722 in Antigua and was educated in England. When she was fifteen, her father moved the family to Wappoo Plantation in South Carolina, hoping that the move would help his ill wife. When he had to leave for military duty, Eliza, who was then sixteen, took over the management of Wappoo and two other plantations, determined to make them successful. Her father sent her several kinds of seed for experimentation. Because of political considerations, indigo proved the most successful. England, dependent on indigo dye for its textile industry, was delighted to import from the colonies rather than from the hated French, who had had a monopoly until that time.

Pinckney began experimenting with indigo in 1738, and her first shipment was a six-pound trial in 1744. She gave seed from that crop to fellow South Carolina plantation owners. As a result exports reached 40,000 pounds in 1746 and 100,000 pounds in 1747. The exportation of indigo remained an industry in the South until late in the nineteenth century when the British turned to India for indigo, and cotton replaced it as the South's main crop.

In 1747 Eliza married Charles Pinckney and continued to experiment on his plantation with flax, hemp, and silk. In 1753 he was appointed commissioner for the colony and they moved to London with their two sons and a daughter. They returned home when the war with France began. Soon afterward Charles died of malaria. She managed his seven plantations until the Revolutionary War, when her home and lands were looted and burned by the British. She was economically ruined and went to live with her widowed daughter. Her sons, although educated in England, were both Patriots. Their various activities included serving as an aide to General George Washington, representing South Carolina at the Constitutional Convention, and serving as governor of South Carolina in 1787. Eliza Pinckney died of cancer in 1793.

Washington was one of her pallbearers. Her letterbook constitutes one of the largest surviving collections of letters by women of this era.

See also: Agriculture/Ranching; Colonial Businesswomen

Further Reading

Dexter, Elisabeth Williams Anthony. *Colonial Women of Affairs: Women in Business and the Professions before 1776*, p. 119–125.

Pinckney, Eliza. *The Letterbook of Eliza Lucas Pinckney.*

Ravenal, Harriott H. *Eliza Pinckney.*

Pinkham, Lydia Estes (1819–1883), Patent Medicine Maker

Lydia Pinkham was the queen of patent medicine. Even though—or maybe because—her formula had little medicinal value and a very high alcohol content, enormous numbers of bottles sold from 1875, when it was invented, and for another hundred years afterward.

Pinkham was born in Lynn, Massachusetts, the tenth of twelve children of a shoemaker. Hers was a staunch abolitionist family. She spent her entire life in Lynn, where she became a schoolteacher and was involved in many causes. In 1843 she married Isaac Pinkham. They had four sons and a daughter.

In the Panic of 1873, Isaac lost everything, including his money, his health, and his energy. The family was destitute, so Lydia's sons thought of selling the herbal medicine she had been concocting and giving away for ten years. She took a recipe by either Dr. John King or George Clarkson Todd and made it her own, mixing unicorn root, pleurisy root, black cohosh, and fenugreek with a liberal amount of alcohol as a solvent and preservative. The mixture was advertised as a cure for "women's weaknesses," or "the miseries," and was used to help cramps, nerves, vapors, anxieties, fainting spells, headaches, digestive disorders, and blood thinning. Eventually Pinkham also prescribed it for male kidney problems. Legend has it that her first sale was in 1875 to a party of women from Salem; she sold them six bottles for $5.00. Mrs. Lydia E. Pinkham's Vegetable Compound had made its debut.

The entire family was involved in the project. Lydia supervised the manufacturing, her sons were in charge of merchandising, and Isaac read to the family as they mixed and bottled. Her sons distributed handbills door-to-door and sold to druggists in Salem, Boston, and Providence. Her son Daniel went to New York City and persuaded Charles Nelson Crittenton, the largest patent medicine broker there, to order the concoction regularly. The company was immediately successful, and the family put all their profits back into it, mainly in newspaper advertising. By 1878 her compound was the most widely advertised product in the country.

In 1879 Pinkham authorized the use of her portrait. Her benign, motherly face began to appear everywhere in conjunction with her "Department of

Advice," in which she answered letters and prescribed good diet, cleanliness, and exercise along with her medicine. She also published a booklet about sex and reproduction.

At the time doctors were looked upon as people to avoid. The practice of medicine was indeed still a practice. Surgery had a 40 percent chance of success, and many people, particularly women, saw doctors as butchers at worst, and unhelpful at best with women's ailments. This accounted for much of the success of Mrs. Pinkham's Compound. Even if it offered no real medical benefit, women felt better, so there was a psychological benefit. The family often used testimonials in their advertising, including one from a Women's Christian Temperance Union official.

> Even if it offered no real medical benefit, women felt better, so there was a psychological benefit.

In 1881 the company incorporated, and by 1883 it was making $300,000 per year. Pinkham never patented her formula but did register the trademark and her picture. When the Federal Drug Administration tried to classify it as an alcoholic beverage, the family cut the alcohol content to 13.5 percent. Lydia died in 1883, little knowing what a bonanza she had created. The medicine sold well into the 1980s, with its heyday the 1920s. In 1898 sales were $1.3 million and in 1925, $3.8 million, but by 1974 they had declined to $750,000. The business remained in the family until 1968, when it was sold to Cooper Laboratories, which continued manufacturing it until the mid-1980s. At the close of the twentieth century it could still be found for sale on the Internet ("Hard-to-Find Products").

As for many women, Lydia Pinkham's business was born of necessity. The times were right, she had a product that was believed to heal, and she had her own business acumen and sons who were brilliant at marketing and advertising.

See also: Advertising Industry; Late Bloomers

Further Reading
"Hard-to-Find Products Gaining Presence Online."
Stage, Sarah. *Female Complaints.*
Washburn, Robert C. *The Life and Times of Lydia Pinkham.*

Pleasant, Mary Ellen (1814–1904), Entrepreneur

A "wealthy entrepreneur, abolitionist, civil rights activist, confidante of the rich, powerful advocate for the weak and disenfranchised—Mary Ellen Pleasant remains one of the most enigmatic figures of the nineteenth-century American West" (Taylor in Riley and Etulain, *By Grit & Grace,* p. 115). She began her entrepreneurial and investment career during the Gold Rush, one of few African American women in San Francisco.

Historians have recently examined her life, and some hard facts have emerged from the deliberate confusion and reimaging in her 1902 autobiography as well as the sensational rumors and outright lies in newspapers of the day. Pleasant's birth and parentage remain in question, although the 1814 date is certain. She may have been a fugitive slave; that would help account for the confusion of her accounts. She was sent to Nantucket to live with a Quaker family when she was six, and there she learned to read and write as well as how to practice good business skills. She later married James W. Smith in Boston. When Smith died he left her a legacy of $15,000, to be used for the abolitionist activities in which they had been involved. Her next marriage was to John James Pleasant, another abolitionist, in 1847. They had a child, Elizabeth, in 1851 and moved to San Francisco in 1852, leaving her behind. In the midst of the Gold Rush, San Francisco had few racial and economic boundaries. There was also a dearth of cooks, and Pleasant auctioned off her services for $500 per month, twice the going rate. Although John and Mary Ellen Pleasant were married for thirty years, they did not live together most of the time because of his work as a ship's cook and his abolitionist activities. Mary Ellen began investing her inheritance, using her contacts with relocated New England abolitionists. She invested in an accounting firm that guaranteed her a 10 percent annual return, speculated in gold and silver, and by 1855 had established three laundries. She was also involved in the antislavery movement. Her first boardinghouse served as a refuge for runaway slaves in the 1850s, and she financially backed many legal challenges to slavery.

In 1858 the Pleasants went to western Canada for two years to meet with a group of supporters of the abolitionist John Brown. Back in San Francisco in 1860, Mary Ellen worked as a housekeeper for wealthy and powerful white families, giving her access to the secrets of political and financial decision making. She continued her investing and entrepreneurial activity and was also involved in civil rights and aid to African Americans, including helping to finance churches and a school. In 1868 she sued San Francisco's streetcar company for refusing to permit her to ride, and won $500. Earlier, she had sued for and won the right for African Americans to have their testimony accepted in California courts.

In the early 1860s Elizabeth came to San Francisco to live with her mother. After she married at age fourteen, Elizabeth and her husband lived with Mary Ellen until Elizabeth's death in 1887. The wedding was reported in the *San Francisco Examiner*.

After the streetcar lawsuit, Pleasant focused on her businesses. She bought three boardinghouses that she turned into luxurious gathering places and supper clubs in the infamous Barbary Coast area. She also opened a saloon and a livery stable and continued operating the laundries. By the 1870s she had accumulated a fortune in mining stocks and property. In 1877 she built a mansion worth $100,000, one of the largest African American–owned houses in the United States.

In 1892 her life began to unravel. Thomas Bell, a prominent banker and a friend since her arrival in San Francisco, who had been living with his family in Pleasant's mansion, died in an accident. Rumors began. Pleasant was accused of murdering him, and she was eventually evicted from her home by Bell's wife in 1899. She also was involved in another legal case, and vilification emanating from one of the lawyers was printed in the newspapers. Her creditors believed his stories and began to sue her. Pleasant lost almost all of her hard-earned wealth to legal fees. In November 1903, impoverished, she moved into the house of friends. Two months later she died.

Quintard Taylor has called the story of Mary Ellen Pleasant a "uniquely western episode" (in Riley and Etulain, p. 132). The boundaries of race and gender did not stop her from accumulating wealth and power. But a tendency to hide her activities behind other people's signatures and to encourage mystery and confusion worked against her in the end.

See also: African American Businesswomen

Further Reading

Bennett, Lerone. "An Historical Detective Story."

Hudson, Lynn M. "A New Look, or 'I'm Not Mammy to Everybody in California': Mary Ellen Pleasant, a Black Entrepreneur."

Taylor, Quintard. "Mary Ellen Pleasant: Entrepreneur and Civil Rights Activist in the Far West." In Glenda Riley and Richard W. Etulain, eds., p. 115–134.

Poon, Christine A. (1953–), Pharmaceuticals Executive

Christine Poon is the worldwide chairman of pharmaceuticals for Johnson & Johnson, heading a $17 billion business that is responsible for 60 percent of the company's profits. She was ranked number 27 on *Fortune's* 2003 list of the most powerful women in American business.

Poon grew up in the Midwest, where she was the only Chinese American person in her school. Her father was a doctor, and Christine's childhood career choice was to be a doctor too. She received a BA in biology from Northwestern University, an MA in biology and biochemistry from St. Louis University, and an MBA from Boston University. Her first job was as a laboratory technician at the University of California. After stints as a chemist at companies in St. Louis and Boston, she began her career in business development at New England Nuclear. She then moved to the biomedical division of DuPont, where she held positions in business development, marketing, sales, and management.

In 1985 she joined Bristol-Myers Squibb. By 1993 she was vice president of marketing for Squibb Diagnostics and, later that year, vice president of business strategy for the U.S. pharmaceutical and specialty pharmaceutical divisions. The following year she was promoted to president and general manager of Bristol-Myers Squibb Pharmaceutical Group in Canada and vice president of intercontinental operations. In 1997 she became president of the company's Canadian and Latin American operations and president of its medical devices group. In 1998, in a reorganization of senior management, she was made president of international medicines. Poon was now one of the highest-ranking women in the pharmaceuticals industry.

She was recruited by Johnson & Johnson in November 2000 as worldwide chairman of its pharmaceutical group and a member of its twelve-person executive committee. In April 2002 she introduced the Together Rx™ Card, a prescription drug savings plan for Medicare enrollees. She was responsible for the acquisition of Scios, a biotech company that manufactured a heart medicine, Alza Centocar, and three other companies to strengthen Johnson & Johnson's offerings of prescription medicines.

One of Poon's strengths is her balance of humility and directness. She loves challenges but does not feel comfortable with public speaking. One reason for her move to Johnson & Johnson was its reputation for diversity. Her leadership style is based on encouraging questions. She promotes curiosity and innovation. Poon was appointed to the board of Liz Claiborne because of her "substantial management expertise and understanding of multicultural dynamics" ("Liz Claiborne").

See also: Asian American Businesswomen

Further Reading
Farmer, Melanie Austria. "The Powerhouse Who Leads a Billion-Dollar Business."
"Liz Claiborne Inc. Elects Christine A. Poon to Board of Directors."
www.jnj.com/our_company/diversity/poon

Popcorn, Faith (1943–), Market Research Consultant

Faith Popcorn is one of the foremost futurists in the United States, a prophet of consumer trends who predicted the popularity of home shopping and gourmet coffees and coined the terms *cocooning* and *conscious consumer.* In 2003 Malini Bhupta called her "the first lady of consumer forecasting, the women with her finger on the pulse of the American consumer" ("Keeping the Faith").

Popcorn was born Faith Plotkin in New York City to lawyer parents. Her father left his criminal law practice to work for a U.S. intelligence agency in Shanghai, and the family was in China until Faith was six, when they caught the last plane out before the communists led by Mao Zedong took over. She returned to New York to be raised by her grandparents. She wanted to be an actress and graduated from the High School of Performing Arts and then, in 1966, from New York University with a degree in theater.

Popcorn began her advertising career that year and spent the next twelve years at four ad agencies learning skills such as copywriting and how to use public relations, create ads, and market a product. She suggested the name Popcorn for herself when one of her bosses couldn't remember Plotkin. In 1969 she changed it legally.

In 1974 she and an office associate formed BrainReserve, a consulting company whose mission is to understand consumer trends and advise companies on ways to meet consumer demands based on the trends. Ninety percent of the staff are women. They analyze psychological, sociological, demographic, and economic factors using a thirty-eight-step methodology that includes 4,000 interviews a year with consumers, brainstorming with experts, and scanning more than 300 publications a month. By 1984 the business was a success. Popcorn bought out her partner and became creative director and president. Two years later she promoted herself to chair and hired a president and chief operating officer.

> They analyze psychological, sociological, demographic, and economic factors using a thirty-eight-step methodology.

During the 1990s she predicted the popularity of salt-free foods, that more attention would be paid to the family, and the growth of preventive medicine. Her clients have included Bacardi Imports, Campbell Soup, Colgate-Palmolive, IBM, E.F. Hutton, and Nestlé. Clients receive six "trendpacks" a year, which focus on emerging trends. BrainReserve also helps to create names for new products, refresh old ones, and polish images and brands.

In 1984 *Fortune* called Popcorn "the Nostradamus of marketing," and in 1986 *Savvy* named her as one of the top three women business owners in the United States. She has written four best-selling books: *The Popcorn Report* (1992), *Clicking* (1996), *EVEolution* (2000), and *Dictionary of the Future* (2001). Her predictions of emerging trends for 2003 included food coaches for dealing with obesity, family first, male vanity, reality politics, and life-lifting.

See also: Consulting

Further Reading:
Bhupta, Malini. "Keeping the Faith."
McGarvey, Robert. "Trend Spotting."
Popcorn, Faith. *Dictionary of the Future*.
———. *The Popcorn Report: Faith Popcorn on the Future of Your Company, Your World, Your Life*.

Porter, Sylvia F. (1913–1991), Financial Columnist

Sylvia Porter, the first woman hired on a newspaper financial desk, pioneered the personal finance newspaper column. Over a fifty-six-year career, she wrote more than thirty books and reached 40 million readers through her nationally syndicated columns. A crusader against economic injustice, she was the most widely read economic reporter in the country.

Porter was born in Patchogue, Long Island, the only daughter of Russian Jewish immigrants. Her father and brother were doctors. Her middle-class family was intellectually and culturally oriented. Sylvia wrote her first book, a novel, at age six. In 1925 her father died, and the collapse of the stock market followed soon after. Her mother, a suffragette, became a milliner to support the family and insisted that her daughter have a career. Sylvia went to Hunter College when she was sixteen and majored first in English literature and history and then in economics. She won a number of cash prizes during her college career that helped fund her education. She was a junior Phi Beta Kappa, graduated with honors in 1932, and received the Hunter College Centennial Medal for noteworthy achievement. She had married Reed Porter the year before her graduation, the first of three marriages.

Porter's first job was an apprenticeship at an investment firm. She worked for other brokerage houses too and learned about bond markets, business cycles, and currency fluctuation. Night courses at the New York University School of Business Administration added to her financial education. She began to write for financial journals under the name S. F. Porter because women were not an accepted part of the economic domain. In 1934 she began a weekly column in *American Banker* on the government securities market. The following year the *New York Post* accepted her articles. This led to a job on the Wall Street beat. In 1938 she became the *Post*'s financial editor and wrote a daily column, Financial Post Marks, later named S. F. Porter Says. Her goal was to educate the public about personal finances and also to expose economic injustices, as she had done earlier in a 1936 article about a bond market racket. At this time, the Great Depression was ending, the United States was preparing for war, and people distrusted the stock market.

In 1939 Porter wrote her first book. Her style was a combination of expert advice and down-to-earth writing designed to inform the layperson. In 1942 she changed her *Post* byline to Sylvia F. Porter. She also became a lecturer and began writing about financial affairs for women's magazines and, two years later, began editing a weekly newsletter for the banking and securities businesses. By 1947 her newspaper column was syndicated nationwide.

From 1948 to 1963 Porter and Jacob Lasser, a tax expert, coauthored practical handbooks about personal and family finances. From 1960 until she died, she wrote her own annual tax guide, *Sylvia Porter's Income Tax Guide*. Her columns began to focus more on the small investor, consumer advocacy, and dealing with changing financial conditions. In 1975 the first edition of her best seller *Sylvia Porter's Money Book* was published. In 1978 her column moved to the New York *Daily News*. From 1983 to 1989 she published *Sylvia Porter's Personal Finance Magazine*. In 1987 she offered portfolio management software, and in

1989 she founded a company that produced magazines, newsletters, audiocassettes, a radio show, videos, software, and the tax guide. Porter died in 1991 of complications from emphysema.

Porter's writing style was clear and to the point. Her goals were to expose economic injustice and to render economics comprehensible to the layperson. She wrote in plain English for the consumer and small investor. She was on the cover of *Time* magazine on November 28, 1960. Elizabeth Whitney said, in the *St. Petersburg Times*, "In putting Sylvia Porter on its cover, *Time* in essence anointed her a living legend" ("Sylvia Porter," p. 11). In 1962 she was named by President John F. Kennedy to the newly created Consumer Advisory Council. In 1974 she was a member of President Gerald Ford's economic summit and the chair of his nonpartisan Citizens' Action Committee. She was awarded fourteen honorary doctorates and won the William Allen White Award for Journalistic Merit. In 1979 she won the Bob Considine Award and was named Woman of the Year in Finance at the first annual Women in Finance Conference. The *World Almanac* put her on its list of most influential women in the United States three years in a row. In 1999 she was one of twelve women on the TJFR Group/MasterCard International list of 100 journalism trailblazers and visionaries.

See also: Finance Industry

Further Reading
Porter, Sylvia Field. *Sylvia Porter's New Money Book for the 80's.*
"Sylvia Porter." In Lynn Gilbert and Gaylen Moore, p. 227–231.
Whitney, Elizabeth. "Sylvia Porter: Living Legend Becomes an Institution."

Post, Marjorie Merriweather (1887–1973), Food Manufacturer

Marjorie Merriweather Post has been called the first woman tycoon. She inherited General Foods Corporation and, after two forays into allowing her husbands to sit on the board of directors in her place—customary at the time—she took over as president and owner from 1935 to her death. Post's father was a farm equipment salesman and frequent traveler prone to depression and digestive problems. In 1893 he decided to move from Illinois, where Marjorie was born, to Battle Creek, Michigan, where he could be treated at John Harvey Kellogg's Sanitarium. Because Marjorie's father disliked coffee, he invented an alternative hot drink, Postum. He followed that up with breakfast cereals including Grape Nuts and Post Toasties. Marjorie licked labels and went door-to-door selling the products. By 1903 the company was worth $10 million.

Marjorie, the only child, was brought up to know the business, frequently accompanying her father to board meetings and on factory tours. After the meetings, he would question her about what had gone on. It is said that she knew every employee and every decision within the company. Her father also taught her to do good with her money.

In 1905 Marjorie's parents divorced, and in 1906 she married Edward Bennett Close, with whom she had two daughters. After her father committed suicide in 1914, she inherited the company. Although her husband sat on the board of directors in her place, he consulted her about

> It is said that she knew every employee and every decision within the company.

every decision, particularly the selection of executives. She and Close were divorced in 1919, and in 1921 she married E. F. Hutton. They had a daughter, Dina Merrill, who became a well-known actress. Hutton took the company public and acquired fifteen other grocery and food companies including the makers of Jell-O, Maxwell House Coffee, Swan's Down Cake Flour, Minute Tapioca, Baker's Chocolate, and Log Cabin Syrup. Post persuaded him to buy the frozen foods company owned by Clarence Birdseye, which he did, for $22 million. In 1929 they changed the name of their company to General Foods Corporation. It was the largest food company in the United States.

In 1935 Post and Hutton divorced and she became director of the company. She was finally its official head, in name as well as in influence and power. General Foods continued to grow under her direction. She retired in 1958 at age 71, the mandatory retirement age, and became director emerita. At the time of her death in 1973, her fortune was estimated at $250 million.

Post was very active in charities, funding a Red Cross hospital in France during World War I, subsidizing a soup kitchen during the Great Depression, giving $1.5 million to the National Symphony Orchestra to sponsor Young American Concerts, and funding the Boy Scouts Center in Washington, D.C., and C.W. Post College. She was also a member of Lady Bird Johnson's More Beautiful Capital campaign in 1965. She won the U.S. Flag Association's Cross of Honor in 1932, the Federation of Women's Clubs Award for Philanthropic Achievement in 1958, and the James Smithson Society Medal. She received honorary degrees from Long Island University, Hobart and William Smith Colleges, and Bucknell University. In 1917 she was part of a delegation that met with President Woodrow Wilson to discuss women's issues, particularly woman suffrage. She was married twice more, to Joseph Davies, U.S. ambassador to the Soviet Union and Belgium, and to Herbert Arthur May. Both marriages ended in divorce, and in 1964 she went back to her maiden name. Her lavish and magnificent estate, Mar-a-Lago, was designated a National Historic Site in 1969.

See also: Food Industry

Further Reading
Post, Marjorie Merriweather. *The Reminiscences of Marjorie Merriweather Post.*
Rubin, Nancy. *American Empress: The Life and Times of Marjorie Merriweather Post.*
Wright, William. *Heiress: The Rich Life of Marjorie Merriweather Post.*

Potter, Myrtle Stephens (1958–), Pharmaceuticals Executive

Myrtle Potter is executive vice president of commercial operations and chief operations officer at Genentech. In 2002 *Fortune* ranked her number 18 on its list of the most powerful black executives in the United States, and the following year she was number 29 on its list of the 50 most powerful women in American business.

Potter grew up in Las Cruces, New Mexico, one of six children. Her family was poor when Myrtle was young, but she learned teamwork through her childhood experiences, sometimes sacrificing her personal wishes for the good of a sibling or the family. Her father retired from the military to own a successful small business. Her mother was a teacher, social worker, and community activist. Both parents imbued their children with the value of personal discipline, achievement, teamwork, and giving to others. When Myrtle was in seventh grade the family moved to a neighborhood with few African Americans, and she got her first taste of racism. Her parents taught the children to ignore it, saying, "They're just ignorant. It has nothing to do with you" (Tichy, *The Cycle of Leadership*, p. 108–109). In high school she was Girls State Governor of New Mexico, a cheerleader, a student body leader, and she received good grades. Her father remortgaged their house to send her to the University of Chicago, where she majored in political science. During college she had a part-time job at the University of Chicago Hospital and an IBM internship. Potter is married and has a son and a daughter.

Her first professional job, beginning in 1980, was as a sales representative for patient care products for Procter & Gamble. In 1982 she went to Merck, rising through the ranks in a variety of sales, marketing, and management positions. By 1992 she was senior director of field sales planning and from 1993 through 1996, vice president, Northeast Region Business Group. From 1996 to May 2000 she held a number of important positions at Bristol-Myers Squibb, beginning as vice president of strategy and economics in the U.S. Pharmaceutical Group. She reevaluated business processes, reorganized most of the operations, and was involved in the marketing of several important new drugs. Toward the end of that period she was promoted to president of the U.S. Cardiovascular/Metabolics Division. As such, Potter was the first African American to head a major pharmaceutical division.

In May 2000 she moved to Genentech in its number two position, as executive vice president of commercial operations and chief operating officer. She is also on its executive committee. She is responsible for all commercial operations, including sales, marketing, and business development. She moved to Genentech for the opportunity to work in both the commercial and the developmental processes. In April 2001 Genentech and Roche won a contract to develop a new cancer drug.

Potter's management style combines leadership and vision with a strong focus on mentoring, teamwork, diversity, and work-life balance. She pushes her employees yet always gives credit where it is due. She cares about each person's development and career and says that her core belief is: "You can do absolutely anything with the right team focused on the right goal, all together working toward a common place" (Tichy, p. 107–108).

Potter's son has a developmental disability, and she was once told that he would "never be able to even place an order at McDonald's." That statement galvanized the family, and he now "excels academically and musically." She and her husband share equally in raising their children, and they are her first priority (Tichy, p. 109–110).

Potter has been on the boards of the California Healthcare Institute and the Delaware Valley Boys and Girls Club. She won the Merck Chairman's Award in the mid-1990s, for her work on an Astra Merck joint venture, and the Bristol-Myers Squibb Leadership Development Award. In 1999 she was lauded by the Association of Black Cardiologists, and in 2000 the Healthcare Business Women's Association named her Woman of the Year. She was also a member of the University of Michigan Business School faculty in 2000. In 2002 *Time* called her a "Global Business Influential."

See also: African American Businesswomen

Further Reading

Madell, Robin. "Uniting People and Products: Myrtle Potter—2000 HBA Woman of the Year."

Taylor, Chris. "Myrtle Potter: COO of Genentech."

Tichy, Noel. *The Cycle of Leadership*, p. 107–110.

Power

According to the *Oxford Large Print Dictionary*, power is "the ability to do something," "vigour, energy, strength," "control, influence," or "authority." The word powerful means "having great power, strength, or influence." The concept of power has long been uncomfortable for most women. The traditional male view has been that power equals control and is evidenced by rank, pay, or ownership. Women see power differently and tend to focus on the ability to influence or make changes.

As more women became involved in business, their discomfort with the concept of power lessened as they began to see that their version could be valid too. In 1986 Kathryn Stechert stated that "many women mistakenly think that vying for power would be something shameful, [that women] want to be liked and fit in" ("Raising Your Power Consciousness," p. 117). Maureen Dowd, five years later, talked about women's approach to power and their fear that it would corrode their femininity ("Power"). But during the late 1990s women began concentrating on power as influence and saw that there were more facets than authority and control, that power could be expertise and competence and the ability to accomplish their own goals as well as the goals of a company.

Since 1998 *Fortune* has published an annual list of the fifty most powerful women in American business. The magazine uses four criteria: (1) a woman's clout in her company, as shown by the revenues and profits controlled; (2) the importance of her business in the global economy; (3) the arc of her career, that is, how quickly she has risen and how high she is likely to go; and (4) her impact on culture and society. An overall criterion is that only women in for-profit companies are considered. Carly Fiorina of Hewlett-Packard was number 1 on the list from 1998 through 2003 (the cutoff for this book), but many women have been dropped or added over the years. There was one African American and one Asian American on the first list; in 2003 there were four of each. It has become more difficult to make the list as women have risen in power in corporate America. In 1998 there were two women CEOs in *Fortune* 500 companies; in 2003 there were six. The list has also mirrored the economy: the seventeen newcomers in 1999 reflected the shift to power through the Internet. The following year there were eighteen newcomers, mainly from the burgeoning high-technology sector. The 2001 list reflected the bursting of the "dot.com" bubble as companies on that exciting edge of the economy failed. The majority of women on it had been with their companies for a long time and had slowly and steadily risen in responsibility and rank.

Although the women on the *Fortune* lists work in a wide variety of businesses, one common theme has emerged. All of them see power as influence, as a way to make a difference, to be able to change the company or the industry or even the world. Fiorina stated in 2000 that "power is the ability to change things" (quoted in Sellers, "The 50 Most Powerful Women in Business," p. 132). Most women are still a little ambivalent about their power. In 2002 Patricia Sellers said, in her annual article accompanying the *Fortune* 500 list, "virtually every woman said she felt pressed to soften the very thing that got her here: her powerful style. But even if these women don't wear their power as comfortably as men do, they've got every bit as much backbone" ("True Grit," p. 105). In 2003 Sellers focused on whether women really want power ("Power"). The discomfort has not disappeared altogether, but the discussion has changed to the personal sacrifices necessary to attain high corporate positions.

See also: Appendix I

Further Reading
Dowd, Maureen. "Power: Are Women Afraid of It—Or Beyond It?"
Langford, Margaret, Orion J. Welch, and Sandra T. Welch. "Men, Women, and the Use of Power: Is It Based on the Person or Situation?"
Sellers, Patricia. "The 50 Most Powerful Women in Business: Secrets of the Fastest-Rising Stars."

———. "Power: Do Women Really Want It?"
———. "These Women Rule."
Stechert, Kathryn B. "Raising Your Power Consciousness."

Pregnancy Discrimination Act

The Pregnancy Discrimination Act of 1978 amended Title VII of the Civil Rights Act of 1964. It expanded the definition of sex discrimination by prohibiting discrimination against female employees because of pregnancy, childbirth, or illnesses related to those events. The act applies to all firms employing fifteen or more people. It also covers hiring, firing, promotion, seniority rights, and benefits. Fuzzy areas still exist around dangerous work environments and state laws.

Further Reading
Schneider and Schneider, p. 212–213.

President's Commission on the Status of Women

In 1961 President John F. Kennedy created the President's Commission on the Status of Women with Executive Order 10980. Its purpose was to investigate discrimination against women and to recommend ways to eliminate it. Esther Peterson, director of the Women's Bureau in the Department of Labor, urged the establishment of the commission. Eleanor Roosevelt was its chair, and it had twenty-six bipartisan members. The commission had seven technical committees: one examined employment policies and practices, for example, and another looked at protective labor legislation. The work of the commission led to the Equal Pay Act of 1963 and an executive order requiring equal employment opportunities for women working under federal contracts. The commission also recommended changes in state laws that excluded women from owning property or a business. The commission was dissolved in 1963, but Kennedy also created the Citizen's Advisory Council on the Status of Women and the Interdepartmental Committee on the Status of Women. As of 2003 there were about 270 state, county, and local President's Commissions on the Status of Women.

See also: Equal Pay Act of 1963

Further Reading
Prussel, Deborah. "Commission on the Status of Women." In www.indiversity.com/villages/woman/article-ID=1274
Read and Witlieb, p. 419.

Pringle, Elizabeth W. Allston (1845–1921), Plantation Owner

Elizabeth Pringle managed two rice plantations in South Carolina from the late 1800s until the advent of mechanized rice cultivation in the Southwest during the early 1920s. Her writings offer a first-hand look at plantation life. Pringle was born in Canaan Seashore, South Carolina, the second daughter of five children. Her father was a prominent owner of rice plantations who wrote a respected book about rice cultivation and was politically active. After the Civil War, Elizabeth taught in a Charleston school that had been founded by her mother. In 1868 she moved back to Chicora Wood, the only plantation left after her father's death. Two years later she married John Julius Pringle, also a rice plantation owner, and moved to his home, almost two hours' travel from Chicora Wood. They were married for six years and lost an infant son. When John died suddenly the couple was in debt. Elizabeth returned to Chicora Wood and helped to manage that plantation.

In 1880 she inherited some money and bought her husband's plantation from his heirs. She did not live there but managed it from Chicora Wood, an exhausting job. She raised rice, livestock, and poultry; planted for fodder; and cultivated peaches, strawberries, and scuppernong grapes. She also managed the workers and did farm chores such as making mattresses from sheep's' wool and helping animals give birth. She was a firm believer in using the newest techniques and scientific methods of agriculture.

In 1896 her mother died, and Pringle began to manage both plantations single-handedly. She was fifty-one and had two major problems: little capital, and a shortage of farm workers. For the next eighteen years the work was difficult and the proceeds barely enough to pay taxes and wages. In 1906 a terrible storm damaged the buildings and the land. At the same time, mechanized rice cultivation was developing in the Southwest. This spelled the end of the Carolina rice plantations and resulted in the financial failure of both of Pringle's plantations. She sold much of the land and farmed what remained during the last ten years of her life. She also wrote essays and books that provide a portrait of daily life on the rice plantations.

Pringle was active in a variety of charities and was state vice-regent of the Mount Vernon Ladies Association of the Union. She died of a heart attack in 1921.

See also: Agriculture/Ranching

Further Reading

Childs, Margaretta P. "Pringle, Elizabeth Waties Allston." In Edward T. James, p. 100–101.

Pringle, Elizabeth W. Allston. *Chronicles of Chicora Wood.*

———. *A Woman Rice Planter.*

Printers, *see* Colonial Businesswomen; Publishing Industry

Private Company, *see* Public Company

Procope, Ernesta G. (circa 1929–), Insurance Executive

Ernesta Procope, often called the "First Lady of Wall Street," founded E.G. Bowman, the largest minority-owned and woman-owned insurance brokerage in the United States. The company was fifty years old in 2002. Procope was born in Brooklyn, New York, to West Indian immigrant parents, the only girl of four children. She loved music, particularly the piano, and when she was thirteen she and eight other children were featured in a Carnegie Hall concert. She attended Brooklyn College, but dropped out to marry Albin Bowman. In 1950 she graduated from Pohs Institute of Insurance and Real Estate and received her real estate license. Bowman encouraged her to enter the insurance business.

After he died in 1952 she opened her company and named it for him. The following year she married John L. Procope, the publisher and editor of the *Amsterdam News*. They have no children. She began the company in a storefront in the Bedford-Stuyvesant area of Brooklyn, selling personal insurance in the neighborhood. In the late 1960s, 80 percent of other insurance companies canceled policies in the area out of fear of riots in the mostly African American neighborhood. Procope discussed the situation with New York governor Nelson Rockefeller, who held hearings and subsequently created the New York State Fair Plan, which guaranteed the availability of homeowners insurance in low-income areas. Procope's company handled all property-casualty insurance for the newly created Bedford-Stuyvesant Restoration Corporation.

In 1970 she began to expand into the commercial insurance market. She also bid for and won the employee benefits package of the Community Development Agency (CDA), the New York City anti-poverty program. A subdivision, Bowman-Procope Associates, now oversees an insurance program covering 17,000 employees.

In 1979 Procope moved the company's offices to Wall Street. In 1980 E.G. Bowman won Northern Border Pipeline as a client, in the largest contract ever signed with a minority business enterprise up to that time. The company also began focusing on specialty niches: churches, municipal construction, and one-stop commercial service. By 1985 it had expanded into national sales as well as into Puerto Rico and Canada and had become a full-service insurance brokerage with a staff of forty. Its accounts are 85 percent commercial with blue-chip clients.

Procope's business philosophy is to hire the best professionals, treat clients' businesses as if they were her own, and provide good service (Leavitt, *American Women Managers and Administrators*, p. 217). Procope radiates elegance and warmth and is intelligent, astute, and ambitious; perseverance is one of her greatest strengths. According to Thura Mack, she "attributes her success to a willingness to work hard and show tenacity in the face of insurmountable odds" (in Smith, *Notable Black American Women*, p. 886). She does not believe that being a woman is one of those of odds, but being African American has been. She is known for mentoring dozens of younger black women in business throughout the years. In 1997 *Fortune* featured her as one of five black mentors.

Procope has received honorary doctorates from three universities and has been on the boards of Avon, Chubb, Cornell University, Columbia Gas System, Equitable Community Home Service Corporation, Salvation Army of Greater New York, the New York Zoological Society, and Adelphi University, where she was briefly chairman. Her awards are legion and include the Sojourner Truth Award from the Negro Business and Professional Women's Club, Woman of the Year in 1972 for *Tuesday at Home*, and the 1976 Business Achievement Award from the National Business League. She was featured in a 1974 cover story in *Black Enterprise* and was one of *Cosmopolitan's* 36 Women of Power in 1975. That year President Gerald Ford appointed her special ambassador to the Republic of Gambia's anniversary of independence. She has won the Catalyst Award for Women Directors of Corporations and, in 1977, the National Council of Negro Women's Distinguished Black Woman in a Corporate Role award. In 1981 she received a Special Woman of the Year commendation from the White House and, in 1991, the NAACP's Distinguished Service Award. In 2002 she was honored by One Hundred Black Men Investors Club and received the Trumpet Award from Turner Broadcasting.

See also: African American Businesswomen; Insurance Industry

Further Reading

Bowers, Barbara. "First Lady of Wall Street."

Branch, Shelly. "A Premium Asset on Wall Street: After 40 Years of Running a Successful Insurance Firm, Ernesta and John Procope Are Expanding Their Financial Empire."

Mack, Thura R. "Ernesta G. Procope." In Jessie Carney Smith, ed., *Notable Black American Women*, p. 885–887.

Proctor, Barbara (1933–), Advertising Executive

In his 1984 State of the Union address, President Ronald Reagan singled out Barbara Proctor as the epitome of the nation's "spirit of enterprise." When she founded her advertising agency in Chicago with an unsecured loan from the Small Business Administration, she was not only the first African American to begin an advertising agency in that city, but also the first African American to work in advertising in Chicago.

Proctor was born to an unmarried sixteen-year-old girl who boarded her in Asheville, North Carolina, when she went to Washington, D.C., to get an education. When Barbara was four, her grandmother found out about her and brought her to Black Mountain, North Carolina, where she was raised. Her grandmother was a profound influence. She was affectionate, proud, and hardworking with high standards and a strong work ethic that she passed on to her granddaughter. They lived in a shack with no running water but worked hard and refused to take handouts. Her grandmother and Lena Horne were Barbara's role models growing up. One of her hopes has always been to be the same kind of role model for some other little girl (Davis, Marianna W., p. 384).

In high school she received good grades, was a cheerleader, and was on the yearbook staff. She was awarded scholarships by three colleges and chose Talladega College in Alabama. Additional expenses were covered partly by her mother and partly by a part-time job. She finished her degree in education and English in three years and stayed an extra year to earn another degree in psychology. During her last year she received the Armstrong Creative Writing Award.

After college Proctor worked at a summer camp in Michigan, stopping off in Chicago on her way back to North Carolina. Having spent all her money, she needed a job and began her first career in the music industry, writing jazz album labels for VeeJay Records. She was also a contributing editor at *Down Beat* magazine and became a respected jazz music critic. She worked her way up to the position of international director at VeeJay, making numerous talent-finding trips to Europe. One accomplishment was to bring the Beatles to the United States in 1962. During this period she married Carl Proctor, had a son, Morgan, and divorced. Because Carl was also active in the music business, she decided to find a different way to make a living.

Advertising agencies were looking for African Americans to hire. One approached her and, although she was humiliated by being a token African American, she took the job because it was an opportunity to learn the advertising business. She found herself fascinated by it. Between 1965 and 1970 she worked for several agencies, learning more at each and winning more than twenty awards for her ads. She also discovered that her personal standards could be a problem when she was fired for refusing to work on a commercial she thought demeaning to the civil rights movement.

In 1970 she started her own agency. She called it Proctor & Gardner so that prospective clients would think there was a Mr. Gardner running things back in the office. She applied for a $100,000 loan from the Small Business Administration (SBA), and when she was asked for collateral, said she had only herself, but to ask around and find out what she was worth. The SBA decided her worth at $80,000, and she was in business. The huge African American consumer market had just been discovered, and Proctor was in the perfect position to specialize in advertising to it. Her first client was Ghana America and the agency grew steadily with clients such as CBS in Chicago, Kraft Foods, Sears of Chicago, Jewel Food Stores, Alberto Culver, and, later, Gallo and Heileman Beer. In 1972 it moved to new offices. By 1973 annual billings were $4.5 million and by 1982, $8 million. Eighty percent of billings were from companies aiming at African American consumers. Proctor refused to work with clients that exploited minorities or women and would not advertise liquor, cigarettes, or drugs because she saw them as detrimental to the economic condition and dignity of African Americans. She has always felt deeply responsible for her ads (Mack in Smith, *Epic Lives*, p. 432, 433). She tries to turn obstacles into advantages and does not blame other people for her misfortunes. Her problem-solving method is timely innovation and strategic planning. In 1984 the company lost its largest account. That was a bad year, but the company's billings had rebounded to $4 million by 1987.

> She called it Proctor & Gardner so that prospective clients would think there was a Mr. Gardner running things back in the office.

In 1995 Proctor & Gardner filed first for Chapter 11 bankruptcy, having more than $1.8 million in debts, and then for Chapter 13 protection. Her Chapter 11 reorganization plan focused on Internet advertising, and she renamed the company Proctor Information Network Inc. In 1996 she started Proctor Communications Network, which was listed in the July 1999 *Standard Directory of Advertising Agencies* as Proctor Communications with approximate annual billings of $12.5 million. She was listed as president and CEO.

Proctor has received many awards during her career, including a Clio, Chicago Advertising Woman of the Year and Blackbook Businesswoman of the Year in 1974, the Mary McLeod Bethune Achievement Award in 1976, the Headline Award and the Charles A. Stevens International Organization of Women Executives Achievement Award in 1978, and the Black Media Award for Outstanding Professional in 1980. She was appointed a member of the White House Task Force for the Small Business Council in 1979. In 1983 the governor of Illinois asked her to cochair a commission to study the role of women in Illinois, the Gannon-Proctor Commission. In 1987 she was named a Hero of the 80s by President Ronald Reagan, who said she "rose from a ghetto shack to build a multimillion-dollar advertising agency in Chicago" (quoted in Klose, "In the Spirit of Enterprise").

Proctor was the first African American woman to be elected president of the Cosmopolitan Chamber of Commerce and sits on its board of directors. Other civic boards on which she sits include People United to Save Humanity, the Better Business Bureau, Northwestern Hospital, Girl Scouts of Chicago, the

Economics Club, and Operation PUSH. Her corporate boards have included Illinois Bell, the Louisville Courier-Journal, Bingham Companies, and the Mid-City Bank of Chicago. She has been on the governing council of the Illinois State Bar Association's Institute for Public Affairs and the national Citizen's Stamp Advisory Committee and a member of the DuSable Museum of Black History, the Chicago Urban League, the National League of Black Women (president from 1978 to 1982), and Chicago Media Women. Proctor is featured in the Smithsonian Institution's Black Women Achievements against the Odds Hall of Fame and is in demand as a speaker.

See also: Advertising Industry; African American Businesswomen

Further Reading

Cahill, Joseph B. "Debt Swamps Star Who Beat the Odds: Proctor Battles to Save Ad Firm; Files Chapter 11."

Ingham, John N., and Lynne B. Feldman. *African-American Business Leaders: A Biographical Dictionary*, p. 364–371.

Klose, Kevin. "In the Spirit of Enterprise: Barbara Proctor and Her Presidential Mention."

Mack, Thura R. "Barbara Gardner Proctor." In Jessie Smith, ed., *Epic Lives: One Hundred Black Women Who Made a Difference*, p. 428–433.

Rich-McCoy, Lois. *Millionairess: Self-Made Women of America*, p. 207–227.

Prostitution

Prostitution has existed as a way of earning a living in the United States since the American colonies were settled. Until the early twentieth century, it was legal although not socially acceptable. It was also very dangerous both for the prostitute and the client. Called the oldest profession, prostitution usually has been the last resort for women needing to make a living. In 1858 a survey of 2,000 prostitutes showed that half had been domestic servants and another quarter had been seamstresses until lured by the higher earnings of prostitution. However, their life expectancy was only four years after entering the profession (Schneider and Schneider, *ABC-CLIO Companion*, p. 216).

During the Westward migration prostitutes abounded. They gathered in mining towns, around army camps, and in the new large cities as they grew. In Helena, Montana, from 1865 to 1886, prostitution was the biggest source of paid employment for African American and white women (Riley, *The Female Frontier*, p. 2). Thousands of Chinese women were kidnapped in China and brought to California to be prostitutes. Western army posts often had "hog ranches" nearby, where prostitutes plied their trade. Certain red-light districts were famous, as were some of the madams who ran the houses of ill-repute: San Francisco's Tenderloin District, Mattie Silks in Denver, and the Everleigh sisters in St. Louis and Chicago.

As towns grew into cities, reform movements began and a variety of laws were enacted against the profession; prostitution, where it survived, went underground. Most brothels run by madams disappeared and new forms of prostitution appeared, including streetwalkers and call-girl operations. While there had been some control over health and cleanliness before, that was lost when the profession became illegal. Throughout most of the twentieth century and now, prostitution was not only criminal in most of the United States, but was increasingly dangerous for reasons of health and violence.

Further Reading

Rosen, Ruth. *The Lost Sisterhood: Prostitution in America, 1900–1918.*

Schneider, Dorothy, and Carl J. Schneider. *ABC-CLIO Companion to Women in the Workplace*, p. 216

Whelehan, Patricia. *An Anthropological Perspective on Prostitution: The World's Oldest Profession.*

Public Company

A public company is one that is owned by people holding stock in the company. Potential shareholders buy shares through one of the stock exchanges. In return, these shareholders receive a stock certificate, an annual report about the company's activities, and the right to vote at the annual shareholder's meeting.

A private company is owned by the founder or co-founders of the company. As small companies grow, its owners may wish to raise money to build larger facilities or to develop new products, and so they "go public"; that is, sell shares of their company on the stock market. They request a valuation and issue an Initial Public Offering (IPO), informing would-be shareholders and the Securities and Exchange Commission (SEC) of their intentions. Many technology companies did this during the dot.com bubble of the late 1990s.

The SEC regulates the stock market and requires public companies to disclose financial information to the public.

See also: Securities and Exchange Commission

Publishing Industry

Publishing has been a more welcoming field for women than many industries. Since the first settlers came to the American colonies, women have been involved in printing and publishing; they have been "printers, compositors, publishers, booksellers, patrons, editors, promoters—entrepreneurs of the word" (Albertine, *A Living of Words*, p. xi). The best-known colonial women printers usually began in a family business that printed forms, laws, meeting records, and newspapers. When their husbands died, they carried on. Eleven women who ran printing presses before 1776 have been recorded by name. Ten women of the period published newspapers. There was at least one woman printer in each colony. These women also printed books and often sold books and stationery in an adjoining store. During the Revolutionary period, many printed religious and political tracts. One of them, Sarah Goddard, printed the Declaration of Independence. After the Revolutionary War and well into the 1800s, many women were active in small printing establishments. However, with the advent of the Industrial Revolution, when machines began doing work once done by hand, women were gradually excluded.

By 1850 there were three leading book-publishing centers: New York City, Philadelphia, and Boston provided 81 percent of the publishing output of the United States. Publishing, however, was known as the "gentleman's profession" (Feldman, Breaking through the Glass Ceiling, p. 82). Women worked for the publishing houses, but as secretaries or in the mailroom. In 1940 *Literary Market Place* listed seventy-eight trade publishers and thirteen woman editors. The majority of the editors worked in children's literature. One exception was Blanche Knopf, who owned Alfred A. Knopf with her husband. By 1957 there were more publishing houses and many more women involved in the industry but, again, mostly in juvenile literature. Women college graduates who aspired to careers in publishing still went first to the mailroom and then to secretarial positions; men graduates headed directly to the editorial department. By the 1970s women had advanced; Time Inc. promoted its first woman vice president, and the Publishers Lunch Club admitted its first woman in 1973. But there was still a male route in a publishing career (college traveler, sales representative, editorial assistant) and a female route (editorial secretary or editorial trainee). Women were paid less and endured overt discrimination. In the 1980s women attempted to unionize and filed sex discrimination lawsuits. Today women are a vital part of the industry and have been accepted in positions of power.

The first woman-owned newspaper in the colonies was the *Philadelphia Mercury*. After its founder died in 1742 his wife took charge. There were many other colonial newspapers owned by women, but after 1800 newspapers became a male bastion. Women published many antislavery, abolitionist, suffrage, and temperance newspapers during the middle 1800s, but they were kept out of mainstream newspapers. In 1868 the first women's newspaper to cover all the news was published by Susan B. Anthony and Elizabeth Cady Stanton. In 1876 Eliza Nicholson inherited the *New Orleans Picayune*, a newspaper that is still published today. In the 1880s women's pages appeared. They were edited by women and included domestic news, advice to the lovelorn, and fashion and society news. Ida Wells-Barnett published an African American newspaper in 1892, and during the Mexican Revolution of 1910 a group of Latina women published political newspapers.

By 1900 there were 2,193 women reporters and editors (Marzolf. p. 43). The National Federation of Press Women was founded in 1937. Helen Rogers Reid ran the *New York Herald Tribune* from 1918 and was acknowledged as a great business executive, but not until the 1970s did women enter newspaper publishing in great numbers. Katherine Graham's *Washington Post* literally changed history with its coverage of the Watergate scandal in 1974. By the 1980s women were assigned a full range of stories, but men still provided most of the commentary on editorial pages.

The first magazine appeared in the colonies in 1741. The first one aimed specifically at women—upper-class women in particular—was the *Lady's Magazine and Repository of Entertaining*, published in 1792 and 1793. The most successful was *Godey's Lady's Book*, published from 1839 to 1898, which sold 150,000 copies a month at its peak. As with newspapers, many magazines published by women focused on issues such as temperance, dress reform, abolition, and equal rights for women. Amelia Bloomer published *The Lily* from 1849 to 1856. Margaret Fuller focused on transcendentalism in *The Dial* from 1840 to 1844, and the *Women's Era* was published by African American women from 1894 to 1903. Miriam Leslie inherited her husband's publishing empire and brought it out of near-bankruptcy. In 1904 the *Ladies Home Journal* was the first to reach a circulation of 1 million.

By 1966 the large magazine publishers began to hire women to sell the small ads at the back of magazines. Women entered magazine publishing in large numbers in the 1970s and finally reached positions of power. Many gained experience working at women's magazines such as *Ms*, *Self*, and *Working Woman*. In 1988, a banner year for women in magazine publishing, at least ten magazines including *TV Guide*, *People*, and *Life* appointed women as publishers.

Further Reading

Albertine, Susan, ed. *A Living of Words: American Women in Print Culture*

Feldman, Gayle. "Breaking through the Glass Ceiling: Women Have Had a Long Hard Struggle to Reach Their Current Status in the Industry."

"Magazines." In *The Reader's Companion to U.S. Women's History*, p. 352–354.

"Newspapers." In *The Reader's Companion to U.S. Women's History*, p. 428–430.

Q

Lois Quam, CEO of Ovations in the United Health Care group, made *Fortune*'s 2003 list of the most powerful women in American business because she won a huge AARP contract for her company. She was ranked number 43.

A Rhodes scholar, Quam received a master's degree in philosophy, politics, and economics from Oxford University. In 1989, when she was a U.S. health economist, she presented a white paper on health care at a conference in London organized by the Oxford Review of Economic Policy. Although studying health care was not her focus, she wanted to help solve the problems in the health care system, so she joined the United Health Group that year as director of research and evaluation. The following year she chaired the Minnesota Health Care Access Commission. The commission worked for more than two years on health care reform and eventually issued recommendations that were enacted into law. In July 1992 Quam established a Center for Health Care Policy and Evaluation at United Health Care. It evaluates performance, outcomes, and cost effectiveness for both company and clients. She was promoted to vice president of public sector services in 1993. She took an extended leave of absence that year to be a senior advisor on President Bill Clinton's White House Task Force on National Health Care Reform and helped design the ill-fated Clinton health care reform plan. Back at United Health Group in 1996, she won the AARP contract and was appointed CEO of the AARP/United Division. She has always been concerned about the availability of health care for senior citizens. In April 1998 she was promoted to CEO of a new division, the Retiree and Senior Services Company. One of its goals was to lower prescription drug costs for this segment of the population. In 1999 the unit evolved into Ovations, of which she is CEO. It employs more than 1,500 people.

Quam is married to Matt Entenza, a member of the Minnesota legislature. They have three sons. She serves on the board of editors of the *British Medical Journal* and in 1999 was named a trustee of the George C. Marshall Foundation.

Further Reading

"Quam Named Trustee of George C. Marshall Foundation."

"United Healthcare Announces Executive Team to Lead Retiree and Senior Services Company."

R

Radio, *see* Broadcasting Industry

Ranching, *see* Agriculture/Ranching

Real Estate

Until the 1960s the real estate business was composed of small local companies that, for the most part, sold houses. The rise of national real estate chains and franchises changed the business. Industry standards, federal regulations, and state laws led to more professionalism among practitioners. During the economic recession of the 1970s women began to enter the field in large numbers. The flexibility of the work schedule was appealing as was the opportunity for part-time employment. By 1982 there were 225,551 woman-owned real estate firms, 19,501 woman-owned real estate operators and lessors, and 204,547 women real estate agents and managers. Real estate ranked sixth among the ten largest industry groups for woman-owned businesses (Fraser, Edie, p. 152). During the 1990s it seemed possible that the industry was resegregating into a predominantly female field, but by the end of the century, the ratio was fifty-eight women to forty-two men (Wharton, p. 136) in the residential real estate sales force. The Women's Council of Realtors offers leadership training, referral, and business relocation.

Commercial real estate is still dominated by men who see women as weak negotiators, and much of their business is done during social occasions such as golf outings, fishing or hunting trips, and sporting events. Clients are mainly corporate men who wish to deal with other men. This area of real estate requires more training and a particularly thick skin. Changes are occurring, but much more slowly than on the residential side.

During the 1990s mortgage brokering came to the fore. Many women opened their own companies and bypassed the glass ceiling of mortgage banking. They established their own organization, the National Association of Mortgage Women.

The main appeal of real estate for women is the flexibility of working hours, even though schedules must be tailored to clients' needs. Most women realtors feel that the job fits their natural abilities such as building relationships with clients, handling myriad details, and understanding clients' housing needs. Drawbacks include pay by commission only, few benefits, and the need for intense training to obtain credentials. It can take two to three years for the work to become profitable.

Many women have seen property ownership as a way out of poverty. This was particularly true for former slaves, like Biddy Mason and Mary Ellen Pleasant. The land rushes of the nineteenth century underscored the importance of owning property. Although most women did not themselves own homes before the 1990s, during the last decades of the twentieth century there was a surge in women's home ownership. In 1997 the federal Department of Housing and Urban Development (HUD) began a program called Home Ownership Opportunities for Women, offering advice and homeowner education. Since then more women are heads of households, and more single women own their own home.

Further Reading

Crumb, Tura. "Rising to the Top: These Women Are Breaking Stereotypes in a Male-Dominated Industry."

National Association of Mortgage Women (www.napmw.org).

"Real Estate." In Edie Fraser, ed., *Risk to Riches: Women and Entrepreneurship in America*, p. 151–152.

Wharton, Carla S. *Framing a Domain for Work and Family: A Study of Women in Residential Real Estate Sales Work.*

Women's Council of Realtors (www.wcr.org).

Reed, Nell Quinlan Donnelly (1889–1991), Fashion Designer

Nell Donnelly Reed was a pioneering manufacturer of women's clothing from 1916 until she retired in 1956. She has been called "the most successful American Businesswoman on pure balance sheet showing" ("Nell Donnelly Reed"). Reed was born on a Kansas farm, the youngest of twelve children.

She was educated first in a convent, then attended high school, and then trained at a business school to be a stenographer. At age seventeen she married Paul Donnelly, who saved money to send her to Lindenwood College in Missouri, where she was the only married student. She graduated in 1909.

Donnelly Garment Company grew out of her failure to find inexpensive but fashionable housedresses. In 1916 she designed what she called "dress aprons"—pretty ruffled dresses—and showed them to the buyer for the George B. Peck Dry Goods store in Kansas City. He agreed to sell them as a test; all twelve dress aprons were sold by noon, and he ordered twelve more. She charged $1 for each; the average price of a dress then was 69 cents. She bought two power sewing machines with $1,270 from her husband, set them up in their attic, and hired two girls to sew. Paul later quit his job and became president of the company; Nell was its secretary and treasurer. He handled the finances; she designed dresses, hired workers, and supervised sales. By the 1920s the business was grossing around $3.5 million a year. This level of business was maintained throughout the Great Depression.

In 1931 Nell Donnelly and her chauffeur were kidnapped, an event headlined in the national news. They were later released unharmed without paying ransom, and the two perpetrators received life sentences. The prosecutor was James A. Reed. Nell married him after a 1932 divorce from Donnelly. She kept the company in the divorce settlement and became its president. She and Reed had one son, David. After Reed died in 1944 she sold the company for more than $1 million dollars but stayed on until she retired in 1956. The new owners changed the company's name and took it public in 1958.

Reed was one of the first women to begin a grassroots company based on a perceived niche. She used production-boosting devices to eliminate waste motion in her factory. She was one of the first business leaders to believe strongly in employee benefits, offering group hospitalization, a subsidized cafeteria, and night courses for workers and scholarships for their children at local colleges.

Reed was involved in the community, serving on the school board and the boards of the Kansas City Art Institute and the Midwest Research Institute. She died in 1991 at age 102.

See also: Fashion Industry

Further Reading
Bird, Caroline. *Enterprising Women*, p. 192–195.
"Nell Donnelly Reed."
Williams, Lena. "Nell Donnelly Reed, 102, Pioneer in Manufacture of Women's Attire."

Reid, Helen Miles Rogers (1882–1970), Newspaper Publisher

Helen Reid was a part of the *New York Herald Tribune* for thirty-seven years and its publisher from 1947 to 1955. The newspaper was losing money when she arrived, and she turned it into a major national daily.

Reid was born in Appleton, Wisconsin, in 1882, the belated eleventh child and sixth daughter of a failed hotel operator. Her father died when she was three. Through an older brother, who was headmaster at a women's seminary, Helen was able to go to high school and later to Barnard College, working her way through with a variety of jobs. After graduating with a BA in zoology, she was hired as a social secretary to Elisabeth Mills Reid, wife of the owner of the *New York Tribune*. Her salary was $100 per month, a princely sum for those days. With a natural affinity for detail and good managerial skills, she ran their three households in Westchester County, New York, in New York City, and in London when Whitelaw Reid was ambassador there. In 1911 she married Ogden Reid, the only son of Elisabeth and Whitelaw. They had three children. Helen received a monthly allowance from her mother-in-law so that she could be independent and help her own family. For the next six years she learned society pursuits such as shooting, golf, and tennis. An avid feminist, she also became involved in suffrage matters. She was elected treasurer for the New York suffrage campaign in 1917.

In 1912 Whitelaw Reid died, and Ogden took over the newspaper. In 1918 Ogden asked Helen to help him put the paper back on track. Her sister moved in with them to help with the children and the housekeeping. Helen quickly became the director of advertising and, in her first two years, increased advertising dollars by 90 percent. Her management was innovative: She met weekly with the salesmen and reviewed their progress, set goals, and offered incentives and pep talks. In 1922 her title was vice president, and she became involved with editorial policies and decisions. She was a moving force behind the purchase of and merger with the *New York Herald* in 1924; the merged newspapers became the *New York Herald Tribune*. By 1928 the paper was making a profit of more than $1 million.

Over the next several years Ogden's health began to fail due to alcoholism, and Helen managed the paper. Her main job was advertising, but she instituted many editorial policies, lured Walter Lippman and Dorothy Thompson as columnists, and began features designed to attract women readers. She developed suburban pages dealing with gardening and homemaking, hired a food writer, and introduced a Sunday literary section and "This Week," which included fiction and articles. In 1930 she began the Forum on Current Events, which continued until 1955. Women's clubs used the issues in the forum as their political agenda during the 1930s and 1940s. She also hired women to write on social and literary issues; the *Herald Tribune* hired more women staff members than any other newspaper in the 1940s.

In 1947 Ogden died, and Helen Reid took over as publisher and owner. The circulation was then 358,000 for the daily edition and 700,000 on Sundays. The Paris edition, begun in 1924, was the leading U.S. newspaper in Europe. The newspaper had a fine reputation for fair treatment of controversial issues and good journalism. It had bought and published several important papers and letters: the Woodrow Wilson letters, the Chaim Weismann papers, and Dwight D. Eisenhower's *Crusade in Europe*. It was also in sound financial shape. Helen remained publisher until 1953, when she became chairman of the board and turned the presidency over to her son Whitelaw. However, she kept the controlling stock and later decided that her younger son, Ogden, might be better suited to run the paper. Unfortunately, neither son was a good business manager, so the family sold the paper to John Hay Whitney. It finally died, a victim of the 1966–1967 New York City newspaper strike.

Helen Reid was an astute businesswoman with a flair for sales, innovation, and creativity and an eye for detail and financial matters. She is credited with bringing the newspaper out of the doldrums and turning it into a national force. She was a lifelong feminist and kept the paper active in philanthropic activities. She continued sponsoring the Fresh Air Fund, which made summer activities outside the city available to New York City poor children, and sponsored book and author luncheons and the Forum on Current Events. She set up the Helen Reid Foundation, which awarded fellowships to journalists, and was a trustee for Barnard College from 1914 to 1956. She hired many women, instituted a liberal maternity leave, and endorsed economic independence and military service for women. She was a liberal Republican with great influence, particularly in New York.

Reid received eleven honorary degrees from colleges and universities including Columbia, Yale, Smith, and New York University. Other awards included the American Women's Association Award, the Cuban Red Cross (in 1937), a gold medal from the Hundred Year Association of New York, and the 1949–1950 seal of the Council against Intolerance in America. In 1943 she was elected the first vice president of the New York Newspaper Women's Club and, in 1950, a fellow of the American Academy of Arts and Sciences. She also received the Theodore Roosevelt Distinguished Service Medal, the National Order of the Legion of Honor, and the Order of the White Rose from Finland. In 1962 a dormitory at Barnard College was named for her.

See also: Publishing Industry

Further Reading

Current Biography Yearbook, 1959, p. 492–494.

Kluger, Richard. *The Paper: The Life and Death of the* New York Herald Tribune.

Renda, Larree M. (1958–), Grocery Executive

Larree Renda worked her way up from a job bagging groceries at Safeway when she was sixteen to the position of executive vice president of retail operations there. One of the most powerful women in the supermarket industry, she was number 48 on *Fortune's* 2001 list of the most powerful women in American business and number 47 on its 2002 list.

Renda was born and raised in Des Moines, Iowa, and began working at Safeway in high school. She never went to college. After marrying her husband, Frank, she moved first to Texas and then California. She moved up steadily into management positions until, in 1993, she became part of Safeway's headquarters staff. In 1994 she was its first woman senior vice president. By 1996 she had gained both acquisition and integration experience, playing an important role in acquiring five grocery chains and integrating them into the Safeway chain. At every level, she was the youngest person to attain her status. She is credited for creating the customer service culture and integrating it into the stores: the "Safeway smile" has become the benchmark for customer retail grocery service. The result has been increased profits and sales and decreased customer complaints.

In 1999 Renda was made executive vice president of retail operations. As such, she is responsible for labor relations, human resources, public affairs, government relations, corporate communications, reengineering, and acquisition transition. She was Safeway's first woman executive vice president and has focused on controlling costs and improving service. In 2001 she was in charge of 1,700 stores with $32 billion in sales.

Renda is responsible for Safeway's community commitment program that has provided funding for cancer research and education in Safeway communities. She sits on the boards of Household International and Casa Ley. She is a trustee and member of the Joint Labor Management Committee of the retail food industry.

See also: Food Industry

Further Reading
"Household Names Larree Renda to Its Board of Directors."
"News of Note."
"Safeway's Exec Honored by *Fortune*."

Resnick, Lynda R. (1943–), Agriculture/Ranching, Direct Mail Executive

Lynda Resnick co-owns Roll International, a Los Angeles–based company made up of three divisions: the Franklin Mint, a direct-mail collectibles business; Teleflora, a flowers wire service; and Paramount Farms, an agribusiness. The three together have placed the company on the *Working Woman* list of top woman-owned companies from 1994 to 2000. In 2000 the company was number 11. Because the Resnicks did not provide the magazine with a sales estimate in 2001 it was not listed that year.

Resnick began her own advertising agency when she was nineteen and later founded an interior-design company. She and her husband were married in 1974 and have five children. They began working together in the early 1980s and have been doing so ever since.

The largest revenue-maker of their company is the Franklin Mint, which they bought in 1985. Lynda Resnick thought that the company could be improved by selling products other than commemorative coins. She immediately expanded its product line to include other collectibles, most notably a Scarlett O'Hara doll priced from $195 to $495. The company has since had sales exceeding $35 million. She also added fine arts and popular culture items. Most are sold through direct mail although there are more than fifty stores in malls, mostly in the Northeast. The Resnicks, who are among the top collectors of fine art in the United States, decided to make art available to the public through licensing agreements with the Louvre in Paris and the Vatican Museum in Rome. In 1996 they paid $211,000 for Jackie Onassis's faux pearls and $151,000 for Princess Diana's pearl-embroidered Elvis dress at auctions. They estimated that reproductions of the necklace would sell 70,000 pieces at $195 each.

In 1995 the company was the largest of its kind, although competitors have made inroads into its profits. It has, however, had problems with licensing agreements, particularly for a Princess Diana doll and a commemorative coin celebrating Tiger Woods. They lost the Tiger Woods suit but won the Princess Diana suit and continue to make and sell the dolls.

Teleflora, the flowers service, continues to grow. Linda Resnick started the company in 1982 and developed flowers-in-a-gift, an idea in which the flower container is an object the recipient will wish to keep. In 1996 it merged with a competitor, Redbook, which had not only agreements with 7,000 more florists but also a technologically up-to-date proprietary ordering service, sorely needed by Teleflora. She is chairwoman of this part of the company.

Paramount Farms owns orchards in California that grow pistachios, almonds, pomegranates, and citrus fruits. The farm grows 20 percent of domestic Sunkist oranges and 60 percent of the pistachios sold in the United States. Its customers are mostly food processors. The Resnicks bought Sunkist Fruit Rolls in 1995 and are testing new nut and fruit snacks. In 2002 they established Pom Wonderful, which makes pomegranate juice.

Resnick collects contemporary art and seventeenth- and eighteenth-century paintings and sculpture. She is the marketing chief in the family, while her husband handles the financial side. She is actively involved in art museums in New York, Los Angeles, and Philadelphia, serving on the board of trustees of the Los Angeles County Museum of Art and acting as a benefactor to various museums. She is on the board of the Aspen Institute. In 1999 Resnick and her husband received the Special Service "Duke" Award from the John Wayne Cancer Institute Auxiliary for their work on behalf of cancer-related causes and institutions.

See also: Agriculture/Ranching; Saleswomen

Further Reading

Bamford, Janet, and Susan McHenry. "The *Working Woman* 50," p. 41.
Bamford, Janet, and Jennifer Pendleton. "The Top 50 Women-Owned Businesses," p. 37.
Karp, David. "Pomegranates for One and All."

Restaurant Industry, *see* Travel Industry

Retailing Industry

According to Kaliski, "retailing is a type of business that sells products and services to consumers for their personal or family use" (p. 47). These businesses range from department stores to discount stores to specialty stores to convenience stores. They are the final stop on the chain of distribution linking the manufacturer to the consumer.

Retailing has a long history in the United States beginning with house-to-house peddlers and tinkers who sold goods and services in the colonies. There were also shopkeepers and "she-merchants" selling a variety of items, including imports from Europe. The peddlers went along with the westward movement and probably founded the first country stores in the emerging new towns. As the military moved in to protect the settlers, another kind of merchant emerged, the sutlers. They moved their stores with the troops, or located near or in the western forts, where they sold liquor, tobacco, books, and sundries. The peak period for country stores was from 1820 to 1860. Department stores grew from country stores selling dry goods, as the towns grew and demand for their goods increased.

Mormons claim that the earliest department store was Zion's Co-operative Mercantile Institution, founded in 1869. Their leader, Brigham Young, insisted on women clerks because he thought they were natural traders. In 1879 Macy's department stores provided a ladies' lunchroom as well as a room for them to rest, visit with one another, or read. Although the colonists used mail to order goods, the large-scale U.S. mail-order business began with Montgomery Ward in 1872, followed shortly thereafter by Sears Roebuck.

During the twentieth century, women worked in retailing, but usually as clerks or buyers. Susan Benson's study of clerks in U.S. department and specialty stores from 1890 to 1960 (in Cott, *History of Women*) points to those stores as major employers in the industry since 1900. Clerks were 90 percent of the store sales force, and more than 66 percent of clerks were women. Socially, "shop girls," as clerks were known, were considered a class or two below their customers. Dorothy Shaver and Beatrice Fox Auerbach, both profiled in this encyclopedia, gained top management positions in the 1940s, but they were two of very few women to do so.

By 1985, 730,000 women owned retail businesses, predominantly selling clothing, food, and home furnishings. Retailing had become an immense industry with numerous product categories. By 1995 annual retail sales were $3 trillion, more than medical, housing, and recreational spending combined. The industry employed more than 20 million people, 20 percent of the total U.S. workforce (Kaliski, p. 749). At *Fortune* 500 retail companies, women held 11.9 percent of the top positions in 1997; in all retail businesses, they held 38.6 percent of managerial positions. Although a higher percentage than in many industries, it seems small in view of the customer base. Moreover, there has been no improvement since 1977, when 40 percent of retail managers were women, and many of them worked in human resources, public relations, and marketing, not areas likely to lead to the executive ranks. In 2001 women were 80 percent of retail customers but held only 16 percent of executive positions.

In a 2001 survey (Moore, Janet D. p. 1D) of 1,251 women retail executives, 77 percent said they succeeded because they exceeded management expectations; 61 percent developed a style with which male managers felt comfortable; 30 percent sought out difficult assignments, and 37 percent had influential mentors. The same barriers emerged as in other industries: male stereotyping and preconceptions, exclusion from informal networks, and few women in the pipeline long enough to rise to management levels. The Network of Executive Women: Consumer Products and Retail Industry (NEW; www.networkofexecutivewomen.com) was formed in 2001 with the goal of attracting, retaining, and advancing women. It provides networking and retail educational opportunities.

See also: Saleswomen

Further Reading
Benson, Susan Porter. "The Clerking Sisterhood." In Nancy F. Cott, ed., p. 514–541.
Moore, Janet. "Where Are the Women?"
"Shattering the Glass Ceiling."

Rhone, Sylvia M. (1952–), Music Industry Executive

Sylvia Rhone became the first African American and the first woman to be chair and CEO of a major record company when she accepted that position at Time Warner's Elektra Entertainment Group in 1994. She is credited with turning the company into one of the premier record labels in the United States. She remains today the highest-ranking African American woman in the recording industry and was number 48 on *Fortune*'s 1998 list of the most powerful women in American business.

Rhone was born in Philadelphia and grew up in Harlem in New York City. After receiving a BS in economics from the Wharton School of Finance and Commerce in 1974, she worked for a year as a commercial lending trainee at Bankers Trust in New York. Because she had always wanted to become involved in the music industry, she took a job as a secretary with Buddha Records. She worked her way up to national promotion coordinator and, later, national promotion manager. In 1976 she was appointed regional promotion manager for ABC Records and beginning in 1978 worked for a year in that position for Ariola Records.

In 1980 she accepted a position as the northeast regional promotion manager in charge of special markets at Time Warner's Elektra Records. In 1983 she became its director of marketing. She credits her experiences along the way as crucial to her knowledge of the record industry. She listened and learned in each job, deepening her experience and readying herself for further opportunities (Davis, Andrea, p. 44). In 1986 she became vice president and general manager of Atlantic's Black Music Operations. Two years later she was a senior vice president with a management staff of twenty. By then she had a reputation as both a team player and a manager with a flair for motivating and building teams. She keeps current with the music scene by going to dance clubs, getting to know disc jockeys, and studying different kinds of music. In 1990 Time Warner established a new division, EastWest America, and she was appointed its co-president and chief executive officer; her counterpart's title was co-president and chief operating officer. In 1991 it became a new division of Atlantic named ATCO/EastWest Records, and she was appointed chairman/ CEO, one of two African Americans to head a major record label that was not Motown oriented. Since she took the position, the company's annual revenues have jumped from $50 million to $79 million.

In late 1993 Rhone was appointed chair and CEO of Elektra Records. She was the first and—at that time only—woman to get to that level in the music industry, a noted male bastion. It took her eighteen years. Since then she has merged three labels (Elektra, East/West, and Sire) into the Elektra Entertainment Group and was credited with sales growth from $1 million to $3 million in her first two years. She was one of the first to realize the potential of rap and hip-hop and signed the top artists. Also recording for the Elektra label are numerous successful artists of other types.

Rhone is known as a skilled marketer and nurturing manager with a flair for picking hit artists. She strongly believes in maintaining a mutual understanding between the artists and the company's executives. She mentors many young African Americans, urging them not to let discrimination distract them but to be determined ("New York's 100 Most Influential Women in Business"). Her hard work, energy, enthusiasm, knowledge, and hands-on support of artists combine to make her one of the most powerful figures in the business.

Rhone won the Herbert H. Wright Award from the National Association of Market Development in 1995 and the Studio Museum Corporate Award in 1996. In 1997 she won the Pioneer Award for distinguished achievement in the recording industry in the areas of contemporary, pop, jazz, and R&B music at the International Achievement in Arts Awards. She was named to the *Black Enterprise* list of the top fifty blacks in corporate America in 2000. In 2000 and in 2002 she made *Hollywood Reporter*'s list of the fifty most powerful women in entertainment. She was featured in Nissan North America's "Black

Experience" advertising campaign, which highlighted notable contemporary blacks. Rhone received an honorary doctorate from Adelphi University in 1996. She sits on the boards of AOL-TV, Phillips-Van Heusen Corporation, the Alvin Ailey American Dance Theater, the Studio Museum of Harlem, the Rock and Roll Hall of Fame, the Phoenix House Fund, and the R & B Foundation. She lives in New York City with her daughter, whom she calls her greatest accomplishment.

See also: African American Businesswomen; Entertainment Industry

Further Reading

Current Biography Yearbook, 1998, p. 43–46.

Davis, Andrea. "Rap-sody & Blue: Sylvia Rhone."

Jeffrey, Don. "Sylvia Rhone Leads Elektra's Turnaround."

"New York's 100 Most Influential Women in Business."

Rice, Linda Johnson (1958–), Magazine Publisher, Cosmetics Manufacturer

Linda Johnson Rice is president and CEO of Johnson Publishing Company, the fourth largest African American–owned company in the United States. Her father, John H. Johnson, founded the company in 1942. It publishes the magazines *EM*, *Jet*, and *Ebony* and manufactures Fashion Fair Cosmetics and Supreme Beauty Products.

Rice was one of two adopted children; her brother died of sickle-cell anemia when he was twenty-five. She was groomed by her father to take over the company and began going to the office when she was seven. In 1970 she graduated from the University of Southern California (USC) with a BA in journalism. That year she became fashion editor and assistant to the president at *Ebony*. She earned her MBA from Kellogg School of Management at Northwestern University at night. Two days after her graduation, her father appointed her president and CEO at *Ebony*. At that time *Ebony* had a monthly circulation of 1.7 million.

> Two days after her graduation, her father appointed her president and CEO at *Ebony*.

One of her first projects was the launch of *Ebony Man* (*EM*). She also began Ebone, a new line of cosmetics for African American women and expanded the Fashion Fair line into department stores in London and Paris. By 1997 the company had developed more cosmetics and skin-care products as well as videos about finance, health, and parenting. In April 2002 she was promoted to president and CEO of Johnson Publishing, the first African American woman CEO of a top-five *Black Enterprise* company. Her father stayed on as chairman and publisher.

It is important to Rice to be a role model for African American women. She has two families: one is her husband, Andre Rice, and her daughter, and the other is her employees. Her management style is more patient than her father's, and her most important advice is to keep a sense of humor. She pays great attention to details and has worked at almost every job in the company. She feels that her breadth of experience matters to her employees. Her favorite activities are the creative process and the free flow of ideas ("*Ebony* Interview with Linda Johnson Rice").

Rice was elected to the board of the Magazine Publishers Association in 1987. She is also on the boards of Continental Bank Corporation in Chicago, Dial Corporation, Bausch & Lomb, Kimberly-Clark, Bank of America Illinois, VIAD, and Quaker Oats. She is on the USC board of trustees for and has been a member of the Committee of 200 since 1989. In 1994 she accompanied Vice President Al Gore to South Africa for the presidential inauguration of Nelson Mandela; she was later invited to President Bill Clinton's state dinner for South African president Thabo Mbeki. In 1999 she won All State Insurance's From Whence Came Award. In 2000 she received the Trumpet Tower of Power Award from the Turner Broadcasting System and the Phenomenal Woman Award from V-103's Expo for Today's Black Women. *Crain's Chicago Business* listed her in its "Who's Who of Chicago Executives" in 2002, and she won the 2003 Robie Award for Achievement in Industry from the Jackie Robinson Foundation. Her philanthropies include the Boys and Girls Clubs of Chicago and the United Negro College Fund.

See also: African American Businesswomen; Publishing Industry

Further Reading
Clarke, Caroline V. "A New Johnson Is CEO."
"*Ebony* Interview with Linda Johnson Rice."
Hochwald, Lambeth. "Heir and Parent: Linda Johnson Rice."
Jenkins, Maureen. "Early Education in Johnson Home."

Rivet, Jeannine M. (1948–), Healthcare Executive

Jeannine Rivet was on *Fortune's* list of the most powerful women in American business from 1998 to 2000. As executive vice president of United Healthcare and CEO of its subsidiary Ingenix, she is one of the highest-ranking women in the healthcare industry.

Rivet graduated from Boston College in 1972. She began her career as a pediatric nurse and then worked as a nursing supervisor. She earned her master's degree in public health from Boston University in 1981. She took several jobs with health-plan companies: associate director of health center administration at Rhode Island Group Health Association, director of clinical services at Group Health Association, senior vice president at Peak Health Plan Ltd., and vice president of group operations at Prudential Insurance Company.

In 1990 she joined United Health Group as vice president of health service operations. She moved up in rank until, in 1998, she became CEO of United Healthcare, then in the middle of a huge restructuring. She was tasked with fixing the unprofitable Medicare HMOs. Her first step was to ask the U.S. Congress to change the reimbursement guidelines. That failed, so she shut down Medicare operations in 86 of the 206 counties then served. She also sold off some smaller businesses and reorganized the remaining Medicare plans. By 2000 profits were rebounding, and in 2001 she was appointed executive vice president of United Healthcare Group, with wide-ranging responsibilities for business services, quality, and representing the company to the pharmaceuticals industry. She also became CEO of Ingenix, a subsidiary that provides healthcare software, databases, and information technology and services.

Rivet has talked about gender discrimination in the form of being left out of meetings, deprived of important reports, and ignored. She dealt with it by telling the men that she did not want their jobs and by organizing the meetings and offering to set up agendas and write the summaries, thus ensuring that she was part of the team. She also made sure that she understood men's language, sports rituals, and clan politics. She mentors three women every year, believing strongly in that process. Her goal at the company and in the country is to change the face of managed care.

Rivet is married and has two stepdaughters and two granddaughters. She was named Twin Cities Woman of the Year in 1999 and the highest-paid female executive in Minnesota in 2000. She sits on the board of Family Meds Group Inc. and on the advisory boards of the American Association of Health Plans and the Katherine J. Densford Center for Nursing Leadership.

Further Reading
Apgar, Sally. "Women on the Line."
"100 Leading Women."
Roth, Andrea, et al. "Jeannine Rivet." In *Profiles in American Enterprise*, Sections 3–2 to 3–4.

Robinson, Janet L. (1950–), Newspaper Publisher

Janet Robinson joined *Fortune*'s list of the most powerful women in American business in 2001 at number 39. In 2002 she was ranked number 28 after having been appointed senior vice president, newspaper operations, at the New York Times Company the previous year. She is responsible for leading all of the company's seventeen newspaper operations, including the *New York Times* and the *Boston Globe*. Due to problems at the *New York Times* she slipped to number 48 on the *Fortune* list in 2003. In February 2004 the *Times* announced that she would be the president and CEO of the New York Times Company when Russell Lewis retired at the end of that year.

Robinson has an unusual background for business: She received an honors BA in English at Salve Regina College in Rhode Island in 1972 and spent the next eleven years as a public school teacher and reading specialist. She taught second grade and then served as an education consultant for the Massachusetts Department of Education. In 1983 she joined the New York Times Company as an account executive for *Tennis Magazine*. She spent the next seven years advancing in advertising with that magazine and *Golf Digest*. In 1990 she was promoted to vice president of the Women's Magazine Group, and in 1992 to group senior vice president for advertising sales and marketing of the group. In 1993, she became a vice president of the *New York Times*, responsible for national advertising, and in 1995 was promoted to senior vice president of advertising for all of the newspaper's advertising.

In 1996 she was appointed president and general manager of the *New York Times*. She is credited with increasing its advertising revenues by 50 percent and turning the newspaper into a truly national publication rather than one primarily oriented to New York City. That year she also completed the Executive Education Program at the Amos Tuck School at Dartmouth College. In February 2001 she became senior vice president, newspaper operations. She instituted a leaner organizational structure and raised the price of the newspaper, which contributed to larger circulation revenues. By 2003 advertising revenues had also improved.

Robinson is known for her high energy and intelligence. She was named as Outstanding Newspaper Executive of 1994 by *Frohlinger's Marketing Report*. She was chairman of the American Advertising Federation board in 1999 and has been a member of the Advertising Club of New York, Advertising Women of New York, and Literacy Volunteers of New York, and on the advisory board of Salve Regina College. She chaired the 2003 Advertising Hall of Fame Council of Judges.

See also: Publishing Industry

Further Reading

Carr, David. "President to Retire from Times Co.: Successor Named."

"Janet L. Robinson Named Senior Vice President, Newspaper Operations: Robinson Announces New Direct Reporting Structure at *The New York Times* Newspaper."

"The New York Times Company Appoints Senior Ad Executive."

Roche, Josephine (1886–1976), Mining Executive

Josephine Roche inherited the Rocky Mountain Fuel Company in 1927 when her father died. She was a social reformer and idealist and ran for governor of Colorado. Roche was born in Nebraska to a wealthy businessman and his wife. Her father owned a large coal-mining operation, and the family moved to Denver in 1906. Josephine developed a social conscience at an early age. When she was twelve, she wanted to visit the mines, but her father said it was not safe. She questioned why it was safe for the miners but not safe for her. She graduated from Vassar in 1908 and began her first job as a probation officer in the Denver Juvenile Court. In 1910 she returned to school and earned a master's degree in sociology at Columbia University. Back in Colorado, she became Denver's first policewoman and was said to have been better at controlling crime than any of the men. However, she was apparently disliked by the people involved in vice, for they saw to it that she was fired.

> She became Denver's first policewoman and was said to have been better at controlling crime than any of the men.

In 1913 and 1914, there was a violent coalfield war in Colorado in mines owned by John D. Rockefeller Jr. It ended in the tragedy that is now called the Ludlow Massacre. Roche sympathized with the strikers and helped the victims' families in various ways, even going to court with them.

In 1915 she served as a special agent for the Commission for Relief in Belgium. Back in Denver she directed the Girls' Department in the Denver Juvenile Court. President Woodrow Wilson appointed her director of the Foreign Language Education Service and a member of the Committee on Public Information. In 1920 she married Edward Bierstadt; they divorced in 1922. Again she returned to the Denver Juvenile Court, this time as a referee.

In 1927 Roche's father died, and she inherited the Rocky Mountain Fuel Company, the second largest coal-mining company in the state. She realized that she could turn her labor beliefs into reality. There was a strike at the mines, and she told the Colorado Industrial Commission that it was justified because of the horrible working conditions and terrible pay. She asked the stockholders to approve unionizing the miners through the United Mine Workers of America. Some refused and sold their shares, which she subsequently bought, becoming the majority stockholder. She reorganized the company, became a vice president, and brokered a historic union contract that paid $7 per day (then the highest mining wage in Colorado), improved working conditions, and guaranteed arbitration. By 1932 the company was prospering. The amount of coal mined had doubled, and workers were employed more days per year and at higher pay with fewer accidents than in any other Colorado company. Roche was also involved in developing the Bituminous Coal Code.

In 1934 she ran for governor of Colorado with the slogan "Roosevelt, Roche and Recovery." Although she carried the cities, she lost the primary election. President Franklin Delano Roosevelt appointed her assistant secretary of the treasury in charge of the U.S. Health Service. She was also on the committee that drafted recommendations for the Social Security Act. In 1935 she resigned from her appointment because the company's general manager died. The Great Depression had hit the coal-mining business, and even though the union loaned her $450,000, the company continued to lose money. She resigned as manager in 1939. In 1944 the company went into bankruptcy and did not recover. She became the first director of the United Mine Workers Welfare and Retirement Fund in 1947 and stayed on until 1971.

Roche was a woman with high social ideals who was willing to put them to the test. Her life was a testament to improving the lives of everyone, particularly people who could not help themselves. She was "a woman of great grace who believed in the most fundamental of human tenets: that the sanctity of the human spirit was the most important thing in life" (Monnett and McCarthy, *Colorado Profiles*, p. 279).

See also: Mining Industry; Western Businesswomen

Further Reading
"Josephine Aspinwall Roche." In John Monnett and Michael McCarthy, p. 279–289.
McGinn, Elinor. *A Wide-Awake Woman: Josephine Roche in the Era of Reform.*
"Roche, Josephine (Aspinwall)." In *Current Biography*, p. 723–725.

Rodale, Ardath (1939–), Publisher

Although Ardath Rodale had been only peripherally involved in her husband Robert's publishing business before 1990, she took it over after he was killed in an automobile accident that year. Rodale Publishing, a magazine and book publisher, has been listed among *Working Woman*'s top woman-owned businesses since 1997.

Rodale Publishing was founded in 1941 by Ardath Rodale's father-in-law. Her husband, Robert, took it over and published its first magazines, *Organic Farming and Gardening* and *Prevention*, in 1952. *Bicycling* began in 1972 and *Runners World* in 1985. After he was killed, and against all advice, she became CEO. She was a two-time cancer survivor with four grown children. Her first act was to set up an executive advisory committee composed of all four children and some of the top division heads. They decided to begin *Men's Health*, which was a success from the beginning. Since then the company has launched *Mountain Bike* and *Heart & Soul* and has published numerous inspirational books. In response to the September 11 terrorist attacks, she published *From the Ashes*, with all the profits going to a charity for the education of the New York City firefighters' families.

The company's sales have grown 56 percent under her leadership. She has carried on her husband's philosophy of better living through good health and self-reliance. She is proud of creating a family atmosphere with a beneficial office design and care for each employee. In 1999 and 2000 *Fortune* named Rodale Publishing one of the best companies to work for. The Rodale Institute receives some of the company profits for the support of its outreach program and chemical-free research farm.

In 1997 Rodale appointed her daughter Maria vice chairman of the board. In 2001 she hired Steven Murphy and in 2002 appointed him president and CEO. Ardath Rodale remains as chairman of the board. The *Central Pennsylvania Business Journal* named her one of the fifty best women in business in the state. Governor Tom Ridge named her a Distinguished Daughter of Pennsylvania, and the Star Group included her in its list of the fifty leading woman entrepreneurs in the world in 1999.

See also: Publishing Industry

Further Reading
Holusha, John. "Folksy Rodale Emerges as Hard-Driving Marketer."
Lowry, Tom. "How Rodale Takes Care of Its Health."
Rodale, Ardath. *Gifts of the Spirit: True Stories to Renew Your Soul.*

Roebling, Mary Gindhart (1906–1994), Banker

Mary Roebling was one of the first women bank presidents and the first woman governor of the American Stock Exchange. An active banker from the 1930s until the 1970s, she was far ahead of the feminist movement.

Roebling was born in West Collingwood, New Jersey, the oldest of four children. Her father was president of the Keystone and Eastern Telephone Company, and her mother was a schoolteacher. Mary's first job was picking strawberries for $1 a box. When she was sixteen she married Arthur Herbert, and they had one daughter. He died of a mustard-gas infection in 1925. Mary took a secretarial job in a brokerage house and studied merchandising and business administration at night at the University of Pennsylvania. She also became a feminist and advocated a woman for U.S. vice president.

In 1931 she married Siegfried Roebling, the grandson of the builder of the Brooklyn Bridge. They had one son. Roebling, who ran Trenton Trust, died of a heart attack in 1931, and his father insisted that Mary take over the bank. He suggested she use her common sense in running it. She went to New York University at night, studying banking and finance, and was privately tutored in law.

Roebling was president of the bank for thirty-five years and chairman of the board from 1941 until 1972. She kept the bank going through the Great Depression and introduced then-unknown practices such as public relations, merchandising, and drive-in banking. She employed only women tellers at the main branch and held financial

> She employed only women tellers at the main branch and held financial teas to market trust funds to wealthy women.

teas to market trust funds to wealthy women. During her tenure assets increased from $17 million to more than $200 million.

In 1972 Trenton Trust merged with the National State Bank in Elizabeth, New Jersey. Roebling became chairman of the merged company in 1976 and was in that position when she retired in 1984 and became chairman emeritus. In 1978 she helped found the Women's Bank of Denver, the first nationally chartered bank founded by a woman.

In a 1960 *Saturday Evening Post* article she was quoted as saying, "Any woman who wants to make her mark in business . . . must make men forget she's a woman between nine and five, and must make them remember she's a woman for the balance of her waking hours" (Tunley, "The Glittering Widow," p. 25). She was known for her business savvy and shrewd appraisal of the financial bottom line. Her parents raised her children while she worked.

President Franklin Delano Roosevelt appointed her to a committee for the China Relief Bill, and President Harry Truman put her on the Citizen's Advisory Committee on Armed Forces Installations. From 1958 to 1962 she was the elected governor of the American Stock Exchange, the first woman in that position. In 1959 the city of Trenton declared a "Mary Roebling Day." She won the Commendatore of the Order of the Star of Solidarity from the president of Italy, the Israel Freedom Medal, the President's Medal and the Outstanding Civilian Service Medal from the U.S. Army, and the Distinguished Service Award from the U.S. Marine Corps. She was an honorary colonel of the New Jersey Blues and held honorary degrees from St. John's University and Bryant College. She was a trustee of Russell Sage College and sat on the boards of several companies and many civic and arts organizations. Three flowers were named for her: a dahlia, an orchid, and a rose.

See also: Banking

Further Reading
"Mary Gindhart Roebling." In *Current Biography Yearbook*, 1960, p. 342–344.
Pace, Eric. "Mary Roebling, 89, First Woman to Head Major U.S. Bank, Dies."
Tunley, Roul. "The Glittering Widow of Trenton, N.J."

Romance, *see* Office Romance

Ronzone, Bertha B. (1885–1969), Retailer, Department Store Owner

Bertha Ronzone was the owner of the largest privately owned department store chain in Nevada at the time of her death. She arrived in the state during the height of the gold-prospecting boom and, rather than pan for gold, became an entrepreneur. Ronzone was born in Iowa, but her family migrated west to California, where she grew up. In 1901 she married A. B. Ronzone, who had come west for gold.

The following spring they took a wooden steamer to Alaska, normally a two-week trip. Just as they saw the lights of Nome, a giant ice floe trapped the ship and drifted out to sea, carrying the ship with it. They were carried so far north that it took seventy-three days to get back to Nome. A brass band and crowds greeted the ship, and the Ronzones received the news that A. B.'s partner had sold their business and left with all the money. They stayed in Alaska for two years before leaving with their new daughter to go to Nevada, which presented a new opportunity to prospect for gold.

They ended up in Manhattan, Nevada, and their second daughter was born. Ronzone began taking in miners' laundry to help make ends meet. She did the wash by hand and soon had nine Paiute women working for her. Her oldest daughter helped by collecting and delivering the clothes. In 1917 Bertha became ill and went to California to recuperate. There she found wonderful sales on socks, in both very small and very large sizes. She shipped them to her daughter, who sold them all to the miners, who were desperate for socks of any size. The venture was so successful that she decided to open a general store to sell clothing and other necessities. With a loan of $500 from a friend, she stocked one room in her house with goods. Even though the mining camp was declining, the store was a success.

In 1923 the Manhattan mine closed. The Ronzones moved to Tonopah, Nevada, and opened another store. In 1929 leaving the Tonopah store in the capable hands of their daughter and her husband, they moved to Las Vegas. The Boulder Dam was going to be built nearby, and they knew there would be a need for another store.

A. B. Ronzone died in 1938 and son Richard joined his mother for two years, but left to go to war. In 1939 her daughter and son-in-law sold the Tonopah store and joined Bertha in Las Vegas. In 1943 she bought a store in Reno, which they operated. In 1946 the Ronzones moved again and opened yet another store. Bertha was active in store operations until her death in 1969.

Bertha Ronzone believed that her success was due to prayer, faith, and determination; it was also due to hard work and initiative and entrepreneurial spirit. In June 1967 the University of Nevada in Las Vegas named her a Distinguished Nevadan, one of the highest state honors; earlier she had been named "Nevada's Golden Rule Pioneer Mother" (*Nevada Women's History Project*).

See also: Retailing Industry; Western Businesswomen

Further Reading

American Mothers' Committee. *Mothers of Achievement in American History 1776–1976: Bi-Centennial Project*, p. 349–350.

Nevada Women's History Project (www.unr.edu/sb204/nwhp).

Rooney, Therese A. (1955–), Insurance Industry Executive

Therese A. Rooney is the chairwoman of the board of Golden Rule Financial, Indiana's largest life and health insurance company. It was number 23 on the 2001 *Working Woman* list of the top woman-owned businesses in the United States.

Rooney was born into the business. Her grandfather started it in 1940 by selling insurance door-to-door with an office at home. Her father joined in 1948 immediately after finishing college, and she began her career there in 1976. She worked her way up to executive vice president, and in 1991 her father stepped down as CEO. He remained chairman of the board, and she became executive vice president and chief operating office. In 1994 she took the position of president and CEO and in 1996, CEO and chair of the board. In 2000 she retired as CEO but remained chair of the board.

The company had estimated sales in 2001 of $1.367 billion and 1,084 employees. It is known for pioneering the concept of medical savings accounts. Ward Group recognized it as one of 50 Life Health Top Performers in 2003, a list it has been on since 1995.

Rooney is interested in education and serves on the board of Project E, a not-for-profit organization whose goal is to improve the educational systems in Indiana.

See also: Insurance Industry

Further Reading
Dunlap, Phil. "Life in Indiana: The State's Largest Life/Health Carriers."
Golden Rule (www.goldenrule.com).

Rosenthal, Ida (1886–1973), Brassiere Manufacturer

Ida Rosenthal invented the brassiere as we know it today and, with it, literally changed the profile of women's fashion. Rosenthal was born near Minsk, Russia, and trained as a dressmaker in Warsaw. She followed her sweetheart, William Rosenthal, to the United States when he fled the Russian czar's draft. She opened a dressmaker's shop in Hoboken, New Jersey, and, in 1906 married William. They had a son, Lewis, and a daughter, Beatrice. William, who had worked in New York's garment district, joined her in the shop. By 1912 they had six employees and a loyal customer base who bought dresses for an average $7 each.

In 1918 the Rosenthals had saved enough to move the shop to New York, where one of her dresses came to the attention of Enid Bissett, the owner of Enid Frocks, a dress boutique. She persuaded Rosenthal to work there, where dresses were priced for the carriage trade at $125 and up. In 1921, Ida and William were offered a partnership in the store. They paid $4,000 for it, their entire life savings.

The shop sold custom-made dresses, focusing on high quality, individualized fashions, and customer satisfaction. The period was the twenties, and flapper styles for boyish figures predominated. The style didn't work for many women, however, particularly those with fuller figures. To make the clothes hang well on their wearers, Ida devised an undergarment with two cups held together by a piece of elastic band. She and Bissett gave them away with the dresses. Soon customers came back to buy just the undergarment for $1 each. William dealt with the construction and also solved sizing problems by devising the cup sizes that are still used today.

> Ida devised an undergarment with two cups held together by a piece of elastic band.

By 1925 brassieres became their major business; they incorporated and called the company Maiden Form. They began manufacturing in Bayonne, New Jersey, with dozens of sewing machines. In 1930 Bissett retired, leaving the business to the Rosenthals. William became president and chief designer, and Ida did the rest: sales, finance, advertising, and public relations. They improved their manufacturing processes by instituting a section-work process with an assembly line. Because each brassiere had at least twenty separate pieces, this worked very well and it too is still used today. In 1938 the company's gross annual income was $4.5 million; by the 1960s, it was $40 million. During the Great Depression they had only one losing year.

World War II brought a reduction in production for many companies, but not for Maiden Form, because Ida persuaded the government that brassieres reduced fatigue for the working female population. The company also supplied WACs and WAVEs with brassieres and soldiers with vests that had special pockets to hold carrier pigeons. It began advertising extensively during the war. In 1949 their famous advertising campaign by Mary Filius, a New York advertising copywriter, debuted. "I dreamed I went shopping in my Maidenform bra" was the first slogan of a twenty-year campaign that would feature women doing various exotic and adventurous things such as racing chariots and winning elections. By the 1960s Maidenform was a household name, and the name of the company was changed to match the brand name. The company employed 5,000 people in twenty-eight plants, warehouses, and offices and had markets in 115 countries.

William died in 1958, and Ida became president. In 1963 she was invited to the Soviet Union as the only woman member of an industrial-study exchange team. When she was eighty she was still making at least two European business trips a year. In 1966 she suffered an incapacitating stroke, and the company was turned over to Joseph Coleman, her daughter Beatrice's husband. He, along with Beatrice and many Rosenthal family members, had worked there for many years. Ida Rosenthal served as chairman of the board until she died in 1973.

The success of Maidenform was due largely to her conservative management as well as innovative manufacturing methods and her inspired invention. Low pricing, volume distribution, and focus on customer satisfaction coupled with repeat business were important factors too. Ida had three goals in running the company: to produce a quality product, to make Maiden Form one of the best-known brands in the world, and to develop a corporate structure that would survive her. The twenties were the right time for her invention, and the advertising campaign was inspired. In the eighties, however, the ads came under fire from feminists.

Both Rosenthals were extremely active philanthropically. They founded Camp Lewis, a Boy Scout Camp in memory of their son Lewis, who died at age twenty-three, established the Judaica and Hebraic Library at New York University, and contributed to the original Albert Einstein Collection of Medicine at Yeshiva University. They were also active in the Anti-Defamation League of B'nai B'rith.

See also: Fashion Industry; Immigrant Businesswomen

Further Reading

Altman, Linda Jacobs. *Women Inventors*, p. 50–60.

"Maidenform's Mrs. R."

Neu, Irene D. "Rosenthal, Ida Cohen." In Barbara Sicherman and Carol Hurd Green, p. 604–605.

Rosie the Riveter (1940–1945), Mythical Female Factory Worker

During every war in U.S. history, women have taken up the slack. Abigail Adams managed the land while John was busy with national politics. Southern women managed the plantations during the Civil War. In the West, women managed homesteads and ranches while the men were off fighting Indians. In World War I more than 1 million women worked in industry during the nineteen months of the war. These World War I women, Rosie the Riveter's forebears, were mostly young and single. They left their jobs after the war but proved they were capable of doing "men's work." They also forced improvements in working conditions that continued after the war was over.

Between World War I and World War II, women who wished to work were discriminated against, poorly paid, and segregated into low-paying professions. As the country began to produce war machinery in 1942, the government mounted a campaign to recruit women. Norman Rockwell painted a cover for the *Saturday Evening Post* of May 29, 1943, of a well-muscled woman factory worker in front of the American flag and "Rosie" on her lunchbox.

Thus Rosie the Riveter was born, and she was successful. In 1940, 12 million women were employed; the number rose to 18.2 million in 1944.

Unlike the previous war, these workers were middle-class and college-educated women; 6 million of them had never before worked outside the home. One and a half million were between the ages of forty-five and sixty-five; a quarter-million were over sixty-five. It was the first time minority women had access to skilled jobs. At the end of the war most of these women were pushed out of their jobs. Their feelings of self-worth and confidence did not diminish, however, and even though there was a backlash against employed women, many think that their independence and pride contributed to the feminist movement of the 1960s, with demands for real equality at work.

In October 2000 the Ford Motor Company, the National Park Service, the National Park Foundation, and the City of Richmond, California, dedicated Rosie the Riveter Memorial Park in Richmond's Marina Bay neighborhood. Work is continuing on exhibits in Ford's Kaiser shipyards in Richmond, California, where many Rosies built war equipment.

See also: Manufacturing

Further Reading

Brown, Carrie. *Rosie's Mom: Forgotten Women Workers of the First World War.*

Gluck, Sherna Berger. *Rosie the Riveter Revisited: Women, the War, and Social Change.*

Rosie the Riveter Trust (www.rosietheriveter.org).

Rowland, Pleasant T. (1941–), Toy Manufacturer

Pleasant Rowland founded the Pleasant Company in 1984, when the only dolls she could find for her niece were the Barbie and Cabbage Patch kids. She decided to make her own dolls, historically accurate and accompanied by storybooks and accessories. Even though she violated every unwritten rule of business and the toy industry, her company was a phenomenal success. It was on the *Working Woman* list of top woman-owned companies from the list's beginnings in 1992 through 1999, when she sold it to Mattel for $750 million.

Rowland was born in Chicago in 1941 to one of the top advertising men of the time. From him she learned about real value, and he imbued her with respect for the creativity and detail necessary to achieve that goal. She learned the rudiments of advertising at the dinner table. After graduating from Wells College in 1962, she taught elementary school for six years. Although she loved teaching and created her own teaching materials, she hated the step system of salaries in which mediocre teachers were rewarded the same as excellent teachers. She saw an ad seeking a TV reporter and decided to apply. She talked to the interviewer about how to teach children to read, got the job, and later became a news anchor. Although it was fun, she felt she wasn't making a difference. Her next career consisted of writing educational programs. She developed two prototype units, which she sold to J.B. Lippincott. She was hired to develop the Addison-Wesley Reading Program and then rejoined the Boston Educational Research Company, her original employer in Boston. She was a vice president there until 1976, when she married Jerry Frautschi and moved to Madison, Wisconsin, where Frautschi owned a printing company. She immersed herself in volunteer work, wrote a guidebook to Colonial Williamsburg, and bought *Children's Magazine Guide*, a children's magazine indexing service. She boosted its circulation before selling it in 1989.

Meanwhile, she was again feeling the need for a more satisfying career, and her abortive 1984 shopping trip triggered a vision of a doll that would have value and be loved and cared for generation after generation. Inspired by a business trip to Colonial Williamsburg with her husband, she conceived of a doll and accompanying storybooks that would tie history and play together. She soon had dolls from three different periods, called the American Girls collection: Kristen, a frontier prairie Swedish-American girl; Samantha, an orphan raised by her Victorian grandfather; and Molly, whose father fought in World War II. Each doll and storybook set cost $82, a fairly high price. The books, accessories (bought separately), and clothing were historically accurate. A matching set of clothes for the young doll owners was also available. More dolls were added later, including Addy, who was born into slavery, and Josefina, a Hispanic girl. Rowland asked a team of prominent African American women to help with Addy's story. The dolls and their accessories are made all over the world, in countries including Germany, China, the Philippines, Taiwan, and Portugal. The doll trunks are made in Wisconsin.

> Her abortive 1984 shopping trip triggered a vision of a doll that would have value and be loved and cared for generation after generation.

The Pleasant Company broke several toy-industry rules. First, its dolls were too expensive. Second, they were marketed initially only through mail order, although the books were available in retail bookstores. Third, they were aimed at girls aged seven through twelve, when girls were thought to lose interest in dolls by age six. Fourth, they were marketed primarily to parents and grandparents, not to the children. Nevertheless, sales boomed and by 1996 the company had sold 3 million dolls and 35 million books. In 1992 Rowland started *American Girl* magazine, which had 675,000 subscribers by 1996.

In 1998 Rowland sold the company to Mattel. Given the anti-Barbie bent of American Girls, selling the company to Barbie's creators was an irony that escaped no one. Jill Barad, Mattel's CEO, promised to keep the company separate and to allow Rowland to run it as an independent division. It would also stay in Wisconsin, and no jobs would be lost. Rowland would have input into Mattel products. She received $750 million for the company and became vice chairman and a board member of Mattel. She shared the money with her long-time employees. In July 2000, after two years with Mattel, she retired.

Rowland's goal for her company was "to create attractive products that really had value, that really taught moral and historical lessons and captured the hearts of young girls"(Ericksen, *What's Luck Got to Do With It?* p. 167). She felt that the company fulfilled all her personal needs: to create, to teach, to lead, to make a difference, and to leave a legacy. She had a reputation for controlling every aspect of the company in a positive way. The company's employees were 85 percent women; two of three vice presidents and seven of nine directors at one time were women.

Rowland has received many awards, including being named one of twelve Outstanding Entrepreneurs in 1990 by the Institute of American Entrepreneurs and the Best & Brightest in Marketing in 1993 by *Advertising Age*, and receiving the Bronze Echo Award in 1991 from the Direct Marketing Association. Her first catalog won the John C. Caples Award for Creative Excellence. Her 1990 holiday catalog won the Gold Award in the American Catalog Awards. She was also named Wisconsin Business Leader of the Year. In keeping with her values, in late 1998 she gave $5 million to the Chicago Botanic Garden in memory of her father. In 1999 Rowland and her husband received the Wisconsin Governor's Award in Support of the Arts. The following year, her foundation gave $3 million to the Milwaukee Art Museum, and in 2001 it gave a $23 million endowment challenge grant to the Madison Community Foundation for a variety of arts groups. That May she bought Mackenzie-Childs, an upstate New York furniture company and its New York retail store, and several other properties in Aurora, New York, the home of Wells College, her alma mater. Her goal was to boost economic activity in the town.

Further Reading

American Girl (www.americangirl.com).

Ericksen, Gregory Y. *What's Luck Got to Do With It? Twelve Entrepreneurs Reveal the Secrets behind Their Success*, p. 165–180.

Forbes Inc. *Forbes Great Minds of Business: Companion to the Public Television Series*, p. 121–212.

Hajewski, Doris. "Mattel Buying State Doll Maker Pleasant Co."

Neal, Mollie. "Cataloger Gets Pleasant Results: Pleasant Co.'s Marketing Strategy."

Rubinstein, Helena (1870–1965), Cosmetics Manufacturer

Helena Rubinstein, like Elizabeth Arden, was a pioneer in the cosmetics industry as we know it today. While Arden began her salons in the United States, Rubinstein started in London and Paris. Rubinstein was born in Cracow, Poland, the eldest of eight daughters. Her father was an egg merchant. She briefly attended the University of Cracow. Toward the end of the

1890s she emigrated to Australia, where she worked in a cafe and then as a governess while she learned English.

In her baggage were twelve pots of her mother's face cream. When Australian friends complimented her on her complexion, she sold the face cream to them. In 1902 she opened a shop in Melbourne, borrowed $1,000 to get more cream, and opened her first salon. She called the cream "Creme Valaze" and taught women how to take care of their skin along with the sale of a jar. She insisted upon this technique for the rest of her life. She also wrote a newspaper article and received 15,000 orders.

In 1904 she left her Australian business in the capable hands of her sisters and went to London with $100,000 to establish European salons. For four years she studied dermatology in Paris and Vienna, and then in 1908 she rented a twenty-room mansion belonging to Lord Salisbury and opened her London salon. The Maison de Beauté was a success from the beginning; elite society women patronized it and paid £200 pounds (U.S.$1,000) for a series of treatments. That year she also married an American journalist, Edward Titus. They had two sons.

In 1912 Rubenstein opened a salon in Paris, but World War I made the timing unfortunate. At the urging of her husband, they moved to the United States, bought a home in Greenwich, Connecticut, sent the boys to boarding schools, and opened a salon in New York City. She expanded into Philadelphia, New Orleans, San Francisco, and Boston, always with young women staff who were trained to give treatments and teach skin care along with selling jars of cream. She also developed and sold other preparations; by the end of her life, she offered 629 products.

Department stores had been clamoring for her products, and in 1917 she began wholesale distribution with the caveat that purchasers be trained to use the creams successfully. She established schools to train the saleswomen, developed a diet plan and a day of beauty (eight hours of treatments), and invented medicated skin creams for skin problems. Her marriage began to show signs of strain, so in 1928 she incorporated, selling 66 percent of the stock to Lehman Brothers for $7.3 million. She soon regretted it because the company tried to shift to lower-priced cosmetics of lesser quality. She tried to buy the stock back without success until the stock market crash in 1929 enabled her to obtain it all for a mere $1.5 million. She always maintained direct control after that.

Rubenstein and Titus were divorced around 1937; the following year she married Prince Gourielli, a Russian who was twenty years younger. She began a line of cosmetics for men in his name, the House of Gourielli. Over the years her business changed its emphasis to manufacturing and wholesale. She kept the salons, but they slowly decreased to just one, in New York City. Her family members were all involved in the business and, at the time of her death in 1965, her cosmetics were sold in more than a hundred countries. She never retired and was doing business from her apartment two days before her death. She wrote five books about beauty and had a huge art collection.

Rubenstein's philanthropy focused on art and medical research. She was painted by some of the greatest artists of the time and founded an art museum in Israel, the Helena Rubinstein Pavilion of Contemporary Art. She established the Helena Rubinstein Foundation to give scholarships and fund other worthy causes. She represented the U.S. cosmetics industry at the American National Exhibition in Moscow in 1959 and was awarded the Italian Star of Solidarity the same year. She received an honorary degree from Wilson College in Chambersburg, Pennsylvania, in 1965. Her personal fortune was estimated at $100 million. Colgate-Palmolive bought the company from her sons in 1973 and still operates it as a subsidiary.

See also: Arden, Elizabeth; Beauty Industry; Immigrant Businesswomen

Further Reading

Fabe, Maxene. *Beauty Millionaire: The Life of Helena Rubinstein.*

Keiffer, E. B. "Madame Rubinstein, the Little Lady from Krakow."

O'Higgins, Patrick. *Madame: An Intimate Biography of Helena Rubinstein.*

Rubinstein, Helena. *My Life for Beauty.*

Rudkin, Margaret Fogarty (1897–1967), Bakery Owner

Margaret Rudkin has been called a late bloomer: She started her bakery business, Pepperidge Farm, when she was forty. She began making bread when a doctor suggested that her youngest son's asthma might be helped if he stopped eating the chemicals found in store-bought bread.

Rudkin was born in New York City, where she lived in a brownstone with her mother, father, and grandmother. When her grandmother died, the family moved to Flushing, Queens, where Margaret graduated from high school and worked in a bank for four years. In 1919 she got a job as a customer's representative for a New York brokerage firm, and in 1923 she married one of the partners, Henry Rudkin. They lived in the city, where they had three sons. In 1929 they moved to a 125-acre farm in Fairfield, Connecticut, and built a Tudor mansion. They called it Pepperidge Farm after the pepperidge (black gum) trees that grew there. Due to the Great Depression and following a serious polo accident by Henry, they cut back, selling four of their five cars and all twelve of their horses. They looked for ways to make money on the farm, beginning with selling apples and turkeys. At this time, their son began to have asthma symptoms. Rudkin experimented with a recipe from *The Boston Cookbook* coupled with memories of her Irish grandmother's baking to make her own bread. After many attempts, she baked a loaf of whole wheat bread that tasted good and seemed to alleviate the asthma symptoms.

> In 1929 they moved to a 125-acre farm . . . and built a Tudor mansion. They called it Pepperidge Farm.

When the doctor saw that her bread seemed to be helping her son, he recommended that she make bread for other patients as well. Her business started as mail order. In August 1937 she sold her first batch of loaves to a Fairfield grocer for a high price. Later that year she persuaded the manager of a New York specialty grocery store to buy twenty-four loaves a day, sending them with her husband when he went to work. Soon she had to hire help and converted the Pepperidge Farm stable and part of the garage into a bakery. The business was a success, appealing to consumers who wanted the same quality as homemade bread and were willing to pay more than twice what commercial bread cost. By the end of 1937 the bakery was producing 4,000 loaves a week. Rudkin received free publicity from a 1937 article in the *New York Journal and American*: "Society Woman Turns Baker to Supply Elite with Healthful Bread." A later *Reader's Digest* article elicited worldwide mail orders (Ratcliff, J. D., p. 102).

By 1940 she had rented buildings in Norwalk, Connecticut, with the capacity to bake 50,000 loaves a week. Her husband became chairman of the board and directed finance and marketing; she was president and supervised personnel and production. Margaret Rudkin remained committed to high quality, natural ingredients, mixing the dough in small batches, and cutting and kneading by hand. She insisted that stores not sell the bread after two days but return it to her; it became poultry stuffing. The Rudkins built another new plant in 1947, and two more, in Pennsylvania and Illinois, within the next five years. In the 1950s her television advertisements were aimed at people interested in nutritious and homemade-tasting food. She also bought a frozen pastry line and cookie recipes. By the late 1950s the company employed 1,000 people, mostly women.

Rudkin expected good work and paid higher-than-average wages. She also instituted bonus and insurance plans for her employees. Her commitment to high quality and her gift for promotion and advertising made the company a success. In 1955 she was presented with the distinguished award to industry from the Women's International Exposition of the Women's National Institute.

In 1960 Pepperidge Farm profits were $1.3 million out of $32 million total sales. The Rudkins sold the company to the Campbell Soup Company for stock worth $28 million. Margaret Rudkin was a director of Campbell Soup and continued to run Pepperidge Farm as an independent subsidiary. In 1962 she turned over the presidency to her son William and took over the chairmanship until she retired in 1966. She died the next year of cancer. She is in the Connecticut Women's Hall of Fame.

See also: Food Industry; Late Bloomers

Further Reading
Bainbridge, John. "Striking a Blow for Grandma."
"Mrs. Rudkin Revisited."
Ratcliff, J. D. "Bread, de Luxe."
Rudkin, Margaret. *The Margaret Rudkin Pepperidge Farm Cookbook.*

Russo, Patricia F. (1952–), Telecommunications Industry Executive

Pat Russo was named to *Fortune*'s list of the most powerful women in American business in 1998, 1999, 2001, 2002, and 2003, when she was ranked number 21. She was the first woman to head a business unit of AT&T. As executive vice president in charge of strategy, business development, and corporate operations, she was the highest ranking officer of Lucent Technologies. She left in June 2001 to become CEO of EastmanKodak, but returned to Lucent six months later as CEO. In 2003 she was elected Lucent's chair.

Russo was born in Trenton, New Jersey, the second of seven children. Her father was a doctor and her mother, a homemaker. She helped to raise two handicapped brothers. She received her BA from Georgetown University in 1973 and went to work for IBM that year. There she worked in a number of sales and marketing management positions. In 1981 she joined AT&T, where she held management positions in strategic planning, marketing, and human resources. In 1990 she became vice president of national sales and service for AT&T's Global Business Communications Systems, where she was a key member of the team responsible for planning and executing the unit's restructuring and successful turnaround. She divested it of unrelated businesses, focused on its core business of voice systems, and began to expand internationally. In 1993 she was promoted to president of the unit, by then the U.S. market leader in business communication systems products. During this time she also completed a one-year postgraduate program in advanced management at Harvard University.

In 1996 AT&T broke up and spun off the manufacturing components, among them the Global Business Communications Systems unit that, as a separate entity, went public under the name Lucent Technologies. Russo remained president of the Lucent Technologies Business Communications Systems unit until she was promoted to the position of executive vice president and chief of staff of Lucent Technologies. Her responsibilities were to direct strategy, business development, public relations, and advertising. She also led development and implementation of new initiatives and worked on employee morale and loyalty. Her boss has commented on her ability to make tough and necessary decisions and her inclusive management style. As a part of her employee program, she saw to it that every employee received stock options, tied raises and bonuses to the company's financial performance, and planned to extend employee stock purchasing plans to cover more than just executives.

In 1997 Lucent underwent a reorganization and Russo's title changed to executive vice president of corporate strategy and staff operations. She was also named to the five-person Office of the CEO. She was the only woman in the group and the highest ranking woman at Lucent. In November 1999 she was promoted to chief executive of services provider networks group, but the following August the position was eliminated in another reorganization. Russo resigned and in December 2000 became chair of Avaya, a Lucent spin-off. In a surprise move, she accepted the position of president and chief operating officer of Eastman Kodak in June 2001. Six months later she returned to Lucent as CEO.

Russo sits on the board of directors at Xerox, Shering-Plough, and the New Jersey Manufacturers Insurance Company. She has been a trustee of the Alliance for Employee Growth and Development, a cooperative venture of AT&T, the Communications Workers of America, and the International Brotherhood of Electrical Workers. In 1999 she won the National Italian American Foundation's Special Achievement Award for Business. *Business Week* listed her as one of its top twenty-five managers in 2002, and President George W. Bush appointed her to the National Security Telecommunications Advisory Committee in May 2003.

Further Reading

Johnson, Linda A. "New CEO Russo Seen as Strong Manager, Morale Builder as Lucent Recovers."

Mehta, Stephanie N. "Pat Russo's Lucent Vision."

Perone, Joseph R. "Pat Russo's Ascension at Lucent Makes Her Likely Candidate for CEO."

Rust, Lois (1934–), Egg Farm Owner

Lois Rust and her Rose Acre Farms have been on the *Working Woman* list of top woman-owned businesses since the list debuted in 1992. Rose Acre Farms, an egg farm, was founded by Rust's husband, David Rust. Lois Rust attended Ball State University and had been married for twenty-five years when her husband announced he wanted a divorce. He drew up the 1987 settlement himself, keeping 51 percent of the preferred stock.

Lois took over the business with 49 percent of the preferred stock and operating control. The divorce was bitter, and in 1989 she and her seven children, who own all the common stock, ousted her ex-husband from management. He was known in the business as an erratic manager; she stabilized and began to expand the business. All seven children help her.

The egg business is precarious; profit margins are very small, and owners are at the mercy of fluctuating prices and the weather. For example, during the summer of 1995 a heat wave killed 750,000 chickens at Rose Acre Farms. However, production was down nationwide because of the weather, so egg prices rose and the company broke even in spite of the disaster. Lois Rust began her management tenure by buying two other farms. By 1999 Rose Acre Farms had twenty-three mechanized poultry farms in three midwestern states with over 13 million laying hens. The company is an integrated producer, which means that it grows some of its own feed grain. Seventy percent of the business comes from shell eggs; the rest is from processed eggs sold to large institutions such as schools, retirement homes, and hospitals. It is the third-largest egg producer in the United States.

The company uses and sells everything the hens produce, from chicken feathers to manure. Its organic fertilizer operation produces more than 30,000 tons of fertilizer each year. In 1998 Rose Acre Farms began to sell "designer" eggs with altered nutritional content caused by an altered hen diet. These eggs are high in vitamin E and omega-3 essential fatty acids and sell for a higher price under the brand name Golden Premium Eggs. The farm has a network of "roving managers" who check the hens constantly for flock health, feeding, disease control, and water supply. They also monitor egg production and feed consumption. Beginning in 1999 Rose Acre Farms was the first producer to mark the laying date on each egg.

See also: Agriculture/Ranching; Food Industry

Further Reading

Lappen, Alyssa, ed. "The *Working Woman* 25," p. 69.
Schmuckler, Eric, and Harris Collingwood. "The Top 50 Women Business Owners,"
    p. 52.

S

Salaries, *see* Compensation

Saleswomen

American women have been selling goods and services since the arrival of the first colonists. African American white, and American Indian women in the colonies sold or bartered baked goods, sold produce in marketplaces, and traded or sold their skills. When businesses grew more sophisticated they hired salespeople, who were usually paid a commission on their sales. Women have been attracted to careers in sales because compensation is usually based on their performance and measured quantitatively. There have been problems, however.

The early saleswomen dealt with discrimination and, sometimes, sexual harassment. In many areas, particularly industrial sales, these still occur. Bobbi Linkemer outlined some concerns of saleswomen in a 1989 article: Their credibility was questioned; they were subjected to unwelcome advances from men, including hotel employees, prospects, clients, and colleagues; there were real dangers while traveling, particularly at night; and heavy sample cases and luggage were difficult for them to handle. Other concerns included possible misperceptions of their relationships with male colleagues or male sales managers and problems relating to work-life balance, particularly children.

Catalyst, in its 1995 report *Knowing the Territory*, stated that experience in sales is often necessary for promotion to senior management and company leadership. In 1992 a Dartnell Corporation survey counted women as 26 percent of business-to-business sales representatives but only 13 percent of sales managers. The number of saleswomen varies by industry; most work in services, apparel, and publishing. By 2002, 36.4 percent of sales officials and managers were women.

Excepting the need for travel, women like sales. Their tendency to be solutions-oriented and their ability to establish relationships are advantages in this arena. Jeanie Casison says that women generally have a passion for and belief in their products or services, which can translate into helping clients pursue goals through using the products ("The Producers," p. 28). Even though men still represent the majority of sales executives, women are not only making progress toward equality but feel much freer from sexism than in the past.

One area of sales that has always attracted women is direct sales. Direct selling includes catalog sales, home parties, television pitches, telephone sales, and Internet sales. There are more than 1,500 legitimate direct-sales companies with a variety of products from cosmetics and cookware to vitamins and weight loss. In 2002 direct selling had sales of nearly $30 billion.

Direct sales have been in use for a long time. The first "Avon lady" began selling in 1886. Around the turn of the nineteenth century, Sarah Walker parlayed her door-to-door sales into a million-dollar fortune, and Sears catalogs outfitted the country. Sales of Girl Scout cookies and Fuller brushes began in the 1920s. The first home sales party was in 1930. The industry boomed with the advent of Tupperware parties in 1951 and has been growing ever since. The chief benefit of direct sales is flexibility, but there are others. Most businesses require minimal overhead, low inventory, and are inexpensive to enter. Companies such as Mary Kay offer inspirational national conferences, training sessions, and seminars.

Women in Sales Association (WIS) promotes the professional development of women in sales through education, speakers, and publications. The Direct Selling Association (www.dsa.org) offers specialized education opportunities, conducts research programs, and compiles statistics.

Further Reading
Casison, Jeanie. "The Producers."
Catalyst. *Knowing the Territory: Women in Sales*.
Linkemer, Bobbi. "Women in Sales: What Do They Really Want?"
Strout, Erin, and Jennifer Gilbert. "Shrinking Violets."

Sammons, Mary F. (1946–), Retail Executive

Mary Sammons, president and CEO of Rite Aid, revitalized that retail chain through restructuring, reducing processes, halting overexpansion, and introducing bath and domestic products. She was ranked number 37 on the 2003 *Fortune* list of the most powerful women in American business.

Sammons was born in Portland, Oregon, and graduated from Marylhurst College with a BA in French and a secondary-level teaching certificate. In 1973 she began her corporate career as a management trainee for Fred Meyer Stores, a discount retail operation in the West. By 1995 she had risen to senior vice president and director of its General Merchandise Group. In 1997 she was also appointed executive vice president of the Home Electronics and Home Group, a new position. The following year she was promoted to the company presidency, responsible for operations and merchandise. In May 1999 Kroger bought Fred Meyer Stores.

The following December Sammons joined Rite Aid as president and chief operating officer, the first woman to attain that level in the company and also the highest-ranking woman in mass retailing. Her goal was to turn around the company, which was then on the brink of bankruptcy. Within three years she had transformed Rite Aid into a profit-making enterprise. She began with a basic change in the culture of the company in which all associates were made to feel needed and confident. She also focused on customer service and service quality through communication and intensive staff training. The improved morale and new focus combined with improved compensation packages and more employee involvement in company policies and procedures was successful. In June 2003 she became president and CEO.

Sammons learned about motivation, morale, and quality service at Fred Meyer and put those lessons to good use at Rite Aid. Her management style is based on teamwork and involving everyone in the business. She has the ability to reach, touch, and motivate people coupled with a strong merchandising intuition. "Open communication" is one of her mantras.

In 2002 MMR named her to its list of six executives who made a difference, and *Chain Drug Review* named her Retailer of the Year "for engineering one of the remarkable recoveries in chain drug annals" (Pinto, "CDR Names Rite Aid's Sammons," p. 3). She was the first woman chair of the National Association of Chain Drug Stores and sits on the executive committee of the Food Industry Leadership Center. While she was in Portland, she was very active in the community and was a trustee of the Portland Art Museum.

See also: Retailing Industry

Further Reading

Pinto, David. "CDR Names Rite Aid's Sammons Retailer of the Year."

"Rite Aid Announces Appointments of Chairman and Chief Executive Officer, and New Senior Management Team, and Engagement of New Auditors."

"Rite Aid President Sets Out to Define a New Culture."

Sandler, Marion O. (1930–), Banker

For more than thirty years, Marion Sandler and her husband have been co-chairmen and co-CEOs of Golden West Financial Corporation, the holding company for Golden West Savings and Loan. For many years she was one of only two or three woman CEOs of a *Fortune* 500 company. *Fortune* named her one of the most powerful women in American business from 1998 through 2002.

Sandler was born in Biddeford, Maine, graduated from Wellesley College in 1952, and did postgraduate work at Harvard University in 1953. She received her MBA from New York University in 1958. In 1953 she became an assistant buyer at Bloomingdale's, and in 1955 she went to Dominick & Dominick as a security analyst. In 1961 she married Herbert Sandler, then a lawyer in New York City. That year she moved to Oppenheimer & Company as a senior financial analyst, where she followed the stocks of savings and loan companies. She noticed one in particular: a sleepy little bank in the San Francisco Bay area named Golden West Savings and Loan. In 1963 Sandler and her husband formed Golden West Financial Corporation and acquired the bank as well as World Savings and Loan Association in neighboring Oakland. Its assets were $38 million.

In 1968 they took the company public with Marion Sandler as the senior vice president and a member of the board of directors and Herbert Sandler as president and CEO. In 1975 it merged with Trans-World Finance Corporation to become the second-largest savings and loan branch network in the United States, with 107 offices in California and Colorado. Earnings had grown from $16.8 million in 1966 to $92 million. Marion became vice chairman of the board of directors and a member of the executive committee as well as co-CEO of the bank. Since then it has consistently been one of the most profitable savings and loans in the country. By the end of 2003 Golden West had $82 billion in assets. There were 414 branches with offices in thirty-two states, making the company one of the largest branch systems in the United States.

Marion and Herbert Sandler operate the company together with equal responsibilities and pay. Their offices are next to each other, and they have a reputation of finishing each other's sentences. They are very conservative; the branches are plain, without extensive decorating, and there are no ATMs. The bottom line is the Sandlers' main concern. They specialize in low-risk residential mortgage loans; in 1990 down payments on 93 percent of their loans were 20 percent. The corporate culture focuses on productivity and expense control. The board of directors was, in 2003, the only *Fortune* 500 board that is composed equally of men and women. Marion Sandler is very proud of that and believes that she and the women on the board serve as role models for other women.

Both Sandlers are socially conscious. They funded the Human Rights Center at the University of California and regularly donate to a political party. They actively and monetarily support international human rights causes. Marion is a member of Phi Beta Kappa and Beta Gamma Sigma and holds an honorary doctorate from Golden Gate University. In 1992 *Business Week* listed her as one of the fifty top women in business. In 1998 *Vanity Fair* named her one of the two hundred most influential women in the United States, and she has been on *Working Woman*'s lists of best-paid corporate women many times.

In 1980 President Jimmy Carter appointed her to the President's Management Improvement Council, and in 1989 she was appointed by the Federal Reserve Board to the Thrifts Institutes Advisory Council to the Federal Reserve Board. She served as its vice president and then as its president. She has been a member of the policy advisory board for the Center for Real Estate and Urban Economics at the University of California in Berkeley, the ad hoc committee to review the School of Business Administration at Berkeley, and the vice chair of the Industrial Advisory Committee for the Federal Savings and Loan Insurance Corporation. She was a member of the Glass Ceiling Commission in 1992 and 1993. In 2001 she was named to the Bay Area Business Hall of Fame and a member of *Working Woman*'s billion-dollar club. In May 2002 she received a lifetime achievement award from the Financial Women's Association of San Francisco. As of January 2003 she was one of the twenty-five richest women with self-made fortunes in the United States according to *Women's Money Magazine* (*PR Newswire*, January 14, 2003).

See also: Banking

Further Reading
Crockett, Barton. "Golden West's Golden Couple Retiring? No Way."
Hiltzik, Michael. "Duo's Success Built on Old-School Approach."
Stevenson, Richard W. "Inside the Nation's Best-Run S & L."

Sanford, Linda S. (1953–), Computer Executive

Linda Sanford, senior vice president of IBM's Enterprise on-Demand Transformation, part of the Storage Systems Group, is one of the highest-ranking women at that company. She was listed on *Fortune*'s list of the most powerful women in American business from 1999 through 2001.

Sanford grew up on a Long Island potato farm, the oldest of five daughters. Their required chores on the farm instilled her with a strong work ethic as well as time management skills. She graduated from St. John's University with a BS in mathematics and a teaching degree, continuing her education later at Rensselaer Polytechnic Institute with a master's degree in operations research.

She joined IBM right out of college in 1975 as an engineer in the typewriter division, developing typewriters and printers. Her first responsibility was to design a color ink-jet printer. After ten years in the engineering division in Colorado, she became executive assistant to the chairman of the board for two years, a position valuable for its broad overview of global operations and contacts with the top executives. In the 1990s, as director of IBM Networking Systems, she was responsible for reinventing the mainframe business. In 1998 she was promoted to general manager of Global Industries, the first woman to hold the job. She was in charge of 17,000 employees. In 2000, in a company reorganization, she became senior vice president and group executive of the IBM Storage Systems Group. As such she was in charge of developing and marketing storage systems and in July 2002 introduced the Enterprise Storage Server Shark. The following January there was another reorganization and she assumed her present position. IBM's strategy has changed to focus on e-commerce on-demand computing, and it is her job to lead this new vision.

Her management style combines tact with great attention to detail and an ability to learn from her mistakes. She has been a role model for women at IBM as it has doubled the number of women managers. She regularly walked the factory floor when she was in charge of mainframes and continually searches for creative ways to deal with problems. She believes in customer service and building customer loyalty.

Sanford sits on the boards of ITT Industries, St. John's University, and Rensselaer Polytechnic Institute. She was inducted into the Women in Technology International (WITI) Hall of Fame in 1996, one of its first ten inductees, and was named one of the ten most influential women in technology by *Working Women* in 1997. In 2002 she was named one of *Network World*'s fifty most powerful people in networking, and she was listed among the *Computerworld* premier 100 IT leaders for 2003.

See also: Information Technology Industry

Further Reading
Godfrey, Nicola. "Key Player."
Krantz, Matt. "IBM's Linda Sanford."

Scardino, Marjorie (1947–), Magazine, Newspaper, and Book Publisher

When Marjorie Scardino became CEO of Pearson PLC in Great Britain she also became the first and only woman to head a major British public company. She was listed as number 10 and number 7, respectively, of *Fortune*'s most powerful women in American business in 1998 and 1999. From 2000 to 2002 *Fortune* named her one of the most powerful international businesswomen.

Scardino was born in Flagstaff, Arizona, and was raised in Texarkana, Texas. She was a barrel racer in rodeos during high school and graduated from Baylor University with degrees in psychology and French. During college she was involved in the civil rights movement and campaigned against poverty. She began law school at George Washington University and married Albert Scardino in 1974. They moved west, and she finished her law degree at the University of San Francisco in 1975. The couple has three children.

In 1978 the Scardinos moved to Savannah, Georgia, and bought the *Georgia Gazette*, an alternative weekly newspaper with a circulation of 2,600. Their editorials were liberal, and in 1984 the paper won a Pulitzer Prize, the first weekly newspaper to do so in twenty years. However, the paper never made a profit, and by 1985 they had accumulated $250,000 in debts.

They closed the paper and moved to New York City. Marjorie joined the Economist Group Inc., the U.S. arm of the *Economist*, which was owned by Pearson. As company president she increased circulation from 100,000 to 230,000 by 1992. The United States became the journal's largest market by targeting affluent businesspeople. In 1992 and 1993 she was worldwide managing director of the Economist Intelligence Unit in New York as its earnings doubled and global circulation increased 20 percent. In 1993, in a move that stunned London, she became CEO of the Economist Group in London, the first woman and the first American in that position in the company's 150-year history. In her four-year tenure she doubled profits while studying the strategy and goals of the company.

In 1997 she was named CEO of Pearson PLC, the $3.5 billion conglomerate that owns *The Economist* as well as many other subsidiaries. She focused on the company's mission, streamlining its various operations into three areas: information, entertainment, and education. She bought Simon & Schuster's educational division, sold Madame Tussaud's and Lazard Investment, and doubled the circulation of the *Financial Times*. She created a new corporate culture that contrasted with the company's traditional stuffiness. She also inaugurated flexible work schedules. Overall, she changed Pearson into a leaner, more focused global publisher and media company.

Scardino's management style is down-to-earth with an emphasis on fairness and equity. She has been seen in public wearing a baseball cap and regularly refers to her rodeo and shrimp-boating experiences. She has described herself as a warrior and adheres to General Douglas MacArthur's maxim "Have a good plan, execute it violently, do it today" (Doward, "Mammon," p. 18). On her first day as CEO, she sent an e-mail to all 17,000 employees introducing herself. She believes that jobs should be fun and stimulating and that there should be "give-backs" to the community. Scardino has balanced the rigors of work and family life with the help of her stay-at-home husband. She also has a rule that if her children call, she talks to them, no matter where she is or what she is doing.

> She has described herself as a warrior and adheres to General Douglas MacArthur's maxim "Have a good plan, execute it violently, do it today."

Her awards are numerous: She is an honorary fellow of the London Business School and has won the Maria and Sidney E. Rolfe Award from the Women's Economic Roundtable and the International Commerce and Leadership Award from New York City Partnership has been Veuve Cliquot Businesswoman of the Year and one of two women on Britain's Power 300. In 1999 *Texas Monthly* named her one of the most important Texans, *Good*

Housekeeping called her the fourth most influential woman in England, *Business Week's* sobriquet was "an executive to watch," and she won the Campaign Gold Award as Media Achievement of the Year. She was also ranked number 11 on the *Sunday Times* Media Power List and number 10 among *Sunday Business's* Media Elite. *Management Today* called her Britain's most powerful businesswoman in 1999, 2000, and 2002. In 2001 she was the first woman to be named European Businessperson of the Year by the Spanish magazine *Futuro*. In February 2002, after taking dual citizenship, she was made a Dame of the British Empire. She sits on several corporate and nonprofit boards of directors, including AOL, Nokia, and Public Radio International.

See also: Publishing Industry

Further Reading
Bulkley, Kate. "Corporate Profile: Pearson—Will Marge Stay in Charge?"
Doward, Jamie. "Mammon: Can Marje Stay in Charge?"
Guyon, Janet. "In Europe: No. 1 Marjorie Scardino, 53."
"Scardino, Marjorie." *Current Biography Yearbook*, April 2000, p. 73–77.

Schary, Hope Skillman (1908–1981), Textile Manufacturer

Hope Skillman Schary became the first woman cotton manufacturer and textile converter when she founded Hope Skillman Inc. in 1942. The company was later renamed Skillmill Inc.

Schary was born in Grand Rapids, Michigan, and grew up in New York City, attending both public and private schools there. After graduating from Goucher College, she married Saul Schary, a painter, in 1934. He died in 1978.

She was one of the first American textile designers and during the 1930s worked as a creative textile stylist for Cohn-Hall-Marx Company and Tabin-Picker Company. In 1942 she started her own company, which developed a reputation for producing cottons of high quality. She was known as a champion of women's rights beginning with the years when she employed only women. From 1958 to 1960 she was president of Fashion Group Inc., an organization of around 5,000 women in the fashion industry.

After Schary retired in the 1960s she became heavily involved in the women's rights movement. She was president of the National Council of Women of the United States, a nonpartisan, nonprofit clearinghouse working on human and women's rights, for two terms, 1970 to 1972 and 1976 to 1978. As president, her duties included sitting on many commissions in Washington, among them the Joint Commission for Correctional Manpower and Training and the Bicentennial Commission. She was the National Council of Women's representative to the International Council of Women for many years and at the time of her death was vice president of that organization.

See also: Fashion Industry; Manufacturing

Further Reading
Diamonstein, Barbaralee. *Open Secrets: Ninety-Four Women in Touch with Our Time.* p. 344–348.
Waggoner, Walter H. "Hope Schary, Leader in Textiles Designing and Women's Rights."

Schiff, Dorothy (1903–1989), Newspaper Publisher

Dorothy Schiff was the first woman newspaper publisher in New York City. She pioneered the tabloid format, putting her financially ailing newspaper, the *New York Post,* on its feet.

Schiff was born to wealth; tutored at home; schooled at Brearly, an exclusive girls school; and took a yearly trip to Europe with her mother. She attended Bryn Mawr for a year but was asked to leave because of poor grades. She married for the first time in 1923, had two children, and lived the life of a socialite during the 1920s. She divorced her first husband, Richard Hall, and in 1932 married George Backer.

During the 1930s she became involved in civic and political activities, particularly in child and women's welfare. She joined the Democratic Party after hearing Franklin Delano Roosevelt speak in 1936 and was thoroughly committed to his New Deal programs. She also became a good friend of both Eleanor and Franklin Roosevelt.

In 1939 Schiff bought a controlling interest in the *New York Post* with her inheritance and installed Backer as president and publisher. She was a director, vice president, and editor. The *Post* was the longest continuously running daily newspaper in the United States, started by Alexander Hamilton in 1801 as a vehicle for opposing Thomas Jefferson's views. It had a history of independent liberal thought, and she continued that tradition. Backer became ill, and she took over as president and publisher in 1942. When they divorced in 1943 she became sole owner and became involved in every facet of running the paper.

She immediately changed the format to tabloid, saying it was easier for subway riders to read, and focused the content on liberal causes, human interest stories, comics, gossip, and scandal. Her readers were mainly working class, and they loved the paper's sensational style. During the 1940s she hired more than fifty columnists including Drew Pearson, Langston Hughes, Sylvia Porter, Jackie Robinson, and Eleanor Roosevelt.

Another marriage to a newspaperman, Theodore Thackrey, foundered in 1949. After that Schiff was once again in total charge: publisher, editor, owner, and also a columnist from 1951 to 1958. In her column she held "conversations" with people such as Fidel Castro, Winston Churchill, and Albert Einstein. She tightened the structure of the paper, increased advertising revenues, raised the cover price, and put the paper on its feet financially. She also survived a disastrous three-month New York newspaper union strike in which the *Post* remained the only afternoon paper in the city.

The 1970s brought increases in the cost of supplies and labor and more rises in the price with subsequent losses in circulation. In 1976 she sold the *Post* to Rupert Murdoch, continuing as a consultant until 1981. Murdoch changed the political focus from liberal to conservative.

When she bought the *Post*, she resigned her many civic activities because of possible conflicts of interest. Before that she sat on the boards of the Henry Street Settlement and the Mount Sinai Hospital. She was also active on the Ellis Island Investigating Committee and the Social Service Committee of Bellevue Hospital and a member of the NAACP, the Women's Trade Union League of New York, and the Women's Division of the Democratic State Committee of New York. In 1937 Mayor Fiorello LaGuardia appointed her to the New York City Board of Child Welfare. She was awarded the Legion d'Honneur by France and established the New York Post Foundation. She was admired by her staff (though not universally) and respected by the business community for her business acumen and ability to survive in the rough New York newspaper market. Schiff died of cancer in 1989.

See also: Publishing Industry

Further Reading

Benjaminson, Peter. *Death in the Afternoon: America's Newspaper Giants Struggle for Survival*.

Diana, M. Casey. "Schiff, Dorothy." In John A. Garraty and Mark C. Carnes, eds., p. 374–376.

Potter, Jeffrey. *Men, Money and Magic: The Story of Dorothy Schiff*.

"Schiff, Dorothy." In *Current Biography Yearbook*, 1965, p. 364–366.

Schoenleber, Gretchen (1890–1953), Chocolate Manufacturer

Gretchen Schoenleber was president of the Ambrosia Chocolate Company for twenty-six years. Elected to the New York Cocoa Exchange, she was the first woman on any commodity exchange. Schoenleber was born in Milwaukee to second-generation German immigrants. Her father founded the Ambrosia Chocolate Company in 1894, when she was a small child. She graduated from the University of Wisconsin in 1911 and taught American history and English in two small Wisconsin towns for a year. In 1912 she joined her father's company as an office employee, and by 1916 she had risen to company secretary, a position she held until 1927, when her father died. She was then elected president.

Schoenleber's accomplishments included a complete modernization of the company as well as a change in customer focus. Previously its customers had been grocery stores that bought solid chocolate candy and packaged chocolate items. She began specializing in chocolate and cocoa products to be used in ice cream, baked goods, and confectionery manufacturing. She built a new plant, enlarging facilities from one 20,000-square-foot building to three buildings totaling 120,000 square feet. She also started a pension trust retirement plan for employees.

In 1935 she was elected to membership in the New York Cocoa Exchange. She was a member of the executive committee of the Cocoa and Chocolate Manufacturers of the United States and was also involved in many civic activities. She was on an advisory group to the Board of Regents of the University of Wisconsin from 1945 to 1953 and chaired the board in the period 1951–1952. In 1953, the year she died, she received the Wisconsin Alumni Association award for distinguished service.

See also: Food Industry; Manufacturing

Further Reading
National Cyclopedia of American Biography, vol. 45, p. 291–292.
Zilboorg, Caroline, ed. *Women's Firsts*, p. 110.

Schwartz, Felice N. (1925–1996), Founder of Catalyst, Consultant

Felice Schwartz, the founder of Catalyst, was inducted into the National Woman's Hall of Fame in 1998 for her pioneering work with women's issues in corporations. The citation reads in part: "[She] helped provide women with better access to the workplace and more opportunities at the top levels of corporate America. . . . [Her] efforts at Catalyst and her pioneering research on job-sharing, dual-career couples, parental leave and other work/family issues have significantly impacted corporate America" (National Women's Hall of Fame). She was sometimes controversial, particularly in her idea of a different career track for women who wish to have children.

> She was sometimes controversial, particularly in her idea of a different career track for women who wish to have children.

Schwartz was born to a wealthy family in New York City and planned to study medicine. However, she was influenced by her professor of religion at Smith College and turned to a career in social reform after graduating in 1945. Appalled by the unequal mix of races at Smith, she worked for the NAACP for a time but became frustrated by its bureaucracy. So she founded the National Scholarship Service and Fund for Negro Students, basing it in Harlem; its goal was to place black students in colleges. In two years she had placed 750 African American students in colleges that had previously accepted none.

In 1951 her father died, leaving his company, Etched Products Corporation, in precarious financial shape. Schwartz stepped in as vice president of production and worked with her brother to put it back on firm footing. Three years later they sold it for a small profit. Then she began an eight-year hiatus from working, staying home with her three small children. During that time, she noticed that many stay-at-home mothers had no idea of what they would do when their children went to school or left home. They felt alienated and frustrated; she saw this as a waste of talent and resolved to do something about it.

In 1962 she founded Catalyst, a nonprofit organization with the goal of helping women re-enter the work force. At that time female workers were 35 percent of the total U.S. workforce. She began by trying to obtain funding from college presidents. She then set up 300 resource centers around the country to facilitate the re-entry process and wrote forty pamphlets outlining job-hunting strategies. These centers served around 12 million women a year. Her initial focus was on part-time jobs; she talked the Boston Department of Public Welfare into advertising for fifty part-time caseworkers, and 1,600 women applied. During the 1970s the economy worsened, and many women had to go back to work, some full-time. Catalyst began to move into the corporate world and pioneered studies of issues that prevented the full utilization of women's talents, such as recruitment, promotion, retention, child-care issues, parental leave, relocation, benefits, and dual-career couples. The strategy was informational, not confrontational. She worked with executives of the companies, many of whom she knew personally from her business days, and tried to effect change from the top and from within.

In 1988 she wrote an article for the January–February 1989 issue of the *Harvard Business Review* suggesting that executives devise a way to accommodate women who wished to concentrate on both career and family ("Management Women"). A *New York Times* reporter picked up on the concept and named it "the mommy track." Feminists were furious. They believed that women could concentrate on both without special treatment and thought this would lead to discrimination. Schwartz believed otherwise and said she was totally misunderstood: Her idea was to remove barriers to advancement and career productivity. The furor lasted several years, and Schwartz has maintained that it opened up a dialogue regarding basic facts of life such as child bearing that led to pressures for working women. Today maternity leave is a common corporate benefit; then, it wasn't.

By 1990 Catalyst employed forty people and had an annual budget of $2 million. Its focus changed again, to concentrate on women executives. Schwartz established the Corporate Board Resource, a database of 1,200 women with outstanding qualities that made them suitable for corporate board positions. In 1977 there were forty-six women on corporate boards; by 1996 there were 400. The organization continued serving as an adviser, a solution-oriented problem solver, and it was highly successful. The appeal to corporations focused on how much economic sense it made to employ women and ensure that they stay. Schwartz retired in 1993, having completed two books. She donated the proceeds of one of them to the Felice N. Schwartz Fund for the Advancement of Women in Business and the Professions so that Catalyst could continue its research.

Schwartz was awarded honorary doctorates by Pace University, Smith College, Marietta College, Chatham College, the City University of New York (CUNY) Graduate Center, and Mount Holyoke College. She served on the advisory boards of the National Women's Political Caucus, the National Network of Hispanic Women, the CUNY Graduate Center, and the Foundation for Students Committee. In 1949 she was awarded the *Mademoiselle* Medal for Singular Achievement in Education for her work with African American students. Many other awards followed: the Smith College Distinguished Alumnae Medal in 1976, the Susan B. Anthony Award from the National Organization for Women in 1981, Human Resources Professional of the Year from the International Association of Personnel Women in 1983, the Boehm Soaring Eagle Award from the National Women's Economic Alliance, and the Sara Lee Corporation Front Runner Award in 1987. From 1994 to 1996 she was a Woodrow Wilson Fellow, and in 1999 she was named posthumously to the National Women's Hall of Fame. She died in 1996 of heart failure after a long illness. She had just finished her third book.

See also: Catalyst; Consulting; Mommy Track; Work-Life Balance

Further Reading

Hopkins, Ellen. "Who Is Felice Schwartz and Why Is She Saying Those Terrible Things about Us?"

National Women's Hall of Fame.

Schwartz, Felice, with Jean Zimmerman. *Breaking with Tradition: Women and Work, the New Facts of Life*.

"Schwartz, Felice N." In *Current Biography Yearbook*, 1993, p. 511–514.

Securities and Exchange Commission (SEC)

The Securities and Exchange Commission (SEC) was established by the U.S. Congress to enforce securities laws that were a result of the 1929 stock market crash. The laws mandated that public companies make financial and other pertinent information available to the public. If a company falsifies information, that action is punishable by jail. Violations also include stock price manipulation, insider trading, and selling shares without proper registration. The SEC requires companies to file quarterly (IOQ) and annual (10K) reports. These can be found on the SEC Web site and in a number of databases.

Further Reading

U.S. Securities and Exchange Commission (www.sec.gov).

Seifert, Kathi P. (1949–), Personal Care Products Executive

Kathi Seifert is executive vice president of the personal care division of Kimberly-Clark, which has annual revenues of nearly $6 billion. She is the second highest ranking person at the company and was number 38 on *Fortune's* list of the fifty most powerful women in American business in 2002.

Seifert graduated from Valparaiso University with a BA in marketing and management and joined Kimberly-Clark in 1978. She began in household products and feminine care and worked her way up through the ranks. In 1988 she became director of new products in the feminine care sector and the following year was named marketing director. In 1992 she was promoted to president of that sector and in 1994 became co-group president of North American Consumer Products with Thomas Falk. Her responsibilities encompassed the household products sector and the safety and quality assurance team. In January 1996, Falk was promoted and Seifert assumed responsibility for infant and child care as well as U.S. consumer sales. In 1998 the company expanded into the European market, and she has been credited for the success of the expansion. In November 1999, she was promoted to executive vice president of the company, and in October 2002 she became executive vice president of the personal care division.

Seifert has been on the board of directors of Eli Lilly, the Aid Association for Lutherans, and Fox Cities Performing Arts Center. In 1999 she was named a "Woman to Watch" by *Advertising Age*. She is very knowledgeable about parenting and women's health issues. She and Kimberly-Clark launched Parentstages.com in partnership with iVillage, UrbanBaby.com, Salon.com, TotalWoman.com, and CBSHealthWatch.com, a Web site that helps parents find and access the best parenting information. She also established a community partnership with the Grand Opera House in OshKosh, Wisconsin, to hold music-listening parties for Kimberly-Clark employees and was a director for Aid Association for Lutherans.

See also: Beauty Industry

Further Reading
Neff, Jack. "Strategic Team Leader Takes on the World."

Self-Employment, *see* Entrepreneurs

Sex Discrimination

According to *The Human Resources Glossary*, sex discrimination is "discrimination, mainly but not exclusively against women, in such areas as denial of employment, quality of employment, differences in wages, pregnancy, and opportunities for advancement" (Tracey, p. 474).

Discrimination against women in business has been a part of the American economic system since the colonies were settled. It continued through World

War II and still exists, although in a more subtle form, today. Women have worked in the business world, and some exceptional women have thrived there, but under blatant sexism. Even after wars, when they were employed in large numbers, women were forced to leave their jobs when the men returned. Unionization attempted to deal with some of the problems, but it was not until the Equal Pay Act of 1963 and the Civil Rights Act of 1964 that the federal government took action. Since then the U.S. Supreme Court and lower courts have upheld antidiscrimination laws and set precedents protecting women from sex discrimination.

See also: Affirmative Action; Civil Rights Act of 1964; Equal Employment Opportunity Commission (EEOC); Equal Pay Act of 1963

Further Reading

Graves, Laura M., and Gary N. Powell. "Effects of Sex-Based Preferential Selection and Discrimination on Job Attitudes."

Kilbourn, Peter T. "For Women in Bias Case Wounds Remain."

Schneider, Dorothy, and Carl J. Schneider. *ABC-CLIO Companion to Women in the Workplace*, p. 237–238.

Wendt, Ann C., William M. Slonaker, and Joseph W. Coleman. "Employment Discrimination Is Sex-Blind."

Sexual Harassment

Sexual harassment is defined by the Equal Employment Opportunity Commission (EEOC) as "unwelcome sexual advances, requests for sexual favors, and other verbal or physical conduct of a sexual nature when submission to or rejection of this conduct (1) explicitly or implicitly affects an individual's employment, (2) unreasonably interferes with an individual's work performance, or (3) creates an intimidating, hostile, or offensive work environment" (Kaliski, p. 765).

According to U.S. law, there are two types of sexual harassment. One is "quid pro quo," which implies a trade involving sex, for example, a demotion because a sexual advance was refused. The second is a "hostile environment," where a workplace is uncomfortable or threatening due to unwelcome sexual behavior such as telling off-color jokes.

Although the term sexual harassment did not come into use until 1975, the behavior has existed throughout history. Title VII of the Civil Rights Act of 1964 laid the foundation by making sex discrimination illegal, but sexual harassment was not explicitly laid out or defined. The court rulings of that time treated lawsuits of this kind as personal disputes between two people. In the 1970s women's rights groups focused on these issues amid much publicity, and in 1980 the federal Office of Personnel Management defined the term and issued guidelines stating that it was unacceptable in the federal workplace;

however, it did not include ways to enforce the guidelines. Also in 1980 the EEOC declared sexual harassment illegal in the workplace.

The first case to come before the U.S. Supreme Court was *Meritor Savings Bank v. Vinson* in 1986. The Court's landmark ruling set the boundaries we have today. It confirmed that Title VII outlawed sexual harassment, defined quid pro quo harassment, and added the concept of hostile environment sexual harassment. The case was not widely publicized but led to discussion about the exact parameters of sexual harassment and the boundaries of employer liability. In 1991 and 1992 two events catapulted the issue into the national spotlight: first, the U.S. Navy Tailhook scandal and then Anita Hill's allegations of sexual harassment against Judge Clarence Thomas during Senate hearings for his nomination to the U.S. Supreme Court. Many women who had remained silent about their experiences began to speak up.

The Civil Rights Act of 1991 expanded the rights of the complainant to the ability to collect damages, and many states established their own laws. In 1993 the U.S. Supreme Court established standards and criteria for investigating sexual harassment, and subsequent decisions further clarified the issue. Of particular interest to businesses was that employers with a known, effective policy could successfully defend themselves.

The number of complaints received by the EEOC has increased since 1985, when there were nine. In 1992, 10,532 complaints were received by the EEOC and related state and local agencies. Of these complaints, 9.1 percent were filed by men. In 2002, 14,396 complaints were received, 14.9 percent filed by men. Settlements have been reached in 1,692 cases, withdrawals of the complaint with benefits occurred in 1,235 cases, while administrative closure resulted in 3,957 cases. The EEOC found no reasonable cause for the complaint in 7,445 cases (47.1 percent), and it agreed that there was cause in 1,463 cases. Successful conciliation was reached in 455 cases and merit resolution was reached in 4,930 cases. Monetary benefits awarded in 2002 totaled $50.3 million.

Corporations and small businesses alike must have a strong sexual harassment policy in order to manage sexual harassment lawsuits. The policy should be clearly written and explain the kinds of prohibited behavior. It needs visible commitment from top management and should be a solid part of the corporate culture. All supervisors, managers, employees, and recruits must have a copy of the policy and be trained on sexual harassment laws, policies, and practices on a regular basis. The company must have a complaint process that assures confidentiality, avoids conflicts of interest, and prohibits retaliation. All complaints need to be investigated swiftly and thoroughly, and action should be taken. Complainants must be advised of further avenues such as the EEOC and the courts if resolution is not possible. Companies should also make periodic checks of the physical facilities to identify possible problems.

Because sexual harassment cases can cause enormous expense (a typical *Fortune* 500 case costs the company $6.7 million), it is imperative that companies be proactive in dealing with the issue. It is important to be aware of the rights of all employees in a complaint and to keep in mind that what is considered harmless by one person may be offensive to another. Sexual harassment can cost a company not only money but also loss of productivity, degeneration of morale, and damage to its reputation.

See also: Civil Rights Act of 1964; Equal Employment Opportunity Commission (EEOC); Office Romance

Further Reading

Brantley, Clarice P., and Rita Shaw Rone. "Sexual Harassment." In Kaliski, p. 765–769.

Hajdin, Mane. *The Law of Sexual Harassment.*

Levy, Anne. *Workplace Sexual Harassment.*

U.S. Equal Employment Opportunity Commission (www.eeoc.gov).

Shaver, Dorothy (1897–1959), Retail Executive

Dorothy Shaver was the first woman president of a mercantile organization doing an annual business of more than $30 million per year. The store was Lord & Taylor. She is credited with both discovering and developing the U.S. fashion industry and creating several new ways for department stores to do business.

Shaver was born in Arkansas to a cultivated, well-read family who believed that children should not only be heard but should be intelligent conversationalists. Each of the five children was expected to bring something to the dinner table of interest to them all. Her father was a federal and circuit court judge, and his father, a Confederate general, lived with the family. Numerous relatives visited often, and the children grew up gregarious and self-confident. She attended the University of Arkansas and the University of Chicago, and in 1920 her sister Elsie, who was artistic, decided to seek her fortune in New York City. Dorothy went with her. They still received an allowance from home and rented the top two stories of a brownstone. It became clear that they would need to earn more money, so Dorothy decided to try to sell dolls that Elsie made. She had read about the success of the Kewpie doll and thought that Elsie's were just as nice. Dorothy began to peddle the dolls, named "The Five Little Shavers," from store to store. A distant cousin stopped by for a visit, and they showed him the dolls. He was Samuel Reyburn, the president of Lord & Taylor. His managers placed the dolls in the Lord & Taylor windows, and they were a success.

By 1924 Elsie had lost interest in making the dolls, and Dorothy received an offer from Lord & Taylor to join its comparison-shopping department. In two months she was made the director. However, she did not believe that comparison-shopping made sense. Her idea was for a department of specialists who would work directly with manufacturers and designers to improve products and provide them exclusively to Lord & Taylor. She put the idea in writing along with an organization chart. She remained head of comparison shopping but was also asked to develop her Bureau of Fashion. It proved to be successful, and other stores were soon following her lead.

In 1927 Shaver was elected to the store's board of directors. In 1928 she took her first trip to Europe and imported a $100,000 collection of modern art and decorative objects from France by artists such as Pablo Picasso, Georges Braque, and Maurice Utrillo. In 1931 she became vice president in charge of advertising, publicity, and the Bureau of Fashion. That year she discovered American fashion designers, who had been neglected and nameless in New York's garment district. From that time she tirelessly promoted American designers and American fashion. Lord & Taylor ran ads featuring "The American Look," and in 1938 she created the annual $1,000 Lord & Taylor American Design awards. She is credited with jump-starting the careers of more than sixty young American designers, including Lily Dache, Anne Fogarty, Nettie Rosenstein, Claire McCardell, and Elizabeth Hawes. The awards were later expanded to reward contributions to other areas and were given to Albert Einstein, Ralph Bunche, and the United Nations. During the period from 1931 to 1945 she also instituted other innovations: the first teen department with specially designed fashions, the "Bird Cage" lunchroom, the Men's Soup Bar, seasonal awnings, unique advertising, and innovative window displays. The most famous was a 1938 Christmas display of nothing but gold bells against a background of black-and-white velvet, all chiming. The bells could be heard on the street and the windows became famous worldwide. She also began the suburban branch program. During World War II she was consultant to the quartermaster general on merchandise and women's uniforms and also did volunteer war work.

In 1945 Shaver was elected president of Lord & Taylor with an annual salary of $110,000, the largest on record for any woman in the United States. The author of the *Life* magazine article announcing this fact also noted that it was only a quarter of the salary paid to a man in a similar job (Perkins, "No. 1," p. 117). Sales and employee numbers began to grow: Sales were $30 million in 1945 with 2,800 employees; $59 million in 1951 with 4,000 employees; and in 1959, the year Shaver died, sales were $100 million with 4,500 employees.

She never married, always living with her sister in a house in New York City and another in the country. Shaver was a trustee of the Parsons School of Design and a fellow of the Metropolitan Museum of Art, where she helped found the Costume Institute; was on the advisory councils of the New York School of Applied Design and the Cooper Union Art School; and served on the board of directors of the Advertising Federation of America, the Menninger Foundation, the Women's Council of New York Public Library, Girl's Clubs of America, and the Museum of Modern Art. She received honorary degrees from six universities and was named chevalier of the French Legion of Honor. She was awarded the Star of Solidarity by Italy.

See also: Retailing Industry

Further Reading

Boynick, David K. *Women Who Led the Way: Eight Pioneers for Equal Rights,* p. 209–235, 240.

Perkins, Jeanne. "No. 1 Career Woman."

Taves, Isabella. *Successful Women and How They Obtained Success,* p. 141–150.

Siebert, Muriel (1932–), Financial Analyst/Stockbroker

Muriel Siebert, known as "The First Woman of Finance," was the first woman to buy a seat on the New York Stock Exchange. She was also the first Wall Street woman billionaire and the first woman to serve as superintendent of New York State's Banking Department. She was inducted into the National Women's Hall of Fame in 1994.

Born the younger of two daughters to a Cleveland dentist and his wife, Siebert won Cleveland's yo-yo championship at the age of ten. In high school she was a star on the tennis team. She attended Western Reserve University from 1949 to 1952, but dropped out when her father died of cancer and she needed to help support her mother and sister. She later headed for New York City with $500 and a used Studebaker and was rejected for jobs at the United Nations and Merrill Lynch because she did not have a college degree. She finally landed a position at Bache & Company as a trainee research analyst for $65 a week after lying about her degree. She covered airlines and motion pictures, two areas no one else wanted, and found that she loved the work. A woman working in a male-dominated environment, she left three companies because men were paid more to do the same job.

In 1961 Siebert became a partner at Finkle & Company. She stayed there for three more years and then worked at Brimberg & Company from 1965 to 1967. A colleague at Brimberg suggested that she buy a seat on the New York Stock Exchange, then costing $445,000. The requirements were that she be twenty-one, a U.S. citizen, professionally competent, wealthy enough to finance the cost, and have a sponsor. The first nine men she approached turned her down, but the tenth agreed. Next she had to obtain a letter from a bank promising to loan her $300,000 of the fee. Most banks would not promise before she had been admitted, but after twenty-two months of frustration, Chase Manhattan agreed. On December 28, 1967, Siebert finally purchased her seat. At that time, the exchange did not even have a women's restroom. It would be ten years before another woman was admitted.

In 1969 she was the first woman to found her own brokerage firm. She was its chair and president until 1977, when she was asked by the governor to be the New York State banking commissioner. She put her company in a blind trust and, from 1977 to 1982, was the first woman to serve as New York's superintendent of banks. She was also director of the New York State Mortgage Agency, the New York City Urban Development Corporation, and the New York City Job Development Authority. No banks failed during her tenure.

In 1983 Siebert returned to her brokerage firm and spent the rest of the decade rebuilding it. By 1996 she employed 120 people and had more than 80,000 accounts. That year she took it public as Siebert Financial Corporation on the NASDAQ Stock Market under SIEB. It was valued at $160 million. She used the money to expand, build the bond business, and become a presence on the Internet. By February 4, 1999, shares had risen from $16³/₄ to $66¹/₄. In October 2000 she created Women's Financial Network at Siebert (WFN), with the goal of offering serious financial education to women. The Web site opened on May 1, 2001.

Siebert has been a pioneer in many ways, but most importantly as the first woman to buy a seat on the New York Stock Exchange. For ten years, it was 1,365 men and her. As of 2002, 12 to 15 percent of the members were women. In her 2002 book *Changing the Rules: Adventures of a Wall Street Maverick* she discusses her experiences. She feels that Wall Street is still an "old boys club" and points out that there still are no women CEOs of major securities firms. She has been interviewed and quoted often and credits her success to hard work, luck, perseverance, and risk. She has been very involved in women's issues and their advancement. She helped found the National Women's Forum, donated generously to the National Museum of Women in the Arts, and has mentored younger women entrepreneurs.

She has held board positions on both profit and nonprofit corporations. In 1994 she established the Siebert Entrepreneurial Philanthropic Plan (SEPP) and set up two other foundations. She regularly lectures at universities. In 1982 she ran for the U.S. Senate, but lost the primary election. Her awards are countless, beginning with the 1977 Spirit of Achievement Award from the Albert Einstein College of Medicine. She is in four women's halls of fame and has three honorary degrees. In 1998 *Time* called her one of its 100 Builders and Titans of the 20th Century. In 2003, 100 Women in Hedge Funds honored her as the "First Woman to Cross the Street." Siebert has never married.

See also: Finance Industry

Further Reading
Cordato, Mary F. "Muriel Siebert." In Schweikert, Larry, ed., p. 394–399.
Kempton, Beverly. "What Does Success Really Mean?" 1993.
"Siebert, Muriel." In *Current Biography Yearbook*, 1997, p. 509–512.
Siebert, Muriel, with Aimee Lee Ball. *Changing the Rules: Adventures of a Wall Street Maverick.*

Sims, Judy, *see* Odom, Judy C.

Small Business Administration (SBA)

The Small Business Administration (SBA) was created by the U.S. Congress in the Small Business Act of July 30, 1953. Its function is to aid, counsel, assist, and protect the interests of small business concerns. The act also mandates that the SBA offer programs that include technical assistance through training and counseling; financial assistance; disaster assistance recovery; advocacy, laws, and regulations; and internal administrative and support assistance. Since 1953 almost 20 million small businesses have received help through one of these programs.

One of the special interests of the SBA is to increase business participation by women. The office has a variety of resources for women owners of small businesses. The Online Women's Business Center offers programs addressing business training and technical assistance. It is a nationwide network of mentoring roundtables and women's business centers in nearly every state and territory. The SBA Office of Women's Business Ownership promotes access to capital and credit, federal contracts, and international trade opportunities. WomenBiz.gov offers helpful information about bidding on government contracts, while Women Entrepreneurship in the 21st Century partners with the U.S. Department of Labor and twenty-three women's business organizations to provide Women-21.gov, a federal resource for targeted information and networking opportunities. The WNET (Women's Network for Entrepreneurial Training) Roundtables provide mentoring and support for women business owners. They can be located through local SBA offices. The SBA also surveys, gathers statistics, and researches issues relevant to woman-owned businesses.

See also: Entrepreneurs; Woman-Owned Businesses

Further Reading
Online Women's Business Center (www.onlinewbc.gov).
Small Business Administration (www.sba.gov).
WNET Roundtables (www.wnet.bz).
Women Entrepreneurship in the 21st Century (www.women-21.gov).
WomenBiz (www.womenbiz.gov).

Sneed, Paula A. (1947–), Food Executive

Paula Sneed is a group vice president of Kraft Foods North America and president of e-commerce and an executive vice president of Kraft Foods. She was ranked number 24 on *Fortune's* list of the most powerful black executives in 2000. Sneed is a native of Everett, Massachusetts, and received a BA from Simmons College in 1969. She worked for a variety of nonprofit companies in Boston doing social service work until 1976, when she went to Harvard Business School to improve her administrative skills. There she had a case study of a General Foods manager wishing to develop a new pet food product, and she was enthralled by marketing and product development. She received her MBA in 1977 and went to work for General Foods as an assistant product manager. She married Lawrence P. Sneed in 1978; they have one daughter.

Sneed rose through the ranks at General Foods, as product manager first of the Main Meals Division and then of the twelve-person Desserts Division. In 1985 General Foods merged with Kraft. Sneed became vice president of consumer affairs, in charge of the test kitchens, consumer nutrition program, product publicity, and the consumer response and information center. She managed one hundred people. In 1990 she advanced to senior vice president of the Food Service Division, and a year later, to executive vice president and general manager of the Desserts Division, the second-most-profitable division in the company. In 1995 she rose to the senior vice presidency of marketing services for Kraft Foods, supervising 500 employees. Also a member of Kraft's operating committee, she launched Kraft Interactive Kitchen in 1996. By the end of the following year the Web site was getting 93,000 hits a day. In May 1999 she was promoted to chief marketing officer, and the following September, she became executive vice president of Kraft Foods and president of e-commerce, a new division. This division is responsible for the 600-person marketing services operation. She has continued on the operating committee.

When Sneed joined General Foods, she wanted to become an officer, so she looked at the company's strategies and promotion lines to see what she needed to do to fulfill her ambitions. Her philosophy, formed during her years of social service, is to dream impossible dreams and then take realistic steps to fulfill them. In a 1997 article she explained how she works and what was important to her ("Carpe Diem"). Her CEO, Betsy Holden, talks of her "unique mix of vision, strategic insight, and business savvy" ("Kraft Foods Names Sneed").

Sneed has been named on many lists: *Black Enterprise's* 1991 list of twenty-one women of power and influence in corporate America, its 1993 list of America's most powerful black executives, and *Ebony's* 1990 and 1991 lists of the top hundred black women in corporate America. While at Harvard, she was MBA of the Year. The YWCA named her to its Academy of Women Achievers in 1990. In 2000 she was on an *Advertising Age* panel about Internet advertising and has become Kraft's spokeswoman for Internet business, leading a session at the inaugural Food eBiz conference in September 2000. She sits on the boards of Charles Schwab, Airgas, and Westchester/Fairfield Inroads. She is on the Dean's Advisory Council at Howard University Business School and holds an honorary DBA from Johnson & Wales University.

See also: African American Businesswomen; Food Industry
Further Reading
Sachdev, Ameet. "Despite Dot-Com Downturn, Internet Dominates Business Market."
Segal, Troy. "American's 50 Most Powerful Women Managers."
Sneed, Paula A. "Carpe Diem: Take Advantage of Time."

Snider, Stacey (1961–), Film Industry Executive

Stacey Snider illustrates the classic Hollywood success story. She began her career in the mailroom and rose to be the chairman of Universal Pictures. She has been on *Fortune*'s list of the most powerful women in American business since 2000. Snider graduated from the University of Pennsylvania with a degree in international relations in 1982 and went on to UCLA Law School, where she earned her JD in 1985. Her first job was in the mailroom at the Triad Agency. She quickly moved up to assistant in the development department.

In 1986 she became director of development for Guber Peters Entertainment Company and then vice president of production. Her responsibilities were negotiating rights to literary manuscripts, developing talent, and supervising production. In 1990 she was promoted to executive vice president and was in charge of production for the movies *Single White Female* and *Remains of the Day*. Two years later she became president of production at TriStar, the highest-ranking woman executive in Hollywood. There she produced a string of hits that included *Sleepless in Seattle* and *My Best Friend's Wedding*.

In 1996 there was a reorganization of the studio, and she left the following year to be co-president of production at Universal Pictures. She steadily rose to the position of chair in November 1999. As such, she has been responsible for all production, marketing, and domestic distribution for the studio. She and Sherry Lansing were the only two women running major studios at that time. Some of her many hits are *Gladiator*, *Erin Brockovich*, *A Beautiful Mind*, *8 Mile*, and *Red Dragon*. In 2000 she testified at the Senate Commerce Committee's hearing on the marketing of violence in media to children.

Snider is known for her literary acumen and instincts for acquiring and developing material. Her skills in project development are renowned. She is a mix of creative execution, business savvy, and team-building talent. She is married and has two daughters, born in 1994 and 1999. In October 2001 she was tied for the most powerful figure in Hollywood in *Entertainment Weekly*'s list, and that December *Hollywood Reporter* named her the most influential woman in show business. She was also a Pier del Sol honoree at the Special Olympics of Southern California.

See also: Entertainment Industry

Further Reading
Furman, Phyllis. "Challenging Role for Movie Exec Snider Seeks Universal Reversal."
"Snider, Stacey." In *Celebrity Biographies*, 2000.
"Stacey Snider Has Been Appointed Co-President, Production for Universal Pictures. . . ."

Srere, Linda Jean (1955–), Advertising Executive

Linda Srere was named the forty-third most powerful woman in American business in 1998 by *Fortune* for her accomplishments in obtaining new clients for Young & Rubicam, the fifth-largest advertising agency in the world. She was president of its New York office until September 1998, when she was promoted to vice chairwoman and chief client officer of Young & Rubicam's holding company. In late 2000 she became president and chief client officer of Young & Rubicam Worldwide. One year later she resigned during a massive company reorganization.

Srere was born in New York City and received her BA from the State University of New York at Oswego. Her mother was an insurance officer at a bank and her father was a salesman and driver for Shell Oil Company. Srere was trained as an elementary school teacher, for which she now credits her skills at listening, encouraging, motivating, and problem solving. Instead of teaching she went to work in advertising as an assistant account executive. After working for several agencies in increasingly responsible positions, she became president of Rosenfeld, Sirowitz, Humphrey, & Strauss in 1990, and then chairman of the New York office of Earle, Palmer, Brown in 1992.

In 1994 Young & Rubicam recruited her as an executive vice president and its director of business development. She was promoted to be the head of global new business in 1995, group managing director in 1996, and, in 1997, president and CEO of the New York office. It was the first time a woman had held that position. In her next promotion, to president and chief client officer, she became responsible for more than 6,000 employees and $7 billion in billing. She is known in this cutthroat industry for her excellence at attracting new clients and was the main force leading the teams that won the accounts of United Airlines, Showtime, Blockbuster Video, Cadbury Beverages, and Citicorp. She has been called a rainmaker, an expert at finding and signing new clients. In 1996 alone she was responsible for bringing more than $500 million in billings to the agency.

> She has been called a rainmaker, an expert at finding and signing new clients.

Srere has a warm, down-to-earth style and casual manner, unusual in the high-powered atmosphere of advertising. She is said to have a gift for putting her finger on the exact needs of a client and obtaining the right information for creating a successful presentation. She is a team builder who puts the right mix of people together for a particular problem. She is liked and respected by her staff and believes strongly in positive feedback. Her philosophy is, "There are no obstacles if our eyes are open to look in the right places for opportunities" ("New York's 100 Most Influential").

In 1996 Srere was elected to the American Advertising Federation's Hall of Achievement for advertising executives forty and younger, and in 1997 she was named Advertising Woman of the Year by Advertising Women of New York. *Crain's New York Business* named her one of New York's Most Influential Women in Business. She is a member of the American Management Association, the Young President's Organization, and Advertising Women of New York. She married Jeremy Brown, the CEO of Earle Palmer Brown Companies, in 1998. She was on the board of TheStreet.com but resigned in October 2000. In June 2001 she was appointed to the board of Electronic Arts.

See also: Advertising Industry

Further Reading
Enrico, Dottie. "Rainmakers: Women Bring a Flood of New Business to Madison Avenue Firms."
Marchetti, Michele. "Here's One Marketer Who Can Sell."
"New York's 100 Most Influential Women in Business."

Staff Managers, *see* Line and Staff Managers

Stay-at-Home Dads, *see* Husbands/Fathers

Steel, Dawn (1946–1997), Film Executive

Dawn Steel was the first woman to head a major motion picture corporation, Columbia Pictures. Her tenure there was short, 1987 to 1990, but while she held that position she was the most powerful woman in Hollywood.

Steel was born in the Bronx, in New York City, and grew up in Great Neck, Long Island, a poor child in a rich neighborhood. Her parents were both businesspeople, but her father had a nervous breakdown when she was ten, and her mother supported the family. Dawn worked from the time she was sixteen. She majored in marketing at Boston University and New York University but was unable to graduate for financial reasons. Her first job was as a receptionist in New York's garment district; she then worked as a researcher and sportswriter for a sports digest book publisher. In 1968 she was hired as a secretary at *Penthouse* magazine and told her mother she was working for a fashion magazine. Eventually she worked her way up to editor and director of merchandising. In 1975 she opened her own merchandising company, Oh, Dawn Inc., and in 1979 she moved to Los Angeles to become a merchandising consultant for *Playboy* magazine.

A year later she went to work at Paramount Pictures and quickly became a protégée of Barry Diller, the tough head of the company. His management style consisted of awarding projects to the person who argued the loudest, and Steel was frequently that person. Her first break was the movie *Flashdance*, for which she spoke vociferously in spite of a lack of enthusiasm of all around her. It became a hit, grossing $95 million at the box office, and it made her name. She followed that success with hits including *The Accused*, *Top Gun* and *Beverly Hills Cop*. In 1980 she was made vice president of production then senior vice president of production, and in 1985, president of production.

In 1985 she met and married her second husband, Charles Roven, a producer. In 1987 they had a daughter, Rebecca. While she was in labor, she was fired from Paramount. She moved to Columbia Pictures as head of the studio, and at that time was the only woman in Hollywood to run one. Among hit films there was *When Harry Met Sally*. She built and jointly operated an on-site day care facility with Warner Brothers that was used by ninety children. In 1990 Sony bought Columbia Pictures, and she was demoted, so she resigned. She and Roven formed Atlas Entertainment in 1994. Two years later she was diagnosed with a brain tumor and she died the following year. She was fifty-one.

Steel was known as "Steely Dawn" because of her abrasive management style. A 1998 *Variety* article called her a "determined tornado with a lot of passion and no room in her life for the words 'no' or 'it can't be done'" ("Dawn Steel," p. 90). She was tenacious and intelligent with a proven ability to work with and attract talent. Her ego was large and her self-confidence legendary, but after childbirth she toned down her personality and became more mellow. Her book *They Can Kill You—But They Can't Eat You* was reviewed as energizing, interesting, and generous-spirited. Steel won the Women in Film Crystal Award in 1989 and was on *Variety*'s list of the hundred top mavens in motion pictures in 1999. *Variety* noted her significance in mentoring other women in the film industry. She was on the board of trustees of the American Film Institute and was a member of the California Abortion Rights Action League and the AIDS Project.

See also: Entertainment Industry

Further Reading
Acker, Ally. *Reel Women: Pioneers of the Cinema 1896 to the Present*, p. 143–145.
Steel, Dawn. *They Can Kill You—But They Can't Eat You: Lessons from the Front*.
Weinraub, Bernard. "Dawn Steel Muses from the Top of Hollywood's Heap."

Steigerwaldt, Donna Wolf (1929–2000), Clothing Manufacturer

Donna Wolf Steigerwaldt's Jockey International has been on the *Working Woman* list of top woman-owned businesses from the list's beginning in 1992. Her company commands about 30 percent of the men's underwear market and, under her leadership, has ventured into women's underwear and sports underwear too.

Steigerwaldt was born in Chicago, received a BA from the University of Colorado in Colorado Springs in 1950 in language with a minor in music, then returned to Chicago to work for Connecticut Mutual Life Insurance Company until 1953. In 1955 she went to work at Jockey International, where her father, Harry Wolf, was in charge. After thirty years of accumulating Jockey stock, he bought the company in the early 1970s. Donna had meanwhile married William Steigerwaldt in 1969, stopped working and become a homemaker and mother raising two daughters. When her father died in 1978 she returned to Jockey as vice chairman. In 1980 she became chairman and CEO. She co-owned the company with her brother and sister but bought out her brother in 1983 and her sister in 1994. Her two daughters are also with the company.

Steigerwaldt continued the company's success by sticking to the basic product and expanding within those limits. In 1982 she introduced Jockey for Her, a line of women's underwear that has been very successful. The year 1992 saw the addition of Jockey for Her Soft Elegance and the first use of Lycra. As the market became more fashion conscious, a licensed Tommy Hilfiger line was added. In the late 1990s she expanded into additional lines. The company has also licensed its name to sportswear and underwear manufacturers for the large chain stores K-Mart and Sam's Club. In 1998 she left day-to-day operations to the other officers but continued to act as a goodwill ambassador for Jockey.

Steigerwaldt had a reputation for being a hands-on manager and a very private person. She received an honorary degree from the University of Colorado in 1987 and is a Paul Harris Fellow of Rotary. She was vice chairman of the board of Carthage College from 1982 to 1992 and was elected its chairman from 1992 to 1997. She was president of the Donna Wolf Steigerwaldt Foundation in Kenosha, Wisconsin, which donated to a $3.5 million expansion of the Mote Marine Aquarium and Laboratory in Sarasota, Florida. Steigerwaldt died in December 2000. Her daughter continues to run Jockey International.

See also: Fashion Industry

Further Reading

Lappen, Alyssa, ed. "The *Working Woman* 25," p. 65.

Schmuckler, Eric, and Harris Collingwood. "The Top 50 Women Business Owners," p. 35.

Steinem, Gloria (1934–), Magazine Publisher

Gloria Steinem is known as one of the original spokespeople of feminism and the co-founder of Ms. magazine, the first women's magazine controlled, written, and edited by women. Ms. was also the first to deal with women's issues such as equal pay, sexual harassment, abortion, and child and day care.

Born in Toledo, Ohio, Steinem had an unsettled childhood, traveling during the winters with her itinerant father who sold antiques from his house trailer. After her parents divorced when she was ten, Gloria took care of her invalid mother. She came from feminist stock: Her paternal grandmother was a president of the Ohio Women's Suffrage League from 1908 to 1911 and one of the U.S. representatives to the International Council of Women. Her sister, Susanne, was nine years older, and when Gloria reached her senior year in high school she lived with Susanne and her family. She was a voracious reader; because her family was on the road so much she rarely went to school, and so she educated herself. She graduated magna cum laude from Smith College in 1956 and was a member of Phi Beta Kappa. After college she won a Chester Bowles Fellowship to go to India for the summer, which instilled in her a strong desire to help the disadvantaged in the world. She stayed in India for two years traveling and studying at universities in Delhi and Calcutta.

When she returned to the United States, she became co-director of Independent Research Service in Cambridge, Massachusetts. Two years later, she moved to New York and took a job at *Esquire*. In 1963 she wrote her famous story about working undercover as a Playboy Bunny. She also interviewed many New York celebrities for *Esquire*, *Vogue*, and the *New York Times*. In 1968 she began writing a column, City Politic, for the newly launched *New York Magazine*. In 1969 she was jolted into feminism at a protest march against New York's abortion laws. Subsequently she co-founded the Women's Strike for Equity with Betty Friedan; the National Women's Political Caucus with Bella Abzug, Betty Friedan, and Shirley Chisholm; and many other feminist groups.

Together with Patricia Carbine, she co-founded Ms. in December 1971 as an insert in *New York*. *Washington Post* publisher Katharine Graham offered $20,000 as seed money. Within eight days 300,000 copies sold out. The publication became a monthly and remained successful throughout the 1970s and into the mid-1980s; by 1977 circulation was 500,000 per issue. Steinem was the magazine's editor through these early years. By 1987, however, Ms. was experiencing financial troubles, so Steinem and Carbine sold it to an Australian conglomerate and Steinem stayed on as a contributing editor and consultant.

Throughout the magazine's tumultuous history, Steinem was its nurturer, serving as a writer and chief editor, consulting editor, and from 1998 to 2001 head of the completely women-run company that then owned it. In December

1998 Steinem, Marcia Gillespie, and a group of women investors named Liberty Media for Women bought *Ms.* from MacDonald Communication. Steinem was president of the magazine and chairperson of Liberty Media for Women (Tichy, p.109–110). In December 2001 the Feminist Majority Foundation assumed ownership of the magazine and moved its offices to Los Angeles. Steinem is still involved with the magazine and appeared on the cover of the thirtieth anniversary issue in March 2002.

Steinem has won many awards, including the Penney-Missouri Journalism Award in 1970, the Ohio Governor's Award for Journalism and *McCall's* "Woman of the Year" in 1972, and a National Fellowship Award in 1974. In 1977 she was appointed to the National Committee of the Observance of International Women's Year by President Jimmy Carter and was awarded a Woodrow Wilson Scholarship to study feminist theory. Other honors include the Lifetime Leadership Award from the *Ms.* Foundation for Women in 1989, being part of *Parade* magazine's informal survey of twenty prominent Americans in 1991, naming to the National Women's Hall of Fame in 1993, the Women's Action Alliance's Silver Anniversary Founder's Award in 1996, naming to the American Society of Magazine Editors' Hall of Fame in 1998, and naming to the Deadline Club Hall of Fame by the Society of Professional Journalists. In 1999 *Biography Magazine* listed her in its end-of-the-century list of visionaries, and she was the keynote speaker at Century 21's conference "The Power of Women." She also won the North American Menopause Society's Celebrating Women at Midlife and Beyond award. In 2000 the U.S. Postal Service held a Women's History Month Event and named her a female trailblazer.

Steinem is still respected as one of the most powerful voices of the feminist movement. She pioneered reforms in many areas, including women's compensation and job advancement.

See also: Publishing Industry

Further Reading

Heilbrun, Carolyn G. *The Education of a Woman: The Life of Gloria Steinem.*

Steinem, Gloria. *Outrageous Acts and Everyday Rebellions.*

Thom, Mary. *Inside Ms.*

"Wake Up and Smell the Estrogen: Ms Magazine Is Back on Newsstands Today; Independent and Women-Owned by Liberty Media for Women, LLC."

Stevens, Anne L. (1948–), Automobile Executive

Anne Stevens is vice president of North American Vehicle Operations of Ford Motor Company, a position that earned her the number 27 ranking on the 2001 list and number 4 ranking on the 2002 list of *Fortune's* most powerful women in American business. According to Ford, as of 2000 she was the highest ranking woman in the automobile industry.

Born in Reading, Pennsylvania, Stevens was a car-racing enthusiast during high school. When she found that girls were not allowed to work at racetracks, she put on a cap to cover her hair and managed to join a mechanic's pit crew. After high school she went into a nursing program, but hated it (Maynard, p. 2). She took at job at Bell Telephone, met and married William Stevens, a telephone repairman, and later had two children. At Bell she was tested for employment interests and found that she was suited for engineering. In 1975 she and her husband enrolled in engineering school and shared one job while they were in school. She graduated from Drexel University in 1980 with a dual degree in mechanical engineering and materials engineering. She did graduate work at Rutgers University and studied six years with W. Edwards Deming, a quality guru.

Stevens began her engineering career with Exxon Chemical Company and worked there ten years in increasingly responsible engineering, manufacturing, and marketing positions. In 1990 she joined Ford as a marketing specialist in the Plastic Products Division, Vehicle Exterior System. In 1992 she became manager of the Quality Services Department at the Saline, Michigan, plant, and three years later, manufacturing manager of Plastic and Trim Products Operations. Next she was appointed plant manager in Enfield, England, the first woman manager for Ford in Europe. She headed the Automotive Components Division. Following a stint at the Dunton, England, operation, she returned to the United States as vice president of North American Assembly Operations and later became executive director of Vehicle Operations. She was the industry's highest-ranking woman, in charge of 68,000 employees at twenty-nine plants that produced more than 4 million cars and trucks a year. By February 2002 she had installed a new quality-control system in all the U.S. plants.

Stevens never felt that there were obstacles to her career because she was a woman (Maynard, p. 2). She was sometimes lonely, but her male colleagues introduced her to other professional women. She has since gathered 400 women at Ford into an informal network. She loves solving problems. Her management style blends toughness with accountability while having a good time. She is known for being open and fair with a strong focus on the customer. Her experience in engineering, business, and manufacturing has been a plus in the automotive industry.

Stevens has been on the boards of Auto Alliance and Lockheed Martin and the advisory board for the Graduate Program at Northwestern University. She was involved in the North London Regeneration Effort and was elected to a two-year term as a councilor for the London Confederation of British Industries. In 2000 she was named one of the top one hundred women executives in the North American Automobile Industry and received the Shingo Leadership Award. In 2001 Northwestern University honored her as that year's Outstanding Business Leader.

See also: Automobile Industry

Further Reading
"Breaking the Mold: Ford's Anne Stevens Is One of a New Breed of Auto Execs with Expertise in Many Disciplines."
Maynard, Micheline. "Private Sector: Comfortable with the Fast Track."
McCormick, John. "Making It Right."

Stewart, Martha (1941–), Home Accessory Merchandiser, Media Executive

Martha Stewart is the ubiquitous founder of Martha Stewart Living Omnimedia. It has been on *Working Woman*'s list of the 500 largest woman-owned companies, and from 1998 through 2001 Stewart was on *Fortune*'s list of the most powerful women in American business. In 2002 she was investigated for insider trading, and in March 2004 she was convicted of conspiracy, making false statements, and obstruction of justice. Her home-living empire suffered as a result of the publicity surrounding the investigation. Subsequently, Stewart served a sentence in a minimum-security corrections facility.

Stewart was born in Jersey City, New Jersey, and grew up in Nutley, New Jersey, the oldest daughter and second child of six children. Her father sold pharmaceuticals and was an avid gardener; her mother taught sixth grade. Stewart liked cooking and gardening from an early age. In elementary school she organized birthday parties for children in the neighborhood. She began modeling when she was thirteen and continued it through college, appearing in some television commercials. She attended Barnard College and graduated in 1963 with a degree in architecture and European history. In 1961 she married Andrew Stewart, a law student at Yale. They have one daughter, Alexis.

After graduation she worked as a stockbroker for eight years. In 1972 she resigned and moved to an old farmhouse in Westport, Connecticut, which she restored. In 1976 she started catering specialty gourmet meals. She partnered with a friend and worked out of her basement, but the partnership did not last. By 1981 she was catering for corporate clients, and by 1986 her annual sales were over $1 million. She also published articles in the *New York Times* and wrote a magazine column. Her first book, *Entertaining*, was published in 1982 and, despite mixed reviews, brought Stewart to national attention. In 1987 she became K-Mart's official spokesperson and launched her own line of products. In

> She published nine books, appeared in television specials, published video- and audiotapes, and launched a bimonthly magazine.

1990 she established Martha Stewart Living Omnimedia, with herself as chairman and CEO. Her syndicated television shows began in 1994 and garnered 5 million viewers per week. Her career flourished in the 1990s. She published nine books, appeared in television specials, published video- and audiotapes, and launched a bimonthly magazine, *Martha Stewart Living*.

She made a ten-year book/magazine partnership with Time-Warner, but bought it back in 1997. By 1999 she had a media empire and was known as the "First Lady of Domesticity" and the best self-marketer in the publishing business. That year she took her company public at $13–$15 per share. She controls 60 percent of the shares. The company has four business segments: publishing, Internet commerce, television, and merchandising. In October 2001 *Fortune* called her "The Princess of Perfection." She calls herself the leading authority for the home.

Stewart is a shrewd marketer and a hardworking perfectionist. Although she is a demanding manager, many of her staff have stayed on for years. She tapped a niche: homemakers and career women wanting elegance. She has convinced millions that they, too, can create an attractive environment. Stewart was divorced in 1989, and her daughter helps with the business.

She has won many awards, beginning in 1961 when she was one of *Glamour's* best-dressed college girls. In 1998 she was named to the National Sales Hall of Fame and was one of *Time's* most influential Americans and among the Hot 100: Entrepreneurial Superstars in *Success*. She was given the American Marketing Association's Edison Achievement Award that year for her influence as a lifestyle authority. In 1999 she was named a visionary business leader, third nationwide in a poll conducted by Yellow Pages. She was also number six of the top ten advertisers in *AdWeek*. In 2001 *Business Week* named her one of its top twenty-five managers. She has won numerous Emmy awards and has been very active with the March of Dimes and the Lupus Foundation.

In December 2001 she was accused of insider trading. Her company's stock has declined, as have advertising revenue and newsstand sales. In a highly publicized trial, Stewart was found guilty on several charges and sentenced to serve time in a minimum-security facility.

See also: Broadcasting Industry; Fashion Industry

Further Reading

Byron, Christopher. *Martha Inc.: The Incredible Story of Martha Stewart Living Omnimedia.*

Martha Stewart (www.marthastewart.com).

Pogrebin, Robin. "Master of Her Own Destiny."

Stewart, Martha. "The Importance of Being Myself."

Stoneman, Abigail (late eighteenth century), Tavern Owner

Abigail Stoneman was one of the first colonial businesswomen in the hospitality industry. She ran a resort for summer visitors in Rhode Island and a series of coffeehouses that also offered dance gatherings. Much of what is known about Stoneman appears in newspaper articles, advertisements, announcements, and so forth. Nothing is recorded of her birth or early life. Her first marriage is thought to have been to Samuel Stoneman, a lieutenant in the Rhode Island regiment during the French and Indian War. She was a widow by 1760, for she is listed alone in the church meeting records in that year. In the November 17, 1766, issue of the *Newport Mercury*, a small news item recounts a robbery at her "large and commodious dwelling." The "gleanings" were around 100 Spanish dollars and some pieces of china (Bridenbaugh, p. 390–391).

In May 1767 she opened the Merchant's Coffee House at the Sign of the King's Arms. She also sold West Indian goods there. In 1768 she bought a house and lands in Middletown, Rhode Island, for £1,400. They were about four miles from Newport, and her intent was to offer dancing and entertainment to summer visitors, mainly from Pennsylvania and South Carolina. She added a ballroom to the property and held dances "in the genteelest manner" (*Newport Mercury*, May 22, 1879). By October 1769, she had moved to Whitehall and opened another place of entertainment, naming it Vauxhall after an entertainment palace in London.

In 1770 she applied for a license to open a coffeehouse in Boston. Named the Royal Exchange, it was on King Street, where the Boston Massacre had taken place six months earlier. Again she renovated and advertised, taking in boarders and/or renters. In June 1772 she opened a teahouse in Middletown, Rhode Island, for the summer season. When the season was over, she rented the property and moved back to Newport, where she opened the British Coffee House. She applied for a liquor license for it. She stayed there during 1772 and 1773, summering in Middletown.

In November 1774 she opened another establishment in Newport, this time near Point-bridge. It had a dancing room with music and was open from six to nine every evening except for Thursdays, the day of the Newport Assembly. She also provided board and lodging for gentlemen, one of whom she married: the "Honorable Sir John Treville, Knight of Malta, Captain of the Cavalry, in the service of his most Christian majesty" (*Newport Mercury*, October 28, 1774). Stoneman sold her house and land in Middletown and two church pews, in the Congregational Meetinghouse and Trinity Church. Because Treville was a British officer, the couple had to flee to New York City, and from there he disappeared into the murk of the Revolutionary War.

Stoneman had very little money left. In a notice appeared in *Rivington's New York Loyal Gazette* of October 25, 1777, she announced that she had "sustained considerable losses during the present rebellion" and was opening a coffeehouse with boarding, the London Coffee-House.

It is difficult to ascertain whether Stoneman abandoned all these places or accumulated them as part of her property. She seems to have done well, and did not change her vocation apart from her second brief marriage to Treville.

Her political sentiments seem to have remained with the British, as evidenced by the names of her establishments. After the 1977 notice she disappears from all records.

See also: Colonial Businesswomen; Entertainment Industry; Travel Industry

Further Reading

Bridenbaugh, Carl. "Stoneman, Abigail." In Edward T. James, p. 390–391.

Zilboorg, Caroline, ed. *Women's Firsts,* p. 120.

Strobel, Pamela B. (1952–), Energy Executive

Pamela Strobel is executive vice president and chief administrative officer of Exelon. She was ranked number 29 on *Fortune's* 2002 list of the most powerful women in American business. Strobel grew up in Chicago, one of several sisters. Her grandmother worked at Commonwealth Edison in 1918 and 1919, and her grandfather was an Illinois Supreme Court Justice. She wanted to be a professional pianist when she was growing up. She studied journalism in college and graduated from the University of Illinois Law School. During her first year there, she met her husband-to-be, Russ, who is now general counsel for Nicor Inc., a utility company. They have two children.

She began working in 1977 with the law firm Sidley & Austin, then with Isham, Lincoln, and Beale after the two firms merged. It represented local news organizations and also did legal work for Commonwealth Edison (ComEd). In 1993 she joined ComEd as its general counsel and later became its chief legal counsel.

In 2000 Unicom (ComEd's parent company) and Peco Energy Company merged to form Exelon, a $15 billion utility company. That October Strobel was named vice chair of Exelon and president of Exelon Energy Delivery. Her job was to run the company's operations. She also led the team that rebuilt its aging system, with the primary goal of a summer with no power outages. In April 2003 she was appointed chief administrative officer of Exelon, responsible for business services, enterprises, and communication. She has also been named chair of the Exelon Corporate Strategy Committee.

Strobel is one of Chicago's most powerful executives. She is a team builder and patient in explaining difficult concepts. Her people skills are her strength, and she blends calm with thoughtfulness. She has been on the boards of IMC Global and Sabre Holdings and chairman of the board of the Joffrey Ballet of Chicago. She is heavily involved in Chicago civic organizations.

See also: Energy Industry

Further Reading

"The 'Exelon Way' Business Model Approved."

Greising, David. "Chicago Tribune David Greising Column."

Williamson, Tammy. "ComEd Spokeswoman Near the Center of Power."

Sueltz, Patricia C. (1952–), Software Executive

Until March 2004 Patricia Sueltz was executive vice president of Sun Microsystem's Enterprise Services Division. Her previous position as head of the Software Systems Division ranked her number 35 in 2000 and number 22 in 2001 on the *Fortune* list of the most powerful women in American business. In March 2004 she left Sun to lead a new company, Salesforce.com.

Sueltz was born in Japan and is a naturalized citizen of the United States. She graduated with a BA in political science from Occidental College in Los Angeles and was a Rockefeller Fellow at the Clarmont School of Theology and Ethics. A former seminarian, her first jobs were at Pacific Telephone & Telegraph in its Installation and Repair Division. She is married to a stay-at-home husband who formerly worked for IBM. They have two daughters.

She joined IBM in 1979 and worked in a variety of product management and technical positions. In 1991 she managed a group of 800 employees in development and marketing for online transaction and message-queuing products. From 1993 to 1995 she was the technical assistant to Louis Gerstner, then IBM's CEO. In 1997, as vice president of Internet Software, she was responsible for creating and implementing the e-business web-server products. The following year she was promoted to general manager of the Java Division and worked with Sun Microsystems on backing Java, quickly becoming the company expert.

In September 1999 Sueltz moved to Sun Microsystems as the president of New Software Products and Platforms. She was responsible for overseeing all of Sun's software businesses and for acquiring new products. In July 2002 she became executive vice president of Enterprise Services, the division responsible for global consulting, training, and support services. She was in charge of 12,000 employees, and her goal was to expand that division. She is a firm backer of open standards for software. In March 2004 she left Sun to lead a new start-up company, Salesforce.com.

Sueltz has been active in Women in Technology International and was on IBM's Women's Diversity Taskforce. She has been on the boards of Delphi Automotive Systems, Amgen, and Sun.

See also: Information Technology Industry

Further Reading
Forgrieve, Janet. "Sun Exec Puts Family First."
Hamilton, David P. "Sun Hires IBM Executive Patricia Sueltz to Take Control of Its Software Division."
"Verses from a Java Gospel."

Sweeney, Anne M. (1958–), Television Executive

Anne Sweeney, one of the most powerful executives in television today, is the president of both ABC Cable Networks Group and Disney Channel

Worldwide. She was number 47 on the original 1998 *Fortune* list of the most powerful women in American business and was number 35 on the 2003 list.

Sweeney was born in Hudson, New York, the oldest of three children. Her parents were elementary school teachers who were proud of their Irish ancestors and had a strong sense of family. She graduated from the College of New Rochelle and went on to receive a master's degree in education from Harvard University in 1980. Her plan was to become a teacher, but one of her graduate courses was taught by Gerry Lesser, a creator of *Sesame Street*, and she became interested in the possibilities of children's television as an educational tool. She married in 1984 and has a son and a daughter.

Sweeney's first job was as a page at ABC-TV in New York when she was twenty. In 1979 she was an unpaid intern for Action for Children's Television. After receiving her master's degree, she worked for three months at Automation House, a company that helped organizations develop television programs. In 1981 she joined Nickelodeon/Nick at Nite, which was just beginning as a network. She worked for head of acquisitions Geraldine Laybourne, who became her mentor, and succeeded her in that position. One of her accomplishments was to bring *The Mary Tyler Moore Show* and *The Bob Newhart Show* to Nick-at-Nite. In 1990, she became vice president of acquisitions and she helped to launch the Comedy Channel.

When she was thirty-six she joined Fox Networks as chairman and CEO. She had always wanted to start something from the beginning, and Fox Basic Cable was her chance. It was the largest launch in cable history. However, by 1996 Fox's goals had changed, and Sweeney left to become president of the Disney Channel. At Disney she again worked with Laybourne. In 1998 Sweeney was promoted to president of Disney/ABC Cable Networks and was in charge of all of ABC's cable networks except ESPN. In January 2000 she launched Soapnet, and in April that year, the Internet site ZoogDisney.com. In October 2000 she was promoted to her current position, where she has the added responsibility for all Disney channels worldwide. In September 2001 she led an on-air campaign designed to help children cope with their emotions following the September 11 terrorist attacks. The following May she developed another public affairs initiative, "Learning Together," designed to increase family involvement in learning. In January 2003 children's television programming and production and the animation divisions were added to her responsibilities.

Sweeney's management style is characterized by her strong belief in teamwork. She lets others do most of the talking and has a reputation as a wonderful team builder. She is tough underneath a sweet manner and is a meticulous planner. She is also known for her single-mindedness and drive and has spent her career working for companies and causes in which she believes. The Fox Network's Rupert Murdoch remarked on her "unique vision in providing new and distinctive programming" (Flint, "Sweeney," p. 20).

Sweeney has won several honors: 1994 Executive of the Year from New York Women in Cable, 1995 Star Award from American Women in Radio and Television, and 1997 Woman of the Year by Women in Cable. She was named to the American Advertising Federation's Hall of Achievement in 1996, *Irish America Magazine*'s Business 100 in 1998, and the Wonder Woman Hall of Fame by *Multichannel News* in 1999. She received the Advocate Leader Award from the Southern California Chapter of Women in Cable and Technology in 1998 and the Joel A. Berger Award from CablePositive for her years of service in fighting AIDS. In October 2002 *Electronic Media* listed her as one of the most powerful women in television. She has been on the board of directors of the Walter Kaitz Foundation, the National Academy of Cable Programming, and Special Olympics, and on the boards of trustees of the College of New Rochelle and the Harvard University Partners Council. She is one of the founding members of Women in Cable.

> Murdoch remarked on her "unique vision in providing new and distinctive programming."

See also: Broadcasting Industry

Further Reading

"Anne Sweeney Named President of ABC Cable Networks Group and President of Disney Channel Worldwide."

"Disney Mogul Sweeney Breaks Mold."

"Sweeney, Anne." In *Celebrity Biographies*, 1999.

T

Teel, Joyce Raley (1930–), Grocery Store Chain Owner

Raley's, the grocery store chain belonging to Joyce Raley Teel, has been listed among the top five companies on the *Working Woman* list of top woman-owned companies several times since 1993. Since she inherited the company in 1991 the number of stores has doubled and the company has become known for its charitable efforts.

Teel was born and brought up in Sacramento, California, the only child of Tom Raley, who founded the chain in 1925. She married Jim Teel when she was nineteen; they had met while both were working in the store. The Teels have five children, four daughters and one son. In 1951 she graduated from Sacramento City College. Over the years she kept asking her father to let her help run the business, but he thought raising children and being a wife were more important. Finally, in 1985 she moved into a vacant office and began convincing him that she was serious. Her job title was director of community relations. Four years later Tom Raley had a massive stroke, and in 1991 he died. Joyce and her husband, who had held a number of progressively responsible positions at Raley's, took over as co-chairs.

One of their first actions was to increase the number of stores. They bought BelAir Markets, adding 17 stores to bring the total to 82. They also initiated a warehouse chain designed to compete with Sam's Club stores and Costco; by 1999 there were four stores in the chain. Other innovations were the addition of dry-cleaning, in-store banking, and child-care centers in some stores. In 1998 they purchased 27 Nob Hill stores in San Francisco and expanded into Nevada. In 1999 they purchased Albertson's Food Markets in Albuquerque and Las Vegas. As of October 2000 they owned 151 stores in four distinct chains and had 18,000 employees and $3 billion in annual sales.

Raley's is a family-owned company and the family is committed to keeping it that way. Estate taxes were paid out of personal moneys and not profits or stock sales; all Teel's children and their spouses have worked or do work in the stores. In 1995 her son Michael, who had been running a food-advertising agency in Seattle, was named chief operating officer. He became president in 1996 and CEO in 1998. In 1996 Joyce Teel began working less in the stores so that she could pursue other interests. She climbed Mount Kilimanjaro in 1996 when she was sixty-five.

One of the most important accomplishments of Teel's management was Raley's involvement with charity and community fundraisers. She co-founded Food for Families, a nonprofit agency that donates food for the hungry in Raley's communities. The agency has raised millions of dollars over the years. Teel also supports Books for Schools and the Anti-Defamation League's World of Difference program, which tries to reduce racial prejudice in schools. For her work in this area she received the league's Distinguished Community Service Award. She was named Businesswoman of the Year in 1994 by the Sacramento Chamber of Commerce and received the William Booth Award from the Salvation Army in 1997. As head of the Thomas Raley Foundation, she has donated millions of dollars to Sacramento charities. She has been on the board of directors of the American Heart Association and the Crocker Art Museum and is a member of the Sutter Hospital Guild, the Cerebral Palsy Guild, and the Sacramento Children's Home. She is perennially listed on the *Forbes* 400 as one of the wealthiest people in the United States. In 2001 the Sacramento Chamber of Commerce named her Sacramentan of the Year. She is an avid hiker and mountain climber and has many grandchildren.

See also: Food Industry

Further Reading
Schmuckler, Eric, and Harris Collingwood. "The Top 50 Women Business Owners," p. 32.
Sutter, Pam. "Joyce Raley Teel."

Telecommuting, *see* Flexible Work Arrangements

Television Industry, *see* Broadcasting Industry

Thomas-Graham, Pamela (1963–), Television Executive

Pamela Thomas-Graham is president and CEO of CNBC, the business and financial channel. She is also the author of two acclaimed mystery novels, *A Darker Shade of Crimson* and *Blue Blood*.

Thomas-Graham was born in Detroit, Michigan, to a middle-class family, the younger of two children. Her father was an engineer and her mother, a social worker. Her family emphasized achieving her best possible, whatever her goal. She was the first person from her high school to attend Harvard University. In fact, she earned three degrees there: an honors degree in economics and joint degrees in business and law. She graduated Phi Beta Kappa and won the Captain Jonathan Fay prize, the highest honor awarded to a female student. In law school, she was the editor of the *Harvard Law Review*. During the summers, she worked for Bain & Company, Goldman Sachs, and Sullivan & Worcester, a Boston law firm. She is married to attorney and author Lawrence Otis Graham. They have one son.

After graduating from Harvard Law School in 1989, she joined a global consulting company, McKinsey & Company. In 1995 she became its first African American woman partner. At the time McKinsey had 600 partners; thirty-four were women and two were African Americans. Thomas-Graham was a leader in the media and entertainment division and began working with the Internet on clients' behalf in 1994.

In September 1999 she was appointed president of CNBC.com, a beginning financial Web site. She was NBC's highest-ranking African American executive. Her goal was to bring the Web site to profitability. She also became an NBC executive vice president in 2000. CNBC.com won *Worth Magazine*'s Reader's Choice Award for Best On-Line Stock Market News. In January 2001 it was folded back into NBC, and Thomas-Graham took the number two spot of president and chief operating officer. Six months later she was promoted to president and CEO of CNBC, the most powerful African American in the cable news industry. When she began, the stock market was booming; two years later it had seriously declined, along with

> She had to cut jobs but used the opportunity to improve programming and focus on analysis and depth.

advertising revenues and viewership. She had to cut jobs, but used the opportunity to improve programming and focus on analysis and depth rather than play-by-play stock market coverage.

Thomas-Graham has been quoted by Suzanne Ryan ("Her Drive") as saying, "I truly believe that if you're going to do something, you should try to do the best you can. . . . My parents worked hard and set high standards. That's a core part of who I am." Her hero is Thurgood Marshall. She says one of her secrets is that she sleeps about four hours per night. She describes herself as determined, ethical, and compassionate. She is also highly intelligent and personable and has the ability to synthesize data and use it to quickly make decisions. She has experienced subtle racism in many small ways, particularly with people not taking her seriously. She has three guiding principles: aim high, find mentors, and maintain balance.

She has won many awards. In 1997 *Crain's New York Business* listed her in "Forty under Forty" and *Global Finance Magazine* placed her among its top twenty women in finance. *Consulting Magazine* called her one of the top ten consultants in the United States in 1999, and she was the 2000 Woman of the Year for the Financial Women's Association. *Black Enterprise* and *Crain's New York Business* also listed her as a top businesswoman that year. She won the 2001 Matrix Award from New York Women in Communications and was listed among *Black Enterprise's* Corporate Executives of the Year. *Electronic Media* listed her among the most powerful women in television and *Ebony*, among the ten most powerful black people in television in 2002. In 2003 she won the Quasar Award from the National Association of Minorities in Communications. She has been on the boards of the New York City Opera, the Harvard Alumni Association, the American Red Cross of Greater New York, and the Inner City Scholarship Fund.

See also: African American Businesswomen; Broadcasting Industry

Further Reading
Clarke, Robyn D. "Excellence by the Graham."
Ryan, Suzanne C. "Her Drive Makes News at CNBC."
"Thomas-Graham, Pamela." In *Current Biography Yearbook*, 2000, p. 552–554.
Thomas-Graham, Pamela. *A Touch of Crimson.*

Ticknor, Carolyn (1948–), Electronics Executive

Carolyn Ticknor was ranked number 22 of the most powerful women in American business by *Fortune* in 1999 and number 37 in 2000. Both rankings were based on her responsibilities at Hewlett-Packard (HP), where she was president of Imaging and Printing Systems, a division accounting for almost half of HP's annual revenues. She was also a vice president of the company.

Ticknor was born in 1948. She received a BA in psychology from the University of Redlands in California, an MA in industrial psychology from San Francisco State, and an MBA from Stanford University. She is married and has two children. Her first job was in management information systems at the Bank of America, where she stayed for five years. In 1977 she moved to Hewlett-Packard's Corporate Computing Center, primarily because she could work there part-time on a flexible schedule and care for her baby. She later was promoted to research and development manager and section manager for the Information Networks Division. There, she was in charge of developing communications products. In 1987 she became the general manager of the Hewlett-Packard Roseville Networks Division.

In 1994 she was promoted to general manager of LaserJet and spearheaded the development of the "mopier," a printer that integrates printing, collating, and stapling of computer-generated documents. Her group also developed scanners. In 1995 she was made vice president of the renamed LaserJet Solutions Group, where she was in charge of research, development, marketing, and manufacturing as well as business strategy. Sales for this group alone in 1997 were $8.7 billion out of the company's total sales of $42 billion.

In 1999 she received a new title, president and CEO of the same division, with the power to operate almost as a separate company through arranging acquisitions and alliances and controlling her own workers. She still reported to Hewlett-Packard CEO Lewis Platt. Later that year Platt retired and Carly Fiorina was hired to replace him. Fiorina kept Ticknor and her co-executive Ann Livermore on the top executive team, and Ticknor received expanded responsibilities as well as a new title, president of Imaging and Printing Systems and vice president of Hewlett-Packard. She was in charge of printers, a $20 billion division, and a reinvention of the printer as part of an e-service center. One of her first accomplishments was to partner with Stamps.com to bundle their Internet Postage Software on HP printers. She retired in January 2001 after twenty-four years with the company. In November 2001 she became a special managing partner for Village Ventures, a network of venture capital funds in Florida.

Ticknor has sat on the boards of directors of FileNET Corporation and Stamps.com. The chairmen of both companies have commented on her skills as a strong and aggressive leader with years of valuable experience. She was elected to the boards of Boise Cascade Corporation in February 2000 and AT&T Wireless in June 2001. She has also served on the Stanford Graduate School of Business Advisory Council and the board of the Lucille Packard Children's Hospital at Stanford.

See also: Information Technology Industry

Further Reading
"Carolyn M. Ticknor Named General Manager of HP's LaserJet Printer Group."
Cleaver, Joanne. "The Top 25 Companies for Executive Women."
Gross, Daniel M. "Next CEOs," p. 50.

Timothy, Ann (1727–1792), Newspaper Publisher, Printer
Timothy, Elizabeth (circa 1700–1757), Newspaper Publisher, Printer

Elizabeth and Ann Timothy were two members of a famous colonial printing family. Elizabeth was Ann's mother-in-law and was the first woman newspaper publisher in the American colonies. Ann was the second South Carolina woman newspaper editor, publisher, and printer.

Elizabeth Timothy was born in Holland and received the usual education given to a woman there, which included a knowledge of accounting. Nothing else is known of her birth and childhood. She married Louis Timothee, a Huguenot, early in the eighteenth century and had four children. They sailed from Rotterdam for Philadelphia in 1731. In the colonies, Louis became

Benjamin Franklin's protégé. They attempted to publish a German-language newspaper, *Philadelphia Zeitung*, but it lasted only two issues; however, the Timothees' association with Franklin continued. In 1733 Louis Timothee contracted with Franklin to continue a printing business and newspaper, the *South Carolina Gazette*, in Charleston, South Carolina. The previous contractor, Thomas Whitmarsh, had died after only one year. The terms of the contract were that Franklin provide the press and type, pay one-third of the maintenance, and in return get one-third of the profits. The contract was for six years with an option to buy at the end of that time.

Louis moved to Charleston, and Elizabeth and their children, now numbering six, followed the next year. In 1734 he changed his name to Lewis Timothy. The weekly newspaper was revived and so was the printing business, which printed mostly official colonial business. He also printed some sermons, hymns, forms for business, and was the postmaster. In 1738 he was killed in an accident, and Elizabeth Timothy, with Franklin's approval, took over the contract in the name of her fourteen-year-old son, Peter. She did not miss a beat, getting the next issue of the newspaper out the following week. Although the quality of both the printing and the news was a little ragged at first, it gradually improved, and the newspaper became very successful. She eventually published it twice a week. She remained the official colonial printer and postmaster and sold various goods provided by Franklin as well as many copies of *Poor Richard's Almanac*. Between 1742 and 1746 the Commons House authorized payments to her of just over £2,406. According to Franklin's autobiography, she was an improvement over her husband, particularly in accounting matters, being prompt and meticulous with accounts and payments. When the contract was finished, she was doing so well that she was able to buy the business with cash.

In 1746 Peter reached his majority and she turned the business over to him. She opened a shop next to the printing establishment, where she sold books and stationery items. In 1748 she moved out of Charleston but returned the year before her death. Her prosperity and success are attested by the property left in her will: three houses, eight slaves, and household furniture and money, all of which she left to her surviving children.

Peter Timothy continued the printing business and the newspaper. He became one of the leading American printers and was well known for his part in the American Revolution. He had married Ann in 1745, shortly before he took over the printing business. He slowly became involved in the patriot cause, and changed the name of the newspaper to *Gazette of the State of South Carolina*. By the time the British took over Charleston in 1780, he had become so well known as a patriot that the family had to flee to Philadelphia. In 1782 he and two daughters were lost at sea.

Ann Timothy had little to do with the business until that time. She had been busy having fifteen children, five of whom survived infancy. However, like many women before her, she took over. She returned to Charleston in

1783 and revived the newspaper under the name *State Gazette of South Carolina.* She partnered with two other people and, again, the result was a bit ragged at first. The format was attractive, with three-column pages and woodcuts for illustrations, and the paper carried a variety of domestic and international news. Advertising usually took up half the space. She also was the state printer and had fifteen imprints under her name between 1783 and 1792. Her other printing consisted of the usual forms, books, sermons, and other documents. She died in 1792, leaving the business to her son, Benjamin Franklin Timothy. He retired in 1802, bringing the Timothy printing dynasty to an end.

The Timothy women have been called the foremothers of American women journalists. They reported on events of their time, wrote homilies and essays, printed first efforts of Southern writers, and relied on news exchanges for national and international news. They did not print editorials. Elizabeth is honored with a plaque at the printing museum at Charles Towne Landing, the site of the first South Carolina colony.

> The Timothy women have been called the foremothers of American women journalists.

See also: Colonial Businesswomen; Publishing Industry

Further Reading

Demeter, Richard. *Primer, Presses and Composing Sticks: Women Printers of the Colonial Period,* p. 13–30.

Dunn, Elizabeth E. In Garraty and Carnes, "Timothy, Elizabeth," p. 689.

McKerns, Joseph P., ed. *Biographical Dictionary of American Journalism,* p. 700–704.

Thomas, Isaiah. *History of Printing in America: With a Biography of Printers & an Account of Newspapers.*

Toben, Doreen A. (1950–), Telecommunications Executive

In 2002 *Fortune* ranked Doreen Toben number 25 on its list of the most powerful women in American business, the highest ranked newcomer to the list that year. She had been named executive vice president and chief financial officer of Verizon Communications the previous April. In 2003 she was ranked number 17.

Toben was born in Curaçao, Venezuela, and raised in Harding Township, New Jersey. She graduated from Rosemont College in 1972 with a degree in political science and from Fairleigh Dickinson University in 1978 with an MBA in finance and marketing. She began her business career in telecommunications in the treasury department of AT&T. Later she became its director of corporate planning.

In 1983 she joined Bell Atlanticom Systems and received a number of promotions there, including division manager of strategic planning, executive director of marketing for Bell Atlantic Enterprises International, and, in 1993, chief financial officer for Bell Atlantic-New Jersey. In May 1995 she became vice president of corporate finance for Bell Atlantic Corporation and, later that year, vice president of finance and controller as well as a member of the executive committee. In January 2000 she was promoted to senior vice president and telecommunications chief financial officer. In this position she was responsible for "internetworking," information services, and the international merger of Bell Atlantic and GTE into Verizon's Telecommunications Group. Her role was pivotal during the transition, and because of her excellent work she rose to become executive vice president and chief financial officer of Verizon Communications. Since then she has successfully focused on reducing debt and improving overall company performance, in keeping with her reputation for strong results and fiscal discipline.

Toben is married with two children and is active in community organizations and the Peddie School in New Jersey. In March 2003 she was honored by Girls Incorporated as an important role model and leader for girls. Under her management, Verizon is very active in offering promotion, mentoring, and networking opportunities for women.

Further Reading
"Bell Atlantic Elects Toben to New Vice President—Corporate Finance Position."
"Verizon Communications Names Doreen A. Toben Chief Financial Officer."

Tomé, Carol B. (1957–), Home Improvement Executive

Carol Tomé made her debut on *Fortune*'s list of the most powerful women in American business in 2001. In 2002 she was number 43. She is executive vice president and the chief financial officer of Home Depot, one of the most successful retail operations of its kind in the United States.

Tomé was born and raised in Jackson, Wyoming, and received a BS in communications from the University of Wyoming and an MBA in finance from the University of Denver. Her first job was as a commercial loan analyst, which she credits for honing her problem-solving skills. In 1981 she joined what was then United Bank of Denver as a vice president of commercial lending. To gain corporate financial experience, in 1988 she joined Manville Corporation, then in the throes of reorganization under the bankruptcy act. Four years later she moved to Riverwood International Corporation, an operating subsidiary of Manville, and was responsible for its initial public offering. In 1994 she was promoted to vice president and treasurer and made responsible for the company's worldwide treasury management activities.

In 1995 Tomé moved to Home Depot as vice president and treasurer, managing its treasury, cash, and capital-structure operations. She was promoted to senior vice president of finance and accounting and treasurer and, in 2001, executive vice president and chief financial officer. When she was appointed, the CEO complimented her on not only knowing all the numbers but also knowing how to make changes at the store level (Harrington, p. 197). Following the financial scandals of 2002 she immediately strengthened the company's ethics code, including more stringent guidelines and accountability in the finance department. She is the highest-ranking woman at Home Depot and is responsible for all its finance functions. Tomé credits her success to her business education as well as good communication and problem-solving skills (Knight, Jennifer, p. 83). She suggests that a way to earn respect of the senior management and board of a company is to work on projects and give presentations, take risks, add value to your activities, and always deliver when you make a commitment. She has a varied background, always learning from her positions: capital-structure issues, domestic finance, and international finance.

She is a volunteer in Atlanta, where she lives, has been a member of the Treasury Management Association and a trustee of the Georgia Substance Abuse Advisory Council, has raised funds for the Woodruff Arts Center, and has sat on the board of trustees of the American Red Cross Metropolitan Chapter and the corporate board of UPS.

See also: Finance Industry; Retailing Industry

Further Reading
"The Home Depot Appoints Carey Executive Vice President—Business Development, Strategy and Corporate Operations; Promotes Tomé to Executive Vice President—Chief Financial Officer."
Knight, Jennifer. "Communication, Problem-Solving Skills Key."

Top Women Business Owners

In 1992 *Working Woman* published its first ranked list of companies in the United States owned by women. There were only 25 in that first list. The next year the list grew to 50, and in October 1997 it expanded to 500 companies. This list's expansion alone indicates a phenomenal growth in business ownership by women.

In 1992 the first twenty-five companies together employed over 13.2 million total workers and comprised 40 percent of all service and retail firms. By 2001 the total company employment for the top 500 woman-owned firms was about 400,000. Combined revenues were $88 billion in 2000 and $96.4 billion in 2001 (Collins, "The Top Women-Owned Businesses," p. 56).

The three major criteria measured in the list were sales, ownership, and title/active management. Sales figures covered the twelve months ending with

December of the previous year. Private company sales figures were checked against industry analysts, and the most conservative estimates were used. Until 1996 these figures as well as employment figures were for the United States only except as noted. The woman owner had to hold a controlling interest. In private companies, this meant at least 20 percent of the stock; in public companies, it meant 10 percent of the stock or the person holding the largest block of the company's stock. Also, the owner had to be involved in day-to-day management activities and hold a title of chief operating officer or above. She could be a co-founder if both partners had management control.

The last issue of *Working Woman* was September 2001. No other magazine continued the list.

See also: Appendix II; Woman-Owned Businesses

Further Reading

Ahlers, Kate O'Brien. "The Top 500 Women-Owned Businesses," (1999 list).

Bamford, Janet. "The *Working Woman* 50: America's Top Woman Business Owners," (1993 list).

Bamford, Janet, and Susan McHenry. "The *Working Woman* 50," (1994 list).

Bamford, Janet, and Jennifer Pendleton. "The 50 Top Women-Owned Businesses," (1997 list).

———. "The *Working Woman* 50 Top Women Business Owners," (1995 list).

Collins, Kathleen, dir. "The Top Women-Owned Businesses," (2001 list).

Freeman, Lisa Lee. "The Top 500 Women-Owned Businesses," (2000 list).

Lappen, Alyssa, ed. "The *Working Woman* 25," (1992 list).

Schmuckler, Eric, and Harris Collingwood. "The Top 50 Women Business Owners," (1996 list).

Seneker, Harold, dir. "The Top 500 Women-Owned Businesses," (1998 list).

Totino, Rose (1915–1994), Pizza Manufacturer

Rose Totino and her husband founded Totino's Pizza, at one time the manufacturer of the largest-selling frozen pizza in the United States. When they sold the company to Pillsbury, she became a vice president of research and development there.

Totino was the daughter of Italian immigrants, fourth in a poor family of seven children. She sold milk for 5¢ a gallon, and the family lived off its garden and chickens. At sixteen Rose quit school to do housework for $2.50 a week. As was customary at the time, her brothers continued their education. She got a better job at a candy factory for 17¢ an hour and soon earned a raise to 37¢ an hour. In 1934 she married Jim Totino, a baker. They had two daughters and Rose became a school volunteer and den mother for a Cub Scout troop. For a special treat, she made little Italian pies for the boys with sugar and cinnamon, as her mother did for Rose when she was young. Treating the boys grew into catering larger affairs with dinner pies. Friends urged her to start selling them, so she and Jim, armed with what is now known as pizza, went to the bank. After the banker tasted one, they received a loan of $1,500.

With this loan, they opened Totino's Italian Kitchen in Minneapolis in 1951. It was planned as take-out only, but people ate there standing up, so they added tables and chairs and eventually expanded into the shop next door. They advertised by handing out samples, and Rose did demonstrations on local television. She figured that sales of 25 pizzas a week would pay the rent. Within three weeks Jim quit his bakery job, and they were in business. He made the crusts while she made sauces and toppings; they averaged 120 pizzas per day. For ten years, they worked long hours, selling 400 to 500 pizzas on weekends yet still running out.

After their request for a loan to expand the business was turned down, the Totinos decided to open a plant making frozen dinners and save the profits for a pizza crust–making machine. Despite advice from a consultant, the frozen dinners were a disaster, and they lost the $50,000 they had saved. By 1962 they were almost bankrupt, so they applied for an SBA loan, mortgaged everything they owned, and began all over again, this time concentrating on frozen, bake-at-home pizzas using prebaked crusts. Within three months the business was a success.

They marketed primarily to Minneapolis and later expanded into Denver. Soon a second plant was needed with a second shift of workers. Totino's Pizza became the biggest selling pizza in the United States. A buyer offered them $1 million, which they turned down.

Jim's health began to fail, and in 1971, needing yet another new plant, they decided to sell. There were many prospective buyers, and they chose Pillsbury because it was local and believed in research and development. Pillsbury paid $20 million in stock and hired Rose as vice president of research and development. She was then sixty and Pillsbury's first female vice president. She toured the country on the talk show circuit; it soon became clear that she was a natural salesperson.

Rose Totino was a successful entrepreneur and, according to her employees, a wonderful manager (Pine, p. 154–155). She chose employees she could trust and then gave them complete responsibility for making decisions and executing them. Her motivational power was renowned. She also believed strongly in giving back to her community, donating 5 percent of pre-tax profits to charity. A Catholic high school near the original plant is now named for the Totinos. A grandson has continued to run the original restaurant. In 1993 Totino was the first woman elected to the Frozen Food Hall of Fame.

See also: Food Industry

Further Reading

Pine, Carol. *Self-Made: The Stories of 12 Minnesota Entrepreneurs*, p. 144–159.

Taylor, Russel R. *Exceptional Entrepreneurial Women: Strategies for Success*, p. 94–102.

Thayer, Warren. "The Story of Rose Totino: From Pauper to Pizza Queen."

Tourism Industry, *see* Travel Industry

Traditional Occupations, *see* Nontraditional Occupations

Travel Industry

The travel industry is wide-ranging, covering a number of interrelated disciplines: tourism; hospitality; leisure activities; restaurants; hotels, motels, and inns; resorts; theme parks; cruises; convention bureaus; and welcome centers. This industry has been strong since the settlement of the American colonies, when both women and men ran lodging- and boardinghouses, inns, and taverns.

African American women were street vendors and sold prepared food; they also opened cook shops. During the nineteenth century they were successful in catering because members of the elite society in the cities deemed African American caterers essential to their parties. One Philadelphia caterer in the 1850s charged as much as $50 a plate. African Americans also established exclusive restaurants and hotels, where only white patrons were allowed. The cook shops catered to other African Americans, however. White tavern-keepers and innkeepers also abounded throughout the eighteenth and nineteenth centuries. During the westward movement and the gold rushes, hotels and inns were established as the towns grew. Both Nellie Cashman and Mary Ellen Pleasant took advantage of the mining booms to run boardinghouses and restaurants.

After the Civil War African American catering declined due to increased competition from white caterers, changing food tastes, racial attitudes, and newly required and expensive liquor licenses. Instead, African Americans built hotels and motels for a African American clientele. This area of the industry grew from the 1870s until the 1950s. Meanwhile, the travel industry as a whole was booming. As towns grew into cities, transportation became easier, and people began to take trips in automobiles. More and more activities were offered under the tourism and hospitality umbrellas. The hotel industry alone expanded from individual hotels and motels into inns, spas, bed-and-breakfasts, resorts, residential hotels, economy chains, and extended-stay motels.

Women were always involved, but as entities grew larger and more complex, men became the managers. However, small travel businesses still flourish, and women run many of them. Women own 33 percent of all restaurants in the United States. Although 55 percent of all lodging employees are women, however, only 15 percent of lodging management positions are held by women. The Hospitality Financial and Technology Professionals (www.hftp.org) provides education, training, and certification programs and maintains a hall of fame.

Further Reading
Rowe, Megan. "When Will Women Hit the Top?"
Walker, Juliet E. K. "Catering, Inns, Hotels," p. 128–134.
VNR's Encyclopedia of Hospitality and Tourism.

Trudell, Cynthia (1953–), Automobile Executive, Boat Executive

In 1999 *Fortune* magazine named Cynthia Trudell the forty-second most powerful woman in American business. She was then chairman and president of Saturn and a vice president of General Motors. In March 2001, in a move that shocked the automobile industry, she was named president of Sea Ray Group, a builder of pleasure boats and subsidiary of Brunswick Corporation.

Trudell was born in 1953 in St. John, New Brunswick, Canada. Her father was a car salesman; she helped him as a child and fell in love with cars. Her first car was her dream car—a yellow 1973 Ford Capri with a stick shift. She earned an undergraduate degree in chemistry in three years at Acadia University in Nova Scotia and received her PhD in physical chemistry from the University of Windsor, Ontario. She was always fascinated with why and how things work, and her first degree led her to the study of automotive emissions. She is married to Brian Trudell, a math teacher. They have one son and one daughter.

Her first job was as a chemical processing engineer for Ford Motor Company from 1979 to 1981. She moved to General Motors in 1981, where she was senior engineering supervisor and superintendent of manufacturing at the Windsor Transmission Plant. She was responsible for 150 workers. She held several manufacturing and plant-manager positions of increasing complexity and responsibility until 1997, when she became president of IBC Vehicles, a wholly owned subsidiary of General Motors in Luton, England. One of her main accomplishments was keeping the peace among five unions at its SUV factory.

In January 1999 she became president and chairman of Saturn and a vice president of General Motors, the first woman to run a major division of an automobile manufacturer. Saturn had never been profitable, and Trudell's mission was to change that and to expand the trademark from one model to include a midsize car and an SUV. She spent the first day walking the assembly lines and talking with the workers. She was able to gain the trust of the union leaders and negotiate a new contract that rewarded productivity; however, the new model was unsuccessful and sales slid, so in March 2001, she left to be president of Sea Ray Group, a part of Brunswick Corporation and the world's largest powerboat builder. It was her first experience with boating. The move was a surprise because she loved the automobile industry, particularly the manufacturing side.

Trudell's specialty is fixing problems, whether they come from labor unions or manufacturing. A self-described "factory rat," she was a trailblazer as a woman with manufacturing expertise. She is customer service-oriented and believes strongly in teamwork. At General Motors, the first thing she did was to paint her office pink.

Trudell was the first woman to run a major division of an automobile manufacturer, the first women to head a major car company, and the first to reach the top in any heavy-manufacturing industry. *Business Week* named her an executive to watch in 1999, and she was nominated to the Automotive Hall of Fame in 2000 with a distinguished service citation. She received an honorary doctorate from Ryerson University in Toronto in 2000 and has been on the board of PepsiCo.

See also: Automobile Industry

Further Reading

Bradsher, Keith. "Private Sector: From Factory to the Top of Saturn."

Ferrar, Rebecca. "President of East Knox County, Tenn., Boating Company Discusses Career."

Miller, Karin. "Trudell Settling in as First Woman to Head Major U.S. Car Company."

Turnbo-Malone, Annie, *see* Malone, Annie Turnbo

V

Vernon, Lillian (1927–), Direct Mail Company Owner

Lillian Vernon, maestro of mail order and queen of catalogs, began her business at her kitchen table. She received $32,000 worth of orders in the first six months. It was the beginning of a direct mail empire that by 1999 had sales over $258 million and employed thousands of people. Lillian Vernon Corporation was on the list of top woman-owned businesses published by *Working Woman* since the list began in 1992.

Vernon was born in Germany to a Jewish industrialist. The family had to flee from the Nazis, going first to Holland in 1932, and to New York City in 1937. Her father opened a zipper-reconditioning business, later moving into leather handbags and belts. By the time Lillian was ten she had learned two languages in addition to German and had adapted to two new cultures as well. This experience helped later when she needed to adapt quickly to a variety of business circumstances. From her father she learned perseverance, tenacity, determination, and how to deal with ambiguity. She would later say that he was her most important role model.

Lillian graduated from high school and attended New York University while working at several jobs at once, but stopped her education in 1951 to marry Sam Hochberg, a woman's clothing retailer. As a young, pregnant housewife, she looked around for a way to augment their income. Pregnant women did not generally work outside the home then, so she used $2,000 the couple had gotten as wedding gifts to place an ad in *Seventeen* magazine and buy supplies. The $475 ad was for a monogrammed handbag priced at $1.99. Her biggest selling points were personalization and a ten-year guarantee. She bought the handbags from her father and did all the work herself at the kitchen table. When sales reached $40,000, her husband joined the company and converted his store into their warehouse. She named the company Vernon Specialties after their hometown, Mount Vernon, New York. She expanded into combs, buttons, pins, and other products and also began manufacturing custom-designed products for cosmetics companies. In 1956 she mailed her first catalog to 125,000 people; it was sixteen black-and-white pages.

In 1965 she changed the name of the company to Lillian Vernon Corporation. In 1969 she and Hochberg were divorced. He kept the manufacturing side, and she kept the catalog business. One year later, sales had risen to $1 million. The same year she married Sam Katz, a marriage that would end in divorce in 1990. During the gas crisis of the early 1970s, shoppers were looking for alternative ways to buy what they needed, and catalog sales boomed. Vernon continued to expand her product lines through buying trips to Europe, sending specialty catalogs as well as the regular mailing. Her two sons joined the business, as president and head of public relations. Her older son later left it to become involved in politics. In 1987 they entered the company on the American Stock Exchange, selling 31 percent of it for $28 million. It was the first company founded by a woman to be listed. They used part of the money to build a state-of-the-art distribution center in Virginia Beach.

The company kept growing through more specialty catalogs, outlet stores, a telemarketing center, a catalog on CD-ROM, and, finally, an online catalog. By the end of 2002 online sales accounted for 19 percent of total sales. The distribution center was expanded twice, to over 1 million square feet. Even though profits declined in the mid-1990s due to high paper and postage costs, sales continued to inch up. By 1998 the company's database numbered more than 19 million people, of whom 4.6 million had placed orders. In 1999, the company processed 290,000 orders and employed 5,100 persons during Christmas week. Company headquarters is in Rye, New York.

Vernon taught herself about the mail-order business, how to start a company, and how to manage a growing company. Her basic principles from the beginning were to sell products she would like to have in her own home; to focus on the possibilities, not the problems; to buy and sell good-quality products; and to offer superior customer service. She has said that her two rules for starting a business are pay as you go, and live like a pauper (Taylor, *Exceptional Entrepreneurial Women*, p. 23). She is a natural entrepreneur powered with strong convictions, an autonomous spirit, and the intuition to make important decisions. In 1998 she married again, this time to Paolo Martino. She has said her first two marriages were casualties of the business.

In 2001 the company was fifty years old. In April 2002 Vernon stepped down as CEO, but remains chairman of the board and focuses on long-term strategies.

Her management style is tough but fair. She has attributed her success to the free personalization, the company's money-back guarantee, her intuitive merchandise selections, and her sense of what the moderate-income woman home shopper wants.

She is a strong believer in giving back to the community. The Lillian Vernon Foundation has donated to a variety of causes including homelessness, flood relief, and more than 500 local charities and civic and religious organizations. She endowed a chair at New York University and bought a townhouse for the school's international center. She has been on the board of directors of the Lincoln Center for the Performing Arts, the Virginia Opera, the Kennedy Center for the Performing Arts, the Children's Museum of Art, New York City Meals-on-Wheels, and the Center of Preventive Psychology. She holds honorary degrees from five colleges. She chaired the White House National Business Women's Council and is a director of New York University and Bryant College. President Bill Clinton appointed her Women's Business Counselor. She was part of inc.com's mentoring program. Her many awards include the Direct Marketing Hall of Fame, the Ellis Island Medal of Honor, the Big Brother/Big Sisters National Hero Award, the American Red Cross Good Neighbor Award, and the Gannett Newspaper Business Leadership Award. She was named to the *Working Woman* Hall of Fame in 1986. In 1999 the National Foundation for Woman Business Owners listed her among its 50 Entrepreneurs of the World and *Biography Magazine* named her one of the top women in the United States. She received Ernst & Young's Lifetime Achievement Award in 2002. She is a member of the Committee of 200 and the Women's Forum.

See also: Immigrant Businesswomen; Saleswomen

Further Reading

Current Biography Yearbook, 1996, p. 606–609.

Landrum, Gene N. *Profiles of Female Genius: Thirteen Creative Women Who Changed the World*, p. 346–358.

Rosenfeld, Megan. "The Woman Who Has Everything: For Lillian Vernon, a Business Empire Made to Order."

Vernon, Lillian. *An Eye for Winners: How I Built One of America's Great Businesses—And So Can You.*

Virtual Teams, *see* Flexible Work Arrangements

W

Wachner, Linda Joy (1946–), Clothing Industry Executive

Linda Wachner, the former president, CEO, and chair of Warnaco and CEO and chair of Authentic Fitness Corporation, was the first woman in the United States to capture a company in a hostile takeover and then successfully take it public. Her accomplishment turned Warnaco around and made her one of the wealthiest CEOs in the country. She was the only woman to appear twice on the same *Working Woman* list of top woman-owned businesses, ranked number 9 as chair and president of Warnaco and number 38 as chair and CEO of Authentic Fitness in 1999.

Wachner was born and raised in New York City by a fur salesman father and a homemaker mother. She had a sister who was eighteen years older, so to all intents and purposes Wachner was raised an only child. When she was eleven, a school accident required her to have corrective spinal surgery, and she spent the next year and a half in a cast from her neck to her knees. She decided then that she wanted her own company, and the subsequent years all led her in that direction.

She grew up focused, self-reliant, and introspective, able to concentrate fiercely on a goal for long periods of time. During high school she dreamed of becoming a fashion buyer, and during college vacations she clerked at Best & Company, a department store. In 1966 she graduated from the State University of New York at Buffalo with a BA in economics and business administration.

Wachner's first position was as a buyer's assistant for Associated Merchandise Corporation for $90 per week. Two years later she moved to Houston to become a junior buyer at Foley's. During her lunch hours, she held informal street surveys about the merchandise. Macy's recruited her back to New York

> When she was eleven . . . she decided that she wanted her own company, and the subsequent years all led her in that direction.

as its bra and girdle buyer, and she began educating herself in all aspects of the garment industry. In 1971 she met Seymour Applebaum, an executive for a dressmaking company, on a buying trip. They married in 1973, when she was twenty-seven and he was sixty. Although he was ill during most of their marriage, he supported her in her dreams of business success, telling her that she could achieve anything she really wanted. He died in 1983.

In 1974 Warnaco asked her to improve its bra business. She devised what is now a basic way to display bras, on hangers rather than in boxes. The bras sold, and Wachner was rewarded with a vice presidency, the first woman vice president at that company. In 1977 she became president of Caron International, a yarn manufacturer, in order to learn the manufacturing side of the business, and in 1979 she went to Max Factor as president and chief operating officer, a job created for her. The company had registered a $16 million loss; her job was to turn it around. She did so, and by 1984 profits were $5 million. When Beatrice Foods took over Max Factor that year, Wachner found financing and tried to buy it back, but Beatrice was not interested. One month later she left.

In 1985 Wachner joined a venture capital company, Adler & Shaykin, and eventually looked at Warnaco. Adler & Shaykin didn't take part in hostile takeovers, so she found financing with a California entrepreneur and began a leveraged buyout, buying enough stock to take over the company. She returned to Warnaco, this time as president and CEO. Her partner was a director but took no part in the day-to-day activities.

She had a reputation as a tough manager at Warnaco, with little patience with failure and mediocrity. Her critics have said that she asked more than it was humanly possible to give consistently. She was a workaholic, working an average of twenty hours per day. Her manner was brusque, frank, and honest; she was quick to criticize, but also quick to praise. Employee turnover was high, particularly in the management tier. Her company motto was "Do it now," and each manager had a spiral notebook with the motto printed on the cover. She turned the company around from heavy debt to high profits and was a respected, if sometimes feared, business leader. In 1997 she was the highest-paid executive in the apparel industry and one of only a handful to head two large, publicly held firms simultaneously. In mid-1998, however, the company's financial troubles became overwhelming, and finally, on June 12, 2001, Warnaco filed for bankruptcy. In November 2001 she was asked to resign as CEO.

Wachner has been on the board of directors at Applied Graphics Technology, Travelers' Insurance, and QVC. She was on the New York Stock Exchange Board but resigned in March 2002. She has been a trustee for the University of Buffalo Foundation, Carnegie Hall, and the Aspen Institute and on the board of overseers of the Memorial Sloan-Kettering Cancer Center. She was a presidential appointee to the federal Advisory Committee for Trade, Policy, and Negotiations. In 1980 she was named Outstanding Woman in Business by the Women's Equity Action League, and in 1986, Woman of the Year by *Ms. Magazine. Savvy* listed her as one of the most powerful women in corporate America in 1989, and *Fortune* called her one of the year's most fascinating businesspeople in 1987 and America's most successful businesswoman in 1992. Also in 1992, *Business Week* listed her as one of the fifty top women in business. One year later *Fortune* called her one of the seven toughest bosses in American business. In 1995 she was named to the YMCA Academy of Women Achievers.

See also: Fashion Industry; Retailing Industry

Further Reading

Landrum, Gene N. *Profiles of Female Genius: Thirteen Creative Women Who Changed the World*, p. 360–372.

Monget, Karyn. "The Wachner Way."

Strom, Stephanie. "Fashion Avenue's $100 Million Woman."

Waldo, Ruth Fanshaw (1885–1975), Advertising Executive

Ruth Waldo was one of the leading women in advertising during the 1930s and 1940s, a period of enormous growth in the industry. She began on the creative side as a copywriter and eventually became the first woman vice president of the advertising agency J. Walter Thompson. Waldo was born in Connecticut, the oldest of three daughters. After receiving an AB in languages from Adelphi College in 1909 and a master's degree from Columbia University in 1910, she worked as a social worker for four years.

Her career in advertising began in 1915 as the result of a friendship with Helen Resor. Resor's husband had bought J. Walter Thompson and invited Waldo to work there as a copywriter. She did, for $15 per week. In the early twentieth century, advertising was totally dependent on printed words and artists' drawings, and Waldo found that she was talented and creative with words and slogans. In the early 1920s she was sent to the London office.

Companies were becoming aware of two business truths: advertising was becoming a necessity, and housewives controlled the spending of more and more of the family income. In 1930 Waldo came back to New York to supervise women's copy for the agency. She was responsible for many advertising campaigns that became household catchphrases. One of the most famous was for Pond's cold cream: "She's lovely! She's engaged! She uses Pond's!" Aimed directly at women, these ads were very successful.

She encouraged her women copywriters to wear hats at work to distinguish them from the secretaries and to underline their status as creative professionals. In 1914 she was appointed vice president, the first woman at that rank in the agency. She was proud of that, and particularly that she was the first of many women to achieve that status.

Waldo was successful in the volatile advertising industry for many reasons. She was creative with words and also had a knack for getting along with difficult people and adapting readily to changes in the world. Her advertising approach changed first with the Great Depression, then with World War II, and then with the advent of television. She never married: Work was her life, and she found it of never-ending interest.

Waldo retired in 1960 and established a trust fund with the principal to be divided at her death between Adelphi University and the American Friends Service Committee. She died in 1975 at age eighty-nine, leaving her nineteenth-century Waldo Homestead to the public.

See also: Advertising Industry

Further Reading
Martin, Albro. "Waldo, Ruth Fanshaw, December 8, 1885–August 30, 1975: Advertising Executive." In Barbara Sicherman and Carol Hurd Green, eds., p. 715–716.
Waldo, Ruth. "Invention—the Essence of Advertising."

Walker, Maggie Lena (1867–1934), Banker, Insurance Industry Pioneer

After Maggie Walker died, a letter from Eleanor Roosevelt was found among her treasures. It said, "I cannot imagine anything more satisfying than a life of the kind of accomplishments which you have had. I congratulate you" (Longwell, *America and Women*, p. 205). This was a fitting tribute for a woman who was the first woman bank president in the United States and single-handedly improved the economic life of African Americans in Richmond, Virginia.

Walker was born in 1867 in segregated Richmond to a free cook's helper in the house of Elizabeth Van Lew, a Union spy during the Civil War and an ardent abolitionist. Her early childhood was a happy one; she received exceptional encouragement in her education and other endeavors. Her mother married the butler, who took a position as headwaiter in the newest hotel in the city. He was murdered in 1876, leaving the family without money, so her mother took in laundry and Walker picked it up and delivered it. She completed high school, graduating from the Normal School at the head of her class in 1883. She was a part of the first school strike in the United States when her class refused to receive their diplomas in the African American church, insisting that they get them in the auditorium where the white students did. They were finally seated in the auditorium, but separated from the white students and their families, in a partial victory. She taught school for three years until she married Armstead Walker in 1886. He was older and a part of Richmond's African American society, where women of that class took their customary place. The Walkers had four children, three boys, one of whom died in infancy, and an adopted daughter.

The life of leisure did not suit Walker. In high school she had joined the Independent Order of St. Luke's, a mutual aid society and insurance provider, and now she became really involved. Due to a Prudential study showing that African Americans were shorter-lived than whites, African Americans could not get life insurance or were offered reduced benefits. As a result, mutual aid societies sprang up around the country, providing care for the sick and destitute and burial benefits. Walker worked her way up in the hierarchy; one of her major accomplishments was starting a juvenile division. In 1899 she was elected right worthy grand secretary, effectively the leader of the organization. Her salary was $8 a month, and her duties were to collect dues, verify cases of illness and death, keep the books, and pay claims.

When she took over, the treasury had $31.61 and about $400 in unpaid bills. There were 1,080 members. Walker began a membership drive, and her charismatic style convinced people to join in droves. In her first year, membership doubled. Members had to believe in a supreme being, and dues were 50¢ per month. The society prospered under her leadership for the next twenty-five years. By 1924 membership had grown to more than 50,000 with assets of $400,000; the 57 local chapters ballooned to 1,500 in twenty-two states, and instead of one clerk, the staff numbered fifty.

Walker's vision encompassed far more than just increasing membership. It focused on African American cooperative enterprise and economic independence from whites—with a dash of women's equality thrown in. She expanded the organization's financial activities and in 1903 started the St. Luke Penny Savings Bank and became its president. She taught herself banking by spending several hours per day at another Richmond bank. Her goals for the bank was to house the society's funds and to help its members save money and buy homes. The bank offered low-cost mortgages; encouraged savings, particularly for children; and eventually became a depository for gas and water payments and for city taxes. It was very influential in segregated Richmond. Federal and state regulations forced it to break its tie with the Independent Order of St. Luke's, and during the Great Depression it merged with other African American–owned banks to form the Consolidated Bank and Trust Company. Walker resigned as president but remained chairman of the board until her death.

Walker also founded a newspaper for the order and opened a department store. The latter foundered after six years due to stiff opposition from white retailers and lack of support from the more affluent African American community. In 1924 the Order of St. Luke honored her at its twenty-fifth anniversary gathering. Active in charitable endeavors, she founded the Richmond Council of Colored Women, was active on NAACP boards both locally and nationally, and ran for public office. She loved children and lived with her extended family. In 1925 she received an honorary degree from Virginia Union University, where she served as a trustee.

In 1934 Walker died of gangrene caused by a 1907 accident. Eventually confined to a wheelchair, she was known in later years as the Lame Lioness. Her funeral was one of the largest ever held in Richmond. Her obituary read, "In solid achievement, [Walker] was one of three or four of the ablest women her race ever produced in America" (Duckworth in Smith, *Notable Black American Women*, p. 1187). Walker was not only an astute businesswoman but also a champion of equal rights for African Americans and women. She helped her people in Richmond both economically and spiritually. She is honored with a street, a high school, and a theater named for her, and the city celebrates Maggie Walker Day. Her house, a national landmark, was featured in a 2000 television special, "Our Heritage: Homes of African American Visionaries." The Consolidated Bank and Trust was still doing business in 2004, the oldest continuously operating African American–owned bank in the United States. Walker was inducted into the Junior Achievement's Global Business Hall of Fame in 2001.

> "In solid achievement, [Walker] was one of three or four of the ablest women her race ever produced in America."

See also: African American Businesswomen; Banking; Insurance Industry

Further Reading

Bird, Caroline. *Enterprising Women*, p. 166–171.

Chandler, Sally. "Maggie Lena Walker (1867–1934): An Abstract of Her Life and Activities."

Dabney, Wendell P. *Maggie L. Walker and the I.O. of St. Luke: The Woman and Her Work.*

Duckworth, Margaret. "Maggie L. Walker." In Jessie Carney Smith, ed., *Notable Black American Women*, p. 1188–1193.

Walker, Sarah Breedlove (Madame C.J.), (1867–1919), Haircare Manufacturer

Sarah Walker was an African American inventor and entrepreneur, manufacturer and philanthropist, the founder of Madame C.J. Walker Manufacturing Company, and the first self-made African American millionaire.

The daughter of Louisiana sharecroppers, Walker was orphaned at six and married at fourteen. Six years later her husband was killed (it was rumored that he was lynched), leaving her barely literate and unskilled with a two-year-old daughter. She made her way up the Mississippi River to St. Louis, where she worked as a washerwoman and a domestic servant. Between 1900 and 1905 she noticed that she was losing her hair, so she began experimenting with the chemicals she used in washing. She eventually developed a hair-care formula for African American women. She later said that the secret ingredient came to her in a dream. Others claimed that she got a hair-care product from Annie Turnbo Malone's Poro Company and analyzed, copied, and sold it. She also improved the hot comb, making it from steel. With the comb and her ointment, she developed the Walker System for straightening hair, which she sold door-to-door. In 1905 she moved to Denver, where she continued door-to-door sales. There she met Charles Walker, who suggested she call herself Madame C.J. Walker. They later married.

As the popularity of her treatment grew, Walker began training agents whom she called hair culturists or scalp culturists. They not only learned hair-care methods but also how to manufacture the products. Walker added lessons in personal hygiene, cleanliness, and a neat appearance. Expansion in the East and South was rapid due to her extensive traveling. In 1906 her daughter, A'Lelia, was put in charge of mail orders in Pittsburgh. In 1908 Sarah Walker set up an office there and founded Lelia College, which offered a $25 correspondence course. By this time a headquarters was needed, and in 1910 she built a large factory in Indianapolis. She eventually added a training center, research laboratory, and an additional beauty school. In 1911 she incorporated and was the sole stockholder. At that time the company employed fifty factory workers and more than 2,000 women agents giving home treatments around the country. She had many products now: hair grower, shampoo, gossine, and tetter salve.

Her next idea was Walker Clubs for her agents. The concept focused on community philanthropy but also included cash prizes for the agents to attend annual national conventions, where they learned new techniques and shared their experiences through personal success stories. By 1917, when the first convention was held, the company was the largest African American–owned business in the United States, earning $500,000 annually. At the time of her death in 1919 Madame C.J. Walker was a millionaire with many real estate holdings. The company went to her daughter. It peaked in 1920 with sales of $595,000; then sales declined as first the Great Depression, then World War II, then postwar competition killed it. In 1985 it was sold.

Madame C.J. Walker is remembered for many reasons. She took pride in being an African American woman and instilled that same pride in her agents. She worked tirelessly and gave back some of what she made through generous contributions to the NAACP and scholarships for women at Tuskegee Institute. For many of her agents, the work was one of the few respectable ways out of domestic servitude. She received substantial posthumous recognition. She was named to the Junior Achievement's Global Business Hall of Fame, and in 1997 she appeared on a U.S. postage stamp. In 1998 she was part of the *Time* 100 Builders and Titans of the 20th Century. Her estate, Lewaro, is a national monument. She is also in the National Women's Hall of Fame. In 1999 *Ebony* voted her one of the 100 Most Fascinating Women of the Twentieth

Century. In 2001 A'Lelia Bundles, her great-great-granddaughter, wrote the first comprehensive biography about her. A park in Denver was named for her in May 2002.

See also: African American Businesswomen; Beauty Industry

Further Reading

Bundles, A'Lelia. *On Her Own Ground: The Life and Times of Madam C.J. Walker.*

Elliott, Joan Curl. "Madame C.J. Walker." In Jessie Carney Smith, ed., *Notable Black American Women*, p. 1184–1188.

Ingham, John N., and Lynne B. Feldman. *African-American Business Leaders: A Biographical Dictionary*, p. 68–69.

Leavitt, Judith A. *American Women Managers and Administrators: A Selective Biographical Dictionary of Twentieth-Century Leaders in Business, Education, and Government.* p. 281–282.

Wallace, Lila Acheson (1889–1984), Magazine Publisher

Lila and DeWitt Wallace founded the *Reader's Digest* in 1921 in the living room of their Greenwich Village apartment. Their first issue had thirty-one articles, one for each day of the month, that DeWitt had condensed in longhand from magazines in the New York Public Library. Lila encouraged him, stuffed envelopes, and sent out subscription appeals. Then they went on a belated honeymoon. When they returned, there was money from 1,500 subscribers, each paying $3 for a year's subscription.

The Wallaces were both born to Presbyterian ministers, Lila in Virden, Manitoba, where her father was studying. The family moved to the United States soon after her birth and eventually settled in Tacoma, Washington. Lila met DeWitt in 1911 when her brother brought him home for a visit. The two were college roommates. After she graduated from the University of Oregon in 1917, she taught high school for two years and then worked for the YWCA in several capacities. In 1920 she was sent to establish an industrial YWCA in cities all over the United States, ending up in New York. Legend has it that DeWitt, who was in St. Paul at the time, ran into her brother and asked about Lila. He sent her a telegram: "Conditions among women workers in St. Paul ghastly. Suggest you investigate" (Roosevelt, *Doers and Dowagers*, p. 190). They were married one year later.

Lila worked at three jobs after they were married, so that DeWitt could pursue his dream of a magazine that condensed important articles. He borrowed $1,500 to put out the first issue. The circulation was 5,000, all that they had printed. The magazine's format never changed while they were alive. His criteria for articles were that they be significant, quotable, and discussable; that the average person could relate to the subject matter; and that they still be interesting in a couple of years. The magazine was a success from the beginning. In 1926 they had 30,000 subscribers, in 1929 there were 300,000 subscribers, and in 1939, over 3 million. As they expanded, they moved into larger quarters, and in the mid-1930s, they built the present plant for $1.5 million on eighty acres in Pleasantville, New York. Lila planned the new building, the landscaping, and the interior decoration on the principle that people deserved a beautiful workplace. She intended to design an industrial showcase and did just that. She also decided on Pegasus for the *Reader's Digest* symbol.

In 1929 the Wallaces had a gross income of over $600,000. That year they began to pay other magazines for reprint rights. They also put *Reader's Digest* on newsstands. In 1933 they began to publish original articles, some of which introduced important writers of the day such as James Michener, Alexander Woollcott, Fulton Oursler, and John Gunther. In 1938 they published the first British edition, and they later expanded into foreign-language editions. They accepted no advertising until 1954 and after that no ads for liquor, cigarettes, or drugs. In 1978 they allowed beer and wine ads, and the next year, hard liquor. Cigarettes were never advertised, and their articles pointed out the dangers of smoking long before the U.S. surgeon general's report. The first annual sweepstakes was held in 1961 in an effort to boost circulation. By 1980 circulation was 18 million in the United States and 12 million abroad, making it the world's largest circulating magazine.

Lila Wallace's responsibility for content was indirect. She sometimes suggested ideas for articles. She was responsible for generous employee benefits including a subsidized cafeteria and bonuses. Also, one child from each worker's family who wished to go to Europe would be supported for a visit of up to six weeks. The only caveat was that they believe in and promote the American way of life.

The Wallaces owned all of the stock of the company: Dewitt had 51 percent and Lila had 49 percent. Some employees were rewarded with non-voting stock. The Wallaces were co-chairmen until 1973, when she resigned but stayed on the board of directors. They donated more than $60 million to institutions including the Metropolitan Museum of Art, the University of Oregon, the Juilliard School of Music; to restorations of The Boscobel Mansion on the Hudson River and Monet's house and grounds at Giverny, France; and to the Save Abu Simbel Fund, Lincoln Center, and the Bronx Zoo. New York City named its floating hospital for her. She was also an avid art collector and displayed some of her collection in offices in the *Reader's Digest* building. When DeWitt died in 1981 Lila became the sole owner of the company. She set up the Lila Wallace–Reader's Digest Fund, which awards grants for improving adult literacy and supports the cultural and performing arts in communities.

In 1954 she joined the board of directors for the New York Central Railroad, the only woman member of a major railroad board. Both Wallaces won an award for distinguished service from the Theodore Roosevelt Association in

1954 and in 1972 were awarded the Medal of Freedom, bestowed by Richard Nixon. In 1980 they were named to the National Business Hall of Fame. They also appear on a postage stamp as part of the Great Americans series.

See also: Publishing Industry

Further Reading

Heidenry, John. *Theirs Was the Kingdom: Lila and Dewitt Wallace and the Story of the Reader's Digest.*

"Wallace, Lila Acheson." In *Current Biography Yearbook,* 1956, p. 637–640.

Wood, James Playsted. *Of Lasting Interest: The Story of the "Reader's Digest."*

Washington, Ruth (1914–1990), Newspaper Publisher

Ruth Washington was the business manager and, after her husband died, publisher of the *Los Angeles Sentinel,* one of the first African American newspapers in Los Angeles. Leon Washington, a noted civil rights activist, had established the paper in 1933, and she kept it alive and flourishing during his illness and after his death.

Washington was born in Salina, Kansas. Her father died in World War I, and her mother, a caterer, raised Ruth and her two sisters. She attended schools in Denver and Kansas City, the Emily Griffith Opportunity School in Denver, and the Metropolitan Business School in Los Angeles. She learned photography retouching and, after graduation, opened Avalon Photographers in 1940. That year she also married Leon Washington.

The photography business was a success, serving African American entertainers and actors as well as families, but Leon had a sudden stroke in 1948, so she took over *Los Angeles Sentinel* while he recuperated. Although she knew nothing about the newspaper business, she learned as she went along, making notes, studying white newspapers for format and other ideas, and, at first, micromanaging until she learned what each department did. She purchased a $25,000 block-long building so the paper could expand. When Leon returned to work she stayed on as business manager. Under her management the number of employees increased from eight to forty-nine. She hired the best staff she could find, including fine African American writers that white newspapers would not employ. Her agenda was to provide community coverage. During the mid-1960s, she met with gang members and told them the *Sentinel* would print their views as a part of her effort to involve and report on the community.

Leon died in 1974 and Ruth became publisher. There was a long court battle over the newspaper. Although he had left her 80 percent of the stock, his sister and a son who owned 20 percent of the stock tried to prove that she was mismanaging the paper. In 1983 she put her friend and longtime attorney, Ken Thomas, in control while she continued as publisher. In 1987 the court case finally concluded with a win for her. She and Thomas remained as publisher and CEO, respectively, until her death.

The newspaper's circulation was at its height during the 1960s, numbering 56,000 readers. It declined during the 1980s and 1990s as the population changed and African Americans moved to the suburbs. It was one of the most influential papers of its time and place. Both Ruth Washington and the paper received many awards and testimonials of appreciation throughout the years.

See also: African American Businesswomen; Publishing Industry

Further Reading

Ehrhart-Morrison, Dorothy. *No Mountain High Enough: Secrets of Successful African American Women*, p. 25, 143–146.

"Ruth Washington Dies; Was *Sentinel* Publisher."

Weinstein, Marta (1957–), Supply Chain Executive

Marta Weinstein and her husband, Steve Weinstein, founded Logistix in 1984. The company, later called iLogistix, was on *Working Woman*'s list of the top woman-owned companies from 1995 until the demise of the magazine and list in 2001. Neither Marta nor Steve Weinstein attended college; in fact, Marta had no formal education after age sixteen.

They began their company doing marketing and promotions for computer companies and soon expanded into providing services such as assembly, materials planning, and some packaging design for software and computer-access kits. Their first large client was Apple Computer, when the Macintosh was launched. Throughout the first half of the 1990s, Apple was their only large client, but after 1995 they expanded into Ireland and broadened services to include Microsoft and other large clients. In 1996 they experienced a 33 percent growth rate that continued into 1997. Both Weinsteins were active until then, but hired an outside CEO in the late 1990s. Steve Weinstein remained as chairman of the board.

In April 2000 the company changed its name to iLogistix to reflect its expanding capabilities in e-commerce, e-fulfillment, and other online activities. Its customers included Qualcomm, Hewlett-Packard, Compaq, Microsoft, Dell, Agilent, Apple, Adobe, and IBM. In 2001 Marta Weinstein returned as CEO. However, the company was in financial trouble due to the depressed electronics industry and the bad economy. That spring it filed for bankruptcy protection. It still had $600 million in sales but large debts too. In July 2002 CMGI bought it for approximately $46 million.

The Weinsteins had no particular expertise when they began their company; they just saw a niche and began providing the services to fill it. They felt that they were a good match since she is conservative and an "inside" person, while he is good at sales and an "outside" person (Bamford, p. 40). They expanded their company successfully for almost twenty years by focusing on improving their services.

See also: Information Technology Industry

Further Reading

Bamford, Janet. "The 51% Solution: Marta Weinstein; Cofounder of Logistix."

Wells, Mary, *see* Lawrence, Mary Wells

Western Businesswomen

During the nineteenth century and the years of the westward movement, women who made money or did business were largely ignored. In fact, until 1850 the U.S. census dismissed them as not gainfully employed. However, women in the West were more free than women in the East, where Victorianism was rearing its repressive head. Many Western women were involved in moneymaking activities. On the wagon trains, they traded or bartered with one another and with American Indians. The farm women, homesteaders, and ranch women also bartered or sold their produce, dairy products, and other domestic goods to help the family income. Many took in boarders. Because the men were away so much of the time, the women often ran the farm, homestead, or ranch.

In the mining camps women were among the prospectors. Many ran restaurants, stores, and post offices to earn money for their claims. Others were prostitutes, or "soiled doves." In Helena, Montana, prostitution was the largest employer of women from 1865 to 1886. Many women's names were on the registers of claims, although some men put women's names on them to distinguish one claim from another. Sally Zanjani found seventy-seven "whose [mining] activities could be dated with reasonable certainty" (*A Mine of Her Own*, p. 301). Dance-hall girls and theater performers were also popular in gold rush boomtowns.

Many women owned ranches and farms. The Homestead Act guaranteed 160 acres to anyone who staked a claim and worked the land for a period of time. Hispanic women had always had the right to own land. Many African Americans saved the money they earned as cooks and laundresses to buy real estate. "When the market economy developed in any given area of the West, the new system revolutionized women's lives" (Riley and Etulain, *By Grit & Grace*, p. x). Towns grew, as did the need for restaurants, hotels, grocery and dry goods stores, seamstresses, and milliners. Women ran post offices and published newspapers. They hired out as cooks and laundresses. One even became a vintner.

Women were scarce in the early West, but they were not pampered. They were, for the most part, self-sufficient and valued for their skills. White women were treated gallantly; many minority women were not. A few, such as Mary Ellen Pleasant and Biddy Mason, managed to prosper in spite of racial prejudice and discriminatory policies. The women who went West, whether married or single (and there were many single women), saw the West as a place of opportunity and independence.

See also: Agriculture/Ranching; Mining Industry; Travel Industry

Further Reading

Gray, Dorothy. *Women of the West.*

Riley, Glenda. *The Female Frontier.*

Zanjani, Sally. *A Mine of Her Own: Women Prospectors in the American West, 1850–1950.*

White, Eartha Mary Magdalene (1876–1974), Entrepreneur, Real Estate Owner

Eartha White is an outstanding example of an entrepreneur who bought small business ventures, built them into successful endeavors, and sold them at a profit, using her profits to make a better life for the community, particularly the African American community of Jacksonville, Florida. Her investment portfolio was eventually worth more than $1 million.

White was born in Jacksonville to a former slave and an unnamed prominent white man and was adopted as a baby by freed slaves Clara and Lafayette White. Her adoptive parents took great pride in their heritage; her father had served in the Civil War in the 34th Regiment, Company D, U.S. Colored Troops. He died when Eartha was five. Her mother worked as a maid, cook, and stewardess for several steamship lines. In 1888 there was an outbreak of yellow fever in Florida, and Clara White moved them both to New York City, where Eartha attended several schools. The last was Madame Thurber's National Conservatory of Music. She took voice lessons and was asked to join the Oriental-American Opera Company, a touring company that traveled to Europe, Asia, and all over the United States. She fell in love and planned to marry, but her fiancé died one month before the wedding. Apparently she swore never to get married. She gave up singing and returned to Jacksonville. The year was 1896.

She taught for a while and worked as a clerk for the Afro-American Life Insurance Company, which was founded by her church. In 1904 she embarked upon her life of entrepreneurship with $150 she had saved from teaching. She opened a department store for the African American community that became very successful, and she began acquiring real estate. She sold the store at a profit and started another venture, and followed the same pattern: buy a small business; build it into a larger, successful business; sell it for a profit; and buy a new business. During her lifetime she owned a dry-goods store, a general store, an employment agency, a taxi service, a janitorial service, a real estate business, and a steam laundry.

White was unusual in that she used all of her profits to support her philanthropic activities. She was known as the "Angel of Mercy" in Jacksonville; she saw acute community needs and did something to help. For years she operated the only orphanage in Florida for African American children. In 1904 she opened the Boy's Improvement Center, for boys who would otherwise have gone to jail. After failing to raise money for a recreational center, she received a donation of land for a park and paid someone from her own funds to run a recreational program. The city eventually took it over. For fifty years, she ran Sunday Bible classes at the county prison.

Her crowning achievement was the establishment of the Clara White Mission, in memory of her mother. She made her home there among Jacksonville's transient and homeless population. During the Great Depression the mission served as a Salvation Army Soup Kitchen and headquarters for various Works Progress Administration activities. Later it housed a home for unwed mothers, an orphanage and placement center for children, a tuberculosis rest home, and the Harriet Beecher Stowe Community Center. In 1976 she established the Eartha M. White Nursing Home for state and county welfare patients, putting up her own money and then receiving federal grants.

White was politically active, on the conservative side at first. She firmly believed in desegregation and protested in a genteel way. She was a charter member of Booker T. Washington's National Business League. She was also active in several World War I activities, and as World War II approached she became more radical. With A. Philip Randolph, she planned a march on Washington. It never took place but led directly to the issuance of Executive Order 8802, which banned discrimination in employment in the defense industry and the federal government. It also established the Fair Employment Practices Committee.

She received many awards, including the Good Citizenship Award from the local Jaycees in 1969, the Lane Bryant Volunteer Award in 1970, an appointment to the President's National Center for Voluntary Action in 1971, and the Booker T. Washington Symbol of Service Award from the National Negro Business League in 1973. White led a long and rewarding life, using her hard-earned money for good works that made a difference to her community and to the United States. She died in 1974.

See also: African American Businesswomen; Entrepreneurs

Further Reading

Perry, Mary Elizabeth. "White, Eartha Mary Magdalene." In John A. Garraty and Mark C. Carnes, eds., p. 190–191.

Schafer, Daniel, "White, Eartha Mary Magdalene." In Barbara Sicherman and Carol Hurd Green, eds., p. 726–728.

Warren, Nagueyalti. "Eartha White." In Jessie Carney Smith, ed., p. 1249–1251.

Whitman, Meg (1956–), Information Technology Executive

Meg Whitman is president and CEO of eBay, among the Internet's busiest and most profitable sites. On the strength of the success of the company's initial public offering, then the most successful IPO of a high-technology company, she was ranked number 5 on the 1999 *Fortune* list of the most powerful women in American business and number 5 on the timedigital.com list of the "D50" executives. In 2003 she was ranked number 2 by *Fortune*.

Whitman was raised on Long Island, the second daughter of a business executive father and a homemaker mother. During her childhood the family were avid campers. Her mother once took a three-month camping trip with her children, a friend, and her friend's five children across Canada and up the Alaskan highway. The family also went on annual camping trips to the Virgin Islands. Camping taught Whitman to adjust and to make do with what was there (Holson, p. 1). Her first job was as a snack bar cook and general manager at a dude ranch in Wyoming. It taught her that hard work makes everything go well and that businesses, even small ones, do not run themselves. She went to Princeton, intending to take premedical courses, but a summer job selling advertising for the university newspaper changed the direction of her studies. She graduated with a degree in economics in 1977, and went on to receive an MBA from Harvard University two years later.

She embarked on a series of corporate marketing positions beginning with a stint at Procter & Gamble as a brand manager. In 1981 Whitman moved to Bain & Company as a vice president and stayed there ten years. In 1979 she married Griffith R. Harsh, IV, and they had two sons. Her next job was for Walt Disney's consumer products division as senior vice president of marketing. Her husband, who is a neurosurgeon, was interning at the time. She moved to Keds in 1993 as a senior vice president and eventually became president of its StrideRite Division. In 1995 she became president of FTD (Florists Transworld Delivery), an association in the process of becoming a private company. A month after she was hired she was made its CEO. She managed the transition and launched a Web site but then resigned, claiming she was unable to fix the business. She moved to Hasbro as president of its preschool division.

In 1995 Pierre Omidyar founded eBay to find buyers for his girlfriend's collection of Pez dispensers. eBay became a successful online auction site, and in 1998 Omidyar hired Whitman as president and CEO to provide business and marketing experience. He stayed as chairman of the board. She began by hiring a marketing expert, changing the site to make it look more professional, and adopting a strategy to prevent fraud. She set up a trust and safety program, hired Lloyd's of London to insure items, and inaugurated the Feedback Forum for buyers and sellers. She moved firearms and pornography to an adults-only site and eventually banned firearms totally. Next, she took the company public in what was then the most exciting high-tech IPO. The stock opened at $6 a share and rose to $18.08 by the end of the day. The next day it jumped to $47.18.

In April 1998 Whitman purchased the auctioneer Butterfield & Butterfield for $260 million, and the following April she signed a three-year contract with AOL. In 1999 she hired Sun Microsystems to maintain eBay's network and created a backup system. She has expanded the kinds of items sold, formed more partnerships, and moved into other countries.

She is an extremely hard worker. When the system crashed, she worked 100 hours a week for four weeks, learning everything about the system so that it would not happen again. Although Whitman had little technology background when she joined eBay, she understood and shared the company's vision and values. She is comfortable with change and can make fast decisions, a necessity in this environment (Sellers, Patricia, p. 96–98).

> She is an extremely hard worker. When the system crashed, she worked 100 hours a week for four weeks.

Whitman has been on the boards of Staples Inc., Bizbuyer.com, and Goldman Sachs, but resigned from the latter in 2002. In 1998 she won the Class of 1998 *People and Product* Award for most likely to succeed, and in 1999 *Business Week* named her a top entrepreneur and a member of the eBiz25. She was the keynote speaker at the Internet Global summit INET '99; one of *Business Week*'s 2001 top twenty-five managers; and eighth on *Time*'s 2001 list of most influential CEOs. In 2002 *Worth Magazine* called her the best overall CEO. Whitman and eBay partnered with SeniorNet in 2000 in the eBay Digital Opportunity Program for Seniors, and after the September 11 terrorist attacks raised $10 million for New York City. Whitman personally gave $30 million to Princeton toward the construction of a new residential college to be named for her.

See also: Information Technology Industry

Further Reading

Cohen, Adam. *The Perfect Store: Inside eBay.*

Holson, Laura M. "Defining the On-Line Chief: Ebay's Meg Whitman Explores Management, Web Style."

Roth, Daniel. "Meg Muscles eBay Uptown."

"Whitman, Meg." In *Current Biography Yearbook*, February 2000, pp. 86–91.

Whittelsey, Abigail Goodrich (1788–1858), Magazine Publisher

Abigail Whittelsey was the first editor of *Mother's Magazine*, the first magazine for mothers. It is unclear whether she was ever its publisher, but she did launch her own magazine, *Mrs. Whittelsey's Magazine for Mothers*, which she published for two years. Whittelsey was born in Connecticut to a minister and his wife, the third of three daughters. Theirs was an educated farm family who read books whenever they could. Abigail attended the local schools. In 1808 she married the Reverend Samuel Whittelsey, and they moved to New Preston, Connecticut, where he was the minister of the Congregational church for ten years. They moved twice more in the next ten years, and she had seven children, two of whom died at an early age.

In 1828 the Whittelseys established a school for girls in Utica, New York. Abigail became interested in the Maternal Association of Utica. It decided to launch a magazine directed at mothers and asked her to be editor. *Mother's Magazine* was the first such publication in the United States. It published articles about discipline, physical care, and the general responsibilities of motherhood. It also espoused better schools, caring for poor children and orphans as well as the children of missionaries, and the formation of maternal associations elsewhere. Its tone was didactic and heavily religious, but the articles were full of commonsense, practical solutions to the problems of raising children. The first issue came out in January 1833.

The following year the Whittelseys moved to New York City and so did the magazine. Whether they became the publishers at this time is not clear, but the magazine continued and by 1837 had a circulation of 10,000. Samuel Whittelsey died in 1842, and Abigail continued it with the aid of her brother-in-law. In 1848 it was sold. The new owner merged it with another magazine, *Mother's Journal*, and she left. In 1850 she began *Mrs. Whittelsey's Magazine for Mothers*, aided by her son Henry. It was similar to the other magazine.

See also: Publishing Industry

Further Reading
McHenry, Robert, ed. *Famous American Women: A Biographical Dictionary from Colonial Times to the Present*, p. 443.
Tyler, Alice Felt. "Whittelsey, Abigail Goodrich." In Edward T. James, ed., p. 604–605.

Williams, Gretchen, *see* Minyard, Liz

Willingham, Deborah (1951–), Software Manufacturing Executive

Before she retired in February 2003 Deborah Willingham was the highest ranking woman at Microsoft. The responsibilities of her positions as vice president of the Enterprise Customer Unit and the Windows Division put her on *Fortune's* 1998 and 1999 lists of the most powerful women in corporate America at numbers 31 and 30, respectively.

Willingham was born in a suburb of Atlanta, Georgia, one of four children. She credits her father with developing her qualities of resilience and perseverance and instilling in her the notion of never being financially dependent on anyone. She graduated from Georgia Institute of Technology with a degree in industrial and systems engineering. She has been married twice and has two sons and a stepson.

After graduation from college she took a job at IBM, where she became known as a problem solver. She held many jobs in management in its hardware manufacturing and development divisions and by 1990 was in charge of the AS-400 manufacturing business. That year the division won the coveted Malcolm Baldrige Award for customer service.

In February 1993 she joined Microsoft, attracted by the possibilities and the company's informal work culture. Her first position was as general manager for end-user support. Her focus was on responsiveness and streamlining the organization. She broadened her scope to include technical support for global and U.S. customers for all electronic services and was soon promoted to vice president of Microsoft Support Services. During the debut of Windows '95, the division handled 20,000 questions daily. In 1996 she became vice president of the Enterprise Customer Unit, which by 1998 was responsible for over a third of the company's $11 billion annual revenues. In her next position she was responsible for marketing Windows 2000. In April 2000 she changed course and became vice president of Human Relations. She began to increase recruiting and mentoring efforts for women employees, particularly for senior management positions. She also introduced new stock options and more flexible vacation schedules. In November 2000 the company granted $100,000 to the Society of Women Engineers for educational programs.

Willingham is approachable and was popular with clients, who liked her empathy and dependability. She has a relaxed style and is quiet but intense. She enjoys a certain amount of creative risk, particularly in problem solving. Her willingness to take on jobs no one else wanted took her far at both IBM and Microsoft. She was very close to her employees, and particularly empathetic to their stress levels. They have talked about how she would devise ways to let them blow off steam at times of high stress. Her focus was always on motivation and leadership, one reason she moved into human relations.

She has said that she had problems balancing her career and personal life, but reached solutions. One incident involved taking a helicopter from a meeting at Bill Gates's compound and back in order to hear her eleven-year-old son's speech at school. She has been on the board of the Seattle YWCA.

See also: Information Technology Industry

Further Reading

Andrews, Paul. "At the Center of Reshaping the New Microsoft—Vice President Deborah Willingham Stresses Service to Corporate Customers."

Dudley, Brier. "Microsoft's Human-Resources Chief to Retire in February."

McGee, Marianne Kolbasuk. "Leaders among Leaders—IT Has Traditionally Been a Man's World, Especially in the Upper Echelons of Management."

Willis, Gertrude Pocte Geddes (1878–1970), Funeral Home and Insurance Company Owner

Gertrude Willis and her husband Clem Geddes founded an insurance company and funeral parlor in New Orleans in 1909. After his death she built it into a major African American–owned insurance companies, one which still exists today.

Willis was born near the small fishing community of Happy Jack, Louisiana, one of three daughters. Her family moved to New Orleans when she was small, and there she received an elementary school education. She married Clem Geddes, one of three sons of a funeral home operator. All three sons went into the business. In 1909 Clem and Gertrude partnered with a local barber, Arnold Moss, to form their own company that sold both insurance and funeral home services. They called their company Geddes and Moss. Clem died in 1913 and Gertrude continued the partnership with Moss until 1940, when she reorganized under the name Gertrude Geddes Willis Funeral Home and Life Insurance Company.

She had married William Willis, a dentist, in 1919. He died in 1947. Although they had no children, other family members have kept her business going, and it was ranked by *Black Enterprise* as the twelfth-largest black-owned company in 1995, with sixty-five employees. The owners trace their roots back to the original Geddes funeral home business and boast of 135 years of service.

Willis was active in many professional and social organizations and was a life member of the NAACP.

See also: African American Businesswomen; Insurance Industry

Further Reading
Alpha Kappa Alpha Sorority. *Women in Business*, p. 24.
Borders, Florence. "Willis, Gertrude Pocte Geddes." In Darlene Clark Hine, ed., *Black Women in America: An Historical Encyclopedia*, p. 1269.

Winblad, Ann L. (1950–), Electronics Manufacturer Executive

Ann Winblad, a pioneer in software portability and information technology, is one of the leading venture capitalists in the software industry. She was ranked number 24 on the 1998 *Fortune* list of the most powerful women in American business.

Winblad was born in Red Wing, Minnesota. Her father was a high school football coach, and she had five sisters and one brother. In high school she was both a cheerleader and valedictorian. She graduated from the College of

St. Catherine's in St. Paul with a degree in mathematics and business administration and continued her education to become the first woman to receive a master's degree in international economics and education from St. Thomas, St. Catherine's affiliate men's college.

Her first jobs were as a computer programmer and then a systems analyst for the Federal Reserve Bank of Minneapolis. In 1976 she and three co-workers founded Open Systems Inc., a company that developed accounting software. She was vice president of marketing and sales and was always the dominating force in the company. In 1984 Wyly Corporation bought the company for $15.5 million. She stayed on as a vice president until 1989, when she founded Hummer Winblad Venture Partners with John Hummer, the first venture capital firm specializing in software. A few of its investments were Wind River Systems, Powersoft Corporation, Arbor Software, and Berkeley Systems. In 1997 it expanded into Internet firms with Napster and Pets.com. As of November 2001 Hummer Winblad had funded more than seventy start-up companies. Some of Winblad's board memberships are the result of funding agreements with the fledgling companies. The company funds an annual February Madness Business Plan Competition for college students in which over one hundred universities participate.

Winblad's management style has been characterized as no-nonsense and hands-on. She is known for her investigative and probing skills. When she began working, women were rare in the high-technology arena. She has said repeatedly that she found being a woman an asset because she was different and thus stood out (Nash, p.12). She is considered one of the most capable and admired experts in the business. She has frequently spoken at conferences.

Winblad has won many awards over the years. In 1996 and 1998 *Vanity Fair* named her one of the fifty leaders of the information age, and in 1998 she was included in its list of the 200 most influential women in the United States. In 1997 she received an entrepreneurship award from the University of St. Thomas, and *Time* named her to its Cyber Elite list in 1997 and 1998. She received the Visionary Award from the Software Development Forum in 1999 and was named to lists of the best by *Forbes*, *Business Week*, and *Fortune* in 2000. She has been on several boards including The Knot, Dean & Deluca, eHow, Liquid Audio, Net Perceptions, and MyPrimeTime.com. She is on the board of trustees of the University of St. Thomas.

See also: Information Technology Industry

Further Reading

Alarilla, Joey G. "Infotech Winblad: Separate the Real Thing from Dotcom Wannabes."

Nash, Jim. "Ann Winblad: A Small-Town Native Leaps Headlong into Big-Time VC World."

Serwer, Andrew. "The Techie: Ann Winblad."

Winblad, Ann L., Samuel D. Edwards, and David R. King. *Object-Oriented Software*.

Winfrey, Oprah (1954–), Television Producer, Entertainment Entrepreneur

Oprah Winfrey is the most successful woman in television, the first African American woman billionaire, the second-richest African American in the United States, and probably one of the most recognizable Americans in the world. Her company, Harpo Entertainment Group, was on the *Working Woman* list of top woman-owned companies since its inception, and Winfrey has been on *Fortune*'s list of the most powerful women in American business since its beginning in 1998. She owns her television talk show and the studio that produces the talk show as well as films, has her own magazine, and is one of three owners of Oxygen, a cable channel for women.

Winfrey was born in Mississippi, the result of a one-day fling. Her mother went north to find work, leaving Oprah to be raised by her grandmother, a poor woman who lived on a pig farm. Her grandmother was a stern woman who taught Oprah how to read and write and how to recite Bible verses by the time she was three. When she was six she joined her mother, who was working as a maid in Milwaukee. At age eight she moved to Nashville to live with her father, but a summer visit to her mother became permanent, starting a dreadful period in her life. She was sexually abused by several family members, ran away several times, left school, and was eventually sent to a detention home that had no room. She was fourteen and pregnant. The detention home sent her back to her father in Nashville. He was married, had a family, and was a business owner, church deacon, and city councilman. Winfrey credits him with turning her life around. Her baby was born prematurely and later died.

An honor student in high school, Oprah was voted most popular and was president of the student council her senior year. She was chosen to attend Nixon's White House Conference on Youth and was active in the speech and drama clubs. After winning a full scholarship to Tennessee State College, she majored in speech and drama there.

She started her first job during high school as a weekend news reporter for WVOL, a black radio station. In 1972 she began her television career with WTVF. She was nineteen, still in college, and earning $15,000 a year. She became the station's first female and first African American news anchor. In 1976 three months before graduation, she moved to Baltimore to be a news anchor. She was fired because she became too emotionally involved with the people in the news; once she cried along with a victim. Because she had a contract she was asked to cohost a morning talk show. She was an instant success.

> She was fired because she became too emotionally involved with the people in the news.

In 1984 she was asked to host a talk show, A.M. *Chicago,* on WLS-TV. Winfrey turned the show around, and a year later its name was changed to *The Oprah Winfrey Show* and expanded to one hour. She began by interviewing celebrities, but it became clear that her real strength was in talking to people in the audience and eliciting their stories. Again, her honest empathy and genuine interest put them at ease; she even opened up her private life to them and, incidentally, the television viewers. In 1985 she began her movie career in *The Color Purple.* In 1986 *The Oprah Winfrey Show* was nationally syndicated. She formed Harpo Entertainment Group and bought a studio for $2 million, becoming the third woman, after Mary Pickford and Lucille Ball, to own her own production studio.

During the late 1980s and early 1990s Winfrey became involved in more projects including co-ownership of a restaurant and Granite Broadcasting Corporation. By 1995 she was reaching 15 to 20 million viewers daily in the United States and abroad. She introduced "Oprah's Book Club" in 1996. In 1998 she began changing the format of her television show to concentrate on finding solutions to problems. Her mission statement now reads: "Entertain while engaging the heart, lifting the spirit, and stimulating the mind" (Oprah.com).

She produced and starred in the movie *Beloved,* closely based on Toni Morrison's book. She and Hearst Magazines started a monthly magazine, *O: The Oprah Magazine.* It was the most successful launch in the history of magazine publishing. Winfrey and two other prominent women in the television industry started a new cable channel for women, Oxygen. She also has a very successful Web site.

Winfrey's management style is characterized by control and generosity. She is a perfectionist; demanding, but fair. She seems to inspire great loyalty among her employees, but also asks them to sign an agreement never to talk about her show or herself. She controls and knows about every aspect of the company and the many projects. She calls her approach humanistic and says she considers how a decision will affect her employees before making it.

Winfrey has won a legion of awards, including the NOW Woman of Achievement Award, nominations for an Academy Award and a Golden Globe Award for her performance in *The Color Purple,* and three Emmys for *The Oprah Winfrey Show* in 1991. She was the first African American woman named to the Television Hall of Fame, in 1993. She won the Horatio Alger Award that year and the British Academy of Film and Television Art's best foreign television program in 1994. She was named to the *Forbes* 400 for the first time in 1995 and was the first woman to lead the *Forbes* list of the forty highest paid entertainers in 1996. She also received the George Foster Peabody Individual Achievement Award in 1996. In 1998 she received the National Academy of Television Arts and Sciences Lifetime Achievement Award, was named to the National Women's Hall of Fame, was the favorite female performer in the People's Choice Awards, was on the cover of *Vogue,* and was the first African American and first woman to be named the most powerful person in the entertainment industry by *Entertainment Weekly*. *Time* named her one of the hundred most influential people of the twentieth century. She has also received awards from the NAACP. In 2000 she was number 3 in the *Forbes* Power 100. That year she also received the Martin Luther King Center's Salute to Greatness Award.

Her philanthropic activities have encompassed many causes. She has established ongoing scholarships at Spelman and Morehouse Colleges and at Tennessee State University. She and her fiancé, Stedman Graham, have begun Families for a Better Life, a nonprofit organization designed to get Chicago families off welfare and out of the projects. She has been a spokesperson for A Better Chance, a program providing college preparatory school scholarships for inner-city youth to which she also has contributed $1 million. She inaugurated Oprah's Angel Network as part of her show, a program that enables her viewers to contribute to Habitat for Humanity houses and college scholarships. The Use Your Life Award each Monday on *The Oprah Winfrey Show* goes to a person who is improving the lives of others. She donates about 10 percent of her annual income to charities.

Oprah Winfrey is one of the most successful businesswomen in history and is continuously originating new projects. She sells herself, her personality, and her celebrity in ever-new formats.

See also: African American Businesswomen; Broadcasting Industry; Entertainment Industry

Further Reading

Brands, H.W. *Masters of Enterprise*, p. 292–302.
Peterson, April. "Oprah: She Came, She Talked, She Conquered."
Powell, Joanna. "Oprah's Awakening: Oprah Winfrey; Interview."
Randolph, Laura B. "Oprah!"
Sellers, Patricia. "The Business of Being Oprah."
www.oprah.com.

Woertz, Patricia (1953–), Oil Industry Executive

In her position as president of Chevron Products, Pat Woertz may be the highest-ranking women in the oil industry and is the only woman to run a major operating company. In 2001 she became an executive vice president of ChevronTexaco. In October 1999 *Fortune* ranked her number 32 on its list of the most powerful woman in American business, and in 2003 her rank was number 9.

Woertz was born in Pittsburgh, Pennsylvania. She received a BA in accounting from Pennsylvania State in 1974 and later graduated from Columbia University's Executive Development Program. She is married and has three children. She worked as a certified public accountant for Ernst and Young until 1977, when she was recruited by Gulf Oil for a position in accounting and auditing. When Gulf was bought by Chevron Corporation in 1984 she was responsible for many of the financial maneuvers necessary for the merger.

At Chevron she has risen through the ranks, first as manager of finance for Chevron Information Technology Company in 1989, and then as manager of strategic planning for Chevron Corporation in 1991. In that position she developed its decentralized strategic planning process. In 1993 she was named president of Chevron Canada, an operation with 430 employees, one refinery, 230 service stations, and revenues of $500 million. She liked the move to the operating side of the business and felt challenged by it. When the company reorganized its management structure in 1995–1996 she took over the dual role of president of Chevron International Oil Company and vice president of Chevron U.S.A. Products Company. As such she had worldwide responsibility for the supply and distribution of Chevron's petroleum products.

In 1998 Woertz was named president of Chevron Products Company, Chevron's largest division, which employs 8,600 people and has 8,000 service stations and six major refineries. It earns around one-fifth of Chevron's income from refining, transporting, marketing, and selling at gasoline stations and is one of the largest marketers of petroleum products in the United States. It is also the largest supplier of California reformulated gasoline (a cleaner-burning fuel) and a large marketer of aviation fuels. In October 2001 after a merger with Texaco, she was named executive vice president, Downstream, and is in charge of ChevronTexaco's $80 billion worldwide refining, marketing, and transportation businesses.

Woertz has been on the board of directors of the American Petroleum Institute and Dynegy Inc., an affiliate of Chevron. She was named one of the fifty smartest women by *Success* magazine.

See also: Energy Industry

Further Reading
"Chevron Names Dave O'Reilly as a Vice Chairman; Patricia Woertz Named President of Products Company."
Pender, Kathleen. "Running with the Wolves."

Woman-Owned Businesses

Since the first settlers came to America, women have owned businesses. In most of the colonies they were owners only if they were single or widowed; otherwise they were part of a family business. It was not until the 1830s, when states began to pass legislation enabling women to own property and to negotiate contracts in their own name, that married women were able to begin businesses. Such married women's property rights acts were the law in most states by 1880. Most women owned small businesses with few employees through the 1950s. Many focused on women's interests, such as catering, shops of various kinds, food services, clothing, newspapers, and magazines or books about women's issues such as suffrage and abstinence.

Woman-owned businesses were not counted separately until 1972, when the U.S. Census Bureau added women- and minority-owned firms to the economic census that took place every five years. In 1972 there were 402,000 woman-owned companies, with receipts of $8.1 billion. These firms comprised 4.6 percent of all businesses in the United States. More than half were in retail trade (133,000) and selected services excluding law and architecture (151,000). Other industries included construction (15,000); manufacturing (8,000); transportation and public utilities (7,000); wholesale trade (5,000); and finance, insurance, and real estate (37,000). The largest area of receipts was retail trade ($4.2 billion) with wholesale trade, manufacturing, and services lagging far behind. Although services was an industry with many firms, profits were very low.

The 1997 Economic Census of woman-owned firms showed large growth both in the number of firms and in receipts. The total number of companies was 5,417,034, with receipts of $818 billion. Again, half were in services (2,981,266) and retail trade (919,990), but other areas showed robust growth as well: agricultural services, forestry, and fishing (74,444); mining (20,030); construction (157,173); manufacturing (121,108); wholesale trade (125,645); and finance, insurance, and real estate (479,469). The largest dollar amount of receipts was in wholesale trade ($188.5 billion), followed by services ($186 billion), retail trade ($152 billion), and manufacturing ($113.7 billion).

These statistics are not directly comparable, however, because the 1972 Economic Census counted every company where a woman was the sole owner, one of two partners, or owned 50 percent or more of the stock. The 1992 Economic Census counted only those firms where the woman owned 51 percent or more of the stock. In 2003 the Center for Women's Business Research counted 10.1 million firms in which 50 percent of the company was owned by a woman or women, nearly 46 percent of all businesses in the United States. This number had grown 37 percent since 1997, a growth rate four times that for male-owned companies. One of every eleven adult women owned a business, and the businesses employed more than 18 million workers. By 2004 one in five was owned by a woman of color.

These woman-owned firms employed a more gender-balanced workforce than businesses owned by men and are more likely to have work-life balance programs such as flexible work arrangements. Their management style was more likely to be team-based and consensus building. Women continue to diversify into previously male-dominated industries in ever-increasing numbers, and their businesses are just "as financially sound and credit-worthy as the average U.S. firm with similar performance on bill payment and similar levels of credit risk." The women owning the companies are also dreaming bigger and expecting faster growth than in the past, when most were content with their small businesses (Center for Women's Business Research).

See also: Entrepreneurs

Further Reading

Brush, Candida G. "Research on Women Business Owners: Past Trends, a New Perspective and Future Directions."

Drachman, Virginia G. *Enterprising Women: 250 Years of American Business.*

Hagan, Oliver, Carol Rivchun, and Donald Sexton, eds. *Women-Owned Businesses.*

Nelton, Sharon. "The Challenge to Women."

President's Interagency Task Force on Women Business Owners. *The Bottom Line: Unequal Enterprise in America; Report of the President's Interagency Task Force on Women Business Owners.*

Women's Banks, *see* Banking

Women's Business Ownership Act

The Women's Business Ownership Act, signed into law on November 2, 1988, was intended to make business and commercial credit lending nondiscriminatory. It also provided $10 million in matching grants to organizations offering management and technical assistance to woman-owned businesses, created a guaranteed miniloan program for loans up to $50,000, provided incentives for lenders to make very small loans, and established a National Women's Business Council and Women's Business Centers. Potential lenders were barred from asking applicants about their marital status and were required to give a written statement detailing reasons if commercial credit was denied.

Women's Online Business Center, *see* Small Business Administration

Woodhull, Victoria Claflin (1838–1927), Stockbroker, Newspaper Publisher

Victoria Woodhull was the first woman stockbroker on Wall Street, the first woman to own a brokerage, the first woman to publish her own house organ, the first woman to speak before a congressional committee, and the first woman to run for president of the United States. She was ahead of her time by about one hundred years, always controversial and involved in lawsuits.

Woodhull was born in Ohio in 1838, the seventh of ten children. The entire family took to the road when she was small, following a suspicious fire at her father's mill. They became a traveling medicine and clairvoyance show, selling quack medicine, spiritualism, and healing. In the 1840s spiritualism was very popular, particularly in the Midwest, so their show was successful. Woodhull later said that she had had visions since she was three, and she held séances while her sister Tennessee laid on healing hands, practiced clairvoyance, and sold elixirs. Neither of them had any formal education. When Victoria was fifteen she married a Dr. Woodhull, who turned out to have no medical practice and be an alcoholic. They moved to California and had two children, a mentally disabled boy and a girl, Zula. Woodhull's alcoholism grew worse, and she divorced him. After returning to the family, she met a Colonel Blood. They signed a paper stating that they intended to marry in 1866.

In 1868 Woodhull announced that her spirit, Demosthenes, had told her to go to New York City, so the family moved. Her father offered Cornelius Vanderbilt Tennessee's spiritualist services in reaching his dead wife. Vanderbilt, then the richest man in the United States, became bewitched by both Tennessee and Victoria. He loaned them money or promised tips in setting up a stock brokerage firm. The sisters began to trade stocks, real estate, bonds, and gold and did very well, particularly in the stock market crash of September 1869. In January 1870 they opened Woodhull, Claflin & Company. They were the first woman stockbrokers on Wall Street. Their pet projects changed from real estate to silver mines to railways. Victoria also added a banking business. Profits mounted but so did rumors, cartoons, articles poking fun at them, and jokes at their expense.

In March of 1870 she announced her candidacy for president of the United States. That May she began a weekly newspaper, *Woodhull & Claflin's Weekly*, in which she crusaded against the shoddy financial practices she had observed. She also used the paper to explain finance to the public, but the content evolved into muckraking as well as articles about free love, birth control, legalization of prostitution, woman suffrage, and other social and economic issues of the day. She embarked on yet another career as a lecturer, again espousing her own views. Her debut in that arena was before the House Judiciary Committee in January 1871, when she tried to make the point that the U.S. Constitution guarantees women the right to vote. She tried to take over the National Woman Suffrage Alliance, headed by Susan B. Anthony. Failing in that, she held her own convention, formed the Equal Rights Party and ran for president with Frederick Douglass as her running mate. He never took part in her campaign, however, and in fact he supported General Ulysses Grant for president. Woodhull made history as the first woman to run for that office.

The next year her life began to unravel. She was vilified and ostracized for her sensational views. Her Wall Street clients began to disappear, and the newspaper became more and more notorious. She published *The Communist Manifesto*, but the final blow came after she published details of the most sensational social scandal of the day, the Beecher-Tilton scandal. She was tricked into sending a copy of the paper through the mail, and she and Tennessee were arrested for mailing obscene material and spent time in jail. The scandal ruined her career, and she was forced to give up her mansion, her office, and her newspaper.

In 1877 Cornelius Vanderbilt died and Victoria and Tennessee went to England, some say financed by the Vanderbilt family, who were engaged in a lengthy fight over his will. Victoria married John Biddulph Martin, a wealthy man, in 1883. They spent most of their lives in litigation over her reputation, but enjoyed the life of English society. She started another magazine, *The Humanitarian*, which tackled the topic of eugenics as well as finance. Her later years were spent in philanthropic endeavors. Victoria Woodhull has been described as a beautiful and fascinating woman. Her views were far ahead of her time. She died in 1927.

See also: Finance Industry; Publishing Industry

Further Reading

Gabriel, Mary. *Notorious Victoria: The Life of Victoria Woodhull Uncensored.*

Goldsmith, Barbara. *Other Powers: The Age of Suffrage, Spiritualism, and the Scandalous Victoria Woodhull.*

Underhill, Lois Beachy. *The Woman Who Ran for President: The Many Lives of Victoria Woodhull.*

Woods, Emily (1961–), Clothing Manufacturer

Until March 2003 Emily Woods was the chairman of J. Crew, the clothing company founded by her father. She helped design the clothing and worked with her father, Arthur Cinadar, on the catalog. The company was number 23 on *Working Woman*'s 2000 list of the top 500 woman-owned companies and number 22 in 2001. It has grown since 1983 into a three-faceted company, selling clothes through its catalog, in retail and factory stores, and over the Internet.

Woods was born in 1961 and graduated from the University of Denver in 1982 with a BA in marketing. The following year she joined her father's company. She helped him design the preppy but casual line of clothing, and he designed the catalog layout. Aimed at 18- to 35-year-olds, it was an immediate success. In 1989 they opened their first three retail stores, and by 1993 there were twenty-five. Store and catalog clothing lines expanded. Her father's title was CEO, and Emily Woods was president. Her two sisters and brother were also involved in the company; even her puppy appeared in the catalog. Sales in 1992 were $571 million, with profits of $14 million.

By 1996 sales had jumped to $808.8 million, but profits had diminished to $12.5 million. The mix of merchandise had changed to include more women's wear. In October 1997 Texas Pacific Group, an investment company, bought 60 percent of the company for $560 million. Woods was named CEO with a lucrative contract that included a $10 million signing bonus. Her father retired with a $5 million noncompete contract, but continued as a consultant. She hired more management, particularly in marketing and advertising; increased advertising; and expanded the number of catalogs and catalog formats. Her plan was to increase the number of retail stores and factory outlets and to expand operations in Japan, Europe, and Australia. In 1999 she became chairman, relinquishing her CEO role.

That year J. Crew opened a flagship store in Rockefeller Center in New York City. By the end of the year the company owned sixty-seven retail stores and forty-two factory outlets. Woods owned 15 percent of the company. The next year she decided to work a four-day week and forgo her design responsibilities. She remained as chairman. In January 2003 Millard Drexler, former CEO of Gap, took over as CEO, the fifth person in that position since Texas Pacific bought the company. The following March Woods resigned as chairman.

Woods was named one of the fifty smartest women in the money business by *Money* magazine in its May 15, 2000 issue ("50 Smartest Women"). When Beringer Wine Estates announced her appointment to its board of directors, it noted her extraordinary perception about emerging trends in customer buying habits and her experience in brand building (King, p. 73). Her business role model is Jack Welch, and her personal role models are Katharine Hepburn and Amelia Earhart, for their strength and style.

See also: Fashion Industry; Retailing Industry

Further Reading
Fiedelholtz, Sara. "Emily Woods: J. Crew's Steady Captain."
King, Rachel. "Beringer Wine Estates Names Emily Woods to Board of Directors."
Moin, David, and Sidney Rutberg. "The Book on J. Crew."

Woods, Jacqueline (1962–), Software Executive

Jacqueline Woods, as vice president of global pricing and licensing strategy at Oracle Inc., was ranked number 39 on *Fortune*'s list of the most powerful black executives in 2002. Woods earned her bachelor of science at the University of California at Davis and received an MBA from the University of Southern California, where she concentrated on marketing and venture management.

She began her career at GTE in marketing, moving up to marketing management positions. She moved to Ameritech as director of product management for Customer Premise Equipment, where she developed, implemented, and managed strategy for the retail business products.

She went to Oracle as director of marketing, was promoted to senior director of marketing, and by 2001 had become vice president of global pricing and licensing strategy. She is responsible for defining and establishing pricing strategies, guidelines, and policies for the entire range of Oracle products. She also chairs the Pricing Committee. She was the company's spokesperson in 2001 when Oracle was widely criticized by users for unfair prices. After Oracle decided to change to a different pricing model, Wood's job was to educate and reassure the customers. She discussed the issues on the E-Business Network; was widely quoted in the media; implemented an Internet site; and produced the Oracle Software Investment Guide, which responded to customer complaints about confusing pricing and policies.

See also: African American Businesswomen; Information Technology Industry

Further Reading
Daniels, Cora. "The Most Powerful Black Executives in America."
http://www.hoovers.com/officers/bio/7/0,3353,14337_130189990,00.htm
"Oracle Guide Aims to Clear Up Policies."

Work-Life Balance

One of the greatest concerns of businesswomen today is the need to balance the demands of their careers with the responsibilities and needs of their families and personal lives. In articles in both academic journals and the popular press, this dilemma is called work-life balance. It has become clear that this is also an issue for men and for companies that wish to attract and retain employees.

In the 1970s women began to enter the workforce in great numbers. In 1977 Rosabeth Moss Kanter published a book, *Work and Family in the United States*, in which she focused on work-life issues in relation to policies and society. A flood of academic research papers followed during the 1980s, and then in the popular press in the 1990s. By then it was clear that companies, if they wished to recruit women, would need to launch programs designed to help women deal with the problems of balancing work life and home life. A business case was made for reducing employee turnover, stress, and absenteeism and improving employee recruitment and retention.

It also became clear that men would benefit from work-life balance programs as well. In 1998 there were 2.1 million single fathers in the workforce. In 1999, 60 percent of mothers with children under age three were in the workforce, 80 percent of women with children aged six through seventeen, and 76.6 percent of all single mothers. According to Laurie Morton, it had become apparent that "'having a life' [was] just as, if not more, important than 'climbing the corporate ladder,' or getting the highest pay. A balanced company culture that can keep talented employees happier will be the one that achieves higher productivity and lower turnover" ("Work-Life Balance?" p. 18).

Work-life balancing programs can be many, including flexible work schedules, part-time arrangements, home office/telecommuting, and company-supported childcare. However, unless the corporate culture wholeheartedly supports the programs, employees will be reluctant to take part for fear that they might be considered slackers, miss a crucial decision, or be passed over for a promotion or an opportunity.

In 2001 Catalyst published a study of women and men professionals of the 2000s (*The Next Generation*). It found that their primary need was programs and policies to help them balance their work and personal lives. These men and women are the children of the 1970s women pioneers who worked hard to prove themselves in the business world. This generation values personal and family commitment above earning a great deal of money, becoming an influential person, or becoming well known. They want their employers to create a flexible environment and will choose positions based on their values; however, 29 percent of them reported severe or very severe workplace interference with their personal lives, while 43 percent said the job interference was moderate. Claudia Wallis, in a 2004 *Time* article ("The Case for Staying Home"), noted that many executive women are opting out of corporate life to raise children. Many women cannot afford that option, however. The workplace, to be productive, is going to have to change.

See also: Employee Benefits; Flexible Work Arrangements

Further Reading
Catalyst. *The Next Generation: Today's Professionals, Tomorrow's Leaders.*
Hansen, Fay. "Truth and Myths about Work/Life Balance."
Morton, Laurie A. "Work-Life Balance? Coming Right Up . . . Is the Corporate Culture Shift Wishful Thinking?"
Parasuraman, Saroj, and Jeffrey H. Greenhaus. *Integrating Work and Family: Challenges and Choices for a Changing World.*
Wallis, Claudia. "The Case for Staying Home."

Working Woman Top 500 Woman-Owned Companies, *see* Top Women Business Owners

---

Wright, Deborah C. (1958–), Banker

In 1984 Deborah Wright became the first African American woman to earn a double degree from Harvard University, an MBA with an emphasis in investment banking, and a law degree. She is currently president and CEO of Carver BanCorp, the holding company for Carver Federal Savings Bank, one of the largest minority-owned banks in the United States.

Wright was born in Bennetsville, South Carolina, and grew up in Dallas, Texas. Her father was a Baptist preacher who later became minister to the Cornerstone Baptist Church in Brooklyn, New York, a prestigious post. Her aunt, Marion Wright Edelman, is nationally known for her work as a children's rights advocate and White House adviser. After graduating from Harvard, Wright worked at First Boston Corporation as an associate in the Corporate Finance Group for three years. She then moved to New York City and a series of public service positions. In 1990 Mayor David Dinkins appointed her to the New York City Planning Commission. Later she was appointed to the New York City Housing Authority Board that was responsible for overseeing new construction and rehabilitation of housing projects. In 1994 Mayor Rudolph Guiliani appointed her commissioner of the Department of Housing Preservation and Development, where she successfully found private moneys and partnered with corporations to enable projects. Two years later she became the founding president and CEO of the Upper Manhattan Empowerment Zone, an improvement opportunity for Harlem. This was the country's largest empowerment zone, with a budget of $250 million. In 1999 the projects were hindered because of political infighting, however.

That April Wright was named president and CEO of Carver BanCorp. The bank was struggling with a large number of unpaid debts and was in the middle of a hostile takeover bid from an African American shareholder in Boston. Wright had no commercial banking experience, a fact that drew criticism from some shareholders, but was appointed because of her success in her public positions, her understanding of finance, and her management skills as well as her deep roots in and commitment to New York City's African American community. Her first priorities were to improve service, then to add new products and services including electronic banking. She was delayed, however, when she soon found herself embroiled in the attempted takeover that was resolved by seating the dissident shareholder and his wife on the board of directors. Not until 2000 could Wright concentrate on her plans. She hired several very experienced upper managers, pared down the number of employees, and restructured management with a focus on good service. She sold two suburban branches and partnered with corporations and Fannie Mae to offer credit card and auto loans and mortgages, thus limiting the risk held by Carver. In October 2001 she opened a new full-service bank in Harlem. By May 2002 Carver BanCorp was profitable again.

Wright sits on several boards of directors: Initiative for a Competitive Inner City, the Municipal Art Society of New York, PENCIL Inc., Newman Real Estate Institute at Baruch College, the Center on Urban and Metropolitan Policy at Brookings Institute, and Kraft Foods.

See also: African American Businesswomen; Banking

Further Reading

Agosta, Veronica. "At Carver, the CEO Has Control: Now Comes the Hardest Part."

"Deborah C. Wright."

Padgett, Tania. "On the Wright Track: Carver Bank CEO Succeeding in Singular Mission to Rejuvenate Fledgling Institution."

Robinson, Edward. "Fighting to Rebuild a Harlem Institution."

Y

Yang, Linda Tsao (1922–), Banker, Consultant

Linda Tsao Yang was the executive director of the Asian Development Bank from 1993 to 1999. Appointed by President Clinton, she was a prominent banker and financial consultant in California.

She was born in Shanghai, one of three sisters and two brothers. Her mother believed it was important for women to be educated and independent. At an early age, she became interested in "issues of social justice regarding women" (Tilek, p. 432) and banking in relation to women. After receiving a BS in economics from St. Johns University in Shanghai, she came to the United States in 1946 to study for her MBA at Columbia University. She also earned a PhD there. She married, had two sons, and spent the next twelve years as a homemaker, but kept up with her profession by attending conferences and seminars and keeping in touch with her colleagues.

In the late 1970s she founded and organized the Mother Lode Savings Bank with a group of her friends. It was intended as a bank that would give special attention to women's needs. Later she sold it to U.S. Bancorp. In 1980 Governor Edmund Brown appointed her Commissioner of the California Savings and Loan. She was the first minority and first woman to be appointed to this position. It was during deregulation and her term was filled with controversy. She was known as a thoughtful problem solver who would spend time thinking through all aspects of the problem and then decide on a course of action. She also has the ability to get consensus, an ability that came into full play during those years. In 1983 she founded Linda Tsao Yang and Associates, a financial consulting practice, which focused on intermediary needs between American financial institutions and Asian investors who wished to invest in the United States.

> She was known as a thoughtful problem solver who would spend time thinking through all aspects of a problem and then decide on a course of action.

President Clinton appointed her as the United States Executive Director of the Asian Development Bank in 1993 for a six-year term. The president of the bank is Japanese, but Yang was the American voice. The goals of the bank are to provide loans and technical assistance that promote development in Asia and the Far East. For example, one loan to Indonesia was aimed at keeping children of both sexes in school for three years during an economic crisis. After her term ended in 2000, she headed a think tank in San Francisco.

Yang sits on the boards of Blue Cross of California and their Budget and Finance Committee, the University of California at Berkeley's Advisory Committee on Real Estate and Urban Economics, and the California Commission on the Teaching Profession. She was the first Asian American to be appointed to the Board of Administration of California's Public Employment Retirement System where she was vice president and vice chair of the investment committee. She was also a director of the 1990 Institute, a California nonprofit think tank as well as the chair of their Research Management Committee.

See also: Asian American businesswomen; Banking

Further Reading
"Clinton Picks Yang as Asian Bank Director."
Tilek, Visi R. "Linda Tsao Yang (1926–)." In Zia, p. 432–433.

Yates, FaEllen, *see* Hubbard, Sonja Y.

York, Denise DeBartolo (1950–), Sports Industry Executive

Denise DeBartolo York took over ownership of the San Francisco 49ers and the Louisiana Downs Racetrack in May 2000 after the settlement of a bitter legal fight with her brother Eddie DeBartolo. In 2001, her new company, the DeBartolo Corporation, was listed for the first time in the *Working Woman* list of the top woman-owned companies. It was 31st.

She was born in Youngstown, Ohio, one of two children. She graduated from St. Mary's University in 1972 and married John York. Her father's company was the world's largest shopping center and development company. He also owned the San Francisco 49ers. When he died at age eighty-five in 1994, he was the ninety-fifth richest person in the United States.

Both children joined the business. Brother Eddie was the president and CEO of Edward J. DeBartolo Realty Corporation, and York was the vice chairman. He ran the football team, although they each owned half of all the businesses. In December 1997 Eddie resigned as head of the football franchise because he was about to be indicted for fraud over a gambling deal in Louisiana. Denise took over as chair and CEO of the team. This was the beginning of a long and bitter feud between the two siblings involving several conflicting charges and countercharges, suits and countersuits, resulting in estrangement between the two.

After her brother was convicted following a plea agreement and banned from the team by the National Football League, she tried to sever all financial ties with him. York and her husband officially took over the team in May 2000. The final agreement about all the properties was not signed until the following year. Eddie kept all the real estate business and Denise kept the San Francisco 49ers and the Louisiana Downs racetrack. Her office is in her father's building in Youngstown. Her brother moved across the street and named his company DeBartolo Property Company.

The other National Football League owners have publicly welcomed the Yorks as owners, gratified that they wanted to put the 49ers franchise back on its feet. One of the first items on the agenda is a new stadium. During the feud, plans for the stadium were abandoned. The need is crucial since the present stadium, Candlestick Park, is in need of repair. In September 2001 the Yorks looked at stadium plans and the 2003 Super Bowl was scheduled in San Francisco. By the following January, they rejected the idea of a self-funded stadium as originally planned and the Super Bowl site was moved to San Diego. Two years later there were still no firm plans for a new stadium.

The Yorks and the San Francisco 49ers helped support several new neighborhood football fields in San Francisco. Denise York has also applied for an Arena Football League expansion team.

Further Reading
"Not Exactly What You'd Call a Weak Sister."
"Sibling Squabble Between DeBartolos Is Ugly Power Play."

Young, Shirley (1935–), Automobile Executive

In 1988, when Shirley Young joined General Motors as the vice president for Consumer Marketing Development, she was the highest ranking woman at the company. Before leaving for General Motors, she was the Chairman of Grey Strategic Marketing at Grey Advertising. She had helped pioneer attitudinal studies at Gray in the late 1950s.

She was born in Shanghai, the daughter of a Chinese diplomat. The family was living in the Philippines during World War II and was interned by the

Japanese when the country was invaded. Her father was executed there. The rest of the family emigrated to the United States when Shirley was ten. Her mother married a diplomat who became the Nationalist Chinese Ambassador to the United States from 1946 to 1956. Young graduated from Wellesley College in 1955 with a BS in economics and a Phi Beta Kappa key. She is married with three children.

Her first job was as a project director with the Alfred Politz Research Organization in 1955. The following year Young was a market research manager with Hudson Paper Corporation. In 1959, she joined Grey Advertising in New York City as a researcher. She held several marketing positions there, eventually becoming the executive vice president of Marketing Planning and Strategy Development and a member of the agency policy council. While in her research position, she helped develop attitudinal studies. In 1983 she became president of Grey Strategic Marketing, a subsidiary of Grey Advertising. She also began consulting with General Motors. In 1988, she was promoted to chairman of Grey Strategic Marketing.

Later that year she moved to General Motors as the vice president for Consumer Market Development but continued consulting with Grey Advertising. Young's responsibilities at General Motors were to help regain market share. The company had a reputation for poor quality at the time, so she began a campaign titled "Putting Quality on the Road." She initiated a program for the entire company emphasizing quality and consumer responsiveness. She became known for what she called "her persistent evangelism" (Landler, p. 52). In 1995 she was appointed to the GM China Operations Team, but kept her other responsibilities. She advised the president of GM China on strategic matters. In 1997, she became the vice president for China Strategic Development and helped shepherd a joint venture there. By 2001 she was a senior advisor to GM-Asia Pacific. She also owns her own business advisory company, Shirley Young Associates.

Young has served on many boards: Holiday Inns, Bell Atlantic, Promus Corporation, Bombay Company, and Dayton-Hudson. She is currently on the boards of Netro Corporation and TeleTech Holdings. She was the chair of the Committee of 100, a national Chinese-American leadership group, a founding member of the Committee of 200, and a trustee of Wellesley College and Interlochen Center for the Arts. She is also on the boards of Catalyst, American Public Radio, and the Shanghai Symphony Orchestra. She holds honorary professorships at universities in Beijing, Shanghai, and Wuhan, China. She was awarded an honorary PhD by Russell Sage College and was vice chair of the nominating committee for the New York Stock Exchange. She was awarded the Catalyst Award for Outstanding Corporate Director in 1981, the Women's Equity Action League in Advertising Award in 1982, and the Wellesley College Alumna Achievement Award in 1986. The following year, she was named Woman of the Year by the Chinese American Planning Council. She has been the American Advertising Federation's Advertising

Woman of the Year and received the Silk Wings Award for achievement in business from the National Network of Asian and Pacific Women. In 1992, *Business Week* listed her as one of the top fifty women in business.

See also: Asian American businesswomen; Automobile industry

Further Reading

Gall, p. 718–719.

Hoffman, Gary. "Shirley Young's GM Crusade."

Landler, Mark, et al. "Shirley Young: Pushing GM's Humble-Pie Strategy."

Appendix I

Fortune Magazine's Fifty Most Powerful Women in American Business, 1998–2003

Ranking	1998	1999	2000	2001	2002	2003
1	Carleton S. Fiorina	Carleton S. Fiorina	Carleton S. Fiorina	Carleton S. Fiorina	Carleton S. Fiorina	Carleton S. Fiorina
2	Oprah Winfrey	Heidi Miller	Debby Hopkins	Meg Whitman	Betsy Holden	Meg Whitman
3	Heidi Miller	Mary Meeker	Meg Whitman	Oprah Winfrey	Meg Whitman	Andrea Jung
4	Shelly Lazarus	Shelly Lazarus	Donna Dubinsky	Andrea Jung	Indra Nooyi	Anne Mulcahy
5	Sherry Lansing	Meg Whitman	Ellen Hancock	Marce S. Fuller	Andrea Jung	Marjorie Magner
6	Jill Barad	Debby Hopkins	Mary Meeker	Anne Mulcahy	Anne Mulcahy	Karen Katen
7	Marilyn Carlson Nelson	Marjorie Scardino	Shelly Lazarus	Karen Katen	Karen Katen	Oprah Winfrey
8	Andrea Jung	Martha Stewart	Abby Joseph Cohen	Pat Woertz	Pat Woertz	Indra Nooyi
9	Abby Joseph Cohen	Nancy Peretsman	Martha Stewart	Betsy Holden	Abigail Johnson	Pat Woertz
10	Marjorie Scardino	Pat Russo	Andrea Jung	Indra Nooyi	Oprah Winfrey	Betsy Holden
11	Martha Stewart	Patricia Dunn	Ann Livermore	Shelly Lazarus	Ann Moore	Abigail Johnson
12	Pat Russo	Abby Joseph Cohen	Patricia Dunn	Abigail Johnson	Judy McGrath	Betsy Bernard
13	Judy Lewent	Ann Livermore	Nancy Peretsman	Martha Stewart	Colleen Barrett	Ann Moore
14	Rebecca Mark	Andrea Jung	Karen Katen	Patricia Dunn	Shelly Lazarus	Sallie Krawcheck
15	Lois Juliber	Sherry Lansing	Oprah Winfrey	Judy McGrath	Pat Russo	Judy McGrath
16	Karen Katen	Karen Katen	Judy McGrath	Sherry Lansing	Betsy Bernard	Shelly Lazarus
17	Ann Moore	Marilyn Carlson Nelson	Sherry Lansing	Louise Kitchen	Amy Brinkley	Doreen Toben
18	Judy McGrath	Judy McGrath	Anne Mulcahy	Lois D. Juliber	Lois D. Juliber	Stacey Snider
19	Darla Moore	Lois D. Juliber	Lois D. Juliber	Marilyn Carlson Nelson	Sherry Lansing	Colleen Barrett
20	Geraldine Laybourne	Geraldine Laybourne	Heidi Miller	Colleen Barrett	Stacey Snider	Sherry Lansing
21	Sheila Birnbaum	Judith Estrin	Ann Moore	Ann Mooore	Judy C. Lewent	Pat Russo
22	Carolyn Ticknor	Cathleen Black	Judy Lewent	Judy Lewent	Marjorie Magner	Amy Brinkley
23	Patti Manuel	Linda Sanford	Betsy Holden	Betsy Bernard	Ann Livermore	Judy Lewent
24	Ann Winblad	Ann Moore	Linda Sanford	Stacey Snider	Cathleen Black	Ann Livermore

Rank						
25	Gail Berman	Doreen Toben	Dina Dublon	Dawn Lepore	Jill Barad	Cathleen Black
26	Cathleen Black	Amy Pascal	Pat Russo	Pat House	Oprah Winfrey	Orit Gadiesh
27	Christine Poon	Vivian Banta	Anne Stevens	Gail McGovern	Judy Lewent	Claire Farley
28	Linda Dillman	Janet Robinson	Ann Livermore	Cathleen Black	Joy Covey	Jamie Gorelick
29	Myrtle Potter	Pam Strobel	Cathleen Black	Jan Brandt	Rebecca Mark	Abigail Johnson
30	Susan Desmond-Hellman	Dina Dublon	Linda Sanford	Dina Dublon	Deborah Willingham	Ann Fudge
31	Susan Arnold	Nancy Peretsman	Amy Brinkley	Stacey Snider	Dina Dublon	Deborah Willingham
32	Lois Juliber	Susan Arnold	Donna Dubinsky	Jeanne Jackson	Deborah Woertz	Jeanne Jackson
33	Dina Dublon	Mary Kay Haben	Marjorie Magner	Amy Brinkley	Lawton Fitt	Martha Ingram
34	Deb Henretta	Deb Henretta	Nancy Peretsman	Cristina Morgan	Ann Fudge	Linda Wachner
35	Anne Sweeney	Carole Black	Dawn Lepore	Patricia Sueltz	Carolyn Ticknor	Lucy Fisher
36	Nancy Pretsman	Jamie Gorelick	Gail McGovern	Sue Bostrom	Dawn Lepore	Carol Bartz
37	Mary Sammons	Marce S. Fuller	Maria Elena Lagomasino	Carolyn Ticknor	Jeannine Rivet	Katherine Dwyer
38	Amy Pascal	Kathi Seifert	Susan Desmond-Hellman	Marge Magner	Jamie Gorelick	Patricia Fili-Krushel
39	Maria Elena Lagomasino	Anne Sweeney	Janet Robinson	Patricia Woertz	Jan Brandt	Esther Dyson
40	Vivian Banta	Marilyn Carlson Nelson	Carol Tome	Jeannine Rivet	Bridget Macaskill	Bridget Macaskill
41	Vanessa Castagna	Anne Stevens	Jamie Gorelick	Linnet Deily	Jeanne Jackson	Judith Estrin
42	Jenny Ming	Sallie Krawcheck	Vivian Banta	Judy Estrin	Cynthia Trudell	Jeannine Rivet
43	Lois Quam	Carol Tome	Carrie Cox	Indra Nooyi	Nina DiSesa	Linda Srere
44	Ursula Burns	Marion Sandler	Anne Sweeney	Marion Sandler	Linda Wachner	Brenda Barnes
45	Marilyn Carlson Nelson	Louise Francesconi	Carole Black	Vivian Banta	Darla Moore	Marion Sandler
46	Ann Fudge	Vanessa Castagna	Marion Sandler	Jamie Gorelick	Marion Sandler	Anthea Disney
47	Louise Francesconi	Larree Renda	Janet Davidson	Orit Gadiesh	Michelle Anthony	Anne Sweeney
48	Janet Robinson	Dawn Lepore	Laree Renda	Vanessa Castagna	Orit Gadiesh	Sylvia Rhone
49	Christina Gold	Fran Keeth	Louise Francesconi	Safra Catz	Carlotte Beers	Teresa Beck
50	Dawn Hudson	Heidi Miller	Abby Joseph Cohen	Betty Cohen	Abigail Johnson	Ellen Marram

Appendix II

Working Woman's Top Thirty Woman Business Owners, 1997–2001

Ranking	1997	1998	1999	2000	2001
1	Martha Ingram	Pat Moran	Pat Moran	Pat Moran	Abigail Johnson
2	Loida Nicolas Lewis	Abigail Johnson	Abigail Johnson	Abigail Johnson	Pat Moran
3	Marian Ilitch	Martha Ingram	Marion O. Sandler	Marilyn Carlson Nelson	Marion O. Sandler
4	Maggie Hardy Magerko	Marilyn Carlson	Marilyn Carlson Nelson	Marion O. Sandler	Marilyn Carlson Nelson
5	Lynda Resnick	Marian Ilitch	Joyce Raley Teel	Joyce Raley Teel	Joyce Raley Teel
6	Antonia Ax:son Johnson	Mary Kay Ash	Katharine Graham	Marian Ilitch	Linda J. Wachner
7	Linda Wachner	Joyce Raley Teel	Marian Ilitch	Linda J. Wachner	Carol Bernick/Bernice Lavin
8	Liz Minyard/Gretchen Minyard Williams	Katharine Graham	Martha R. Ingram	Martha R. Ingram	Antonia Ax:son Johnson
9	Gay Love	Bernice Lavin/Carol Bernick	Linda J. Wachner	Bernice Lavin/Carol Bernick	Martha Rivers Ingram
10	Donna Karan	Maggie Hardy Magerko	Bernice Lavin/Carol Bernick	Maggie Hardy Magerko	Maggie Hardy Magerko
11	Ardath Rodale	Lynda Resnick	Maggie Hardy Magerko	Lynda R. Resnick	Dorrit J. Bern
12	Christine Liang	Linda Wachner	Lynda R. Resnick	Lily Bentas	Lily Bentas
13	Donna Wolf Steigerwaldt	Elaine S. Frank	Lily Bentas	Antonia Ax:son Johnson	Patricia Gallup
14	Helen Copley	Antonia Ax:son Johnson	Elaine S. Frank	Liz Minyard/Gretchen Williams	Elaine S. Frank
15	Jenny Craig	Lily Bentas	Antonia Ax:son Johnson	Dorrit J. Bern	Thai Lee
16	Irma Elder	Donna Sutherland Pearson	Dorrit J. Bern	Elaine S. Frank	Liz Minyard/Gretchen Williams
17	Patricia Gallup	Liz Minyard/Gretchen M. Williams	Liz Minyard/Gretchen M. Williams	Patricia Gallup	Judy Odom Sims
18	Barbara Levy Kipper	Gay Love	Gay Love	Leona Helmsley	Tami Longaberger
19	Jane O'Dell	Judy Odom Sims	Judy Sims	Gay Love	Gay Love
20	Ellen Gordon	Emily Woods	Emily Woods	Judy Odom Sims	Christine Liang
21	Annabelle Lundy Fetterman	Donna Karan	Christina Liang	Thai Lee	Marian Ilitch
22	Doris Christopher	Christine Liang	Patricia Gallup	Tami Longaberger	Emily Woods
23	Gertrude Boyle	Patricia Gallup	Therese A. Rooney	Emily Woods	Therese A. Rooney
24	Ebba Hoffman/Sharon Hoffman Avent	Donna Wolf Steigerwaldt	Donna Karan	Christine Liang	Doris Christopher
25	Rachelle Friedman	Lynn Johnson	Donna Wolf Steigerwaldt	Therese A. Rooney	Donna Karan
26	Kathy Prasnicki Lehne	Ardath Rodale	Mari Hulman George	Donna Karan	Barbara Levy Kipper
27	Pleasant Rowland	Helen Copley	Ardath Rodale	Barbara Levy Kipper	S. Hubbard/S. Floyd, F. Yates
28	Nanci Mackenzie	Bettye Martin Musham	Helen Copley	Doris Christopher	Marta Weinstein
29	Marta Weinstein	Doris Christopher	Doris Christopher	Jane O'Dell	Jane O'Dell
30	Lillian Vernon	Irma Elder	Orit Gadiesh	Marta Weinstein	Helen Copley

Appendix III

African American
Brown, Clara
Brunson, Dorothy E.
Burns, Ursula M.
Cholmondeley, Paula
Corbi, Lana
Eldridge, Elleanor
Fields, Mary
Fudge, Ann M.
Gaines, Brenda J.
Harris, Carla A.
Hughes, Catherine L.
Keckley, Elizabeth Hobbs
Malone, Annie Turnbo
Mason, Biddy
McCabe, Jewell Jackson
Morgan, Rose
Pleasant, Mary Ellen
Potter, Myrtle Stephens
Procope, Ernesta B.
Proctor, Barbara
Rhone, Sylvia M.
Rice, Linda Johnson
Sneed, Paula A.
Thomas-Graham, Pamela
Walker, Maggie Lena
Walker, Sarah Breedlove
    (Madame C.J.)

Washington, Ruth
White, Eartha Mary Magdalene
Willis, Gertrude Pocte Geddes
Winfrey, Oprah
Woods, Jacqueline
Wright, Deborah C.

American Indian
Ainse, Sally
Alberty, Eliza Missouri Bushyhead
Bosomworth, Mary Musgrove
    (Cousaponokeesa)
Bryan, Lisa Little Chief
Davis, Alice Brown
Howard, Agnes Hodgkinson
Martinez, Maria Montoya
Netnokwa

Asian American
Brown, Julie Nguyen
Campbell, Phyllis Takisaki
Chang, Jo Mei
Chen, Joyce
Goon, Toy Len
Jung, Andrea
Lau, Joanna
Lewis, Loida Nicolas
Liang, Christine

Ming, Jenny J.
Natori, Josie
Poon, Christine A.
Yang, Linda Tsao
Young, Shirley

Austrian American
Carnegie, Hattie
Grossinger, Jenny

British American
Brent, Margaret
Estaugh, Elizabeth Haddon
Macaskill, Bridget
Moody, Lady Deborah
Pinckney, Eliza Lucas

Canadian American
Arden, Elizabeth
Pickford, Mary
Poon, Christina A.
Trudell, Cynthia
Wallace, Lila Acheson

Caribbean American
Cholmondeley, Paula

Dutch American
Timothy, Elizabeth

German American
Boyle, Gertrude
DeHaan, Crystal
Ehmann, Freda
Leeds, Lilo
Ottendorfer, Anna Sartorius Uhl
Philipse, Margaret Hardenbrook
Vernon, Lillian

Indian American
Bajaj, Kavelle
Nooyi, Indra K.

Irish American
Cashman, Nellie
Haughery, Margaret Gaffney
Pelham, Mary Singleton Copley
Reed, Nell Quinlan Donnelly

Israeli American
Dublon, Dina
Estrin, Judy
Friedman, Rachelle
Gadiesh, Orit

Italian American
Boehm, Helen F.

Latina
Aguirre, Pamela
Alvarado, Linda
Balverde-Sanchez, Laura
Banuelos, Romana Acosta
Barcelo, Maria Gertrudis
Elder, Irma
Haubegger, Christy
Hinojosa de Balli, Rosa Maria
Lagomasino, Maria Elena

Lithuanian American
Bryant, Lane

Philippino American
Lewis, Loida Nicolas
Natori, Josie

Polish American
Adler, Polly
Rubinstein, Helena

Russian American
Adler, Polly
Blumkin, Rose

Scottish American
Aitken, Jane

Appendix IV

**Colonial Businesswomen
1539–1800 (I)**
Ainse, Sally
Aitken, Jane
Alexander, Mary Spratt
   Provoost
Astor, Sarah Todd
Bosomworth, Mary Musgrove
   (Cousaponokeesa)
Brent, Margaret
Butterworth, Mary
Eldridge, Elleanor
Estaugh, Elizabeth Haddon
Franklin, Ann Smith
Goddard, Mary Katherine
Goddard, Sarah Updike
Greene, Catherine Littlefield
Hinojosa de Balli, Rosa Maria
Masters, Sybilla
Moody, Lady Deborah
Netnokwa
Nuthead, Dinah
Pelham, Mary Singleton Copley
Philipse, Margaret Hardenbroeck
Pinckney, Eliza Lucas
Stoneman, Abigail
Timothy, Ann

Timothy, Elizabeth

**Preindustrial Businesswomen
1800–1830 (II)**
Ainse, Sally
Aitken, Jane
Astor, Sarah Todd
Eldridge, Elleanor
Lukens, Rebecca Pennock
Netnokwa
Whittelsey, Abigail Goodrich

**Industrial Businesswomen
1830–1880 (III)**
Alberty, Eliza Missouri Bushyhead
Barcelo, Maria Gertrudis
Boit, Elizabeth Eaton
Bradwell, Myra Colby
Brown, Clara
Cashman, Nellie
Davis, Alice Brown
Demorest, Ellen Curtis
Green, Henrietta
Haughery, Margaret Gaffney
Keckley, Elizabeth Hobbs
King, Henrietta Chamberlain
Knight, Margaret
LaForge, Margaret Getchell

Lukens, Rebecca Pennock
Mason, Biddy
Nicholson, Eliza Jane Poitevant
   Holbrook
Ottendorfer, Anna Sartorius Uhl
Pinkham, Lydia Estes
Pleasant, Mary Ellen
Pringle, Elizabeth W. Allston
Whittelsey, Abigail Goodrich
Woodhull, Victoria Claflin

**Corporate Businesswomen
1880–1930 (IV)**
Adams, Evangeline
Albee, Mrs. P.F.E.
Alberty, Eliza Missouri Bushyhead
Anderson, Margaret C.
Andress, Mary Vail
Arden, Elizabeth
Ayer, Harriet Hubbard
Beach, Sylvia
Bissell, Anna
Boit, Elizabeth Eaton
Bradwell, Myra Colby
Bryant, Lane
Carnegie, Hattie
Cashman, Nellie
Davis, Alice Brown
Demorest, Ellen Curtis
Ehmann, Freda
Everleigh, Ada and Minna
Evinrude, Bess
Fields, Mary
Gilbreth, Lillian Moller
Gleason, Kate
Goon, Toy Len
Green, Henrietta
Greene, Mary Becker
Greenfield, Marguerite
Grossinger, Jennie
Keckley, Elizabeth Hobbs
King, Henrietta Chamberlain
Knight, Margaret
Knopf, Blanche Wolf
Knox, Rose Markward
Laimbeer, Nathalie Schenck
Lauder, Estee
Leslie, Miriam Follin

Malone, Annie Turnbo
Martinez, Maria Montoya
Mason, Biddy
Muller, Gertrude Agnes
Nicholson, Eliza Jane Poitevent
   Holbrook
Phillips, Lena Madesin
Pickford, Mary
Pinkham, Lydia Estes
Pleasant, Mary Ellen
Post, Marjorie Merriweather
Pringle, Elizabeth W. Allston
Reed, Nell Quinlan Donnelly
Reid, Helen Miles Rogers
Roche, Josephine
Roebling, Mary Gindhart
Ronzone, Bertha B.
Rosenthal, Ida
Rubinstein, Helena
Schoenleber, Gretchen
Shaver, Dorothy
Waldo, Ruth Fanshaw
Walker, Maggie Lena
Walker, Sarah Breedlove
   (Madame C.J.)
Wallace, Lila Acheson
White, Eartha Mary Magdalene
Willis, Gertrude Pocte Geddes
Woodhull, Victoria Claflin

**Midcentury Businesswomen
1930–1963 (V)**
Adams, Harriet Stratemeyer
Adler, Polly
Andress, Mary Vail
Arden, Elizabeth
Auerbach, Beatrice Fox
Ball, Lucille
Banuelos, Romana Acosta
Beech, Olive Ann
Bishop, Hazel Gladys
Blumkin, Rose
Boehm, Helen F.
Bryant, Lane
Bullitt, Dorothy Stimson
Carnegie, Hattie
Chen, Joyce
Claiborne, Liz

Clark, Catherine Taft
Cooney, Joan Ganz
Copley, Helen Kinney
Fetterman, Annabelle Lundy
Gilbreth, Lillian Moller
Goon, Toy Len
Graham, Bette Nesmith
Greene, Mary Becker
Grossinger, Jennie
Handler, Ruth
Hoffman, Ebba C.
Howard, Agnes Hodgkinson
Ilitch, Marian
Johnson, Claudia Alta (Lady Bird)
Knopf, Blanche Wolf
Knox, Rose Markward
Lauder, Estee
Lavin, Bernice Elizabeth
Lawrence, Mary Wells
Lewis, Harriet Gerber
Malone, Annie Turnbo
Martinez, Maria Montoya
Morgan, Rose
Muller, Gertrude Agnes
Nicholson, Eliza Jane Poitevent
    Holbrook
Patterson, Eleanor Medill
Payson, Joan Whitney
Phillips, Lena Madesin
Pickford, Mary
Post, Marjorie Merriweather
Proctor, Barbara
Reed, Nell Quinlan Donnelly
Reid, Helen Miles Rogers
Roche, Josephine
Roebling, Mary Gindhart
Ronzone, Bertha B.
Rosenthal, Ida
Rubinstein, Helena
Rudkin, Margaret Fogarty
Sandler, Marion O.
Schary, Hope Skillman
Schiff, Dorothy
Schoenleber, Gretchen
Schwartz, Felice N.
Seibert, Muriel
Shaver, Dorothy

Steigerwaldt, Donna Wolf
Totino, Rose
Vernon, Lillian
Waldo, Ruth Fanshaw
Wallace, Lila Acheson
Washington, Ruth
White, Eartha Mary Magdalene
Willis, Gertrude Pocte Geddes
Young, Shirley

**Modern Businesswomen
1963–1985 (VI)**
Adams, Harriet Stratemeyer
Alvarado, Linda
Arden, Elizabeth
Arnold, Susan E.
Ash, Mary Kay
Avent, Sharon Hoffman
Ball, Lucille
Banuelos, Romana Acosta
Barad, Jill Elikann
Barnes, Brenda C.
Barrett, Colleen C.
Bartz, Carol A.
Beck, Teresa
Beech, Olive Ann
Beers, Charlotte L.
Berman, Gail
Bern, Dorrit J.
Bernard, Betsy J.
Bernick, Carol Lavin
Birnbaum, Sheila
Bishop, Hazel Gladys
Black, Carole Lynn
Black, Cathleen Prunty
Blumkin, Rose
Boehm, Helen F.
Boyle, Gertrude
Brandt, Jan
Brinkley, Amy Woods
Brunson, Dorothy E.
Bullitt, Dorothy Stimson
Burns, Ursula M.
Campbell, Phyllis Takisaki
Carsey, Marcy
Castagna, Vanessa
Chen, Joyce
Cholmondeley, Paula

Christopher, Doris
Claiborne, Liz
Clark, Catherine Taft
Cohen, Abby Joseph
Cohen, Betty Susan
Cooney, Joan Ganz
Copley, Helen Kinney
Craig, Jenny
Davidson, Janet G.
DeHaan, Christel
Deily, Linnet
DiSesa, Nina
Disney, Anthea
Dubinsky, Donna
Dublon, Dina
Dunn, Patricia C.
Dwyer, Katherine M.
Dyson, Esther
Estrin, Judy
Fetterman, Annabelle Lundy
Fields, Debbi
Fili-Krushel, Patricia
Fiorina, Carleton S.
Fitt, Lawton W.
Friedman, Rachelle
Fudge, Ann M.
Gadiesh, Orit
Gilbreth, Lillian Moller
Gold, Christina A.
Goon, Toy Len
Gordon, Ellen Rubin
Graham, Bette Nesmith
Graham, Katharine
Grogan, Barbara B.
Grossinger, Jennie
Haben, Mary Kay
Hancock, Ellen
Handler, Ruth
Hart, Patti S.
Helmsley, Leona
Hoffman, Ebba
Hopkins, Deborah C.
House, Pat
Howard, Agnes Hodgkinson
Hudson, Dawn
Hughes, Catherine L.
Hulman, Mary Fendrich

Ilitch, Marian
Ingram, Martha
Jackson, Jeanne
Johnson, Abigail
Johnson, Antonia Ax:son
Johnson, Claudia Alta (Lady Bird)
Juliber, Lois D.
Jung, Andrea
Kanter, Rosabeth Moss
Karan, Donna
Katen, Karen L.
Keeth, Fran (Martha Frances)
Koplovitz, Kay
Lagomasino, Maria Elena
Lansing, Sherry
Lau, Joanna
Lauder, Estee
Lavin, Bernice Elizabeth
Lawrence, Mary Wells
Laybourne, Geraldine B.
Lazarus, Rochelle P.
Leeds, Lilo
Lehne, Kathy Prasnicki
Lepore, Dawn G.
Lewent, Judy C.
Lewis, Harriet Gerber
Love, Gay McLawhorn
Macaskill, Bridget
Magerko, Maggie
Magner, Marjorie
Mark, Rebecca
Marram, Ellen R.
Martinez, Maria Montoya
McCabe, Jewell Jackson
McGovern, Gail J.
McGrath, Judy
Miller, Heidi G.
Ming, Jenny J.
Minyard, Liz
Moore, Ann S.
Moore, Darla D.
Moran, Pat
Morgan, Cristina
Morgan, Rose
Mulcahy, Anne
Musham, Bettye Martin
Natori, Josie

Nelson, Marilyn Carlson
Nooyi, Indra K.
O'Dell, Jane
Odom, Judy C.
Owen, Dian Graves
Pascal, Amy
Payson, Joan Whitney
Peretsman, Nancy
Poon, Christine A.
Popcorn, Faith
Porter, Sylvia F.
Post, Marjorie Merriweather
Potter, Myrtle Stephens
Procope, Ernesta G.
Proctor, Barbara
Resnick, Lynda R.
Rhone, Sylvia M.
Rice, Linda Johnson
Rodale, Ardath
Roebling, Mary Gindhart
Rooney, Therese A.
Rosenthal, Ida
Rowland, Pleasant T.
Russo, Patricia F.
Sammons, Mary F.
Sandler, Marion O.
Sanford, Linda S.
Scardino, Marjorie
Schiff, Dorothy
Schwartz, Felice N.
Seifert, Kathi P.
Siebert, Muriel
Sneed, Paula A.
Steel, Dawn
Steigerwaldt, Donna Wolf
Steinem, Gloria
Stevens, Anne L.
Stewart, Martha
Sueltz, Patricia C.
Sweeney, Anne M.
Teel, Joyce Raley
Ticknor, Carolyn
Toben, Doreen A.
Totino, Rose
Trudell, Cynthia
Vernon, Lillian
Wachner, Linda Joy

Wallace, Lila Acheson
Washington, Ruth
White, Eartha Mary Magdalene
Whitman, Meg
Williams, Gretchen
Willis, Gertrude Pocte Geddes
Winblad, Ann L.
Winfrey, Oprah
Woertz, Patricia
Yang, Linda Tsao
Young, Shirley

Contemporary Businesswomen 1985 to Present (VII)

Aguirre, Pamela
Alvarado, Linda
Anthony, Michele
Arnold, Susan E.
Ash, Mary Kay
Avent, Sharon Hoffman
Bajaj, Kavelle
Balverde-Sanchez, Laura
Banta, Vivian
Banuelos, Romana Acosta
Barad, Jill Elikann
Barnes, Brenda C.
Barrett, Colleen C.
Bartz, Carol A.
Beck, Teresa
Beers, Charlotte L.
Bentas, Lily
Berman, Gail
Bern, Dorrit J.
Bernard, Betsy J.
Bernick, Carol Lavin
Birnbaum, Sheila
Black, Carole Lynn
Black, Cathleen Prunty
Blumkin, Rose
Boehm, Helen F.
Bostrom, Sue
Boyle, Gertrude
Brandt, Jan
Brinkley, Amy Woods
Brown, Julie Nguyen
Brunson, Dorothy E.
Bryan, Lisa Little Chief
Burns, Ursula M.

Campbell, Phyllis Takasaki
Carsey, Marcy
Castagna, Vanessa
Catz, Safra
Chang, JoMei
Chen, Joyce
Cholmondeley, Paula
Christopher, Doris
Cohen, Abby Joseph
Cohen, Betty Susan
Cooney, Joan Ganz
Copley, Helen Kinney
Corbi, Lana
Covey, Joy
Cox, Carrie Smith
Craig, Jenny
Davidson, Janet G.
DeHaan, Christel
Deily, Linnet
Desmond-Hellmann, Susan D.
Dillman, Linda
DiSesa, Nina
Disney, Anthea
Dubinsky, Donna
Dublon, Dina
Dunn, Patricia C.
Dwyer, Katherine M.
Dyson, Esther
Elder, Irma
Estrin, Judy
Farley, Claire S.
Fetterman, Annabelle Lundy
Fields, Debbi
Fili-Krushel, Patricia
Fiorina, Carleton S.
Fisher, Lucy
Fitt, Lawton W.
Floyd, Stacy Y.
Francesconi, Louise L.
Friedman, Rachelle
Fudge, Ann M.
Fuller, S. Marce
Gadiesh, Orit
Gaines, Brenda J.
Gallup, Patricia
George, Mari Hulman
Gold, Christina A.

Gordon, Ellen Rubin
Gorelick, Jamie
Graham, Katharine
Grogan, Barbara B.
Haben, Mary Kay
Hancock, Ellen
Handler, Ruth
Harris, Carla A.
Hart, Patti S.
Haubegger, Christy
Helmsley, Leona
Henretta, Deb
Hoffman, Ebba C.
Holden, Betsy D.
Hopkins, Deborah C.
House, Pat
Howard, Agnes Hodgkinson
Hubbard, Sonja Y.
Hudson, Dawn
Hughes, Catherine L.
Hulman, Mary Fendrich
Ilitch, Marian
Ingram, Martha
Jackson, Jeanne
Johnson, Abigail Pierrepont
Johnson, Antonia Ax:son
Johnson, Claudia Alta (Lady Bird)
Juliber, Lois D.
Jung, Andrea
Kanter, Rosabeth Moss
Karan, Donna
Katen, Karen L.
Keeth, Fran (Martha Frances)
Kipper, Barbara Levy
Kitchen, Louise
Koplovitz, Kay
Krawcheck, Sallie L.
Lagomasino, Maria Elena
Lansing, Sherry
Lau, Joanna
Lavin, Bernice Elizabeth
Laybourne, Geraldine B.
Lazarus, Rochelle P.
Lee, Thai
Leeds, Lilo
Lehne, Kathy Prasnicki
Lepore, Dawn G.

Lewent, Judy C.
Lewis, Harriet Gerber
Lewis, Loida Nicolas
Liang, Christine
Livermore, Ann
Longaberger, Tami
Love, Gay McLawhorn
Macaskill, Bridget
Mackenzie, Nanci
Magerko, Maggie
Magner, Marjorie
Mark, Rebecca
Marram, Ellen
McCabe, Jewell Jackson
McGovern, Gail J.
McGrath, Judy
Meeker, Mary G.
Miller, Heidi G.
Ming, Jenny J.
Minyard, Liz
Moore, Ann S.
Moore, Darla D.
Moran, Pat
Morgan, Cristina
Mulcahy, Anne
Musham, Bettye Martin
Natori, Josie
Nelson, Marilyn Carlson
Nooyi, Indra K.
O'Dell, Jane
Odom, Judy C.
Owen, Dian Graves
Pascal, Amy
Pearson, Donna Sutherland
Peretsman, Nancy
Poon, Christine A.
Popcorn, Faith
Potter, Myrtle Stephens
Procope, Ernesta G.
Proctor, Barbara
Quam, Lois
Renda, Larree M.
Resnick, Lynda R.
Rhone, Sylvia M.
Rice, Linda Johnson
Rivet, Jeannine M.

Robinson, Janet L.
Rodale, Ardath
Rooney, Therese A.
Rowland, Pleasant T.
Russo, Patricia F.
Rust, Lois
Sammons, Mary F.
Sandler, Marion O.
Sanford, Linda S.
Scardino, Marjorie
Seifert, Kathi P.
Siebert, Muriel
Sneed, Paula A.
Snider, Stacey
Srere, Linda Jean
Steel, Dawn
Steigerwaldt, Donna Wolf
Steinem, Gloria
Stevens, Anne L.
Stewart, Martha
Strobel, Pamela B.
Sueltz, Patricia C.
Sweeney, Anne M.
Teel, Joyce Raley
Thomas-Graham, Pamela
Ticknor, Carolyn
Toben, Doreen A.
Tomé, Carol B.
Trudell, Cynthia
Vernon, Lillian
Wachner, Linda Joy
Weinstein, Marta
Whitman, Meg
Williams, Gretchen
Willingham, Deborah
Winblad, Ann L.
Winfrey, Oprah
Woertz, Patricia
Woods, Emily
Woods, Jacqueline
Wright, Deborah C.
Yang, Linda Tsao
Yates, FaEllen
York, Denise DeBartolo
Young, Shirley

Appendix V

Accounting
Cholmondeley, Paula
Hopkins, Deborah C.

Advertising
Beers, Charlotte L.
DiSesa, Nina
Lawrence, Mary Wells
Lazarus, Rochelle P.
Proctor, Barbara
Srere, Linda Jean
Waldo, Ruth Fanshaw
Young, Shirley

Agriculture
Ehmann, Freda
Estaugh, Elizabeth Haddon
Greene, Catherine Littlefield
Pinckney, Eliza Lucas
Pringle, Elizabeth W. Allston
Resnick, Lynda R.
Rust, Lois

Aircraft Manufacturing
Beech, Olive Ann

Appliances
Bissell, Anna
Christopher, Doris

Evinrude, Bess
Lewis, Harriet Gerber
Muller, Gertrude Agnes

Astrology
Adams, Evangeline

**Automobiles/Dealers/Repairs/
Supplies**
Aguirre, Pamela
Brown, Julie Nguyen
Elder, Irma
Moran, Pat
O'Dell, Jane
Trudell, Cynthia
Young, Shirley

Baking
Clark, Catherine Taft
Haughery, Margaret Gaffney
Rudkin, Margaret Fogarty

Banking
Andress, Mary Vail
Bloch, Julia Chang
Brinkley, Amy Woods
Campbell, Phyllis Takasaki
Dublon, Dina
Gaines, Brenda J.

Gorelick, Jamie
Hopkins, Deborah C.
Lagomasino, Maria Elena
Laimbeer, Nathalie Schenck
Magner, Marjorie
Miller, Heidi G.
Roebling, Mary Gindhart
Sandler, Marion O.
Walker, Maggie Lena
Wright, Deborah C.
Yang, Linda Tsao

Boat Manufacturing
Trudell, Cynthia

Book Publishing
Adams, Harriet Stratemeyer
Beach, Sylvia
Knopf, Blanche Wolf
Rodale, Ardath

Broadcasting
Brunson, Dorothy E.
Bullitt, Dorothy Stimson
Hughes, Catherine L.
Johnson, Claudia Alta (Lady Bird)

Chemicals
Keeth, Fran (Mary Frances)

Construction
Alvarado, Linda
Grogan, Barbara B.

Consulting
Barnes, Brenda C.
Gadiesh, Orit
Gilbreth, Lillian Moller
Kanter, Rosabeth Moss
McCabe, Jewell Jackson
Phillips, Lena Madesin
Popcorn, Faith
Schwartz, Felice N.
Thomas-Graham, Pamela

Cosmetics
Albee, Mrs. P. F. E.
Arden, Elizabeth
Ash, Mary Kay
Ayer, Harriet Hubbard
Bishop, Hazel Gladys

Dwyer, Katherine M.
Jung, Andrea
Lauder, Estee
Rubinstein, Helena

Counterfeit Money
Butterworth, Mary

Defense
Francesconi, Louise L.
Lau, Joanna

Distribution
Ingram, Martha
Kipper, Barbara Levy

Electronics
Bajaj, Kavelle
Dubinsky, Donna
Fiorina, Carleton S.
Gallup, Patricia
Hancock, Ellen
Lau, Joanna
Livermore, Ann
Sanford, Linda S.
Ticknor, Carolyn

Energy/Gas/Oil
Farley, Claire S.
Kitchen, Louise
Lehne, Kathy Prasnicki
Mackenzie, Nanci
Mark, Rebecca
Strobel, Pamela B.
Woertz, Patricia

Entrepreneurism
Elldridge, Elleanor
Estrin, Judy
Fields, Mary
Pleasant, Mary Ellen
White, Eartha Mary Magdalene

Fashion/Clothing Design
Boit, Elizabeth Eaton
Boyle, Gertrude
Bryant, Lane
Carnegie, Hattie
Claiborne, Liz
Demorest, Ellen Curtis
Karan, Donna

Keckley, Elizabeth Hobbs
Natori, Josie
Reed, Nell Quinlan Donnelly
Rosenthal, Ida
Schary, Hope Skillman
Steigerwaldt, Donna Wolf
Wachner, Linda Joy
Woods, Emily

Films
Fisher, Lucy
Lansing, Sherry
Pascal, Amy
Pickford, Mary
Snider, Stacey
Steel, Dawn

Finance
Cohen, Abby Joseph
Deily, Linnet
Dunn, Patricia C.
Fitt, Lawton W.
Gadiesh, Orit
Green, Henrietta
Harris, Carla A.
Johnson, Abigail Pierrepont
Krawcheck, Sallie L.
Lepore, Dawn
Macaskill, Bridget
McGovern, Gail J.
Meeker, Mary G.
Moore, Darla D.
Morgan, Cristina
Peretsman, Nancy
Porter, Sylvia F.
Siebert, Muriel
Winblad, Ann L.
Woodhull, Victoria Claflin

Food
Balverde-Sanchez, Laura
Banuelos, Romana Acosta
Beck, Teresa
Bryan, Lisa Little Chief
Chen, Joyce
Ehmann, Freda
Fetterman, Annabelle Lundy
Fields, Debbie
Fudge, Ann M.

Gordon, Ellen Rubin
Haben, Mary Kay
Holden, Betsy
Hudson, Dawn
Ilitch, Marian
Knox, Rose Markward
Lewis, Loida Nicolas
Marram, Ellen R.
Nooyi, Indra K.
Post, Marjorie Merriweather
Rust, Lois
Schoenleber, Gretchen
Sneed, Paula A.
Totino, Rose

Gambling
Barcelo, Maria Gertrudes

Grocery Stores
Bentas, Lily
Floyd, Stacy Y.
Hubbard, Sonja Y.
Minyard, Liz
Renda, Larree M.
Teel, Joyce Raley
Williams, Gretchen
Yates, FaEllen

Haircare
Malone, Annie Turnbo
Morgan, Rose
Walker, Sarah Breedlove
  (Madame C.J.)

Healthcare
Handler, Ruth
Owen, Dian Graves
Quam, Lois
Rivet, Jeannine M.

Home Accessories
Longaberger, Tami
Resnick, Lynda R.
Stewart, Martha

Hospitality
Alberty, Eliza Missouri Bushyhead
Grossinger, Jennie
Helmsley, Leona
Nelson, Marilyn Carlson

Pleasant, Mary Ellen
Stoneman, Abigail

Imports
Alexander, Mary Spratt Provoost
Liang, Christine

Information Technology
Bostrom, Sue
Brandt, Jan
Catz, Safra
Covey, Joy
Dyson, Esther
Estrin, Judy
Hart, Patti S.
Whitman, Meg

Insurance
Banta, Vivian
Procope, Ernesta B.
Rooney, Therese A.
Walker, Maggie Lena
Willis, Gertrude Pocte Geddes

Inventing
Graham, Bette Nesmith
Knight, Margaret
Masters, Sybilla
Muller, Gertrude Agnes

Iron Production
Lukens, Rebecca Pennock

Madam
Adler, Polly
Everleigh, Ada
Everleigh, Minna

Magazine Publishing
Anderson, Margaret C.
Black, Cathleen Prunty
Haubegger, Christy
Leeds, Lilo
Leslie, Miriam Follin
Moore, Ann S.
Rice, Linda Johnson
Scardino, Marjorie
Steinem, Gloria
Wallace, Lila Acheson
Whittelsey, Abigail Goodrich

Mail Order/Home Selling
Ash, Mary Kay
Christopher, Doris
Gallup, Patricia
Vernon, Lillian
Woods, Emily

Merchant/Trader
Ainse, Sally
Alexander, Mary Spratt Provoost
Astor, Sarah Todd
Bosomworth, Mary Musgrove
   (Cousaponokeesa)
Davis, Alice Brown
LaForge, Margaret Getchell
Masters, Sybilla
Netnokwa
Pelham, Mary Singleton Copley
Philipse, Margaret Hardenbrook

Mining
Brown, Clara
Cashman, Nellie
Roche, Josephine

Music
Anthony, Michele
Friedman, Rachelle
Rhone, Sylvia

Newspaper Publishing
Black, Cathleen Prunty
Bradwell, Myra Colby
Copley, Helen Kinney
Disney, Anthea
Graham, Katharine
Leslie, Miriam Follin
Nicholson, Eliza Jane Poitevant
   Holbrook
Ottendorfer, Anna Sartorius Uhl
Patterson, Eleanor Medill
Reid, Helen Miles Rogers
Robinson, Janet
Scardino, Marjorie
Schiff, Dorothy
Washington, Ruth

Office Supplies
Avent, Sharon Hoffman
Burns, Ursula M.

Graham, Bette Nesmith
Hoffman, Ebba C.
Mulcahy, Anne

Packaging
Love, Gay McLawhorn

Pharmaceuticals
Cox, Carrie Smith
Desmond-Hellman, Susan D.
Katen, Karen L.
Lewent, Judy C.
Pinkham, Lydia Estes
Poon, Christine A.
Potter, Myrtle S.

Porcelain Art
Boehm, Helen F.

Pottery
Martinez, Maria Montoya

Printing
Aitken, Jane
Franklin, Ann Smith
Goddard, Mary Katherine
Goddard, Sarah Updike
Timothy, Ann
Timothy, Elizabeth

Ranching
Bosomworth, Mary Musgrove
  (Cousaponokeesa)
Hinojosa de Balli, Rosa Maria
Howard, Agnes Hodgkinson
King, Henrietta Chamberlain

Real Estate
Brent, Margaret
Brown, Clara
DeHaan, Christel
Eldridge, Elleanor
Estaugh, Elizabeth Haddon
Gleason, Kate
Helmsley, Leona
Mason, Biddy
Moody, Lady Deborah
Pleasant, Mary Ellen
White, Eartha Mary Magdalene

Restaurants
Chen, Joyce
Ilitch, Marian
Totino, Rose

Retail
Auerbach, Beatrice Fox
Bern, Dorrit J.
Blumkin, Rose
Castagna, Vanessa
Dillman, Linda
Jackson, Jeanne
Magerko, Maggie
Ming, Jenny J.
Pearson, Donna Sutherland
Ronzone, Bertha B.
Sammons, Mary F.
Shaver, Dorothy
Tomé, Carol B.

Services
Craig, Jenny
Goon, Toy Len
Greenfield, Marguerite
O'Dell, Jane
Weinstein, Marta

Software
Bartz, Carol A.
Catz, Safra
Chang, JoMei
Estrin, Judy
Lee, Thai
Odom, Judy C.
Sueltz, Patricia C.
Willingham, Deborah
Winblad, Ann L.
Woods, Jacqueline

Sports
George, Mari Hulman
Hulman, Mary Fendrich
Payson, Joan Whitney
York, Denise DeBartolo

Telecommunications
Bernard, Betsy J.
Davidson, Janet G.
Gold, Christina A.
Hart, Patti S.

Johnson, Antonia Ax:son
McGovern, Gail J.
Russo, Patricia F.
Toben, Doreen A.

Television
Ball, Lucille
Berman, Gail
Black, Carole Lynn
Carsey, Marcy
Cohen, Betty Susan
Cooney, Joan Ganz
Corbi, Lana
Fili-Krushel, Patricia
Koplovitz, Kay
Lansing, Sherry
Laybourne, Geraldine B.
McGrath, Judy
Sweeney, Anne M.
Thomas-Graham, Pamela
Winfrey, Oprah

Toiletries
Arnold, Susan E.
Bernick, Carol Lavin
Henretta, Deb
Juliber, Lois D.
Lavin, Bernice Elizabeth
Seifert, Kathi P.

Toys
Barad, Jill Elikann
Handler, Ruth
Rowland, Pleasant T.

Transportation
Barrett, Colleen
Greene, Mary Becker
O'Dell, Jane

Travel
DeHaan, Christel
Nelson, Marilyn Carlson

Appendix VI

Mary Kay Ash
Olive Beech
Liz Claiborne
Vieve Gove
Florence N. Graham
   (Elizabeth Arden)
Katharine Graham
Ruth Handler

Martha Ingram
Estee Lauder
Rebecca Lukens
Madame C. J. (Sarah)
   Walker
Maggie Lena Walker
Lila Acheson Wallace

Bibliography

ABI/INFORM. Ann Arbor, MI: Bell & Howell Information and Learning, 1971–.

Acker, Ally. *Reel Women: Pioneers of the Cinema, 1896 to the Present*. New York: Continuum, 1991.

Adalian, Josef, and Michael Schneider. "Berman Braves Dangers at Fox Top." *Variety* (May 29, 2000): 17.

Adams, David J. "Agnes Howard—A Woman Meeting the Challenges of Today's Ranching." *The Dakota Farmer* (November 1976): 14–15.

Adams, Evangeline. *The Bowl of Heaven*. Santa Fe, NM: Sun Publishing Company, 1926.

Adams, Russell L. *Great Negroes, Past and Present*. Chicago: Afro-American Publishing Co., 1964.

Adler, Polly. *A House Is Not a Home*. New York: Rinehart, 1953.

Advancing Women in Business: The Catalyst Guide. San Francisco: Jossey-Bass, 1998.

Aepel, Timothy. "Nail-Tough Daughter Mirrors Dad; She Runs 84 Lumber with an Iron Touch." *Denver Rocky Mountain News*, April 25, 1997, sec. A.

"Aerogen Elects Susan Desmond-Hellmann, M.D., M.P.H. to Board of Directors." *PR Newswire*, September 14, 2000. (Retrieved from *LEXIS-NEXIS Academic Universe* October 18, 2001.)

Agosta, Veronica. "At Carver, the CEO Has Control: Now Comes the Hardest Part." *American Banker* (October 30, 2000): 1.

Ahlers, Kate O'Brien, et al. "The Top 500 Women-Owned Businesses." *Working Woman* (June 1999).

Alarilla, Joey G. "Infotech Winblad: Separate the Real Thing from Dotcom Wannabes." *Philippine Daily Inquirer* (February 5, 2001).

Albertine, Susan, ed. *A Living of Words: American Women in Print Culture*. Knoxville, TN: University of Tennessee Press, 1995.

"Alberto-Culver Company." *Soap Cosmetics Chemical Specialties* (July 1996): 71. (Retrieved from *LEXIS-NEXIS Academic Universe* April 26, 1999.)

Alberts, Laurie. "Petticoats and Pickaxes." *Alaska Journal* 7 (Summer 1977): 146–159.

Albrecht, Brian E. "One Touch Mama Builds a Business: Making a Success from Outerwear." *The Cleveland Plain Dealer*, September 28, 1993, final edition, p. 1C.

Alexander, Garth. "The Cream of Wall St." *Sunday Times*, September 17, 1995, Business. (Retrieved from *LEXIS–NEXIS Academic Universe* April 26, 1999.)

Alioto, Maryann. "Anthea Disney." *Directors & Boards* (Winter 1999): 54–56.

———. "Brenda Barnes; Former President and CEO of Pepsi-Cola North America." *Directors & Boards* 22, no. 4 (June 22, 1998): 49.

"All Smiles and Mantra; Profile Ann Livermore, Hewlett-Packard." Inside Trace. *Financial Times*, November 9, 1998.

Allen, Margaret. "Southwest Airlines Head Takes Flight with Ground Control." *Houston Business Journal* 32 (August 24, 2001).

"Allen & Co.'s Nancy Peretsman and New York Stock Exchange's Catherine R. Kinney Named Financial Women's Association's 'Women of the Year.'" *Business Wire*, May 18, 2001. (Retrieved from *LEXIS-NEXIS Academic Universe* June 4, 2002.)

Alley, Robert S. *Women Television Producers: Transformation of the Male Medium.* Rochester, NY: University of Rochester Press, 2001.

Allison, Melissa. "Women in Banking's Upper Ranks Still Rare, But They Prefer to Focus on the Future." Business Plus. *Boulder Daily Camera*, October 2, 2000.

Alpha Kappa Alpha Sorority. *Women in Business*. Heritage Series 3. Chicago: Alpha Kappa Alpha Sorority, 1970.

Alter, Judy. *Extraordinary Women of the American West.* Danbury, CT: Children's Press, 1999.

Altman, Linda Jacobs. *Women Inventors*. New York: Facts on File, 1997.

Ambrose, Susan A., et al. *Journeys of Women in Science and Engineering.* Philadelphia: Temple University Press, 1997.

Amende, Coral. *Legends in Their Own Time.* New York: Prentice Hall, 1994.

American Business Leaders. Santa Barbara, CA: ABC-CLIO, 1999.

American Mothers' Committee. *Mothers of Achievement in American History 1776–1976: Bi-Centennial Project.* Rutland, VT: C.E. Tuttle Co., 1974–1976.

Amory, Cleveland. "Mrs. Payson's Ball Park." *Vogue* (September 15, 1964): 144–145.

Amory, Martha Babcock. *The Domestic and Artistic Life of John Singleton Copley, R.A.* Boston: Houghton, Mifflin, 1882.

Anders, George. *Perfect Enough: Carly Fiorina and the Reinvention of Hewlett-Packard.* New York: Portfolio, 2003.

Anderson, Margaret C. *The Autobiography.* 3 vols. Vol. 1, *My Thirty Years War*; Vol. 2, *The Fiery Fountains*; Vol. 3, *The Strange Necessity*. New York: Horizon Press, 1970.

———. *Forbidden Fires.* Tallahassee, FL: Naiad, 1996.

Andrews, Edmund L. "Patents: New Exhibit Shows History of Women Inventors." *New York Times*, January 20, 1990, sec. 1.

Andrews, Paul. "At the Center of Reshaping the New Microsoft—Vice President Deborah Willingham Stresses Service to Corporate Customers." *Seattle Times*, July 27, 1998, sec. A.

Angell, Mike. "Cisco: Net's Productivity Potential Untapped." *Investor's Business News Daily*, February 6, 2003, sec. A.

Angelo, Jean, et al. "Fast Trackers in Magazine Publishing." *Folio: The Magazine for Magazine Management* 16, no. 12 (December 1987): 94–118.

"Anne Sweeney Named President of ABC Cable Networks Group and President of Disney Channels Worldwide." *Business Wire*, October 10, 2000. (Retrieved from *LEXIS-NEXIS Academic Universe* January 10, 2001.)

Antilla, Susan. *Tales from the Boom-Boom Room: Women vs. Wall Street.* Princeton, NJ: Bloomberg Press, 2002.

"AOL Invests in Diversity; Hires Female H.R. Chief." Business & Technology. *Newsday,* June 29, 2001, sec. A.

Apgar, Sally. "Women on the Line." News, Stepping Up. *Minneapolis Star Tribune,* July 27, 1997, sec. A.

Applegate, Edd, ed. *The Ad Men and Women: A Biographical Dictionary of Advertising.* Westport, CT: Greenwood Press, 1994.

Araneta, Rana Lee. "Dressing Up for Success (Again)." *Working Woman* (June 2001): 4.

Archer, Jules. *The Unpopular Ones.* New York: Crowell-Collier Press, 1968.

"Arkansas Business Rankings: Wealthiest Arkansas Families." *Arkansas Business* 17:30 (July 24, 2000): 2/+. (Retrieved from Business and Company Resource Center, March 27, 2003.)

Aron, Laurie Joan. "Six Power Women: New York Women Who Are Emerging as Influential." *Crain's New York Business* (September 25, 2000): 34.

Aronoff, Craig, and John L. Ward, eds. *Contemporary Entrepreneurs: Profiles of Entrepreneurs and the Businesses They Started, Representing 74 Companies in 30 Industries.* Detroit: Omnigraphics, 1992.

"As Leaders, Women Rule." *Business Week* (November 20, 2000): 74.

Asbury, E. "Grand Old Lady of Johnstown." *Collier's* (January 1, 1949): 20–22.

Ash, Mary Kay. *Mary Kay: The Success Story of America's Most Dynamic Business Woman.* New York: Harper & Row, 1981.

Associations Unlimited. Farmington Hills, MI: Gale Group, 2000.

Atkinson, Steven D., and Judith Hudson, eds. *Women Online: Research in Women's Studies Using Online Databases.* New York: Haworth Press, 1990.

Auletta, Ken. *The Highwaymen: Warriors of the Information Superhighway.* New York: Random House, 1997.

Avery, Christine, and Diane Zabel. *The Flexible Workplace: A Sourcebook of Information and Research.* Westport, CT: Quorum Books, 2001.

Ayer, Margaret Hubbard, and Isabella Taves. *The Three Lives of Harriet Hubbard Ayer.* London: W.H. Allen, 1957.

Babco, Eleanor L., and Nathan E. Bell, eds. *Professional Women & Minorities,* 14th ed. Washington, DC: Commission on Professionals in Science and Technology, 2002.

Backover, Andrew. "AT&T Consumer Chief Loves a Challenge." Money. *USA Today,* August 15, 2001, sec. B.

Bainbridge, John. "Striking a Blow for Grandma." *New Yorker* (May 22, 1948): 38–40.

Baker, Beth. "First Lady to the Bar." Horizon. *Washington Post,* December 9, 1998, final edition, sec. H.

Ball, Lucille, with Betty Hannah Hoffman. *Love, Lucy.* New York: G.P. Putnam's Sons, 1996.

Bamford, Janet. "The 51% Solution: Marta Weinstein; Cofounder of Logistix." *Working Woman* (May 1995): 40.

———. "The *Working Woman* 50: America's Top Women Business Owners." *Working Woman* (May 1993): 49–62.

Bamford, Janet, and Susan McHenry. "The *Working Woman* 50." *Working Woman* (May 1994): 39–52.

————. "The *Working Woman* 50 Top Women Business Owners." *Working Woman* (May 1995): 37–48.

Bamford, Janet, and Jennifer Pendleton. "The Top 50 Women-Owned Businesses." *Working Woman* (October 1997): 34–61.

Banchera, Paola. "Raytheon Workers in Tucson, Ariz., Cheered by Missile Test." *Arizona Daily Star*, July, 17, 2001. (Retrieved from *LEXIS-NEXIS Academic Universe* April 29, 2004.)

Banner, Lois. *American Beauty*. Chicago: University of Chicago Press, 1983.

Barbosa, David. "Private Sector; Teacher, Cheerleader and CEO." *New York Times*, May 28, 2000, sec. 3.

Barker-Benfield, G.J., and Catherine Clinton. *Portraits of American Women: From Settlement to the Present*. New York: St. Martin's Press, 1991.

Barkholz, David. "An American Success Story: Ex-Refugee Now Hires Others." *Crain's Detroit Business* (June 5, 1989): 1–2.

Barrenechea, Mark J. *E-Business or Out of Business: Oracle's Roadmap for Profiting in the New Economy*. New York: McGraw-Hill, 2001.

Barriers to Women's Upward Mobility: Corporate Managers Speak Out; A Position Paper. New York: Catalyst, 1983.

Bass, Evan. "Former Cisco CTO Now CEO of Fourth Start-Up: Packet Design, Inc." *Fiber Optics News* (June 19, 2000). (Retrieved from *LEXIS-NEXIS Academic Universe* December 13, 2000.)

Bataille, Gretchen M., and Laurie Lisa, eds. *Native American Women: A Biographical Dictionary*. 2nd ed. New York: Garland Publishing, 1993.

Bates, Alan, and Clarke Hawley. *Moonlight at 8:30: The Excursion Boat Story*. Louisville, KY: Art-Print & Publishing Co., 1994.

Bauer, Hambla. "High Priestess of Beauty." *Saturday Evening Post* (April 24, 1948): 20–27.

Beach, Sylvia. *Shakespeare and Company*. New York: Harcourt Brace, 1959.

Beckham, Stephen Dow. *Many Faces: An Anthology of Oregon Autobiography*. Corvallis, OR: Oregon State University Press, 1993.

Beckles, Frances N. *20 Black Contemporary Women: A Profile of Contemporary Black Maryland Women*. Baltimore: Gateway Press, 1978.

"Bell Atlantic Elects Toben to New Vice President—Corporate Finance Position." *PR Newswire*, May 4, 1995. (Retrieved from *LEXIS-NEXIS Academic Universe* October 3, 2002.)

Bell, Ella L. J. Edmondson, and Stella M. Nkomo. *Our Separate Ways: Black and White Women and the Struggle for Professional Identity*. Cambridge, MA: Harvard Business School, 2001.

Benjaminson, Peter. *Death in the Afternoon: America's Newspaper Giants Struggle for Survival*. Kansas City: Andrews, McMeel & Parker, 1984.

Bennett, Lerone. "An Historical Detective Story." *Ebony* (April/May 1979): 71–86, 90–96.

Berenson, Alex. "From Low-Key Boutique to Pressure-Cooker Firm." *New York Times*, October 31, 2002, sec. C.

Berger, Lance A., and Dorothy R., eds. *The Compensation Handbook*. New York: McGraw-Hill, 1999.

Bergman, Anne. "Honoree Profile: Marcy Carsey: Television Honoree." *Daily Variety*, September 8, 2000, special sec., p. B2.

Berman, Phyllis. "Fat City." *Forbes* (February 17, 1992): 72–74.

Bernhut, Stephen. "Orit Gadiesh: Taking Charge in Uncertain Times." *Ivey Business Journal* 66, no. 3 (January–February 2002): 28–34.

Bernick, Carol Lavin. "When Your Culture Needs a Makeover." *Harvard Business Review* 79, no. 6 (June 2001): 53–60.

Bernstein, Carl, and Bob Woodward. *All the President's Men.* New York: Simon and Schuster, 1974.

"Betting on Farm Girl Grit: Smead's Ebba Hoffman." *Working Woman* (May 1994): 5.

Bettner, Jill Donahue, et al. "Now They're Not Laughing." *Forbes* 132, no. 12 (November 21, 1983): 116–130.

"Betty Cohen Stepping Down as President of Cartoon Network Worldwide to Pursue Next Venture within AOL Time Warner/Turner Broadcasting Family." *Business Wire,* June 15, 2001. (Retrieved from *LEXIS-NEXIS Academic Universe* April 29, 2002.)

Beyond Excellence: The Superachievers. Boston: Nathan/Tyler, 1986.

Bhupta, Malini. "Keeping the Faith." *Asia Africa Intelligence Wire,* January 8, 2003. (Retrieved from *Business & Company Resource Center* March 3, 2003.)

Bianco, Anthony. "Inside a $15 Billion Dynasty." *Business Week* (September 29, 1997): 64–76.

———. "The Prophet of Wall Street." *Business Week* (June 1, 1998): 124–134.

Billard, Mary. "Women on the Verge of Being CEO." *Business Month* (April 1990): 26–41.

Billington, Monroe Lee, and Roger D. Hardaway, eds. *African Americans on the Western Frontier.* Boulder, CO: University Press of Colorado, 1998.

Biographical Cyclopaedia of American Women. New York: Halvord Publishing Co., 1924–.

Biography and Genealogy Master Index. Farmington Hills, MI: Gale Group, 2001.

Biography Index. Bronx, NY: H.W. Wilson, 1984–.

Bird, Caroline. *Enterprising Women.* New York: W.W. Norton & Co., 1976.

Bishop, Joan. "Game of Freeze-Out: Marguerite Greenfield and Her Battle with the Great Northern Railway, 1920–1929." *Montana: The Magazine of Western History* (Summer 1985): 14–27.

Bisoux, Tricia, "A New E-Attitude." *BizEd* (January/February 2002): 15–17.

Black, Carole, and Coeli Carr. "Executive Life: The Boss; Risks Are Allowed." *New York Times,* April 7, 2000, sec. 3.

Block, Valerie. "Multimedia Effort Aims to Empower Business Women: *Working Woman* Network Debuts Web Site." *Crain's New York Business* (August 14, 2000): 4.

Bodipo-Memba, Alejandro. "Detroit Auto Supplier's Bankruptcy Filing Offers Sad Ending for Family Dream." *Detroit Free Press,* October 15, 2001.

Boehm, Helen F. *With a Little Luck—An American Odyssey.* New York: Rawson, 1985.

Bois, Danuta. "Mary Musgrove (Cousaponokeesa)." In www.DistinguishedWomen.com/biographies/html. (Retrieved May 11, 2000.)

Boland, Vincent. "Bull in a Bear Market Remains Undeterred: The Interview." *Financial Times,* December 23, 2002.

Bollier, David. *Aiming Higher: 25 Stories of How Companies Prosper by Combining Sound Management and Social Vision.* New York: AMACOM, 1996.

Bonk, Jenny. "Irma Elder: Strength of a Jaguar." *AmericanWomen Motorscene* 11, no. 1 (February 1999): 8.

Book, Esther Wachs. "Leadership for the Millenium." *Working Woman* (March 1998): 29–34.

———. *Why the Best Man for the Job Is a Woman: The Unique Female Qualities of Leadership.* New York: HarperBusiness, 2000.

Books in Print. New Providence, NJ: R.R. Bowker, 1998–.

Booth, Robin W. *Famous African Americans: In Fine Arts, Sports, Science and Politics.* Austin, TX: Steck-Vaughn, 1997.

Born, Matt. "Media News: The Most Powerful Woman in Britain?" *Daily Telegraph,* April 14, 2000.

Bott, Jennifer. "Big Three Automakers Find Few Qualified Women to Fill Top Posts." *Knight-Ridder/Tribune Business News,* October 11, 1998. (Retrieved from *Business & Company Resource Center* February 17, 2000.)

Bowers, Barbara. "First Lady of Wall Street." *Best's Review* 103, no. 3 (July 2002): 39–43.

Bowman, Garda, et al. "Are Women Executives People?" *Harvard Business Review* (July–August 1965): 14–20.

Boynick, David K. *Women Who Led the Way: Eight Pioneers for Equal Rights.* New York: Crowell, 1959.

Bradsher, Keith. "From Factory to the Top of Saturn," Private Sector. *New York Times,* December 20, 1998, sec. 3.

Brady, Diane. "From Nabisco to Tropicana to . . . efdex?" *Business Week* (September 20, 1999): 100.

Brady, Kathleen. "The CEO of Comedy." *Working Woman* 11 (October 1986): 92–96.

Branch, Shelly. "A Premium Asset on Wall Street: After 40 Years of Running a Successful Insurance Firm, Ernesta and John Procope Are Expanding Their Financial Empire." *Black Enterprise* (December 1993): 100–105.

Brands, H.W. *Masters of Enterprise.* Philadelphia: The Free Press, 1999.

Brawley, Benjamin Griffith. *Negro Builders and Heroes.* Chapel Hill: University of North Carolina Press, 1965. First published 1937.

"Breaking the Mold: Ford's Anne Stevens Is One of a New Breed of Auto Execs with Expertise in Many Disciplines." *Automotive News* (April 3, 2000): 3.

Bredin, Alice. *The Home Office Solution.* New York: John Wiley & Sons, 1998.

Briggs, Bill. "Pampered Parents? Childless Employees Beginning to Grumble about Inequalities." *Denver Post,* July 9, 2000, Sunday Lifestyles sec.

Brodsky, Norm. "Who Are the Real Entrepreneurs?" *Inc.* (December 1996): 33.

Brokaw, Leslie. "Case in Point." *Inc.* (December 1995): 88.

Bronikowski, Lynn. "Woman of Vision." *ColoradoBiz* 27, no. 5 (May 2000).

Brooker, Katrina. "It Took a Lady to Save Avon: Elegant and Poised, with a Will of Iron, Andrea Jung Knows How to Win." *Fortune* (October 15, 2001): 202–208.

Brooks, John, ed. *Autobiography of American Business.* Garden City, NY: Doubleday & Co., 1974.

Brooks, Nancy Rivera. "Business a Grind for Chorizo Queen." *Los Angeles Times,* December 15, 1987, Business sec., home edition.

Brown, Carrie. *Rosie's Mom: Forgotten Women Workers of the First World War.* Boston: Northeastern University Press, 2002.

Brown, Carolyn. "They've Got the Power." *Black Enterprise* (August 1996): 63–66.

Brown, Hallie Q., comp. *Homespun Heroines and Other Women of Distinction.* New York: Oxford University Press, 1988.

Brush, Candida G. "Research on Women Business Owners: Past Trends, a New Perspective and Future Directions. *Entrepreneurship Theory and Practice* (Summer 1992): 5–30.

Bruyn, Kathleen. *"Aunt" Clara Brown: Story of a Black Pioneer.* Boulder, CO: Pruett Publishing Co., 1970.

BSR Staff. "Diversity." BSR White Papers. Business for Social Responsibility. http:// bsr.org/BSRResources/WhitePaperDetail.cfm?DocumentID=353. (Retrieved February 5, 2003.)

Buechner, M.M., et al. "Inside the Top Fifty *Time Digital* Cyber Elite." *Time Digital* (October 5, 1998): 29–55.

Bulkley, Kate. "Corporate Profile: Pearson—Will Marge Stay in Charge?" *The Independent,* September 19, 2001, Business sec.

Bundles, A'Lelia. *On Her Own Ground: The Life and Times of Madam C.J. Walker.* New York: Simon & Schuster, 2000.

Burke, Ronald J., and Debra L. Nelson, eds. *Advancing Women's Careers.* Malden, MA: Blackwell Publishers, 2002.

Burkett, Elinor. *The Baby Boon.* New York: Free Press, 2000.

Burns, Greg. "She's on a Roll; Decades of Waiting Make Success Even Sweeter for Tootsie President." People Plus. *Chicago Sun-Times,* October 31, 1993, late sports final edition.

Burrows, Peter. *Backfire: Carly Fiorina's High-Stakes Battle for the Soul of Hewlett-Packard.* New York: Wiley, 2003.

———. "The Hottest Property in the Valley?" *Business Week* (August 30, 1999).

Burstyn, Joan N., ed. *Past and Promise: Lives of New Jersey Women.* Women's History Project of New Jersey. Metuchen, NJ: Scarecrow Press, 1990.

Business and Company Resource Center. Farmington Hills, MI: Gale Group, 1980–.

Business Dateline. Ann Arbor, MI: Bell & Howell Information and Learning, 1985–.

"Business 100: A Celebration of Irish American Corporate Success." *Irish America Magazine* (December/January 2000): 37–62.

Business: The Ultimate Resource. Cambridge, MA: Perseus Publishing, 2002.

Butter, Andrea, and David Pogue. *Piloting Palm.* New York: John Wiley & Sons, 2002.

Buttner, E. Holly. "Examining Female Entrepreneurs' Management Style: An Application of a Relational Frame." *Journal of Business Ethics* 29, no. 3 (February 2001): 253–269.

Byrne, Pamela R., and Susan K. Kinnell, eds. *Women in North America; Summaries of Biographical Articles in History Journals.* People in History Series. Santa Barbara, CA: ABC-CLIO, 1988.

Byron, Christopher. *Martha Inc.: The Incredible Story of Martha Stewart Living Omnimedia.* New York: Wiley, 2002.

Cagle, Jess. "The Women Who Run Hollywood: The 'Boys Club' That Dominates the Film Industry Is Making Way for Three Women with Attitude—and a String of Hits." *Time,* July 29, 2002: 52–54.

Cahill, Jospeh B. "Debt Swamps Star Who Beat the Odds: Proctor Battles to Save Ad Firm; Files Chapter 11." *Crain's Chicago Business* (September 18, 1995): 1.

Cahn, Steven M., ed. *The Affirmative Action Debate.* 2nd ed. New York: Routledge, 2002.

Calvey, Mark. "ExecutiveProfile: Patricia Dunn." *San Francisco Business Times* (September 21, 2001): 11.

Caminiti, Susan. "Turnaround Titan." *Working Woman* (December/January 1999): 54–57.

———. "What It Takes to Make It on Wall Street." *Working Woman* (March 1999): 57–61.

———. "Writing Her Own Ticket." *Working Woman* (September 2000): 21–22.

Canedy, Dana. "Passed Over Before, a Woman Is Named Chief Executive." *New York Times,* November 11, 1999, late edition.

Cannon, Carl M. "The Adams Chronicle." *Working Woman* (October 1997): 24–27.

Cantwell, Alice. "Hall of Fame Pays Tribute to the Heroines of Maritime." *Journal of Commerce,* August 18, 1995 sec. A.

Capell, Kerry. "It Sure Ain't the Ladies' Auxiliary." *Business Week* (May 12, 1997): 127.

Carberry, Sonja. "Innovators Ole and Bess Evinrude." Leaders and Success. *Investors Business Daily,* July 6, 1999, sec. A.

Careers and the MBA 30th Anniversary Issue: The Changing Face of the MBA 30, no. 2. Cambridge, MA: Crimson & Brown Associates, 1998.

Carey, Charles W., Jr. *American Inventors, Entrepreneurs, and Business Visionaries.* New York: Facts on File, 2002.

Carey, Robert. "Geraldine Laybourne—a.k.a. the Velvet Hammer—Uses Her Teaching Background and a Culture of Fun to Keep Children's Television Nickelodeon Creative, Productive and Profitable." *Sales & Marketing Management* 147, no. 12 (December 1995): 14.

Carlassare, Elizabeth. *DotCom Divas: E-Business Insights from the Visionary Women Founders of 20 Net Ventures.* New York: McGraw-Hill, 2001.

Carlin, John. "Queen of the Netarati: John Carlin on a Woman Whose Intimidating Intelligence Dominates all Things Digital; Profile: Esther Dyson." *The Independent* (October 19, 1997): 3.

"Carolyn M. Ticknor Named General Manager of HP's LaserJet Printer Group." *Business Wire,* January 5, 1994. (Retrieved from *LEXIS-NEXIS Academic Universe* June 7, 1999.)

Carr, David. "President to Retire from Times Co.: Successor Named." *New York Times,* February 20, 2004, sec. C.

Carrington, Evelyn M., ed. *Women in Early Texas.* Austin, TX: Texas State Historical Association, 1994.

Carter, Bill. "ABC-TV Gets a New President with Wider Duties." *New York Times,* August 1, 1998, sec. D.

———. "Cadillac-Sized Hits by the VW of Producers: Carsey-Werner Keeps Its Independence and Still Picks Television's Winners." Business/Financial Desk. *New York Times,* January 22, 1996, sec. D.

Carter, Joan Harrell. "Commuter Marriages." *Black Enterprise* (February 1992): 247–248.

Casison, Jeanie. "The Producers." *Incentive* 178, no. 2 (February 2004): 28–32.

Cassidy, John. "The Woman in the Bubble: Internet Analyst M. Meeker." *New Yorker* (April 26–May 3, 1999).

Catalyst. *Cracking the Glass Ceiling: Catalyst's Research on Women in Corporate Management, 1995–2000.* New York: Catalyst, 2000.

Catalyst. *Creating Successful Mentoring Programs: A Catalyst Guide.* New York: Catalyst, 2002.

Catalyst. *Knowing the Territory: Women in Sales*. New York: Catalyst, 1995.

Catalyst. *The Next Generation: Today's Professionals, Tomorrow's Leaders*. New York: Catalyst, 2001.

Catalyst. *A New Approach to Flexibility: Managing the Work/Time Equation*. New York: Catalyst, 1998.

Cateura, Linda. *Growing Up Italian*. New York: Morrow, 1987.

Caudron, Shari. "The Concrete Ceiling." *Industry Week* 243, no. 13 (July 4, 1994): 31–34.

———. "Constructive Criticism." *Industry Week* 242, no. 12 (June 21, 1993): 12–14.

Cawley, Janet. "The 50 Most Famous People of the Century." *Biography Magazine* (December 1999): 74–80.

———. "The Most Powerful Women in America." *Biography Magazine* (April 1999): 68–80.

———. "The 25 Most Influential Women in America." *Biography Magazine* (June 2002): 64–74.

Celebrity Biographies. Baseline II Inc. (Retrieved from *LEXIS-NEXIS Academic Universe*, various dates.)

Center for Women's Business Research (www.nfwbo.org).

Census of Women Directors of the Fortune 1000. New York: Catalyst, 1993–.

"CFO's Faith in Future Worth Millions: Joy Covey Must Convince Investors to Accept Losses for Several Years While Amazon.com Inc. Rebuilds Its Role on the Internet." *Ottawa Citizen*, March 27, 1999, sec. E.

Chandler, Sally. "Maggie Lena Walker (1867–1934): An Abstract of Her Life and Activities." Master's thesis, Virginia Commonwealth University, 1975.

Chapin, Howard M. *Ann Franklin of Newport: Printer, 1736–1763*. Cambridge, MA: 1924.

Chappell, Lindsay. "Daughter Keeps Dynasty Going; Pat Moran Answered Dad's Call." *Automotive News* (February 28, 2000): 38.

Chappelle, Tony. "Time to Take the Spotlight at TLC." *New York Times*, November 27, 1994, sec. 3.

Chaput, Don. "In Search of Silver and Gold." *American History* 30 (January/February 1996): 36–40.

Check, Dawn Lynn. "Easy Does It: Products from the Pampered Chef Eases Meal-Making for Busy Families." *Pittsburgh Post-Gazette*, September 22, 1996, food sec., five star edition.

Chen, Helen. *Helen Chen's Chinese Home Cooking*. 1994.

Chen, Joyce. *Joyce Chen's Cookbook*. New York: Barnes & Noble, 1983.

Cheney, L. V. "Mrs. Frank Leslie's Illustrated Newspaper." *American Heritage* 26 (October 1975): 42–48.

"Chevron Names Dave O'Reilly As a Vice Chairman; Patricia Woertz Named President of Products Company." *Canada NewsWire*, October, 28, 1998. (Retrieved from *LEXIS-NEXIS Academic Universe* October 7, 2004.)

Christopher, Doris. *Come to the Table: A Celebration of Family Life*. New York: Warner Books, 1999.

Chunovic, Louis. "Most Powerful Women in Television." *Electronic Media* 21, no. 41 (October 14, 2002). (Retrieved from *Business & Company Resource Center* March 24, 2003.)

———. "Plugging Hallmark into Cable Market: President and CEO Lana Corbi Has Sights Set on a Higher Brand Profile." *Electronic Media* 21 (January 21, 2002): 28.

"Citigroup Names Marge Magner to Oversee Primerica Financial Services and Citibanking, North America." *Business Wire*, December 3, 1999. (Retrieved from *LEXIS-NEXIS Academic Universe* October 18, 2000.)

Clair, Blanche, and Dorothy Dignam. *Advertising Careers for Women*. New York: Harper & Brothers, 1939.

Clarke, Caroline V. "Carla Harris Uses Her Prowess to Make Billion-Dollar Deals and Uplift Youth." *Black Enterprise* (February 2003): 104–105.

———. "A New Johnson Is CEO." *Black Enterprise* (June 2002): 136.

Clarke, Robyn D. "Excellence by the Graham." *Black Enterprise* (September 2001): 78–79.

———. "High-Frequency Profits." *Black Enterprise* (June 2000): 130–136.

Cleary, David Powers. *Great American Brands*. New York: Fairchild Publications, 1981.

Cleaver, Joanne. "The Top 25 Companies for Executive Women." *Working Women* (December/January 2001): 58–74.

"Clinton Picks Yang as Asian Bank Director." *Los Angeles Times*, July 13, 1993, sec. D.

Clymer, Eleanor Lowenton. *Modern American Career Women*. New York: Dodd, Mead, 1959.

"Cocktails at Charlotte's with Martha and Darla." *Fortune* (August 5, 1996): 56–58.

Coeyman, Marjorie. "No Man's Land: Women Are Emerging as a Force at all Levels of the Industry." *Restaurant Business* 96, no. 12 (June 15, 1997): 44–53.

Cohen, Adam. *The Perfect Store: Inside eBay*. Boston: Little Brown, 2002.

Cohen, David. "Hands-on Leader Brings Out Best in Sony's Team." *Variety* (August 19, 2002): A16–A18.

Cohen, Deborah L. "Kraft CEO Is Ready to Enter the Food Fray." *Crain's Chicago Business* (May 22, 2002): 4.

Cohen, Scott. *Meet The Makers: The People Behind the Product*. New York: St. Martin's Press, 1979.

Coleman, Lisa. "I Went Out and Did It." *Forbes* (August 17, 1992): 102–103.

Coleman, Susan. "Access to Capital and Terms of Credit: A Comparison of Men- and Women-Owned Businesses." *Journal of Small Business Management* 38, no. 3 (July 2000): 37–52.

Collingwood, Harris. "The Toughest Job in the Phone Business." *Working Woman* (June 1997): 23–26.

Collins, Kathleen, "The Top Women-Owned Businesses." *Working Woman* (June 2001): 45–69.

Collins, Sharon. *Black Corporate Executives: The Making and Breaking of a Black Middle Class*. Philadelphia: Temple University Press, 1977.

The Complete Marquis Who's Who Biographies. (Retrieved from *LEXIS-NEXIS Academic Universe*, April 29, 1999.)

Conant, Jennet. "Sherry Lansing." *Harpers Bazaar* (January 1994): 112–113.

Connecticut Women's Hall of Fame. http://www.cwhf.org/browse/dir.html.

Contemporary Black Biography. Vol. 1. Detroit: Gale Research, 1992.

Contemporary Women's Issues. Responsive Database Services, 1992–.

"A Conversation with Vanessa Castagna." *Chain Store Age Executive with Shopping Center Age* 76 (January 2000): 60.

Coolidge, Shelley Donald. "Trading 30,000 Staff for 3 Kids." Business & Money. *Christian Science Monitor*, October 8, 1997.

Cooper, Gary. "Stage Coach Mary: Gun Toting Montanan Delivered the U.S. Mail." As Told to Marc Crawford. *Ebony* (October 1959): 97–100.

Cooper, Jim. "The USA According to Kay." *Brandweek* 39, no. 18 (May 4, 1998): 54–46.

Cooper, Victor H. *A Dangerous Woman: New York's First Lady Liberty; The Life and Times of Lady Deborah Moody; Her Search for Freedom of Religion in Colonial America*. Bowie, MD: Heritage Books, 1995.

Copple, Brandon. "Shelf-Determination." *Forbes* (April 15, 2002): 131–142.

Corcoran, Elizabeth. "Goodwill Ambassador: Cisco's Fastest-Rising Star Brings in Business But Doesn't Sell Routers." *Forbes* (November 13, 2000): 124–128.

Corr, Casey O. *KING: The Bullitts of Seattle and Their Communications Empire*. Seattle: University of Washington Press, 1996.

Cott, Nancy F., ed. *History of Women in the United States: Historical Articles on Women's Lives and Activities*. Vol. 8, *Professional and White-Collar Employments*. Parts 1 and 2. Munich, Germany: K.G. Saur, 1993.

Council on Economic Priorities. *Women and Minorities in Banking: Shortchanged Update*. New York: Praeger, 1977.

Cox, Dan. "Sony Reels in Fisher." *Daily Variety*, October 19, 1995, p. 1.

Crawford, Ann Fears. *Women in Texas: Their Lives, Their Experiences, Their Accomplishments*. Austin, TX: State House Press, 1992.

"Creative Artists Agency Hires *Latina Magazine* Founder Christy Haubegger." *Business Wire*, February 12, 2003. (Retrieved from Lexis–Nexis Academic *Universe* April 5, 2003.)

Crockett, Barton. "Golden West's Golden Couple Retiring? No Way." *American Banker* 161, no. 135 (July 17, 1996): 1–2.

Crumb, Tyra. "Rising to the Top: These Women Are Breaking Stereotypes in a Male-Dominated Industry. *Dallas Business Journal* 15, no. 46 (July 17, 1992): 17–20.

Current Biography. New York: H.W. Wilson, 1940–1999.

Current Biography Yearbook. New York: H.W. Wilson, 1955–.

Cyclopaedia of American Biography. New York: The Press Association Compilers, 1915–1931.

Dabney, Thomas Ewing. *One Hundred Great Years: The Story of the Times-Picayune from Its Founding to 1940*. New York: Greenwood Press, 1944.

Dabney, Wendell P. *Maggie Walker and the I. O. of St. Luke: The Woman and Her Work*. Cincinnatti: The Dabney Publishing Co., 1927.

Daniel, Carter A. *MBA: The First Century*. Lewisburg, PA: Bucknell University Press, 1998.

Daniel, Jere. "The Loan Ranger: Banker Darla Moore Rescues Collapsing Corporations and Their Honchos from the Terrors of Bankruptcy." *Executive Female* 14, no. 3 (May 1991): 37.

Daniel, Jo Beth. "To Serve and Protect." *Working Woman* (April 2000): 78–80.

Daniels, Cora. "The Most Powerful Black Executives in America." *Fortune* (July 22, 2002): 60–80.

Dannett, Sylvia G. L. *Profiles of Negro Womanhood*. New York: M.W. Lads, 1964.

Darrow, Barbara. "Sortware Spectrum: Moving to Services at Net Speed." *Computer Reseller News*, April 26, 1999. (Retrieved from *LEXIS-NEXIS Academic Universe* April 30, 2004.)

DataTimes Newspaper Abstracts and Index. Ann Arbor, MI: Bell & Howell Information and Learning, 1986–.

Davidson, Marilyn J. *The Black and Ethnic Minority Woman Manager: Cracking the Concrete Ceiling.* London: Paul Chapman Publishing, 1997.

Davies-Netzley, Sally Ann. *Gendered Capital: Entrepreneurial Women in American Society.* New York: Garland, 2000.

Davis, Andrea. "Rap-sody & Blue: Sylvia Rhone." *Executive Female* 13, no. 3 (May 1990): 40.

Davis, Elizabeth Logan. *Mothers of America.* Fleming H. Revell Company, 1954.

Davis, Marianna W., ed. *Contributions of Black Women to America.* Vol. 1, *The Arts, Media, Business, Law, Sports.* Columbia, SC: Kenday Press, 1982.

Davis, William. *The Innovators: The Essential Guide to Business Thinkers, Achievers and Entrepreneurs.* New York: AMACOM, 1987.

"Dawn Steel." *Variety* (January 5, 1998): 90.

De Rouffignac, Ann. "Kathy Lehne Takes Sun Coast Resources Inc. to the Top." *Houston Business Journal* 26, no. 16 (September 6, 1996): S4.

Deal, Terrence E., and Allan A. Kennedy. *Corporate Cultures: The Rites and Rituals of Corporate Life.* Reading, MA: Addison-Wesley, 1982.

———. *The New Corporate Cultures: Revitalizing the Workplace after Downsizing, Mergers, and Reengineering.* Reading, MA: Perseus Books, 1999.

"Deborah C. Wright." *Executive Female* (February 2000): 12.

Decker, Jeffrey Louis. *Made in America: Self-Styled Success from Horatio Alger to Oprah Winfrey.* Minneapolis: University of Minnesota Press, 1997.

Demeter, Richard. *Primer, Presses and Composing Sticks: Women Printers of the Colonial Period.* Hicksville, NY: Exposition Press, 1979.

DePauw, Linda Grant. *Founding Mothers: Women in the Revolutionary Era.* Boston: Houghton Mifflin, 1975.

———. *Remember the Ladies: Women in America, 1750–1815.* New York: Viking Press, 1976.

Derdak, Thomas, ed. *International Directory of Company Histories.* Chicago: St. James Press, 1988–.

Deutsch, Claudia. "Affirmative Action: Selling to Big Companies Cautiously in the Mainstream; Minorities Move Ahead as Political Currents Shift." *New York Times,* June 7, 1995, sec D.

———. "At Xerox, the Chief Earns (Grudging) Respect." *New York Times,* June 2, 2002, sec. D.

———. "Profile: Relighting the Fires at Avon Products." *New York Times,* April 3, 1994, sec. 3.

Dexter, Elisabeth Williams Anthony. *Career Women of America, 1776–1840.* Francestown, NH: M. Jones Co., 1950.

———. *Colonial Women of Affairs: Women in Business and the Professions before 1776.* New York: A.M. Kelley, 1972. First published 1931.

Diamonstein, Barbaralee. *Open Secrets: Ninety-Four Women in Touch with Our Time.* New York: Viking, 1972.

Dictionary of American Biography. New York: C. Scribner's Sons, 1928–1958.

Dictionary of American Biography Supplements. New York: C. Scribner's Sons, 1973–.

Didio, Laura. "Corporate Strategist: Dawn Lepore." *Computerworld* 31, no. 48 (December 1, 1997): 37.

Dietrich, Joy. "Women Reach High." *Advertising Age International* (January 2000): 22–23.

"Digital 50." *Time Digital* (October, 4, 1999): 36–40.

Dingle, Derek K. "TLC's Final Act." *Black Enterprise* (September 1999): 118–119.

Dishon, Betty. "A Woman in the Ice Business." *American Magazine* (May 1921): 54.

"Disney Mogul Sweeney Breaks Mold." *Boston Globe*, April 17, 1998, sec. F.

Dissertations Abstracts Online. Ann Arbor, MI: Bell & Howell Information and Learning, 1861–.

"Diversity Dialogues." *Working Mother* (November 2003): 65–74.

Dobbs, Kevin. "Training: The Last, Best Hope for the Nation's Poorest?" *Training* 37, no. 7 (July 2000): 56–63.

Dobrzynski, Judith H. "Way beyond the Glass Ceiling." *New York Times*, May 11, 1995, sec. D.

Dogar, Rana. "The Top 500 Women-Owned Businesses." *Working Woman* (May 1998): 35–80.

Donovan, Carrie. "Designer Donna Karan: How a Fashion Star Is Born." Magazine Desk. *New York Times*, May 4, 1986, late city edition, sec. 6.

Doward, Jamie. "Mammon: Can Marge Stay in Charge?" *The Observer*, March 9, 2003.

Dowd, Maureen. "Power: Are Women Afraid of It—Or Beyond It?" *Working Woman* (November 1991): 98–99.

———. "Rich Little Rich Girl." *New York Times*, February 12, 1995, Section 7, p. 9, col. 1.

Drachman, Virginia G. *Enterprising Women: 250 Years of American Business*. Chapel Hill, NC: University of North Carolina Press, 2002.

Drago, Harry Sinclair. *Notorious Ladies of the Frontier*. New York: Dodd, Mead, 1969.

Driscoll, Dawn-Marie, and Carol R. Goldberg. *Members of the Club: The Coming of Age of Executive Women*. New York: The Free Press, 1993.

Dubeck, Paula J., and Kathryn Borman, eds. *Women and Work: A Handbook*. New York: Garland Publishing, 1996.

Dudley, Brier. "Microsoft's Human-Resources Chief to Retire in February." *Seattle Times*, November 14, 2002. (Retrieved from *LEXIS-NEXIS Academic Universe* March 27, 2003.)

Duff, Carolyn. *Learning from Other Women*. New York: AMACOM, 1999.

Dunlap, Phil. "Life in Indiana: The State's Largest Life/Health Insurance Carriers." *Indiana Business Magazine* 40, no. 9 (September 1996): 20–29.

Durso, Joseph. "Joan Whitney Payson: America's Sublime Amateur—of Baseball, Racing, Art; Saint Joan of the Mets." *Vogue* (June 1, 1970): 93–95.

Dwyer, Kelly Pate. "Fortune Smiles on Colorado Woman: Magazine Puts Exec in Top 50." *Denver Post*, October 5, 2003, sec. K.

Dyson, Esther. *Release 2.1: A Design for Living in the Digital Age*. New York: Broadway Books, 1998.

"The e.biz 25: The Most Influential People in Electronic Business." *E.biz Supplement* (September 27, 1999): 32–50.

"*Ebony* Interview with Linda Johnson Rice." *Ebony* (November 1992): 208–209.

Edgecliffe-Johnson, Andrew. "Two Brains May Be Better Than One Big Cheese." Inside Track. *Financial Times*, September 3, 2001, edition 1.

Editors of *The Wall Street Journal*. *The New Millionaires and How They Made Their Fortunes*. New York: B. Geis Associates, 1961.

Educational Foundation for Women in Accounting. "Statistical Survey." www. efwa.org/statsurvey.htm. 1996. (Retrieved on December 15, 2003.)

Ehrhart-Morrison, Dorothy. *No Mountain High Enough: Secrets of Successful African American Women*. Berkeley, CA: Conari Press, 1997.

Elkind, Peter. "Where Mary Went Wrong." *Fortune* (May 14, 2001): 68–82.

Elliott, Stuart. "From One Woman to Another, Ogilvy & Mather Is Making History." Business/Financial Desk. *New York Times*, September 9, 1996, late edition, sec. D.

Emert, Carol. "JoMei Chang: Boundless Ambition." *San Francisco*, September 9, 2001, sec. E. (Retrieved from *LEXIS-NEXIS Academic Universe* March 19, 2003.)

Encyclopedia of American Biography: New Series. New York: American Historical Society, 1936.

Engle, Paul. *Women in the American Revolution*. Chicago: Follett, 1976.

Enrico, Dottie. "Rainmakers: Women Bring a Flood of New Business to Madison Avenue Firms." *USA Today*, October 27, 1997, sec. B.

Ericksen, Gregory K. *What's Luck Got to Do With It? Twelve Entrepreneurs Reveal the Secrets Behind Their Success*. New York: John Wiley & Sons, 1997.

———. *Women Entrepreneurs Only: 12 Women Entrepreneurs Tell the Stories of Their Success*. New York: John Wiley & Sons, 1999.

"Executive Profile." *San Francisco Business Chronicle* 11, no. 42 (May 30, 1997): 10.

"The 'Exelon Way' Business Model Approved." *PR Newswire*, April 29, 2003. (Retrieved from *LEXIS-NEXIS Academic Universe* November 25, 2003.)

Eyman, Scott. *Mary Pickford, America's Sweetheart*. New York: D. I. Fine, 1990.

Fabe, Maxene. *Beauty Millionaire: The Life of Helena Rubinstein*. New York: Crowell, 1972.

Fabrikant, Geraldine. "Making Sure the Rich Stay Rich, Even in Crisis." *New York Times*, October 7, 2001, sec 3.

Faircloth, Anne. "The Class of '83." *Fortune* (October 12, 1998): 126–128.

———. "Minding Martha's Business." *Fortune* (September 29, 1997): 173–176.

"Fannie Mae's Vice Chair Jamie Gorelick to Step Down in July." *Business Wire*, January 10, 2003. (Retrieved from *LEXIS-NEXIS Academic Universe*, April 4, 2003.)

Faragher, John Mack, ed. *The Encyclopedia of Colonial and Revolutionary America*. New York: Facts on File, 1990.

Farmer, Melanie Austria. "The Powerhouse Who Leads a Billion-Dollar Business." *DiversityInc.* (July 2003). (Retrieved from www.jnj.com October 13, 2003.)

Farrar, Rebecca. "President of East Knox County, Tenn., Boating Company Discusses Career." *Knoxville News-Sentinel*, December 27, 2002. (Retrieved from *LEXIS-NEXIS Academic Universe* March 26, 2003.)

Fasci, Martha A., and Jude Valdez. "A Performance Contrast of Male- and Female-Owned Small Accounting Practices." *Journal of Small Business Management* (July 1998): 1–7.

Feagans, Brian. "In the Swine Business, Little Guys Are Few." *Sunday Star-News*, October 31, 1999, sec. A.

Feder, Barnaby J. "A Retailer's Home Grown Business." *New York Times*, June 17, 1994, sec. D.

Felder, Deborah G. *The 100 Most Influential Women of All Time: A Ranking Past and Present*. Secaucus, NJ: Carol Publishing Group, 1996.

Feldman, Gayle. "Breaking Through the Glass Ceiling: Women Have Had a Long Hard Struggle to Reach Their Current Status in the Industry." *Publishers Weekly* 244, no. 31 (July 1997): 82–88.

Fenster, Julie M. *In the Words of Great Business Leaders.* New York: John Wiley & Sons, 2000.

Ferris, Jeri, and Ralph L. Ramsted. *With Open Hands: The Story of Biddy Mason.* Minneapolis: Carolrhoda Books, 1999.

Fiedelholtz, Sara. "Emily Woods: J. Crew's Steady Captain." *Women's Wear Daily* (September 1, 1993): 10–12.

Fields, Debbi, and Alan Furst. *One Smart Cookie.* New York: Simon and Schuster, 1987.

"50 Smartest Women in the Money Business (and What You Can Learn from Them)." *Money* (May 15, 2000): 76–78.

Finn, Robin. "The Woman behind Lifetime's Surge." *New York Times,* February 6, 2001, late edition, sec. B.

Finnigan, Annie. "Benefits under Fire." *Working Woman* (July/August 2001): 54–57, 78.

———. "Different Strokes." *Working Woman* (April 2001): 42–48.

"First: They're Hot (or Not); In 2000, They're the People to Watch." *Fortune* (January 10, 2000): 22–28.

Fischer, Alan D. "Tucson Mom Is Also Raytheon Head, Takes Job in Stride." *Arizona Daily Star,* December 17, 2002. (Retrieved from *LEXIS-NEXIS Academic Universe* April 4, 2003.)

Fischer, Christiane. *Let Them Speak for Themselves; Women in the American West, 1849–1900.* Hamden, CT: Archon Books, 1977.

Fischler, Elizabeth. "Making a Difference: Another in a Series of Articles about Men and Women Who Have Changed Life on Long Island." *New York Times,* February 13, 2000, sec. L.

Fisher, Anne. "Women Need at Least One Mentor and One Pantsuit." *Fortune* (October 12, 1998): 208.

Fisher, Kenneth L. *100 Minds That Made the Market.* Woodside, CA: Business Classics, 1995.

Fisk, Holly Celeste. "With Relish." *Entrepreneur* (May 1997): 24.

Fitch, Noel Riley. *Sylvia Beach and the Lost Generation: A History of Literary Paris in the Twenties and Thirties.* New York: Norton, 1983.

Fitzgerald, Beth. "CEO of Prudential's Financial Services Unit Started as Part-Time Consultant." *Star-Ledger,* August 22, 2000. (Retrieved from *Lexis-Nexis Academic Universe* October 18, 2000.)

Flaherty, Tina Santi. "Gender Communication: Mute Issue?" *Executive Female* 23, no. 3 (April 2000): 14–15.

Flanner, J. "Life on a Cloud." *New Yorker* (June 3, 1974): 44–46.

Fleming, Jane Hill. "Women Evolve to Survive in Competitive Workforce." *National Underwriter* 99, no. 37 (September 11, 1995): 29, 32–35.

Flint, Joe. "Sweeney to Head Fox Cable Channel." *Broadcasting & Cable* 123, no. 23 (June 7, 1993): 20.

Florence, Mari. *Sex at Work: Attraction, Orientation, Harassment, Flirtation and Discrimination.* Los Angeles: Silver Lake, 2001.

Flynn, Michael. "Cissie." *Time* 52 (August 2, 1948): 36.

Fogarty, Mark. "Bypassing the Industry's Glass Ceiling." *U.S. Banker* (March 1999). (Retrieved from Business and Company Resource Center, February 22, 2001.)

"The *Forbes* 400: The Richest People in America." *Forbes* (October 12, 1998): 280–330.

Forbes Inc. *Forbes Great Minds of Business: Companion to the Public Television Series.* New York: John Wiley & Sons, 1997.

Foreman, Carolyn Thomas. "Aunt Eliza of Tahlequah." *Chronicles of Oklahoma* 9 (March 1931): 43–55.

Foremski, Tom. "Serial Entrepreneur Strikes Again." Inside Track. *Financial Times,* August 7, 2000, p. 1.

Forest, Stephanie Anderson. "Paddling as Fast as She Can." *Business Week* (May 1, 2000): 89.

Forest, Stephanie Anderson. "Software Spectrum: Have They Got a Program for You." *Business Week* (May 25, 1992): 91.

Forgrieve, Janet. "Pioneering Cable Exec Gets Help from Kids: Keynote Speaker for Athena Awards Lunch Began at Nickelodeon." *Rocky Mountain News,* August 15, 2003, sec. B.

———. "Sun Exec Puts Family First." *Rocky Mountain News,* July 1, 2002, sec. B.

Fowler, Tom. "Barreling Back: Dot-Com CEO Back in Oil Industry She Loves." *Houston Chronicle,* January 10, 2001, p. 1.

Fox, Mary Virginia. *A Queen Named King: Henrietta of the King Ranch.* Austin, TX: Eakin Press, 1986.

Frank, Robert. *Parenting Partners: How to Encourage Dads to Participate in the Daily Lives of Their Children.* New York: St. Martin's Press, 2000.

Frankel, Mark. "Letting Go." *Working Woman* (June 2001): 50–53.

Franklin, Mary Beth. "The Dream Lives On: Immigrant from India Founds a Business and Finds Herself." Womanews. *Chicago Tribune,* July 17, 1994, Chicagoland final edition.

Franks, James A. *Mary Fields: The Story of Black Mary.* Santa Cruz, CA: Wild Goose Press, 2002.

Fraser, Edie, ed. *Risk to Riches: Women and Entrepreneurship in America.* Washington, DC: Institute for Enterprise Advancement, 1986.

Fraser, Jill Andresky. "Indecent Exposure." *Inc.* (December 1997): 151.

———. "Just Say No." *Inc.* (August 1996): 98.

Freeman, Laurie. "Carol Bernick: Alberto VP Stays Busy with Product Development, Helping Raise Funds for Chicago Women's Hospital." *Advertising Age* (July 17, 1989): 32.

Freeman, Lisa Lee. "CEO of Sex." *Working Woman* (March 1999): 29–31.

———. "The Top 500 Women-Owned Businesses." *Working Woman* (June 2000): 51–94.

Frezza, Bill. "Champions of the New Economy Get Rich the Old-Fashioned Way." *Internet Week* (August 28, 2000): 29.

Friedman, Jane M. *America's First Woman Lawyer: The Biography of Myra Bradwell.* Buffalo, NY: Prometheus Books, 1993.

Frois, Jeanne. *Louisianans All.* Gretna, LA: Pelican Publishing Co., 1992.

Fucini, Joseph J., and Suzy. *Entrepreneurs: The Men and Women behind Famous Brand Names and How They Made It.* Boston: GK Hall, 1985.

Fudge, Ann M. "The Boss: Nuns, Bicycles and Berries." *New York Times,* January 12, 2000, sec. C.

Fuentes, Sonia Pressman. "The EEOC, NOW, and Me: My Work in Women's Rights." *Iris—A Journal about Women,* no. 34 (1996): 13–20.

Fuller, Jennifer Mann. "Sutherland Lumber Often Takes the Quiet Way." *Kansas City Star*, September 23, 1997, sec. E.

Furman, Phyllis. "Challenging Role for Movie Exec Snider, Seeks Universal Reversal." *New York Daily News*, December 7, 1998.

Fusaro, Dave. "For the Love of Cheese." *Dairy Foods* 100, no. 9 (September 1999): J.

Gabriel, Frederick P., Jr. "Fast Track: Abby Johnson: Promotion Goes beyond Dad's Fidelity." *Investment News* (May 28, 2001): 16.

Gabriel, Mary. *Notorious Victoria: The Life of Victoria Woodhull, Uncensored.* Chapel Hill, NC : Algonquin Books of Chapel Hill, 1998.

Gall, Susan, ed. *Reference Library of Asian America.* Detroit: Gale Research, 1995.

Gallagher, Carol, with Susan K. Golant. *Going to the Top: A Road Map for Success from America's Leading Women Executives.* New York: Viking, 2000.

Gallese, Liz Roman. "Corporate Women on the Move." *Business Month* 133, no. 4 (April 1989): 30–35.

Gamber, Wendy. *The Female Economy: The Millinery and Dressmaking Trades, 1860–1930.* Urbana: University of Illinois Press, 1997.

Garraty, John A., and Mark C. Carnes, eds. *American National Biography.* New York: Oxford University Press, 1999.

Garry, Michael. "Wal-Mart's CIO Dillman Details RFID Tag Plans." *Supermarket News* (June 16, 2003): 1.

Gaw, Jonathan. "The Spine behind the Ingram Empire." Financial Desk. *Los Angeles Times*, June 6, 1999, sec. C.

Geitz, Christopher. "Fisher a Catch for Sony Pix." *Daily Variety* June 18, 1998, special section. (Retrieved from *LEXIS-NEXIS Academic Universe* December 19, 2000.)

General Business File. Farmington Hill, MI: Gale Group, 1980–.

Gerstner, John. "The Civilization of Cyberspace: Interview with Cyberspace Specialist Esther Dyson." *Communication World* 15, no. 6 (June 16,1998): 37–38.

"Getting Boeing to Fly Right." *Business Week* (September 27, 1999): 104.

Gilbert, Jennifer. "AOL's Marketing Builds Service into Powerhouse." *Advertising Age* (March 6, 2000): S2.

Gilbert, Lynn, and Gaylen Moore. *Particular Passions: Talks with Women Who Have Shaped Our Times.* New York: C.N. Potter, 1981.

Gilbreth, Frank Bunker, and Ernestine Gilbreth Carey. *Belles on Their Toes.* New York: T.Y. Crowell Co., 1950.

———. *Cheaper by the Dozen.* New York: T.Y. Crowell Co., 1948.

Gilbreth, Lillian. *As I Remember: An Autobiography.* Norcross, GA: Engineering and Management Press, 1998.

Gildersleeve, Genieve N. *Women in Banking: A History of the National Association of Bank Women.* Washington, DC: Public Affairs Press, 1959.

Gill, Brendan. *Late Bloomers.* New York: Artisan, 1996.

Gill, Libby. *Stay-at-Home Dads: The Essential Guide to Creating the New Family.* New York: Plume, 2001.

Gillmore, Inez Haynes. *Angels and Amazons: A Hundred Years of American Women.* New York: Arno Press, 1974. First published 1933.

Giscombe, Katherine, and Mary C. Mattis. "Leveling the Playing Field for Women of Color in Corporate Management: Is the Business Case Enough?" *Journal of Business Ethics* 37, no. 1 (April 2002): 103–119.

Gite, Lloyd, and Dawn M. Baskerville. "Black Women Entrepreneurs on the Rise." *Black Enterprise* (August 1996): 72–82.

Gittell, Jody Hoffer. *The Southwest Airlines Way: Using the Power of Relationships to Achieve High Performance.* New York: McGraw-Hill, 2003.

Gluck, Sherna Berger. *Rosie the Riveter Revisited: Women, the War, and Social Change.* Boston: Twayne Publishers, 1987.

Godfrey, Nicola. "Key Player." *Working Woman* (December/January 2000): 32–34.

Goffee, Robert, and Richard Scase. *Women in Charge: The Experiences of Female Entrepreneurs.* London/Boston: George Allen & Unwin, 1985.

Gold, Jacqueline S. "Chase's Private Bank Chief Applies Life Lessons, Has a 'Blast.'" *American Banker* (November 29, 1999): 7.

Goldberg, Laura. "Southwest's New Co-Pilots: As New President, Barrett Plans to Keep Helping Airline 'Customers.'" *Houston Chronicle*, April 22, 2001, Sunday 2 star edition.

Golden, Kristen, and Barbara Findlen. *Remarkable Women of the Twentieth Century: 100 Portraits of Achievement.* New York: Friedman/Fairfax Publishers, 1998.

Goldman, Abigail. "1999/2000 Review & Outlook: People to Watch in 2000." *Los Angeles Times*, January 2, 2000, sec. C.

Goldsmith, Barbara. *Other Powers: The Age of Suffrage, Spiritualism, and the Scandalous Victoria Woodhull.* New York: Knopf, 1998.

"Golf & Business." *Fortune* (April 1, 2002): 177–184.

Graham, Katharine. *Personal History.* New York: Knopf, 1997.

Graham, Sandy. "Out of the Limelight: Where Are They Now?" *Colorado Business* 22, no. 6 (June 1995).

Granatstein, Lisa. "*People* Person." *Brandweek* 40, no. 10 (March 8, 1999): 50–51.

Grande, Carlos. "Publisher with a Strong Penchant for Oprah: Interview with Cathleen Black, Hearst Magazines." *Financial Times*, February 11, 2003. (Retrieved from *LEXIS-NEXIS Academic Universe* March 10, 2003.)

Graves, Laura M., and Gary N. Powell. "Effects of Sex-Based Preferential Selection and Discrimination on Job Attitudes." *Human Relations* 47, no. 2 (February 1994): 133–158.

Gray, Dorothy. *Women of the West.* Millbrae, CA: Les Femmes Publishers, 1976.

Gray, P.B. "Juiced Up." *Working Woman* (December/January 1999): 59–61.

Greco, JoAnn. "Mattel Faces a Baby Bust." *Journal of Business Strategy* (September/October 1998): 23–24.

Green, Frances W. *Memoirs of Elleanor Eldridge.* Providence: B.T. Albro, 1843.

Green, Leslie. "Hopkins Credits Walsh College for Her Success." *Crain's Detroit Business* (June 26, 2000): 33.

———. "NorthCastle Ropes in New Partner." *Buyouts*, September 25, 2000. (Retrieved from *LEXIS-NEXIS Academic Universe*, January 5, 2001.)

Green, Patricia G., et al. "Patterns of Venture Capital Funding: Is Gender a Factor?" *Venture Capital* 3, no. 1 (2001): 63–83.

Greene, Katherine, and Richard. "The Best-Paid Women in Corporate America." *Working Woman* (January 1994): 28–32.

———. "The Top-Paid Women in Corporate America." *Working Woman* (February 1996): 40–45.

———. "The 20 Top-Paid Women in Corporate America." *Working Woman* (January 1995): 36–38.

Greising, David. "Chicago Tribune David Greising Column." *Knight-Ridder/Tribune Business News*, October 16, 2000. (Retrieved from *Business & Company Resource Center* October 16, 2002.)

Griffin, Lynne, and Kelly McCann. *The Book of Women*. Holbrook, MA: Bob Adams, 1992.

Griffiths, Sian, ed. *Beyond the Glass Ceiling: Forty Women Whose Ideas Shape the Modern World*. New York: Manchester University Press, 1996.

The Grolier Library of North American Biographies. Vol. 3. *Entrepreneurs and Inventors*. Danbury, CT: Grolier Educational Corporation, 1994.

Gross, Daniel M. "The Next CEOs." *Working Woman* (December/January 1999): 40–50.

Grossinger, Tania. *Growing up at Grossinger's*. New York: David McKay, 1975.

Guilford, Dave. "Rough Start Made Elder an Expert on Turnover." *Automotive News* (February 2, 1998): 106–108.

Gutner, Toddi. "Progress? Not as Much as You Thought." *Business Week* (February 18, 2002): 108.

———. "The Rose-Colored Glass Ceiling." *Business Week* (September 2, 2002): 101.

Guyon, Janet. "In Europe: No. 1 Marjorie Scardino, 53." *Fortune* (October 16, 2000): 170–172.

Guzzardi, Walter. "Wisdom from the Giants of Business." *Fortune* (July 3, 1989): 78–86.

Habela, Hala. "Expert: Don't Get Emotional with Investments." *Dallas Business Journal* 24, no. 38 (May 4, 2001): 23.

Haben, Mary Kay. "Shattering the Glass Ceiling." *The Executive Speaker* 22, no. 1 (January 2001): 3.

Hagan, Oliver, et al., eds. *Women-Owned Businesses*. New York: Praeger, 1989.

Hajdin, Mane. *The Law of Sexual Harassment*. Selinsgrove, PA: Susquehanna University Press, 2002.

Hajewski, Doris. "Mattel Buying State Doll Maker Pleasant Co." *Milwaukee Journal Sentinel*, June 16, 1998, final edition, p. 1.

Haley, Delphine. *Dorothy Stimson Bullitt; An Uncommon Life*. Seattle: Sasquatch Books, 1995.

Halkias, Maria. "Wal-Mart Exec Becomes J.C. Penney's CEO." *Dallas Morning News*, July 15, 1999.

Hall, Douglas T. "Promoting Work/Family Balance: An Organizational Change Approach." *Organizational Dynamics* 18, no. 3 (January 1990): 4–19.

Hall, Lee. "Pamela Thomas-Graham." *Electronic Media* 22, no. 3 (January 20, 2003): 60.

Hallett, Anthony, and Diane Hallett. Entrepreneur Magazine *Encyclopedia of Entrepreneurs*. New York: John Wiley & Sons, 1997.

Hamilton, David P. "Sun Hires IBM Executive Patricia Sueltz to Take Control of Its Software Division." *Wall Street Journal*, September 29, 1999, eastern edition, sec. B.

Hammer, Richard. *The Helmsleys: The Rise and Fall of Harry and Leona*. New York: Signet, 1991.

Hammond, Teena. "Banana Republic Eyes New Formats and Revived Catalog." *Women's Wear Daily* (April 21, 1997): 1–4.

Hanaford, Phebe. *Daughters of America; or, Women of the Century*. Augusta, ME: True, 1883.

Handbook of Texas Online. www.tsha.utexas.edu/handbook/online (Retrieved April 29, 2004.)

Handler, Elliott. *The Impossible Really Is Possible: The Story of Mattel*. New York: Newcomen Society in North America, 1968.

Handler, Ruth, with Jacqueline Shannon. *Dream Doll: The Ruth Handler Story*. Stamford, CT: Longmeadow Press, 1994.

Hannon, Kerry. "Why Women Put Stock in NASDAQ." *Working Woman* (March 1996).

Hansen, Fay. "Truth and Myths about Work/Life Balance." *Workforce* 81, no. 13 (December 2002): 34–40.

"Happiness Headquarters." *Time* (November 29, 1937): 55.

"Hard-to-Find Products Gaining Presence Online." *Canada Newswire*, November 22, 2000. (Retrieved from *LEXIS-NEXIS Academic Universe*, January 1, 2001.)

Hardy, Quentin. "Cover Story: All Carly All the Time." *Forbes* (December 3, 1999): 138–144.

Harrell, Wilson. "Female of the Species: Entrepreneurship; Do Men and Women Do It Differently?" *Success* 44, no. 7 (September 1997): 104.

Harriman, Margaret Case. "Profiles: Glamour, Inc." *New Yorker* (April 6, 1935): 20–26.

Harrington, Ann. "The Power 50." *Fortune* (October 15, 2001): 194–201.

Harrison, James Henry. *Pearl Rivers, Publisher of the Picayune*. New Orleans: Department of Education, Tulane University, 1932.

Harrison, Roger. *Consultant's Journey: A Dance of Work and Spirit*. San Francisco: Jossey-Bass, 1995.

Hartman, Mary S., ed. *Talking Leadership: Conversations with Powerful Women*. New Brunswick, NJ: Rutgers University Press, 1999.

Hartnett, Michael. "Rose Blumkin: Retailing in the 90s Means Something Different." *Stores* 71, no. 1 (January 1992): 168–172.

Harton, Tom. "DeHaan Has RCI on a Roll after 1st Year at the Helm." *Indiana Business Journal* 11, no. 16 (July 30, 1990): 1A–2A.

Hartwell, Dickson. "No Prissy Is Cissy." *Collier's* (November 30, 1994): 21, 72–78.

Haukebo, Kirsten. "Revamped Chamber Gets First Pep Talk." *The Courier-Journal*, March 17, 1998, sec. C.

Haven, Kendall. *Amazing American Women*. Englewood, CO: Libraries Unlimited, 1995.

Hayes, Cassandra. "Sister CEOs Speak Out." *Black Enterprise* (August 1996): 68–70.

Hayes, Cassandra, ed. "20 Black Women of Power & Influence." *Black Enterprise* (August 1997): 60–82.

———. "Ursula M. Burns: Vice President and General Manager, Departmental Copier Business, Xerox." *Black Enterprise* (August 1997): 62.

Hays, Constance. "Bridging a 'Generation Next' Gap," Private Sector, *New York Times*, January 31, 1999, sec. 3.

Healy, Beth. "Fidelity Executive Quits to Teach at Harvard." *Boston Globe*, April 11, 2002, sec. C.

Healy, Paul F. *Cissy: The Biography of Eleanor M. "Cissy" Patterson*. New York: Doubleday, 1966.

Heidenry, John. *Theirs Was the Kingdom: Lila and Dewitt Wallace and the Story of Reader's Digest*. New York: W.W. Norton, 1993.

Heilbrun, Carolyn G. *The Education of a Woman: The Life of Gloria Steinem*. New York: Dial Press, 1995.

"Helen K. Copley Steps Down as Chairman, Publisher; Son to Succeed Her." *Associated Press,* April 30, 2001. (Retrieved from *LEXIS-NEXIS Academic Universe,* April 29, 2002.)

Helgesen, Sally. *The Female Advantage: Women's Ways of Leadership.* New York: Doubleday Currency, 1995.

Hellman, Geoffrey T. "Profiles: Publisher." *New Yorker* (December 4, 1948): 40–47.

Helms, Marilyn M. "Women and Entrepreneurship: The Appealing Alternative. *Business Perspectives* 10, no. 1 (1997): 16–20.

Henrici, Lois Oldham. *Representative Women: Being a Little Gallery of Pen Portraits.* Kansas City, MO: The Crafters Publishers, 1913.

Herera, Sue. *Women of the Street: Making It on Wall Street—The World's Toughest Business.* New York: Wiley & Sons, 1997.

———— and Ron Insana. "Sallie Krawcheck of Sanford Bernstein on Independence of Research Analysts." *CNBC News Transcripts,* Business Center, August 1, 2002. (Retrieved from *LEXIS-NEXIS Academic Universe* October 6, 2002.)

Herman, Steve. "Woman Who Issued Command 'Gentlemen, Start Your Engines,' Dies. *Associated Press,* April, 11, 1998. (Retrieved from *LEXIS-NEXIS Academic Universe* May 5, 2002.)

Hiltzik, Michael. "Duo's Success Built on Old-School Approach." *Los Angeles Times,* March 3, 2003, sec. 3.

————. "A Veteran of the Fast Track Following Her Own Path." *Los Angeles Times,* April 3, 2003, sec. 3.

Hine, Darlene Clark, ed. *Black Women in America: An Historical Encyclopedia.* Brooklyn: Carlson Publishing, 1993.

————, ed. *Facts on File Encyclopedia of Black Women in America.* Volume 3: Business and Professions. New York: Facts on File Publications, 1997.

Hirsch, E.D., Jr., et al. *The Dictionary of Cultural Literacy.* Boston: Houghton Mifflin, 1988.

Hochwald, Lambeth. "Heir and Parent: Linda Johnson Rice." *Folio: The Magazine for Magazine Management* 23, no. 12 (July 1, 1994): 72.

Hoffman, Gary. "Shirley Young's GM Crusade." *Corporate Detroit* 8, no. 2 (February 1991): 9–10.

Hoffman, Jan. "Executive Names Her Own Price and Style," Public Lives, *New York Times,* March 3, 2000, sec. B.

Hofmeister, Sallie. "Kids' TV—She Walks the Walk." *LA Times Magazine* (September 8, 1996): 10–11.

Hoge, Alice A. *Cissy Patterson.* New York: Random House, 1966.

Holbrook, Stewart Hall. *Age of the Moguls.* Garden City, NY: Doubleday, 1953.

Holliday, Karen Kahler. "Breaking into the Old Boys' Club." *US Banker* (November 1997): 32–40.

Holmes, Stanley. "Gert Gets the Last Laugh!" *Business Week* (June 10, 2002): 100.

Holson, Laura M. "Defining the On-Line Chief: ebay's Meg Whitman Explores Management, Web Style." *New York Times,* May 10, 1999, state edition–final, sec. 3.

Holusha, John. "Folksy Rodale Emerges as Hard-Driving Marketer." *New York Times,* June 27, 1992, sec. 1.

"The Home Depot Appoints Carey Executive Vice President—Business Development, Strategy and Corporate Operations; Promotes Tomé to Executive Vice President—Chief Financial Officer." Financial News. *PR Newswire,* May 4, 2001. (Retrieved from *LEXIS-NEXIS Academic Universe* October 9, 2001.)

Hooks, Karen L. "Diversity, Family Issues and the Big 6." *Journal of Accountancy* (July 1996): 51–56.

Hopkins, Ellen. "Who Is Felice Schwartz and Why Is She Saying These Terrible Things about Us?" *Working Woman* (October 1990): 116–118.

Hopkins, Jim. "Vaudeville Daughter Now Star Player in Mutual Fund World." Money. *USA Today*, June 2, 2000, sec. B.

"Household Names Larree Renda to Its Board of Directors." *PR Newswire*, September 24, 2001. (Retrieved from *LEXIS-NEXIS Academic Universe* June 4, 2002.)

"How Mrs. Fields Cooked Up Success." Woman News. *Montreal Gazette*, February 1, 1999, final edition, sec. E.

"How World's Top Woman Ad Executive Hit the Heights; Marketing: Ogilvy & Mather's CEO Charlotte Beers Is Smart, Has Rapport with Clients and Gives Her Staff Credit, Observers Say." *Los Angeles Times*, May 4, 1992, home edition, sec. D.

Howe, Peter J. "Executive Reflects on Painful Challenges to Recovery at Lucent." *Boston Globe*, July 23, 2001. (Retrieved from *LEXIS-NEXIS Academic Universe* October 24, 2001.)

http://www.hoovers.com/officers/bio/1/0.3353.10521_12902156.00.html. (Retrieved October 21, 2001.)

http://www.hoovers.com/officers/bio/1/0,3353,11261_12895791,00.html. (Retrieved October 21, 2001.)

http://www.hoovers.com/officers/bio/4/0.3353.58444_12940162.00.html. (Retrieved from *Hoovers Online*, October 11, 2001.)

http://www.hoovers.com/officers/bio/7/0,3353,14337_130189990,00.htm. (Retrieved December 3, 2002.)

Hua, Vanessa. "CEO Quits Santa Clara's Exodus Communications." *San Francisco Chronicle*, September 5, 2001, sec. C.

Hubbard, Elbert and Alice. *An Appreciation*. East Aurora, NY: Roycrofters, 1911.

Hudson, Lynn M. *The Making of "Mammy Pleasant": A Black Entrepreneur in Nineteenth-Century San Francisco*. Champaign: University of Illinois Press, 2002.

———. "A New Look, or 'I'm Not Mammy to Everybody in California': Mary Ellen Pleasant, a Black Entrepreneur." *Journal of the West* 32 (July 1993): 35–40.

"Hunt-Scanlon to Name Indra K. Nooyi of PepsiCo as Human Capital Award Recipient at February Conference." *Business Wire*, January 2, 2001. (Retrieved from *LEXIS-NEXIS Academic Universe* January 2, 2001.)

Hymowitz, Carol. "In the U.S., What Will It Take to Create Diverse Boardrooms? *Wall Street Journal*, July 8, 2003, sec. B.

——— and Timothy D. Schellhardt. "The Glass Ceiling: Why Women Can't Seem to Break the Invisible Barrier That Blocks Them from the Top Jobs." The Corporate Woman (Special report). *Wall Street Journal*, March 24, 1986, eastern edition. (Retrieved from *Proquest Newspapers* March 3, 2003.)

——— and Michaele Weissman. *A History of Women in America*. New York: Bantam Books, 1978.

"I Am a Famous Woman in this Industry." *Fortune* 18 (October 1938): 58–65.

"In Brief: Ex-Citi Exec Miller Quits Priceline." *American Banker* (November 3, 2000): 24.

In Finance: Muriel Seibert, the First Woman to Own a Seat on the New York Stock Exchange, and Carol O'Cleireacain, the Finance Minister and Budget Director of

New York, Talk About Women in Finance. Women to Women Series. Interviewer: Frances Degen Horowitz. New York: City University of New York, 1995. Videocassette.

"In High Demand; Automakers Roll Out the Red Carpet for Talented Minority and Women Engineers." *Ward's Auto World* (March 1, 2001). (Retrieved from *Business & Company Resource Center* September 28, 2003.)

"Indiana's Entrepreneurs of the Year Awards, 1991." *Indiana Business Magazine* 35, no. 9 (September 1991): 8–9.

Ingham, John N. *Biographical Dictionary of American Business Leaders*. Westport, CT: Greenwood Press, 1983.

——— and Lynne B. Feldman. *African-American Business Leaders: A Biographical Dictionary*. Westport, CT: Greenwood Press, 1994.

Ingram, Martha Rivers. *E. Bronson Ingram: Complete These Unfinished Tasks of Mine*. Franklin, TN: Hillsboro Press, Providence House Publishers, 2002.

Innis, Doris Funnye, and Juliana Wu. *Profiles in Black: Biographical Sketches of 100 Living Black Unsung Heroes*. New York: CORE Publications, 1976.

"Investment-Banker/Singer's Debut Music CD Carla's First Christmas." *Business Wire*, November 1, 2000. (Retrieved from *LEXIS-NEXIS Academic Universe* December 1, 2002.)

Ireland, Norma Olin. *Index to Women of the World from Ancient to Modern Times: Biographies and Portraits*. Westwood, MA: F.W. Faxon, 1970.

———. *Index to Women of the World from Ancient to Modern Times: A Supplement*. Metuchen, NJ: Scarecrow Press, 1988.

Israel, Lee. *Estee Lauder: Beyond the Magic (An Unauthorized Biography)*. New York: Macmillan Publishing, 1985.

Jabbonsky, Larry. "What Makes Brenda Run?" *Beverage World* (October 1994): 42–43.

James, Edward T., ed. *Notable American Women 1607–1950: A Biographical Dictionary*. Cambridge, MA: Belknap Press of Harvard University Press, 1971.

James, Frank E. "Furniture Czarina, Still a Live Wire at 90: A Retail Phenomenon Oversees Her Empire." *Wall Street Journal*, May 23, 1984.

"Jamie Gorelick Named Vice Chair of Fannie Mae." *PR Newswire*, May 7, 1997. (Retrieved from *LEXIS-NEXIS Academic Universe* June 11, 1999.)

"Janet L. Robinson Named Senior Vice President, Newspaper Operations: Robinson Announces New Direct Reporting Structure at The New York Times Newspaper." *Business Wire*, February 12, 2001. (Retrieved from *LEXIS-NEXIS Academic Universe*, October 8, 2004.)

Jarnow, Jeannette, and Kitty G. Dickson. *Inside the Fashion Business*. 6th ed. Upper Saddle River, NJ: Prentice Hall, 1997.

"J.C. Penney Names Vanessa Castagna Executive Vice President and Chief Operations Officer of J.C. Penney Stores." *PR Newswire*, July 14, 1999. (Retrieved from *LEXIS-NEXIS Academic Universe*, October 16, 2000.)

Jeffrey, Don. "Sylvia Thone Leads Elektra's Turnaround." *Billboard* (November 9, 1996): 1–5.

Jeffrey, Laura. *Great American Businesswomen*. Springfield, NJ: Enslow Publishing, 1996.

Jenkins, Maureen. "Early Education in the Johnson Home." *Chicago Sun-Times* May 11, 1997, late sports final edition, p. 15.

Johansen, Bruce E., and Donald A. Grinde, Jr. *The Encyclopedia of Native American Biography*. New York: Henry Holt, 1997.

Johnson, Curtiss C. *America's First Lady Boss."* Norwalk, CT: Silvermine Publishers, 1965.

Johnson, K. "Making Movie Magic." *Harpers Bazaar* (August 1989): 126–129.

Johnson, Linda A. "New CEO Russo Seen as a Strong Manager, Morale Builder as Lucent Recovers." *Associated Press State & Local Wire*, June 4, 2002. Business News. (Retrieved from *LEXIS-NEXIS Academic Universe* June 6, 2002.)

Johnson, Steve. "Women Building Toward Respected Role in Construction." *San Jose Mercury News*, September 2, 2003. (Retrieved from *Lexis/Nexis*, January 18, 2004.)

Johnston, Johanna. *Women Themselves.* New York: Dodd, Mead, 1973.

Jones, Del. "Avon Takes Breast Cancer Personally: CEO Andrea Jung Leads Company's Fundraising Efforts." *USA Today*, March 7, 2000, sec. B.

Jones, Sarah P. *"Herald* Business Profile: Crises Create Opportunity & Challenge." Finance. *Boston Herald*, November 6, 1995.

Jordan, Jacob. "Wall Street Financier, Darla Hall, Has All the Right Connections." Associated Press State and Local Wire, October 7, 2002. (Retrieved from *Lexis/Nexis Academic Universe*, October 1, 2004.)

Jurgens, Rick. "Making Your Mark Quietly." *Contra Costa Times*, December 10, 2000. (Retrieved from *LEXIS-NEXIS Academic Universe* December 10, 2000.)

Kadlec, Daniel. "Sallie Krawcheck: CEO of Citigroup's New Smith Barney Unit." *Time* (December 2, 2002): 52.

Kaliski, Burton S., ed. *Encyclopedia of Busine$$ and Finance.* New York: Macmillan Reference USA, 2001.

Kaminski, Buron S. *Encyclopedia of Busine$$ and Finance.* New York: Macmillan Reference USA, 2001.

Kanellos, Nicolas. *The Hispanic Almanac: From Columbus to Corporate America.* Detroit: Invisible Ink, 1994.

Kanner, Bernice. "Trumpet of the Swan." *Chief Executive (U.S.)* (June 1997): 23–24.

———. "The Weaver." *Chief Executive* (June 2000): 24–25.

Kanter, Rosabeth Moss. *Work and Family in the United States.* New York: Basic Books, 1977.

Kanter, Rosabeth Moss. *The Change Masters.* New York: Simon Schuster, 1983.

Kanter, Rosabeth Moss. *Work and Family in the United States.* New York: Russell Sage Foundation, 1997.

Kaplan, James. "Amateur's Hour: Who Says It Takes Years of on-the-Job Experience to Run a Business?" *Working Woman* (October 1997): 28–29.

———. "The Queen of Cartoons." *TV Guide* (March 14–20, 1998): 30–33.

Kaplan, Karen. "Female CEO Describes View from the Top: Internet; Ellen Hancock of Exodus Says West Coast Entrepreneurial Culture Takes Some Getting Used To." *Los Angeles Times* November 23, 1998, sec. C.

Kapner, Suzanne. "Marian and Michael Ilitch: Secretary-Treasurer and Chairman, Respectively, Little Caesar Enterprises, Detroit." *Nation's Restaurant News* 29 (January 1995): 105–107.

Karp, David. "Pomegranates for One and All." *New York Times*, October 30, 2002, sec. F. (Retrieved from *LEXIS-NEXIS Academic Universe* March 14, 2003.)

Karst, Gene, and Martin J. Jones. *Who's Who in Professional Baseball.* New Rochelle, NY: Arlington House, 1973.

"Kathy Dyer, President of Revlon Cosmetics, USA, Receives Achiever Award from Cosmetic Executive Women, Inc." *PR Newswire,* June 23, 1997. (Retrieved from *LEXIS-NEXIS Academic Universe,* September 9, 1999.)

Katz, Richard. "Regency on Hot Streak." *Daily Variety* (May 24, 1999): 1.

Katz, William Loren. *Black People Who Made the Old West.* New York: Crowell, 1987.

Keckley, Elizabeth. *Behind the Scenes; or, Thirty Years a Slave and Four Years in the White House.* New York: Arno Press, 1968.

Keeth, Fran, with Eve Tahmincioglu. "In Shock, and in Charge." *New York Times* January 20, 2002, sec. 3.

Keiffer, E.B. "Madame Rubinstein, the Little Lady from Krakow." *Life* (July 21, 1941): 36–40.

Kempton, Beverly. "What Does Success Really Mean?" *Executive Female* 16, no. 1 (January–February 1993): 38–42.

Kennedy, June O. *Mary Alexander, 1693–1760: Colonial Merchant and Mother of William Alexander, Lord Stirling.* Women's Project of New Jersey, 1987.

Kennedy, Patricia. "Voices in the Shadows." *Archivist* 20, no. 1 (1993): 2–4.

Kessel, Mark. "Pat Russo's Lucent Vision." *Fortune* (April 15, 2002): 126–130.

Ketchum, Richard. *Faces from the Past.* New York: American Heritage Press, 1970.

Kilbourn, Peter T. "For Women in Bias Case Wounds Remain." *New York Times,* vol. 149, n. 55, March 24, 2000: p. 337.

King, Anita. "Black Mary: A Westerner with Style." *Essence* (January 1974): 23, 91.

King, R. J. "Auto Supplier Shifts Gears: Mexican Industries Grows–and Changes Its Fortune." *Detroit News,* February 9, 1999, sec. B.

King, Rachel. "Beringer Wine Estates Names Emily Woods to Board of Directors." *Business Wire,* January 14, 1998. (Retrieved from *Lexis/Nexis Academic Universe,* June 3, 1999.)

King, Teresa Tyson, and Jane B. Stockard. "The Woman CPA: Career and Family." *The CPA Journal* 60, no. 6 (June 1990): 22–27.

Kipping, Matthias and Lars Engwall, eds. *Management Consulting: Emergence and Dynamics of a Knowledge Industry.* New York: Oxford University Press, 2002.

Kissell, Margo Rutledge. "Mr. Mom: Local Organization Helps Stay-at-home Dads Fight Isolation." *Dayton Daily News,* June 15, 2003, p. A1.

Klemsrud, Judy. "Leona Helmsley: Power Becomes Her." *New York Times,* July 22, 1980, sec. B.

Klis, Mike. "Minority Owner, Major Accomplishment." Sport. *Denver Post,* November 16, 1999, sec. D.

Klose, Kevin. "In the Spirit of Enterprise: Barbara Proctor and Her Presidential Mention." *Washington Post,* January 27, 1984, sec. D.

Kluger, Richard. *The Paper: The Life and Death of the* New York Herald Tribune. New York: Knopf, 1986.

Knight, Jennifer. "Communication, Problem-Solving Skills Key." *Corporate Cashflow Magazine* 15m no. 11 (October 1994): 83–84.

Kohn, Ken. "Are You Ready for Economic-Risk Management?" *Institutional Investor* (September 1990): 203+.

Kolb, Robert W., ed. *The International Finance Reader.* Miami, FL: Kolb Publishing Co., 1991.

Koplovitz, Kay. *Bold Women, Big Ideas: Learning to Play the High-Risk Entrepreneurial Game.* New York: PublicAffairs, 2002.

Kopytoff, Verne. "Patti Hart: Hart at Home." *San Francisco Chronicle*, May 14, 2001, sec. D.

Kornblum, Janet. "She's Sitting on Top of the High-Tech World." Money. *USA Today*, April 22, 1999, sec. B.

Koselka, Rita. "A Real Amazon." *Forbes* (April 5, 1999): 50.

Koss-Feder, Laura. "Road Rules." *Working Mother* (March 2001): 40–45.

"Kraft Foods Names Sneed as President of New E-Commerce Division." *Business Wire*, August 31, 1999. (Retrieved from *LEXIS-NEXIS Academic Universe* February 7, 2002.)

Krantz, Matt. "IBM's Linda Sanford." *Investor's Business Daily*, May 24, 1999, sec. A.

Krotz, Joanna L. "All Aboard." *Working Woman* (April 1999): 64–70.

Kuczynski, Alex. "Building on Borrowed Cachet: Cathleen Black Shakes Up the Culture at Hearst Magazines." *New York Times,* January 3, 1999, sec. C.

Kwolek-Folland, Angel. *Engendering Business: Men and Women in the Corporate Office, 1870–1930.* Baltimore: Johns Hopkins University Press, 1994.

———. *Incorporating Women: A History of Women and Business in the United States.* New York: Twayne Publishers, 1998.

Labich, Kenneth Fierman, et al. "The Year's Most Fascinating People." *Fortune* (January 1, 1990): 62–72.

Landler, Mark, et al. "Shirley Young: Pushing GM's Humble-Pie Strategy." *Business Week* (June 11, 1990): 52.

Landmarks in Modern American Business. 3 vols. Pasadena, CA: Salem Press, 2000.

Landrum, Gene N. *Profiles of Female Genius: Thirteen Creative Women Who Changed the World.* Amherst, NY: Prometheus Books, 1994.

Langford, Margaret, et al. "Men, Women, and the Use of Power: Is It Based on the Person or the Situation?" *Equal Opportunities International* 17, no. 1 (1998): 1–12.

Lappen, Alyssa, ed. "The *Working Woman* 25." *Working Woman* (May 1992): 63–69.

Larson, Chris. "The Fight for Fair Pay." *Executive Female* (August/September 2002): 12–16.

Larson, Megan. "Job of a Lifetime." *Brandweek* 41, no. 19 (May 8, 2000): 21–22.

Larson, Soren. "Jung's Focus: Avon Product Line." *Women's Wear Daily* (February 24. 1995): 9–10.

LaTeef, Nelda. *Working Women for the 21st Century: 50 Women Reveal Their Pathways to Success.* Charlotte, VT: Williamson, 1992.

Lauder, Estee. *Estee: A Success Story.* New York: Random House, 1985.

Lavelle, Louis. "Angling for a Board Seat?" *Business Week* (December 16, 2002): 138–141.

Lawlor, Julia. "Is There Balm after the Storm?" *Red Herring* (October 2000): 394–398.

Lawrence, Mary Wells. *A Big Life (in Advertising).* New York: Alfred A. Knopf, 2002.

Lazarus, David. "Wal-Mart Names Web Chief; Jackson Headed Gap's Internet Wing." *San Francisco Chronicle,* March 2, 2000, sec. C.

Lear, Robert W., and Boris Yavitz. "The Five Best and Five Worst Boards of 1999." *Chief Executive* (October 1999): 48.

Leavitt, Judith A. *American Women Managers and Administrators: A Selective Biographical Dictionary of 20th Century Leaders in Business, Education and Government.* Westport, CT: Greenwood Press, 1985.

LeBeau, Christina. "As Car Dealers, Women Are Scarce, But Successful." *New York Times,* January 12, 2003.

Lecompte, Janet. "La Tules and the Americans." *Arizona and the West* 20, no. 3 (Autumn 1978): 215–230.

Leder, Lawrence H. *Robert Livingston, 1654–1728, and the Politics of Colonial New York.* Chapel Hill: University of North Carolina Press, 1961.

Lee, Chris. "The Feminization of Management." *Training* 31, no. 11 (November 1994): 25–32.

Lee, Louise. "A Savvy Captain for Old Navy." *Business Week,* no. 3654 (November 8, 1999): 130.

Lehman, Cheryl R. "'Herstory' in Accounting: The First Eighty Years." *Accounting, Organizations and Society* 17, no. 3/4 (1992): 261–285.

Leibovich, Mark. "Apple's Chief Technology Officer Faces Challenge of Her Life." *Knight-Ridder/Tribune Business News,* January 20, 1997, p. 120.

Lemieux, Gloria A. "PC Connection, Inc." International Directory of Company Histories, 37. (Retrieved from Business and Company Resource Center, September 9, 2003.)

Lesonsky, Rieva. "Talking Back (Commentary on Women Entrepreneurship)." *Entrepreneur* 25, no. 12 (November 1997): 62.

"Levi Strauss & Co. Names Pat House to Board of Directors." *Business Wire,* July 2, 2003. (Retrieved from *LEXIS-NEXIS Academic Universe* July 27, 2003.)

Levy, Anne. *Workplace Sexual Harassment.* Upper Saddle River, NJ: Prentice Hall, 2002.

Lewis, Alfred Allen, and Constance Woodworth. *Miss Elizabeth Arden.* New York: Coward, McCann, 1972.

Lewis, Arthur H. *The Day They Shook the Plum Tree.* New York: Harcourt, Brace & World, 1963.

Lewis, Peter H. "Sound Bytes: She Defines AutoDesk and Women's Issues, Too." *New York Times,* November 11, 1993. Late edition, sec. 3.

LEXIS-NEXIS Academic Universe. Dayton, OH: LEXIS-NEXIS, 1985–2004.

LEXIS-NEXIS Online Database. Dayton, OH: LEXIS-NEXIS, 1985–2004.

LEXIS-NEXIS Statistical Universe. Dayton, OH: LEXIS-NEXIS, 1985–2004.

Linderman, Kathryn. "Ranching Entrepreneur Henrietta King: Determination Helped Build a Million-Acre-Plus Cattle Empire in Texas." *Investor's Business Daily,* August 22, 2000, sec, A.

Linkemer, Bobbi. "Women in Sales: What Do They Really Want?" *Sales & Marketing Management* 141, no. 1 (January 1989): 61–66.

Literary Market Place. New York: R.R. Bowker, 1940–.

Littleton, Cynthia. "An Animated Conversation with Betty Cohen." *Broadcasting & Cable* 127, no. 23 (June 2, 1997): 26–30.

"Liz Claiborne Inc. Elects Christine A. Poon to Board of Directors." *PR Newswire,* January 25, 2000. (Retrieved from *LEXIS/NEXIS Academic Universe* October 4, 2003.)

Lloyd, Kate. "The *Working Woman* Hall of Fame." *Working Woman* (November 1986): 157–162.

Lockwood, Lisa. "Women CEOs: Arrival Time." *WWD* (December 20, 1999): 12.

Loewenberg, Bert James, and Ruth Bogin, eds. *Black Women in Nineteenth-Century Life.* University Park, PA: Pennsylvania State University Press, 1976.

Logan, Mary Simmerson. *The Part Taken by Women in American History*. New York: Arno Press, 1972.

Logan, Rayford W., and Michael R. Winson, eds. *Dictionary of American Negro Biography*. New York: Norton, 1982.

Longaberger, Dave. *Longaberger: An American Success Story*. New York: Harper Business, 2001.

Longaberger, Tami. "Diversity: It's Right, It's Here, Embrace It." *Vital Speeches of the Day* 67, no. 3 (November 15, 2000): 89–90.

Longstreet, Stephen. *The Queen Bees: The Women Who Shaped America*. Indianapolis: Bobbs-Merrill, 1979.

Longwell, Marjorie. *America and Women: Fictionized Biography*. Philadelphia: Dorrance, 1962.

Loos, Barbara. "For Women, Getting Hired Is the Easy Part." *Fortune* (November 24, 1986): 160.

Lowe, Denise. *Women and American Television: An Encyclopedia*. Santa Barbara, CA: ABC-CLIO, 1999.

Lowry, Tom. "How Rodale Takes Care of Its Health." *Business Week* (July 23, 2001): 79.

Lublin, Joann S. "How One CEO Juggles a Job and a Family Miles Apart." *Wall Street Journal*, October 8, 1997, eastern edition, sec. B.

"Lucent Technologies Names Frank D'Amelio Chief Financial Officer: Company Combines Switching and Data Networking Units; Names Janet Davidson to Lead New Unit." *PR Newswire*, May 6, 2001. (Retrieved from *LEXIS-NEXIS Academic Universe*, October 24, 2001.)

"Lucy Fisher to Partner with Douglas Wick." Entertainmentwire. *Business Wire*, December 9, 1999. (Retrieved from *LEXIS-NEXIS Academic Universe*, December 19, 2000.)

Lueck, Guadra. *50 Years of Good Taste: A Delicious History of Minyard Food Stores*. Coppell, TX: Minyard Food Stores, 1982.

Lynch, Karen. "The Start Up and the Grown Up—A 30-Year IBM Veteran, Ellen Hancock Gets Exodus Down to Business." *Tele.com* (December 6, 1999): 44.

MacDonald, Anne L. *Feminine Intuition: How Women Inventors Changed America*. New York: Ballantine Books, 1992.

Machan, Dyan. "Death Angel's Endearing Side." *Forbes* (March 8, 1999): 70–71.

———. "Executive Mom." *Forbes* (November 30, 1998): 66.

———. "Smarter Than Herbert's Dog." *Forbes* (May 3, 1999): 50.

Mack, Toni. "High Finance with a Touch of Theater." *Forbes* (May 18, 1998): 140–147.

Mackenzie, Len, and Nanci Mackenzie. "The Real Fuel in the Gas Industry." *Pipeline & Gas Journal* 226, no. 11 (November 1999): S3.

Macksey, Joan, and Kenneth. *Guinness Guide to Feminine Achievements: The Book of Woman's Achievements*. New York: Stein & Day, 1975.

MacPhee, William. *Rare Breed: The Entrepreneur, an American Culture*. Chicago: Probus Publishing, 1987.

"Mad Ave: A Star Is Reborn." *Business Week* (July 26, 1999): 54–64.

Madell, Robin. "Uniting People and Products: Myrtle Potter—2000 HBA Woman of the Year." *Pharmaceutical Executive* 20, no. 4 (April 2000): 48.

Mahoney, Tom. "$49,000,000 Business in Round Figures." *Independent Woman* 29 (October 1950): 310–311.

"Maidenform's Mrs. R." *Fortune* (July 1959): 75–77.

Malinowski, Sharon, ed. *Notable Native Americans*. Detroit: Gale Research, 1995.

Mamis, Robert A. "Master of Bootstrapping Administration." *Inc.* (August 1995): 40–44.

———. "Real Service." *Inc.* (May 1989): 80–87.

Mankiller, Wilma, et al., eds. *Reader's Companion to U.S. Women's History*. Boston: Houghton Mifflin, 1998.

Mansfield, Stephanie. "Hollywood's Leading Lady." *Working Woman* 20 (April 1995): 34–39.

———. "The Porcelain Powerhouse: Helen Boehm, Riding Her Birds to Riches and High Places." *Washington Post*, March 28, 1985, final edition, sec. B.

Many Faces: An Anthology of Oregon Autobiography. Corvallis, OR: Oregon State University Press, 1993.

"Marce Fuller: CEO and President, Mirant." *Utility Business* (June 1, 2001): 61.

Marchetti, Michele. "Here's One Marketer Who Can Sell." *Sales & Marketing Management* 151, no. 3 (March 1999): 24.

Markoff, John. "Private Sector; Trailblazer in the Silicon Jungle." Money & Business/Financial Desk. *New York Times*, November 1, 1998, sec. 3.

Marquardt, Michael J., and Nancy O. Berger. *Global Leaders for the Twenty-First Century*. Albany: State University of New York Press, 2000.

Marriott, Alice. *Maria, the Potter of San Ildefonso*. Norman: University of Oklahoma Press, 1948.

Marshall, Caroline. "Shelly Lazarus—After 28 Years, O&M's Leader Is Steeped in Its Culture." *Campaign* (April 29, 2001): 14–15.

"Martha Frances (Fran) Keeth Joins Mobil as Controller." *Business Wire*, August 26, 1996. (Retrieved from *LEXIS-NEXIS Academic Universe* October 13, 2002.)

Martin, Justin. "Tomorrow's CEOs: Meet Six Young Managers Who Have What It Takes to Lead in the 21st Century." *Fortune* (June 24, 1996): 76–78.

Martin, Pamela, and Beverly Foster. "Bank of America's New Look at Risk: an Interview with Amy Brinkley." *The RMA Journal* 84, no. 5 (February 2002): 8–15.

Marzolf, Marion. *Up from the Footnote A History of Women Journalists*. New York: Hastings House, 1977.

Maters, Kim. "It's How You Play the Game." *Working Woman* (May 1990): 88–92.

Maynard, Micheline. "Comfortable with the Fast Track," Private Sector, *New York Times*, July 22, 2001, late edition–final, sec. 3.

Mayer, Caroline. "Women, Building Careers One House at a Time." *Washington Post*, February 24, 1966, p. E1.

McCallum, Jane Y. *Women Pioneers*. Richmond, VA: Johnson Publishing Company, 1929.

McConville, Jim. "McGrath Mandate: Pick Up the Tempo at VH1." *Hollywood Reporter* (March 19, 2002). (Retrieved from *LEXIS-NEXIS Academic Universe*, May 25, 2002.)

McCormick, John. "Making It Right." *Automotive Industries* 181, no. 6 (June, 2001): 41–42.

McDonald, Marci. "A Start-Up of Her Own." *U.S. News & World Report* (May 15, 2000): 34–42.

McDonough, John "Creating an Environment 'Where People Can do Great Work': Shelly Lazarus Talks About the Challenges and Satisfactions of Her Role as CEO of Ogilvy & Mather." *Advertising Age* (September 21, 1998), sec. C.

McDowell, Barbara, and Hana Umlauf. *Good Housekeeping Woman's Almanac*. New York: Newspaper Enterprise Association, 1977.

McFarland, Lynne Joy, and others. *21st Century Leadership: Dialogues with 199 Top Leaders*. New York: The Leadership Press, 1993.

McGarvey, Robert. "Trend Spotting." *Entrepreneur* (December 1996): 144–149.

McGee, Marianne Kolbasuk. "Leaders among Leaders—IT Has Traditionally Been a Man's World, Especially in the Upper Echelons of Management." *Information Week* (October 9, 2000). (Retrieved from *LEXIS-NEXIS Academic Universe* January 12, 2001.)

McGinn, Elinor. *A Wide-Awake Woman: Josephine Roche in the Era of Reform*. Denver: Colorado Historical Society, 2002.

McGrath, Kimberley A., ed. *World of Invention*. Detroit: Gale Research, 1999.

McHenry, Robert, ed. *Famous American Women: A Biographical Dictionary from Colonial Times to the Present*. Originally published in 1980 as *Liberty's Women*. New York: Dover, 1983.

McKerns, Joseph P., ed. *Biographical Dictionary of American Journalism*. New York: Greenwood Press, 1989.

McLuskey, Krista. *Entrepreneurs*. New York: Crabtree, 1999.

Meeker, Mary with Chris DePuy. *The Internet Report*. New York: HarperBusiness, 1995.

Meer, Aziza K. "I-Net's Bajaj Built Company from Basement Up." *Washington Post*, October 21, 1991, sec. F.

Mehegan, Sean. "Andrea Jung." *Brandweek* 37, no. 39 (October 7, 1996): S98–102.

Mehta, Stephanie. "What Minority Employees Really Want." *Fortune* (July 19, 2000): 181–186.

Meier, Matt S. *Mexican American Biographies; A Historical Dictionary, 1835–1987*. New York: Greenwood Press, 1988.

———. *Notable Latino Americans: A Biographical Dictionary*. Westport, CT: Greenwood Press, 1997.

Mermigas, Diane. "Art of the Media Deal: Nancy Peretsman Brings Credibility and Carefully Crafted Vision to World of Mergers and Acquisitions." *Electronic Media* (May 20, 2002): 24.

Merriden, Trevor. "Rosabeth Moss Kanter." *Management Today* (February 1997): 58.

Merrill, Ann. "Bridging the Generations: Consensus-Building, People Skills Are Key Tools in Nelson's Style." Marketplace. *Star Tribune*, September 21, 1997, sec. D.

Mesdag, Lisa Miller. "From Barbie Dolls to Real Life." *Fortune* (September 8, 1980): 88.

Meyer, Edith Patterson. *Petticoat Patriots of the American Revolution*. New York: Vanguard Press, 1976.

"Michele Anthony Appointed Executive Vice President, Sony Music." *Business Wire*, January 26, 1993. (Retrieved from *LEXIS-NEXIS Academic Universe* October 7, 2004.)

Mikaelian, A. *Women Who Mean Business: Success Stories of Women Over Forty*. New York: Morrow, 2000.

Miller, Karin. "Trudell Settling in as First Woman to Head Major U.S. Car Company. *Associated Press State & Local Wire*, June 4, 1999: AM Cycle. (Retrieved from *LEXIS-NEXIS Academic Universe*, October 13, 1999.)

Miller, Ronald Dean. *Shady Ladies of the West*. Los Angeles: Westernlore Press, 1964.

Millstein, Beth, and Jeanne Bodin. *We the American Women: A Documentary History*. New York: J.S. Ozer, 1977.

Ming, Jenny J., with Amy Zipkin. "The Boss; Tying the Two Strands," Executive Life, *New York Times,* October 27, 2002, sec. 3.

Mintz, Bill. "Bank Executive Deily Leaving after Buyout; First Interstate to Pay Her $5.5 Million." *Houston Chronicle,* March 14, 1996, 3 star ed.

———. "Prescription for Growth: Owen to Merge with Cardinal Health." *Houston Chronicle,* November 28, 1996, p. 1.

Mirabella, Grace. "Beauty Queen Estee Lauder." *Time* 152, no. 23 (December 7, 1998): 183.

Mitchell, Niki Butler. *The New Color of Success.* Rocklin, CA: Prima Publishing, 2000.

Mofford, Juliet H. "Women in the Workplace." *Women's History* 2, no. 1 (Spring–Summer 1996). www.thehistorynet.com/WomensHistory/.

Moin, David, and Sidney Rutberg. "The Book on J. Crew." *Women's Wear Daily* (September 1, 1993): 6–8.

Money. Annual Index. Chicago: Time Inc., 1972–.

"Money Moms." *Working Mother* (December 2000/January 2001): 73.

Monget, Karyn. "The Wachner Way." *Women's Wear Daily* (February 10, 1998): 14–16.

Monnett, John, and Michael McCarthy. *Colorado Profiles: Men and Women Who Shaped the Centennial State.* Boulder, CO: University Press of Colorado, 1987.

Moon, Mike. "Rose Morgan: Success in Grand Style." *Essence* (June 1981): 34–44.

Moore, Dorothy P., and E. Holly Buttner. *Women Entrepreneurs: Moving beyond the Glass Ceiling.* Thousand Oaks, CA: Sage Publications, 1997.

Moore, Dorothy Perrin. *Careerpreneurs: Lessons from Leading Woman Entrepreneurs on Building a Career without Boundaries.* Palo Alto, CA: Davies-Black, 2000.

Moore, Janet. "Where Are the Women?" *Minneapolis Star Tribune,* August 5, 2001, sec. D.

Moore, Martha T., and David Proctor. "Special 4-Day Report: The Mommy Track." *USA Today,* March 3, 1989. (Retrieved from *LEXIS/NEXIS Academic Universe* June 16, 2003.)

Moreno, Katarzyna. "Underestimated." *Forbes* (May 14, 2001): 34.

Morgan, Rose. "An Interview with Rose Morgan," by James Briggs Murray. Four videocassettes (U-Matic), 87 minutes. Schomburg Center for Research in Black Culture, 1988.

Morris, Betsy. "Tales of the Trailblazers: *Fortune* Revisits Harvard's Women MBAs of 1973." *Fortune* (October 12, 1998): 107–120.

———. "Trophy Husbands." *Fortune* (October 14, 2002): 79–98.

Morris, Kathleen. "The Rise of Jill Barad." *Business Week* (May 25, 1998): 112–119.

Morris, Michele. "The St. Joan of Television." *Working Woman* (May 1986): 70–74.

Morton, Laurie A. "Work-Life Balance? Coming Right Up . . . Is the Corporate Culture Shift Wishful Thinking?" Master's thesis, University of Pennsylvania, 1999.

Moskowitz, Milton, Robert Levering, Michael Katz. *Everybody's Business: An Almanac.* San Francisco: Harper & Row, 1980.

Moskowitz, Milton, et al. *Everybody's Business: A Field Guide to the 400 Leading Companies in America.* New York: Doubleday/Currency, 1990.

Moskowitz, Milton, et al. *Everybody's Business Scoreboard.* San Francisco: Harper & Row, 1983.

"Mrs. Rudkin Revisited." *New Yorker* (November 16, 1963): 42–44.

"MTV President Hitting All the Right Notes: Judy McGrath Has Tripled Revenue at the Cable Channel." *Los Angeles Times,* May 30, 2000, sec. C.

Much, Marilyn, and Toni Apgar. "Direct from O&M New York: Shelly Lazarus." *Direct* 3, no. 9 (September 1991): 16.

Muir, Charles S. *Women, the Makers of History*. New York: Vantage Press, 1956.

Mulvihill, Maggie. "At the Bar: Legal Actions Fueling Feud within Family." *Boston Herald*, September 26, 2000.

Murray, Margo. *Beyond the Myths and Magic of Mentoring*. Rev. ed. San Francisco: Jossey-Bass, 2001.

Nash, Jim. "Ann Winblad: A Small-Town Native Leaps Headlong into Big-Time VC World." *The Business Journal* 11, no. 24 (September 27, 1993): 12–13.

"National Coalition of 100 Black Women Hosts First Awards Luncheon." *Southwest Newswire*, January 22, 1986. (Retrieved from *LEXIS-NEXIS Academic Universe*, July 19, 2002.)

National Cyclopedia of American Biography. 77 Volumes. Clifton, NJ: J.T. White, 1893–1984.

National Foundation for Women Business Owners. *Women Business Owners of Color: Challenges and Accomplishments*. Silver Spring, MD: National Foundation for Women Business Owners, 1997.

National Women's Hall of Fame. http://www.greatwomen.org.

"Natori's 25 Year Mystique." *WWD* (November 25, 2002): 6.

Neal, Mollie. "Cataloger Gets Pleasant Results: Pleasant Co.'s Marketing Strategy." *Cataloging Age* 8, no. 9 (September 1991): 87.

Neff, Jack. "No Downtime Face Time." *Advertising Age* (November 26, 2001): 8.

———. "Strategic Team Leader Takes on the World." *Advertising Age* (February 8, 1999): S8.

———. "Susan Arnold: President, P&G Global Skincare; Skincare Chief Pushing P&G Forward." *Advertising Age* 71 (February 7, 2000): S4.

Neidle, Cecyle. *America's Immigrant Women*. Boston: Twayne, 1975.

"Nell Donnelly Reed." *Fortune* (September 1935): 91.

Nelson, Emily. "Diaper Sales Sagging, P&G Thinks Young to Reposition Pampers—How to Sell Premium Brand in Penny-Pinching Times? Casting It as a Lifestyle—'Actually a Piece of Clothing.'" *Wall Street Journal*, December 27, 2001, eastern edition, sec. A.

Nelson, Marilyn Carlson. "Faith in Yourself: Never, Ever, Ever Give Up." *Vital Speeches of the Day* 67, no. 22 (September 1, 2001): 697.

Nelson, Patricia M., ed. *Affirmative Action Revisited*. New York: Nova Science, 2001.

Nelson, Robert T. "Banker Leaves with a Deposit of Goodwill." *Seattle Times*, May 27, 2001, sec. D.

Nelton, Sharon. "The Challenge to Women." *Nation's Business* 78, no. 7 (July 1990): 16–22.

Nemy, Enid. "Mary Kay Ash, Who Built a Cosmetics Empire and Adored Pink, Is Dead at 83." *New York Times*, November 23, 2001, sec. D.

"A Network of Her Own." *Inc.* (September 2000). (Retrieved from *Proquest* March 15, 2002.)

Neuborne, Ellen. "Mad Ave: A Star Is Reborn." *Business Week* (July 26, 1999): 54–64.

Nevada Women's History Project. www.unr.edu/sb204/nwhp. (Retrieved March 11, 1998.)

A New Approach to Flexibility: Managing the Work/Time Equation. New York: Catalyst, 1997.

"New Guides to Help Lead the Way for Growth in Entrepreneurship among American Indians." *PR Newswire,* September 6, 2001. (Retrieved from *LEXIS-NEXIS Academic Universe* May 12, 2001.)

"A New Kind of Oil Dynasty." *Working Woman* (May 1994): 48.

"The New York Times Company Appoints Senior Ad Executive." *PR Newswire,* May 5, 1993. (Retrieved from *LEXIS-NEXIS Academic Universe* October 18, 2001.)

"New York's 100 Most Influential Women in Business." *Crain's New York Business* (September 27, 1999). (Retrieved from *LEXIS-NEXIS Academic Universe* June 23, 2002.)

Newcomb, Peter. "High-Octane Octogenarian." *Forbes* (October 28, 1985): 340–343.

Nichols, Nancy A. "Scientific Management at Merck: An Interview with CFO Judy Lewent." *Harvard Business Review* (January/February 1994).

Nickell, Joe. *Wonder Workers! How They Perform the Impossible.* Buffalo, NY: Prometheus Books, 1991.

Nierenberg, Andrea R. *Nonstop Networking.* Sterling, VA: Capital Books, 2002.

Nilles, Jack M. *Managing Telework: Strategies for Managing the Virtual Workforce.* New York: Wiley, 1998.

1999 Catalyst Census of Women Corporate Officers and Top Earners. New York: Catalyst, 1999.

Nissenson, Samuel. *The Patroon's Domain.* New York: Columbia University Press, 1937.

Noel, Thomas J. *Colorado Givers: A History of Philanthropic Heroes.* Niwot, CO: University Press of Colorado, 1998.

Noguchi, Yuki. "The Money of Color: Built on High-Wattage Black Advocacy, Radio One Is Turning Its Dial to the Bottom Line." *Washington Post,* January 24, 2000.

"Not Exactly What You'd Call a Weak Sister." *Business Week* (August 16, 1999): 61.

Nulty, Peter. "The National Business Hall of Fame." *Fortune* (April 4, 1994): 118–128.

Oana, Katherine D. *Women in Their Own Business.* Skokie, IL: VGM Career Horizons, 1982.

OCLC FirstSearch. Dublin, OH: OCLC Online Computer Library Center, 1992–.

OCLC WorldCat. Dublin, OH: OCLC Online Computer Library Center, 1978–.

O'Dell, Cary. *Women Pioneers in Television: Biographies of Fifteen Industry Leaders.* Jefferson, NC: McFarland & Company, 1997.

O'Donnell, Jayne. "#1: Pat Moran, CEO, JM Family Enterprises." *Working Woman* (June 1999): 38–39.

"Office Depot Adds Two New Members to Its Board of Directors." *Business Wire,* February 20, 2002. (Retrieved from *LEXIS-NEXIS Academic Universe* November 28, 2002.)

O'Higgins, Patrick. *Madame: An Intimate Biography of Helena Rubinstein.* New York: Viking Press, 1971.

Oldham, Ellen M. "Early Women Printers of America." *BPL Quarterly,* January and April, 1958.

O'Leary, Noreen. "The Deal Maker: Mike Greenlees Won His Bid for BDDP. Now He's Eager to Play His Global Hand." *Adweek Eastern Edition* 38, no. 25 (June 23, 1997): 26–34.

Olsen, Frank H. *Inventors Who Left Their Brands on America.* New York: Bantam, 1991.

"100 Leading Women." *Business Insurance,* (October 2, 2000): 50.

O'Neal, Bill. *Historic Ranches of the Old West.* Austin, TX: Eakin Press, 1997.

O'Neil, Lois Decker, ed. *The Women's Book of World Records and Achievements*. Garden City, NY: Anchor Press/Doubleday, 1979.

Opdycke, Sandra. *The Routledge Historical Atlas of Women in America*. New York: Routledge, 2000.

Oppedisano, Jeannette M. *Historical Encyclopedia of American Women Entrepreneurs, 1776 to the Present*. Westport, CT: Greenwood Press, 2000.

"Oprah Makes a Billion." *PR Newswire*, January 14, 2003. (Retrieved from *Lexis/Nexis Academic Universe*, March 26, 2003.)

"Oracle Guide Aims to Clear Up Policies." *EWeek* (August 28, 2002). (Retrieved from *Business and Company Resource Center* November 25, 2002.)

Oracle Corporation. "Jacqueline Woods." (Retrieved from Hoover's Online, October 1, 2004.)

Overholt, Alison, ed. "Unit of One." *Fast Company*, (August 2001): 55–65.

Ovington, Mary. *Portraits in Color*. New York: Viking Press, 1927.

Oxford Large Print Dictionary. Compiled by Jayce M. Hawkins. Oxford, England: Oxford University Press, 1988.

Pace, Eric. "Mary Roebling, 89, First Woman to Head Major U.S. Bank, Dies." *New York Times*, October 27, 1994, sec. D.

Padgett, Tania. "On the Wright Track: Carver Bank CEO Succeeding in Singular Mission to Rejuvenate Fledgling Institution." *Newsday* (March 18, 2002): sec. D.

"Palm Pioneers: The PalmPilot's Parents Created One of the Greatest Hits in High Tech. What Can They Do for an Encore?" *FSB* 9, no. 8 (November 1, 1999): 52–53.

Palmer, Rosemary. *Mrs. Ebba C. Hoffman: Celebrating 40 Years for Leadership and Dedication to the Smead Manufacturing Company*. Hastings, MN: Smead Manufacturing Company, 1995.

"Pamela Aguirre: A Daughter Leads Company Synonymous with Her Father into Its Own." *Detroit News*, October 20, 1997, special section.

Papa, Mary Bader. "A Son Named Marilyn." *Corporate Report—Minnesota* 21, no. 3 (March 1990): 27–34.

Papachristou, Judith. *Women Together: A History of the Women's Movement in the United States*. New York: Knopf, 1976.

Parasuraman, Saroj, and Jeffrey H. Greenhaus. *Integrating Work and Family: Challenges and Choices for a Changing World*. Westport, CT: Quorum Books, 1997.

Parshalle, Eve. *The Kashmir Bridge—Women*. Los Angeles: Oxford University Press, 1965.

"Paula Cholmondeley: Vice President and Residential Insulation, Owens Corning." *Black Enterprise* (August 1997): 62.

Peiss, Kathy Lee. *Hope in a Jar: The Making of America's Beauty Culture*. New York: Metropolitan Books, 1998.

Pender, Kathleen. "Running with the Wolves." *San Francisco Chronicle*, December 18, 1995, sec. B.

"PepsiCo Inc. Announces Executive Appointments for New Division." Associated Press, June 7, 2002. (Retrieved from *LEXIS/NEXIS Academic Universe* October 10, 2003.)

"Pepsi's Dawn Hudson: Concentrating on What Consumers Want." *Brandweek* 39, no. 46 (December 7, 1998): 16–17.

Perkins, Jeanne. "No. 1 Career Woman." *Life* (May 12, 1947): 116–118.

Perone, Joseph R. "Pat Russo's Ascension at Lucent Makes Her Likely Candidate for CEO." *Star-Ledger*, November 21, 1999. (Retrieved from *LEXIS-NEXIS Academic Universe* January 10, 2001.)

Peterson, April. "Oprah: She Came, She Talked, She Conquered." *Biography Magazine* (March 1999): 36–44.

Peterson, Susan. *The Living Tradition of Maria Martinez*. Tokyo: Kodansha America, 1977.

———. "Smead Manufacturing Stays in the Family; Following in Her Mother's Footsteps, Smead President Takes Leadership Role." *Minneapolis Star Tribune*, October 5, 1998, metro edition, sec. D.

"Pfizer's Pep Pill." *Business Week* (January 11, 1999): 69.

"Pharmacia and Upjohn Appoints New Head of Global Business." *PR Newswire*, August 28 1997. (Retrieved from *LEXIS-NEXIS Academic Universe*, October 24, 2001.)

"Physician First." *Pharmaceutical Executive* 21, no. 4 (April 2001). (Retrieved from *Business & Company Resource Center* November 29, 2002.)

Pickford, Mary. *Sunshine and Shadow*. Garden City, NY: Doubleday, 1955.

Piersen, William D. *From Africa to America*. New York: Twayne Publishers, 1996.

Pile, Robert B. *Top Entrepreneurs and Their Businesses*. Minneapolis: Oliver Press, 1993.

Pilgrim, Kitty. "Vitria-CEO, CNNFN." CableNews Network Financial. Capital Ideas (September 22, 1999). Transcript #99092204FN-107. (Retrieved from *LEXIS-NEXIS Academic Universe* January 5, 2001.)

Pinckney, Eliza. *The Letterbook of Eliza Lucas Pinckney*. Chapel Hill, NC: University of North Carolina Press, 1972.

Pine, Carol. *Self-Made: The Stories of 12 Minnesota Entrepreneurs*. Minneapolis: Dorn Books, 1982.

Pinto, David. "CDR Names Rite Aid's Sammons Retailer of Year." *Chain Drug Review* 24, no. 1 (January 7, 2002): 3–6.

Platt, Adam. "Special Kay; *Washington Post* Publisher Katharine Graham." *Harper's Bazaar* (February 1997): 108–110.

Playing Through: The Rise of American Golf. Supplement to *American Heritage Magazine*, 2002.

Ploski, Harry A., and James Williams, eds. *The Negro Almanac: A Reference Work on the African American*. Detroit: Gale Research, 1983.

Plummer, Deborah L., ed. *Handbook of Diversity Management: Beyond Awareness to Competency Based Learning*. Lanham, MD: University Press of America, 2003.

Pogrebin, Robin. "Master of Her Own Destiny." *New York Times*, February 8, 1998, sec. 3.

Pomerantz, Joel. *Jennie and the Story of Grossinger's*. New York: Grosset and Dunlap, 1970.

Poor, Scott Robert. *Herstory*. Freeport, IL: Peekan Publications, 1990.

Popcorn, Faith. *Dictionary of the Future*. Hyperion, 2001.

———. *The Popcorn Report: Faith Popcorn on the Future of Your Company, Your World, Your Life*. New York: HarperBusiness, 1992.

Porter, Gladys L. *Three Negro Pioneers in Beauty Culture*. New York: Vantage Press, 1966.

Porter, Sylvia Field. *Sylvia Porter's New Money Book for the 80's*. Garden City, NY: Doubleday, 1979.

Post, Marjorie Merriweather. *The Reminiscences of Marjorie Merriweather Post.* New York: Oral History Research Office of Columbia University, 1964, 1975.

"A Potent Ingredient in Pepsi's Formula." *Business Week* (April 10, 2000): 180.

Potter, Jeffrey. *Men, Money and Magic: The Story of Dorothy Schiff.* New York: Coward, McCann & Geoghegan, 1976.

Powell, Bonnie Azab. "H&Q's Dynamic Duo Leads the Bank Merge Lane." *Red Herring* (November 2001). (Retrieved from *LEXIS NEXIS Academic Universe* March 23, 2003.)

Powell, J. Robin. *The Working Woman's Guide to Managing Stress.* Englewood Cliffs, NJ: Prentice Hall, 1994.

Powell, Joanna. "Oprah's Awakening: Oprah Winfrey; Interview." *Good Housekeeping* (December 1998): 113–115.

"Power Lunch." *Working Woman* (June 2001): 46–51.

Powers, David Cleary. *Great American Brands.* New York: Fairchild Publications, 1981.

Powers, Dennis M. *The Office Romance: Playing with Fire without Getting Burned.* New York: AMACOM, 1999.

President's Interagency Task Force on Women Business Owners. *The Bottom Line: Unequal Enterprise in America; Report of the President's Interagency Task Force on Women Business Owners.* Washington, DC, 1978.

Preston, Wheeler. *American Biographies.* New York: Harper & Brothers, 1940.

Pringle, Elizabeth W. Allston. *Chronicles of Chicora Wood.* New York: C. Scribner's Sons, 1922.

———. *A Woman Rice Planter.* Cambridge, MA: Belknap Press of Harvard University Press, 1961.

"Profiles: Luxury, Inc." *New Yorker* (March 31, 1934): 23–27.

Profiles in American Enterprise. BCOR 1100, Fall 2001. Boulder, CO: C.G. Press, 2001.

Proquest Newspapers. Ann Arbor, MI: Proquest Information and Learning Co., 2000–.

"Quam Named Trustee of George C. Marshall Foundation." *PR Newswire,* July 23, 1999. (Retrieved from *LEXIS/NEXIS Academic Universe,* October 4, 2003.)

"The Queen of Hearst." *Irish America Magazine,* December/January 2000, 42–44.

Quintanilla, Michael. "With *Latina,* Christy Haubegger Aims for Women Like Her— Bilingual, Bicultural and Underrated." *Los Angeles Times,* August 7, 1997, sec. E.

Ramirez, Anthony. "America's Super Minority: Asian Americans Have Wasted No Time Laying Claim to the American Dream." *Fortune* (November 24, 1986): 148–162.

Randolph, Laura B. "Oprah!" *Ebony* (July 1995): 22–24.

Ratcliff, J.D. "Bread, de Luxe." *Reader's Digest* 35 (December 1939): 102–105.

Rathbun, Elizabeth A. "Woman's Work Still Excludes Top Jobs." *Broadcasting & Cable* 128, no. 32 (August 3, 1998): 22–23.

Raven, Susan, and Alison Weir. *Women of Achievement: Thirty-Five Centuries of History.* New York: Harmony Books, 1981.

Ravenal, Harriott H. *Eliza Pinckney.* New York: Charles Scribner's Sons, 1891.

Read, Phyllis J., and Bernard L. Witlieb. *The Book of Women's Firsts: Breakthrough Achievements of Almost 1,000 American Women.* New York: Random House, 1992.

Reasons, George. *They Had a Dream.* Los Angeles: Los Angeles Times Syndicate, 1969.

Rediger, Pat. *Great African Americans in Business.* New York: Crabtree Publishing Co., 1996.

Reifert, Gail, and Eugene M. Dermody. *Women Who Fought: An American History.* Norwalk, CT: Dermody, 1978.

Reilly, Peter. *Flexibility at Work: Balancing the Interests of Employer and Employee.* Burlington, VT: Ashgate Publishing, 2001.

Reskin, Barbara F., and Patricia Roos. *Job Queues: Explaining Women's Inroads into Male Occupations.* Philadelphia: Temple University Press, 1990.

Ress, David. "Prudential Taps Executive to Lead Individual Service Unit." *Star-Ledger*, March 24, 2000. (Retrieved from *LEXIS-NEXIS Academic Universe*, October 18, 2000.)

Reynolds, Rhonda. "25 Black Women Who Have Made a Difference in Business." *Black Enterprise* (August 1994): 76–81.

Rice, Lynnette. "Fox's Corbi to Rejoin Loesch." *Hollywood Reporter*, March 10, 1999. (Retrieved from *LEXIS-NEXIS Academic Universe* November 28, 2002.)

Rich-McCoy, Lois. *Millionairess: Self-Made Women of America.* New York: Harper & Row, 1978.

Richtel, Matt. "Private Sector; Crisis Control at Warp Speed." *New York Times*, September 2, 2001, sec. 3.

Rifkin, Glenn. "Profile: Don't Ever Judge This Consultant by Her Cover." Financial Desk. *New York Times*, May 1, 1994, Sunday late edition, sec. 3.

Rigg, Cynthia. "Electronics Store Is a World Apart: J&R Grows in One Simple Location." *Crain's New York Business* (March 22, 1999): 3.

Riley, Glenda. *The Female Frontier.* Lawrence, KS: University Press of Kansas, 1988.

Riley, Glenda, and Richard W. Etulain, eds. *By Grit & Grace: Eleven Women Who Shaped the American West.* Golden, CO: Fulcrum, 1997.

Rimm, Sylvia. *See Jane Win: The Rimm Report on How 1,000 Girls Became Successful Women.* New York, Crown Publishers, 1999.

"Rising from the Ranks: Fran Keeth." *Chemical Marketing Reporter* 261, no. 19 (May 13, 2002): 29.

Risk to Riche$: Women and Entrepreneurship in America: A Special Report. Washington, DC: Institute for Enterprise Advancement, 1986.

"Rite Aid Announces Appointments of Chairman and Chief Executive Officer, and New Senior Management Team, and Engagement of New Auditors." *Business Wire*, December 6, 1999. (Retrieved from *LEXIS/NEXIS Academic Universe* October 4, 2003.)

"Rite Aid President Sets Out to Define a New Culture." *Drug Store News* 22, no. 19 (December 18, 2000): 16.

Rivera, Eddie. "Christine Liang: Going for Broke, Owner of Asia Source Inc." *Transpacific* 65 (March 1996): 78.

Roberts, Sally. "Women Making Strides in Industry Leadership, But Obstacles Remain." *Business Insurance* 34 (October 2, 2000): 11.

Robertson, W. "Ten Highest-Ranking Women in Big Business." *Fortune* 87 (April 1973): 84.

Robinson, Edward. "Fighting to Rebuild a Harlem Institution." *Fortune* (May 24, 1999): 46–47.

Robinson, Richard, comp. *U.S. Business History, 1602–1988: A Chronology.* New York: Greenwood Press, 1990.

Rochlin, Harriet. "The Amazing Adventures of a Good Woman." *Journal of the West* 12 (April 1973): 281–295.

———. "Lost Women: Nellie Cashman, Gold Digger of '77." *Ms.* (December 1974): 106–108.

Rodale, Ardath. *Gifts of the Spirit: True Stories to Renew Your Soul.* New York, NY: Daybreak Books, 1997.

Rodengen, Jeffrey L. *Evinrude, Johnson and the Legend of OMC.* Fort Lauderdale, FL: Write Stuff Syndicate, 1993.

Rogers, Marie E. *The Harlem Renaissance: An Annotated Reference Guide.* Englewood, CO: Libraries Unlimited, 1998.

Roosevelt, Eleanor, and Lorena B. Hickok. *Ladies of Courage.* New York: E.P. Putnam, 1954.

Roosevelt, Felicia Warburg. *Doers and Dowagers.* Garden City, NY: Doubleday, 1975.

Roots by the River. Mission, TX: Border Kingdom, 1978.

"Rosabeth Moss Kanter. Pioneer of Empowerment and Change Management." In *Business: The Ultimate Resource,* p. 1008–1009.

"Rosabeth Moss Kanter: The Professor as Business Leader." *Ivey Business Journal,* 66, no. 5 (May 2002): 56–64.

Rosenbloom, Jerry S., ed. *The Handbook of Employee Benefits: Design, Funding, and Administration.* 5th ed. New York: McGraw-Hill, 2001.

Rosen, Ruth. *The Lost Sisterhood: Prostitution in America, 1900–1918.* Baltimore: Johns Hopkins University Press, 1982.

Rosener, Judy B. "Ways Women Lead." *Harvard Business Review* 68, no. 6 (November/December 1990): 119–126.

Rosenfeld, Megan. "The Woman Who Has Everything: For Lillian Vernon, a Business Empire Made to Order." Style. *Washington Post,* August 22, 2000, sec. C.

Ross, Ishbel. *Charmers and Cranks: Twelve Famous American Women Who Defied the Conventions.* New York: Harper & Row, 1965.

———. *Crusaders and Crinolines: The Life and Times of Ellen Curtis Demorest and William Jennings Demorest.* New York: Harper and Row, 1963.

Ross, Marilyn. *Shameless Marketing for Brazen Hussies™.* Buena Vista, CA: Communication Creativity, 2000.

Rostky, George. "A 25-Year Love Affair." *Electronic Engineering Times* (October 30, 1997). (Retrieved from *LEXIS-NEXIS Academic Universe,* December 4, 2001.)

Roth, Daniel. "Meg Muscles eBay Uptown." *Fortune* (July 5, 1999): 81–88.

Rowbotham, Sheila. *A Century of Women: The History of Women in Britain and the United States in the Twentieth Century.* New York: Penguin, 1997.

Rowe, Megan. "When Will Women Hit the Top?" *Lodging Hospitality* 55, no. 13 (1999): 39–42.

Rowland, Mary. "The Mastermind of a Media Empire." *Working Woman* (November 1989): 114–118.

Rubin, Nancy. *American Empress: The Life and Times of Marjorie Merriweather Post.* New York: Villard Books, 1995.

Rubinstein, Helena. *My Life for Beauty.* New York: Simon and Schuster, 1964.

Rudkin, Margaret. *The Margaret Rudkin Pepperidge Farm Cookbook.* New York: Atheneum, 1963.

Russell, Jan Jarboe. *Lady Bird: A Biography of Mrs. Johnson.* New York: Scribner, 1999.

"Ruth Washington Dies; Was *Sentinel* Publisher." *Los Angeles Times,* December, 1, 1990. (Retrieved from *LEXIS-NEXIS Academic Universe* August 5, 1998.)

Rutherford, Sarah. "Organizational Cultures, Women Managers and Exclusion." *Women in Management Review* 16, no. 8 (2001): 371–382.

Ryan, Suzanne C. "Her Drive Makes News at CNBC." *Boston Globe*, December 4, 2001, sec. D.

Rynecki, David. "The Bernstein Way: There Is a Firm That Does Research Right; Inside the Best Little Shop on Wall Street." *Fortune* (June 10, 2002): 85–87.

Sachdev, Ameet. "Despite Dot-Com Downturn, Internet Dominates Business Market." *Knight-Ridder/Tribune Business News*, December 3, 2000. (Retrieved from *Business & Company Resource Center* November 29, 2002.)

"Safeway's Exec Honored by *Fortune*." *MMR* 18, no. 17 (November 26, 2001): 34.

Saito-Chung, David. "Enron's Ken Lay Focus on Finding Best People Helps Keep His Energy Company at the Top." *Investor's Business Daily*, December 12, 2000, sec. A.

Salem, Dorothy C., ed. *African American Women: A Biographical Dictionary*. New York: Garland Publishing, 1993.

Sanders, Coyne Steven. *Desilu: The Story of Lucille Ball and Desi Arnaz*. New York: Quill, 1993.

Sanford, Lynne. "20 under 30." *Working Woman* (September 1999): 44–56.

Sanger, Elizabeth. "L.I. Stocks/CMP Media Shares the Wealth." *Newsday* (September 22, 1997): 18.

Sanger, Elizabeth, James Bernstein, and Tania Padgett. "Long Island Inc." *Newsday*, April 23, 2002, sec. A.

Sansolo, Michael. "In One Woman's Opinion: Should There Be More Female Executives in the Industry? Liz Minyard Makes It Clear Why the Answer Must Be Yes!" *Progressive Grocer* 71, no. 7 (July 1993): 44–45.

Saporta, Maria. "One of the Most Unknown Secrets Blazing an Exciting Path at Mirant." *Atlanta Journal and Constitution*, May 22, 2001, home edition, sec. D.

Satzman, Darrell. "Crowning Achievement: Armed with Family Fare, Veteran TV Executive Leads New Hallmark Channel into Competitive Cable World." *Los Angeles Business Journal* 24, no. 2 (January 14, 2002): 19.

Sawyer, Arlene. "More Women Running Stores with GM Branding." *Automotive News* 77, no. 6046 (June 30, 2003): 20–25.

Schiro, Anne-Marie. "Natori Planning to Cast a Wider Net." *New York Times*, April 25, 1992, sec. 1.

Schleier, Curt. "Kraft Foods' Ann Fudge." Leaders and Success. *Investor's Business Daily*, June 7, 1999, sec. A.

Schlesinger, Arthur Meier. *New Viewpoints in American History*. New York: The Macmillan Company, 1922.

Schmitt, Eric. "Washington at Work: Pentagon Lawyer Quietly Gets Notice as a Rising Star in the Administration." *New York Times*, February 1, 1994, late edition, sec. A.

Schmuckler, Eric. "Cookin' with Gas: Nanci Mackenzie." *Working Woman* (May 1996): 45.

Schmuckler, Eric, and Harris Collingwood. "The Top 50 Women Business Owners." *Working Woman* (May 1996): 31–52.

Schneider, Dorothy, and Carl J. Schneider. *ABC-CLIO Companion to Women in the Workplace*. Santa Barbara, CA: ABC-CLIO, 1993.

"Scholarships and More for Women." *Journal of Accountancy* (November 1998): 22.

Schuch, Beverly. "Bain & Co., CNNfn." CNNfn, February 24, 1999, 8:31 PM EST. (Retrieved from *LEXIS-NEXIS Academic Universe* December 21, 2000.)

Schuyler, Nina, and Vivian Barad. "It's Not Just E-Male." *Working Woman* (June 1996): 38–49.

"Schwab Announces Organizational Changes to Reflect Company's Growing Scale, Scope and Opportunity." Financial News. *PR Newswire,* October 3, 2000. (Retrieved from *LEXIS-NEXIS Academic Universe* June 4, 2003.)

"Schwab Tech Group Focuses on Client Support." *Securities Industry News,* October 29, 2001. (Retrieved from *LEXIS-NEXIS Academic Universe,* May 20, 2002.)

Schwartz, Felice, with Jean Zimmerman. *Breaking with Tradition: Women and Work, the New Facts of Life.* New York: Warner Books, 1992.

Schwartz, Felice N. "Management Women and the New Facts of Life." *Harvard Business Review* (January-February 1989): 65–76.

Schweikart, Larry, ed. *Banking and Finance 1913–1989.* Encyclopedia of American Business History and Biography Series. New York: Facts on File, 1990.

———. *Banking and Finance to 1913.* Encyclopedia of American Business History and Biography Series. New York: Facts on File, 1990.

Scott, Matthew S., et al. "B.E. Wall St. All-Stars: From Investment Banking to Asset Management, These 50 MVPs Score Big in the Financial Markets." *Black Enterprise* 10 (October 2002): 65–76.

Segal, Troy. "America's 50 Most Powerful Women Managers." *Executive Female* 17, no. 5 (September–October 1994): 35–42.

Seger, Linda. *When Women Call the Shots.* New York: Henry Holt, 1996.

Seger, Linda, and Mollie Gregory. "Femme Toppers Blaze Trails for New Generation of Women Exex." *Variety* (August 19, 2002): 56–59.

Seglin, Jeffrey L. "Her Hopes, Her Dreams." *Folio* (October 2002): 10.

Sellers, Patricia. "Behind Every Successful Woman There is . . . a Woman." *Fortune* (October 25, 1999): 129–134.

———. "The Business of Being Oprah." *Fortune* (April 1, 2002): 50–64.

———. "The 50 Most Powerful Women in American Business." *Fortune* (October 12, 1998): 76–95.

———. "The 50 Most Powerful Women in American Business." *Fortune* (October 13, 2003): 103–110.

———. "The 50 Most Powerful Women in Business: Secrets of the Fastest-Rising Stars." *Fortune* (October 16, 2000): 131–160.

———. "Power: Do Women Really Want It?" *Fortune* (October 13, 2003): 80–100.

———. "Powerful Women: Patient But Not Passive." *Fortune* (October 15, 2001): 188–192.

———. "The Rag Trade's Reluctant Revolutionary." *Fortune* (January 5, 1987): 36–38.

———. "These Women Rule." *Fortune* (October 25, 1999): 94–126.

———. "True Grit." *Fortune* (October 14, 2002): 101–112.

———. "Women, Sex and Power." *Fortune* (August 5, 1996): 42–52.

Sellers, Patricia, and Rajiv Rao. "Don't Mess with Darla." *Fortune* (September 8, 1997): 62–65.

Seneker, Harold, et al. "Great Family Fortunes." *Forbes* (October 22, 1990): 281–298.

Seneker, Harold, dir. "The Top 500 Women-Owned Businesses." *Working Woman,* May 1998, p. 35–76.

Sergio, Lisa. *A Measure Filled: The Life of Lena Madesin Phillips Drawn from Her Autobiography*. Washington, DC: R.B. Luce, 1972.

Serwer, Andrew. "The Techie: Ann Winblad." *Money* (October 1998): 119–120.

———. "The Ultimate Investment Club." *Money* (October 1998): 107–127.

Sewell, Tim. "Women Accountants Society on Recruiting Mission." *Memphis Business Journal* 18, no. 48 (April 7, 1997): 16.

Shapero, Albert. "Have You Got What It Takes to Start Your Own Business?" *Savvy* (April 1980): 33–37.

Sharp-Zickerman, Nancy. "Billion-Dollar Club." *Working Woman* (June 2001): 54–55.

"Shattering the Glass Ceiling." *Chain Store Age* (January 2000): 57–61.

Shaw, Anita. "Celebrating 75 Years." *Soap & Cosmetics* 75, no. 10 (October 1999): 24–25.

Shepard, Richard F. "Jennie Grossinger Dies at 80 in Her Resort Home in Catskills." *New York Times Biographical Edition* (November 1972), p. 1965.

Sher, Margery Leveen, and Madeline Fried. *Childcare Options: A Workplace Initiative for the 21st Century*. Phoenix, AZ: Oryx Press, 1994.

Sherefkin, Robert. "Plastech Is Moving to Dearborn: Parts Supplier Wants to Be Close to Ford." *Crain's Detroit Business* 13 (March 17, 1997): 3.

Sherr, Lynn, and Jurate Kazickas. *The American Women's Gazetteer*. New York: Bantam Books, 1976.

Sherrow, Victoria. *A to Z of American Women Business Leaders and Entrepreneurs*. New York: Facts on File, 2002.

———. *Encyclopedia of Women and Sports*. Santa Barbara, CA: ABC-CLIO, 1996.

Shim, Soyeon, and Mary Ann Eastlick. "Characteristics of Hispanic Female Business Owners: An Exploratory Study." *Journal of Small Business Management* (July 1998): 18–34.

Shirley, Gayle C. *More Than Petticoats: Remarkable Montana Women*. Helena, MT: Falcon Publishing, 1995.

"Sibling Squabble between DeBartolos Is Ugly Power Play." *Times-Picayune*, July 4, 1999, Sports, p. C2.

Sicherman, Barbara, and Carol Hurd Green, eds. *Notable American Women: The Modern Period*. Cambridge, MA: Belknap Press of Harvard University Press, 1980.

Siebel, Thomas M. and Pat House. *Cyber Rules: Strategies for Excelling at E-Business*. New York: Currency/Doubleday, 1999.

Siebert, Muriel, with Aimee Lee Ball. *Changing the Rules: Adventures of a Wall Street Maverick*. New York: The Free Press, 2002.

Sieder, Jill Jordan. "Donna Karan's Chic Design for Success: The Fashion Entrepreneur Tailors Her Business Plan and Stitches a Global Empire Together." *U.S. News & World Report* (December 18, 1995): 59–61.

Signorelli, Nancy, ed. *Women in Communication*. Westport, CT: Greenwood Press, 1996.

Silcoff, Sean, and Andrew Wahl. "Save Teleglobe?" *Canadian Business* 72, no. 18 (November 12, 1999): 45.

Silver, A. David. *Entrepreneurial Megabucks: The 100 Greatest Entrepreneurs of the Last 25 Years*. New York: John Wiley & Sons, 1985.

Simmons, Wilson, III. *Inside Corporate America: A Guide for African Americans*. New York: Berkeley Publishing, 1996.

Simpson, Peggy. "The Revolutionary of Radio: Dorothy Brunson; Women Who Have Changed the World." *Working Woman* (August 1986): 46–48.

Sit, Mary. "The View from the Top: Orit Gadiesh Rises to Head Bain & Co. in Boston." *Boston Globe*, March 31, 1992.

Sizer, Mona D. *The King Ranch Story: Truth and Myth*. Plano, TX: Republic of Texas Press, 1999.

Smallwood, David. *Profiles of Great African Americans*. Lincolnwood, IL: Publications International, 1998.

"Smead Manufacturing Company Announces New President, CEO: Mother/Daughter Team Continues Leadership." *PR Newswire*, July 27, 1998. (Retrieved from *LEXIS-NEXIS Academic Universe* March 22, 1999.)

Smith, Dena. "Black Women Get a Shot at the Corporate Game: Golf." *Atlanta Journal and Constitution*, September 24, 1994, sec. B.

Smith, Geoffrey. "A Quick Scramble up Fidelity's Ladder." *Business Week* (February 21, 2000): 146.

Smith, Jerd. "Shattered Glass: Talented Qwest Exec Credits Federal Order for Women's Advance." *Denver Rocky Mountain News*, March 20, 2000, final business edition, sec. B.

Smith, Jessie, ed. *Epic Lives: One Hundred Black Women Who Made a Difference*. Detroit: Visible Ink Press, 1993.

Smith, Jessie, with Caper L. Jordan, Robert L. Johns, eds. *Black Firsts: 2000 Years of Extraordinary Achievement*. Detroit: Visible Ink Press, 1994.

Smith, Jessie Carney, ed. *Notable Black American Women*. Detroit: Gale Research, 1992.

Smith, Page. *Daughters of the Promised Land: Women in American History*. Boston: Little, Brown, 1970.

Sneed, Paula A. "Carpe Diem: Take Advantage of Time." *Journal of Advertising Research* 37, no. 1 (January–February 1997): 2–6.

Snodgrass, Mary Ellen. *Late Achievers: Famous People Who Succeeded Late in Life*. Englewood, CO: Libraries Unlimited, 1992.

Sochen, June. *Herstory: A Woman's View of American History*. New York: Alfred Publishing Co., 1974.

"Society Woman Turns Baker to Supply Elite with Healthful Bread." *New York Journal and American* (November 20, 1937).

"Software House International Signs On as Unicenter TNG Channel Partner." *Business Wire*, November 11, 1998. (Retrieved from *LEXIS-NEXIS Academic Universe* July 20, 2003.)

"Software Spectrum: Retail Entrepreneurs of the Year: Company Profile." *Chain Store Age Executive with Shopping Center Age* 68, no. 12 (December 1992): 43.

Solomon, Jolie. "Operation Rescue." *Working Woman* (May 1996): 54–60.

Sommerfeld, Frank. "The Inevitable Fall." *Crain's New York Business* (May 23, 1988).

Sontag, Deborah. "A 'Queen' in Lonely Seclusion Is Now a Lonely Widow." *New York Times*, January 12, 1997, sec. 1.

"The Southern California Woman: On the Job; Making It; The Personal Stories of Six Women Who Have Found Success in Individual Ways; Laura Balverde-Sanchez; Sausage Entrepreneur." *Los Angeles Times*, December 4, 1988, Sunday magazine, home edition, p. 32.

"Southern Company Names Fuller Executive Vice President." *PR Newswire*, November 4, 1999. Financial News. (Retrieved from *LEXIS-NEXIS Universe* October 19, 2001.)

Sova, Dawn B. *Women in Hollywood: From Vamp to Studio Head.* New York: Fromm International, 1998.

Sparkes, Boyden, and Samuel Taylor Moore. *Hetty Green: The Witch of Wall Street.* Garden City, NY: Doubleday, Doran, 1930.

Spawn, Carol and Willman. "The Aitken Shop: Identification of an Eighteenth-Century Bindery and Its Tools." *Papers of the Bibliographical Society of America* (Fourth Quarter, 1963).

"Special Report: Katharine Graham, 1917–2001." *Newsweek* (July 30, 2001): 42–64.

Sperling, Nicole. "Jeanne Jackson Says Walmart.com is Not Damaged Goods." *Red Herring* (December 19, 2000): 28–29.

Spivey, Richard L. *Maria.* 2nd ed. Flagstaff, AZ: Northland Publishers, 1989.

Spradling, Mary Mace, ed. *In Black and White: A Guide to Magazine Articles, Newspaper Articles and Books Concerning More Than 15,000 Black Individuals and Groups.* Detroit: Gale Research, 1971–.

Sprague, Peg. "Weighing Your Childcare Options." *HR Focus* 75, no. 4 (April 1998): 13–14.

Spruill, Julia Cherry. "Mistress Margaret Brent, Spinster." *Maryland Historical Magazine* (December 1934): 259–268.

Sroge, Maxwell. *The United States Mail Order Industry.* 2nd ed. Lincolnwood, IL: NTC Business Books, 1994.

"Stacey Snider Has Been Appointed Co-President, Production for Universal Pictures." *PR Newswire*, December 5, 1996. Financial News. (Retrieved from *LEXIS-NEXIS Academic Universe* October 16, 2000.)

Stage, Sarah. *Female Complaints.* New York: W.W. Norton, 1981.

Stanley, Allessandra. "The Oxygen TV Channel Is Bowing to Tastes." *New York Times*, February 25, 2002, sec. C.

Stechert, Kathryn B. "Raising Your Power Consciousness." *Working Woman* (April 1986). (Retrieved from *LEXIS/NEXIS Academic Universe* June 16, 1999.)

Steel, Dawn. *They Can Kill You—But They Can't Eat You: Lessons from the Front.* New York: Pocket Books, 1993.

Stein, Leon, ed. *Lives to Remember.* New York: Arno Press, 1974.

Steinem, Gloria. *Outrageous Acts and Everyday Rebellions.* 2nd ed. New York: H. Holt, 1995. First published 1983 by Holt, Rinehart.

Steiner, Rupert. "Briton Who Took Trading Online." *Sunday Times*, December 2, 2001. Business Section. (Retrieved from *LEXIS-NEXIS Academic Universe*, February 22, 2002.)

Stephens, Autumn. *Wild Women: Crusaders, Curmudgeons, and Completely Corsetless Ladies in the Otherwise Virtuous Victorian Era.* Berkeley, CA: Conari Press, 1992.

Stern, Madeleine B. *Purple Passage: The Life of Mrs. Frank Leslie.* Norman, OK: University of Oklahoma Press, 1953.

———. *We the Women: Career Firsts of Nineteenth-Century America.* New York: Schulte, 1962.

Stevenson, Richard W. "Inside the Nation's Best-Run S & L." Financial Desk. *New York Times*, September 9, 1990, late edition, sec. 3.

Stewart, Martha. "The Importance of Being Myself." *Cosmopolitan*, (July 1997): 34.

"Stories Along the Trail: The Cherokee 'Trail of Tears' Eliza Missouri Bushyhead." In www.rosecity.net/tears/trail/eliza. (Retrieved October 7, 2004.)

Stirpe, Amanda. "Mulcahy's Message: Persistence Pays." *Computer Reseller News* (March 27, 2000): 59.

Stoddard, Hope. *Famous American Women*. New York: Crowell, 1970.

Strausse, Flora. *Margaret Haughery: Bread Woman of New Orleans*. New York: P.J. Kenedy, 1961.

Strom, Sharon Hartman. *Beyond the Typewriter: Gender, Class, and the Origins of Modern Office Work, 1900–1930*. Urbana, IL: University of Illinois Press, 1992.

Strom, Stephanie. "Fashion Avenue's $100 Million Woman." *New York Times Biographical Service* 23 (May 1992): 646–648.

Strout, Erin, and Jennifer Gilbert. "Shrinking Violets." *Sales & Marketing Management* 155, no. 5 (May 2003): 46–52.

Struggs, Callie Foster. *Women in Contemporary Business*. Mesquite, AZ: Ide House, 1982.

Suggs, Welch. "Gas Trader Fits Service to Customers' Needs." *Dallas Business Journal* 20, no. 44 (July 4, 1997): B1–B3.

Suplee, Curt. "Nancy Drew's Story: Recalling the Woman behind the Adventurer; The Woman behind Nancy Drew." *Washington Post*, March 30, 1982, sec. B.

"Sutherland Lumber Company L.P." (Retrieved from *Business & Company Resource Center*, June 1, 2003.)

Sutter, Pam. "Joyce Raley Teel." *Sacramento Bee*, June 6, 1999, metro final edition, sec. D.

Sutton, Carlotte Decker and Kris K. Moore. "Executive Women—20 Years Later." *Harvard Business Review* 63, no. 5 (September/October 1985): 42–66.

Swartz, Mimi, with Sherron Watkins. *Power Failure: The Inside Story of the Collapse of Enron*. New York: Doubleday, 2003.

Sweeney, Patricia E. *Biographies of American Women: An Annotated Bibibliography*. Santa Barbara, CA: ABC-CLIO, 1990.

Swisher, Kara. *AOL.com: How Steve Case Beat Bill Gates, Nailed the Netheads, and Made Millions in the War for the Web*. New York: Times Books, 1998.

Symonds, William C., et al. "Sex on the Job." *Business Week* (February 16, 1998): 30–31.

Tait, Nikki. "Matriarch of Good Relations: Profile Marilyn Carlson Nelson." Inside Track, *Financial Times* (London), June 28, 1999, p. 13.

Talley, Karen. "Chase CFO Puts the Emphasis on Productivity; Says Units That Do Not Make Money Risk Losing Their Funding." *American Banker* (January 20, 1999): 26.

———. "Hidden Asset: Citigroup's Little-Known CFO." *American Banker* (August 4, 1999): 3.

Tannen, Deborah. *Talking from 9 to 5: How Women's and Men's Conversational Styles Affect Who Gets Heard, Who Gets Credit, and What Gets Done at Work*. New York: Morrow, 1994.

Tannen, Mary. "Hazel Bishop, 92, An Innovator Who Made Lipstick Kissproof." *New York Times*, December 12, 1998, sec. B.

Tanner, John. *A Narrative of the Captivity and Adventures of John Tanner during Thirty Years' Residence among the Indians in the Interior of North America*, ed. Edwin James. Minneapolis: Ross and Haines, 1956.

Tardiff, Joseph C., and L. Mpho Mabunda, eds. *Dictionary of Hispanic Biography*. New York: Gale Research, 1996.

Taub, Harold Jaediker. *Waldorf-in-the-Catskills; The Grossinger Legend*. New York: Sterling Publishing, 1952.

Taves, Isabella. *Successful Women and How They Obtained Success*. New York: E.P. Dutton & Co., 1945.

Taylor, Chris. "Myrtle Potter: COO of Genentech." *Time* (December 2, 2002): 67.

Taylor, Russel R. *Exceptional Entrepreneurial Women: Strategies for Success*. New York: Quorum Books, 1988.

Telgen, Diane, and Jim Kamp, eds. *Latinas!: Women of Achievement*. Detroit: Visible Ink Press, 1996.

———. *Notable Hispanic American Women*. Detroit: Gale Research, 1993.

"Telocity Names Former Sprint Executive Patti Manuel as CEO and President." *Business Wire*, June 1, 1999. (Retrieved from *LEXIS-NEXIS Academic Universe* January 5, 2001.)

"The Ten Most Important Women in Tech." *Working Woman* (September 1997): 54–59.

"Teresa Beck Is Elected to Board of Lexmark International." *Business Wire*, April 27, 2000. (Retrieved from *LEXIS-NEXIS Academic Universe* April 17, 2002.)

"Teresa Beck Joins Textron's Board." *Business Wire*, October 28, 1996. (Retrieved from *LEXIS-NEXIS Academic Universe* April 5, 1999.)

Texeira, Erin. "A Delicate Balance." *Working Mother* (June/July 2003): 62–70, 117–118.

Thayer, Warren. "The Story of Rose Totino: From Pauper to Pizza Queen." *Frozen Food Age* 42, no. 7 (February 1994): 1, 34–35.

Thom, Mary. *Inside Ms*. New York: Henry Holt and Company, 1997.

Thomas, Isaiah. *History of Printing in America: With a Biography of Printers & an Account of Newspapers*, ed. Marcus A. McCorison from the 2nd ed. New York: Weathervane Books, 1970. First published 1910.

Thomas-Graham, Pamela. *A Touch of Crimson*. New York: Simon & Schuster, 1998.

Thompson, Anne. "A League of Her Own: Columbia Hits 'Panic Room,' 'Spider-Man' and 'MIB II' Indicate Savvy Topper's Smart Choices." *Variety* (August 19, 2002): A2–A6.

Thompson, Stephanie. "Mary Kay Haben." *Brandweek* 38, no. 38 (1997 Supplement: SuperBrands 98): 80–84.

Thorp, Margaret Farrand. *Female Persuasion: Six Strong-Minded Women*. New Haven, CT: Yale University Press, 1949.

Thrapp, Dan L. *Encyclopedia of Frontier Biography*. 3 vols. Glendale, CA: Arthur H. Clark, 1988.

Tichy, Noel. *The Cycle of Leadership*. New York: HarperBusiness, 2002.

Tifft, Susan E., and Janet Bamford. "Board Gains; Corporate Boards of Directors." *Working Woman* (February 1994). (Retrieved from *LEXIS/NEXIS Academic Universe*, November 11, 1998.)

Tode, Chantal. "Alberto-Culver: Doing It Quietly; Health and Beauty Aids Report." *WWD* (October 24, 1997): 8–9.

Toops, Diane. "On a Roll: Candymakers Ellen and Melvin Gordon, Tootsie Roll's Leaders, Keep Brand on Track in Its 100th Year." *Food Processing* 57, no. 12 (December 1996): 22–23.

"The Top 500 Women-Owned Businesses" *Working Woman* (May 1998): 35–80.

"Top 20 Visionaries." *VARBusiness* (November 26, 2001): 45.

"The Top 25 Managers: The Top Entrepreneurs." *Business Week* (January 8, 2001): 82.

"Toy Len Goon, 101; Won '52 Mother of the Year Honor." *Boston Globe,* May 30, 1993, city edition.

Tracey, William R., ed. *The Human Resources Glossary.* 2nd ed. Boca Raton, FL: St. Lucie Press, 1998.

Traiman, Steve. "J&R Music World's 30th Anniversary: A New York City Mainstay." *Billboard* (October 27, 2001). (Retrieved from *LEXIS-NEXIS Academic Universe* April 23, 2002.)

Travers, Bridget, and Jeffrey Muhr, eds. *World of Invention.* Detroit: Gale Research, 1994.

Tucker, Randy. "Cornbelt CEO Makes List for Third Time." *Omaha World Herald,* April 23, 1996.

Tunley, Roul. "The Glittering Widow of Trenton, N.J." *Saturday Evening Post* (May 21, 1960): 23–25, 72.

"Turning Points: Frank Talk from Top Execs about the Moments That Changed Their Careers Forever." *Executive Female* 20, no. 4 (July–August 1997): 48–54.

"The 25 Top Executives of the Year." *Business Week* (January 11, 1999): 58–64.

Twitchell, Ralph Emerson. *Old Santa Fe: The Story of New Mexico's Ancient Capital.* Santa Fe: Santa Fe New Mexican Publishing, 1925.

Tyler, Francine Thistle. "Successful Exec Makes Every Moment Count." *Seattle Times,* October 3, 1994, sec. E.

Tyrkus, Michael J., ed. *Gay and Lesbian Biography.* Detroit: St. James Press, 1997.

Tyson, Laura D'Andrea. "Voices." *Working Woman* (September 2001): 54.

Ubinas, Helen. "Bringing Up Her Baby: Publisher Finds Growing Niche for *Latina Magazine.*" *Hartford Courant,* June 26, 1998, sec. F.

Uglow, Jennifer, comp. and ed. *Continuum Dictionary of Women's Biography,* exp. ed. New York: Continuum, 1989

———. *International Dictionary of Women's Biography.* New York: Macmillan, 1982. First published as *The Macmillan Dictionary of Women's Biography.*

Ulrich, Laurel Thatcher. *Good Wives: Image and Reality in the Lives of Women in Northern New England, 1650–1750.* New York: Alfred A. Knopf, 1982.

Underhill, Lois Beachy. *The Woman Who Ran for President: The Many Lives of Victoria Woodhull.* Bridgehampton, NY: Bridge Works Publishing, 1995.

"United Healthcare Announces Executive Team to Lead Retiree and Senior Services Company." *PR Newswire,* April 22, 1998. (Retrieved from *LEXIS/NEXIS Academic Universe,* October 4, 2003.)

U.S. Bureau of the Census. *1972 Economic Census.* Washington, DC, 1972.

U.S. Bureau of the Census. *1997 Economic Census.* Washington, DC, 1997.

U.S. Bureau of the Census, *Survey of Minority-owned Business Enterprises.* Washington, DC: Government Printing Office, 1994.

U.S. Federal Glass Ceiling Commission. *Good for Business: Making Full Use of the Nation's Human Capital; The Environmental Scan: A Fact-Finding Report of the Federal Glass Ceiling Commission.* Washington, DC, 1995.

———. *A Solid Investment: Making Full Use of the Nation's Human Capital; Recommendations of the Federal Glass Ceiling Commission.* Washington, DC, 1995.

U.S. Government Manual. Washington, DC: U.S. Government Printing Office, 1997/98.

Usborne, David. "She's Got It Made: Abby Cohen Lives in Queens and Goes to Work on a Bus, But She's the Wonderwoman of Wall Street." *The Independent* (March 21, 1999): 1–2.

Vare, Ethlie Ann, and Greg Ptacek. *Mothers of Invention: From the Bra to the Bomb; Forgotten Women and Their Unforgettable Ideas.* New York: Morrow, 1988.

———. *Patently Female: From AZT to TV Dinners; Stories of Woman Inventors and Their Breakthrough Ideas.* New York: John Wiley & Sons, 2002.

Varnell, Jeanne. *Women of Consequence: The Colorado Women's Hall of Fame.* Boulder, CO: Johnson Books, 1999.

Veiders, Christina, Micheal Garry, Stephanie Loughran. "SN's Power 50 (Part Two) Wal-Mart." *Supermarket News* (July 21, 2003): 22.

Verbanas, Patti. "Using Mergers as a Career Stepping Stone." *Corporate Cashflow Magazine* 16, no. 12 (December 2995): 48.

"Verizon Communications Names Doreen A. Toben Chief Financial Officer." *PR Newswire*, April 30, 2002. (Retrieved from *LEXIS-NEXIS Academic Universe* October 3, 2002.)

Vernon, Lillian. *An Eye for Winners: How I Built One of America's Great Businesses— And So Can You.* New York: HarperBusiness, 1997.

"Verses from a Java Gospel." *eWeek.* (July 10, 2000): 42.

VNR's Encyclopedia of Hospitality and Tourism. New York: Van Nostrand Reinhold, 1993.

Waggoner, Walter H. "Hope Schary, Leader in Textiles Designing and Women's Rights." *New York Times*, May 28, 1981, late city edition, sec. D.

Wajcman, Judy. *Managing Like a Man: Women and Men in Corporate Management.* University Park, PA: Pennsylvania State University Press, 1998.

"Wake Up and Smell the Estrogen: Ms Magazine Is Back on the Newsstands Today; Independent and Women-Owned by Liberty Media for Women, LLC." *PR Newswire*, March 30, 1999. (Retrieved from *LEXIS-NEXIS Academic Universe* May 22, 2000.)

Waldo, Ruth. "Invention—the Essence of Advertising." *J. Walter Thompson News Bulletin* (December 1929): 9–12.

Walker, Juliet, ed. *Encyclopedia of African American Business History.* Westport, CT: Greenwood Press, 1999.

Walker, Juliet E. K. *The History of Black Business in America: Capitalism, Race, Entrepreneurship.* New York: MacMillan Library Reference USA, 1998.

Walkup, Carolyn. "Women in Leadership: The Battle to Advance Continues." *Restaurant News* 34, no. 24 (2000): 112.

Wall Street Journal Almanac. New York: Ballantine Books, 1998.

Wallace, Claudia. "The Case for Staying Home." *Time* (March 22, 2004): 51–59.

Walsh, Mary Williams. "For Women at the Top, Something Is Missing: Social, Wifely Support." *New York Times*, June 24, 2001. (Retrieved from *Proquest* December 24, 2002.)

Warren, Ruth. *Pictorial History of Women in America.* New York: Crown Publishers, 1975.

Wascoe, Dan, Jr. "Ebba C. Hoffman, Company Head, Dies." *Minneapolis Star Tribune*, February 8, 1999, metro edition, sec. B.

Washburn, Charles. *Come into My Parlor: A Biography of the Aristocratic Everleigh Sisters of Chicago.* New York: Bridgehead Books, 1934.

Washburn, Robert C. *The Life and Times of Lydia Pinkham*. New York: G.P. Putnam's Sons, 1931.

Watson, Emmett. "Dorothy Bullitt Placed KING-TV in a Class by Itself." *Seattle Times*, August 26, 1990, final edition, sec. B.

Watson, Lloyd. "Chevron Exec is Industry's Top Female Operating Chief." *San Francisco Chronicle*, August 11, 1993, p. B3.

Watson, Lucinda. *How They Achieved: Stories of Personal and Business Success*. New York: John Wiley & Sons, 2000.

Ways, Max. "A Hall of Fame for Business Leadership." *Fortune* (January 1975): 64–73.

Weber, Joseph. "I Am Intense, Aggressive, and Hard-Charging." *Business Week* (April 30, 1990): 58–59.

"WebSmart." *Business Week* (September 29, 2003): 122.

Weil, Dan. "B of A Products Chief Seeks to Orchestrate Offering." *American Banker* 164 (September 2, 1999): 1.

Weiland, Jeanne. "Joyce Chen." *Nation's Restaurant News* 30 (February 1996): 56.

Weimer, De'Ann. "Daughter Knows Best." *Business Week* (April 19, 1999): 132–133.

Weinraub, Bernard. "Dawn Steel Muses from the Top of Hollywood's Heap." *New York Times*, August 30, 1993, sec. C.

Wells, Judy. "Experience Still Does the Talking: EVE Awards Speaker Has Been There, Done That." *Florida Times-Union*, June 8, 1997, sec. F.

Wells, Melanie. "Ad Exec in Business for Image." Money. *USA Today*, May 14, 1996, sec. B.

Wells, Sandra J. *Women Entrepreneurs: Developing Leadership for Success*. New York: Garland Publishing, 1998.

Wendt, Ann C., Joseph W. Coleman, William M. Slonaker. "Employment Discrimination Is Sex-Blind." *Advanced Management Journal* 58, no. 2 (Spring 1993): 28–34.

West, Diane. "HBA's 'Woman of the Year' Remembers Her Retail Pharmacy Roots." *Drug Store News* 23, no. 9 (July 23, 2001): 15.

Wharton, Carla S. *Framing a Domain for Work and Family: A Study of Women in Residential Real Estate Sales Work*. Lanham, MD: Lexington Books, 2002.

Wheeler, Carol. "She Thinks Like a CEO (Because She Is One)." *Executive Female* 19, no. 5 (September–October 1996): 32–35.

Whelehan, Patricia. *An Anthropological Perspective on Prostitution: The World's Oldest Profession*. Lewiston, NY: Edwin Mellen Press, 2001.

White, Julia. "Woman Spirit, Sally Ainse." in http://www.meyna.com/oneida.html. (Retrieved October 7, 2004.)

White, Margaret Blackburn. "The Invisible Minority: American Indian Women in Corporate America." *Diversity Factor* 7, no. 4 (Summer 1999): 2–8.

White, Nicola, and Ian Griffiths, ed. *The Fashion Business: Theory, Practice, Image*. Oxford; New York: Berg, 2000.

Whitely, Sharon, et al. *The Old Girls' Network: Insider Advice for Women Building Businesses*. New York: Basic Books, 2003.

Whitfield, Eileen. *Pickford: The Woman Who Made Hollywood*. Lexington, KY: University Press of Kentucky, 1997.

Whitman, Alden. *Obituary Book*. New York: Stein and Day, 1971.

"Whitman, Meg." *Current Biography* (February 2000): 86–91.

Whitney, Elizabeth. "Sylvia Porter: Living Legend Becomes an Institution." *St. Petersburg Times*, February 26, 1989, Sunday city edition, sec. I.

Who's Who in America. Chicago: Marquis Who's Who, 1900–.

Who's Who in Finance and Industry. Chicago: Marquis Who's Who, 1972/73–.

Widmer, Mary Lou. *Margaret, Friend of Orphans*. Gretna, LA: Pelican, 1996.

Wilkinson, Stephan. "The Practical Genius of Penny Candy." *Working Woman* (April 1989): 98–102.

Willard, Frances Elizabeth, and Mary A. Livermore, eds. *American Women: Fifteen Hundred Biographies with Over 1,400 Portraits; A Comprehensive Encyclopedia of the Lives and Achievements of American Women during the Nineteenth Century*. Detroit: Gale Research, 1973–.

Williams, Lena. "Nell Donnelly Reed, 102, Pioneer in Manufacture of Women's Attire." *New York Times*, September 10, 1991, sec. B.

Williams, Selma R. *Demeter's Daughters: The Women Who Founded America, 1587–1787*. New York: Atheneum, 1976.

Williamson, Tammy. "ComEd Spokeswoman Near the Center of Power." *Chicago Sun-Times*, December 18, 2001.

Willis, Clint. "The 10 Most Admired Women Managers in America." *Working Woman* (December 1993): 44–56.

Wilson Business Abstracts. Bronx, NY: H.W. Wilson, 1986–.

Wilson, Marianne. "Thinking Big." *Chain Store Age* (July 1, 2001): 47.

Wilson, Vincent, Jr. *The Book of Distinguished American Women*. Brookeville, MD: American Research Associates, 1992.

Winblad, Ann L., et al. *Object-Oriented Software*. Reading, MA: Addison-Wesley, 1990.

Winegarten, Ruthe. *Governor Ann Richards and Other Texas Women: From Indians to Astronauts*. 2nd ed. Austin, TX: Eakin Press, 1993.

Winkleman, Michael, and Mary Huhn. "The Seventh Annual Women's Survey." *Adweek Western Advertising News* 39, no. 23 (June 5, 1989): w4–9.

Winters, Rebecca. "Who Needs an MBA?" *Time* (May 17, 1999): 92A–99A.

Wittke, Carl Frederick. *The German-Language Press in America*. Lexington, KY: University of Kentucky Press, 1957.

Wolcott, Robert Wilson. *Woman in Steel: Rebecca Lukens (1794–1854)*. Princeton, NJ: Princeton University Press, Newcomen Society of England, American Branch, 1948.

"Woman Chemist Hits Lipstick Jackpot." *Business Week* (March 17, 1951): 41–45.

Women and the MBA: Gateway to Opportunity. New York: Catalyst, 2000.

"Women in Business: III." *Fortune* (September 1935): 81–83, 86, 88, 91.

Women in the Space Program; Daughters as Caregivers; The Mommy Track; The Rainy Season. Audiocassette. Troy, NY: Sage Colleges, WAMC Public Radio, 1989.

"Women Lag in Technology & Engineering: New Report Challenges Educators, Policy Makers and Industry Executives to Advance Women and Girls." *The Progressive Woman* (Holiday, 2001): 27–32.

"Women Move Up in Manufacturing: Forget Those Images of U.S. Factories as Male-Dominated and Meet Some Unsung Women behind a Lot of the Surging Productivity." *Fortune* (May 15, 2000). (Retrieved from *Business & Company Resource Center* August 24, 2002.)

Women of Color Executives: Their Voices, Their Journeys. New York: Catalyst, 2001.

Women of Color in Corporate Management: Three Years Later. New York: Catalyst, 2002.

"Women Still a Long Way from Achieving Parity in the Workplace with Male Counterparts." *PR Newswire*, May 19, 2003. (Retrieved from *LEXIS-NEXIS Academic Universe* March 22, 2004.)

"Women to Watch: *Ad Age* Special Report." *Advertising Age* 68 (February 3, 1997): S1–S14.

Women's History 1, no. 1, 1995.

Woo, Suzanne. *On Course for Business: Women and Golf.* New York: John Wiley & Sons, 2002.

Wood, Donna, ed. *Research Centers Directory.* Detroit: Gale Group, 2000.

Wood, James Playsted. *Of Lasting Interest: The Story of the Reader's Digest.* Garden City, NY: Doubleday, 1958.

Woodward, Chris. "There's Something Familiar about Kelleher's Successors." Money. *USA Today*, March 20, 2001, final edition, sec. B.

Woodward, Helen Beal. *The Bold Women.* New York: Farrar, Straus, and Young, 1953.

Woolley, Jessie T. "An Interview with Ann Fudge." *Careers and the MBA* 30, no. 2 (Fall 1998): 60–62.

World Almanac and Book of Facts. New York: Newspaper Enterprise Association, 1998.

World Almanac Biographical Dictionary. New York: World Almanac, 1990.

Woyski, Margaret S. "Women and Mining in the Old West." *Journal of the West* 20 (April 1981): 38–47.

Wright, Barbara. "How to Beat Out Big-Name Competition." *Working Woman* (May 1988): 55–57.

Wright, Conrad Edick, and Katheryn P. Viens, eds. *Entrepreneurs: The Boston Business Community, 1700–1850.* Boston: Massachusetts Historical Society, 1997.

Wright, William. *Heiress: The Rich Life of Marjorie Merriweather Post.* Washington, DC: New Republic Books, 1978.

www.abwa.org. (Retrieved December 15, 2003.)

www.aflcio.org/women. (Retrieved December 15, 2003.)

www.aimd.org. (Retrieved January 4, 2004.)

www.americangirl.com. (Retrieved October 8, 2004.)

www.aswa.org. (Retrieved December 15, 2003.)

www.avon.com. (Retrieved December 15, 2003.)

www.awed.org. (Retrieved April 20, 2004.)

www.awib.org. (Retrieved April 27, 2001.)

www.charmingshoppes.com. (Retrieved December 15, 2003.)

www.corp.aol.com/whoweare/who-bios/brandt.html. (Retrieved December 15, 2003.)

www.DistinguishedWomen.com/biographies/musgrove-m.html. (Retrieved May 11, 2000.)

www.dsa.org. (Retrieved October 8, 2004.)

www.earlyradiohistory.us. (Retrieved December 15, 2003.)

www.eeoc.gov. (Retrieved January 24, 2004.)

www.efwa.org. (Retrieved December 15, 2003.)

www.enterprisingwomenexhibit.org. (Retrieved April 29, 2004.)

www.fanniemae.com/mews/media/executives/j_gorelick.html. (Retrieved December 15, 2003.)

www.fwi.org. (Retrieved February 8, 2004.)

www.girlgeeks.com/innergeek/inspiringwomen/morgan.html. (Retrieved December 15, 2003.)

www.goldenrule.com. (Retrieved December 15, 2003.)

www.greatwomen.org. (Retrieved December 15, 2003.)

www.handspring.com. (Retrieved December 15, 2003.)

www.hftp.org. (Retrieved October 8, 2004.)

www.imdiversity.com. (Retrieved December 11, 2003.)

www.indiversity.com/villages/woman/article-ID=1274 (Retrieved October 8, 2004.)

www.ja.org/nbhof. (Retrieved December 15, 2003.)

www.janr.com. (Retrieved December 15, 2003.)

www.jnj.com. (Retrieved December 15, 2003.)

www.journeywoman.com. (Retrieved March 1, 2004.)

www.lexisnexis.com/academic/. (Retrieved December 10, 2003.)

www.lexisnexis.com/academic/2upa/aph/pcmstatuswomen.asp. (Retrieved October 8, 2004.)

www.longaberger.com. (Retrieved December 15, 2003.)

www.marthastewart.com. (Retrieved September 7, 2001.)

www.nafe.com. (Retrieved April 30, 2004.)

www.nasphq.com. (Retrieved February 20, 2004.)

www.nawbo.org. (Retrieved February 20, 2004.)

www.ncbw.org/aboutus/biojewell2.html. (Retrieved February 15, 2003.)

www.networkofexecutivewomen.com. (Retrieved October 8, 2004.)

www.nfwbo.org. (Retrieved April 28, 2004.)

www.9to5.org. (Retrieved March 12, 2004.)

www.now.org. (Retrieved March 12, 2004.)

www.onlinewbc.gov. (Retrieved March 17, 2004.)

www.oprah.com. (Retrieved December 15, 2003.)

www.oracle.com. (Retrieved December 15, 2003.)

www.pcconnection.com. (Retrieved December 15, 2003.)

www.printpack.com. (Retrieved December 15, 2003.)

www.radio-one.com. (Retrieved December 15, 2003.)

www.rosietheriveter.org. (Retrieved October 8, 2004.)

www.sba.gov. (Retrieved March 27, 2004.)

www.sec.gov. (Retrieved December 15, 2003.)

www.shi.com. (Retrieved December 15, 2003.)

www.sutherlandlumber.com

www.thehistorynet.com/Women'sHistory. (Retrieved December 14, 2002.)

www.tvhistory.tv. (Retrieved December 15, 2003.)

www.vitria.com/home/management.html. (Retrieved December 15, 2003.)

www.wcr.org. (Retrieved October 8, 2004.)

www.wimonline.org. (Retrieved February 20, 2004.)

www.wnet.bz. (Retrieved March 27, 2004.)

www.women-21.gov. (Retrieved March 27, 2004.)

www.womenbiz.gov. (Retrieved March 27, 2004.)

www.womenintheeconomy.org. (Retrieved October 8, 2004.)

www.womensalliance.org. (Retrieved December 15, 2003.)

Wyatt, Edward. "Mutual Funds; Making Way for Fidelity's Heir Apparent." *New York Times*, February 15, 1998, late edition, sec. 3.

Wyckoff, Peter. "Queen Midas: Hetty Robinson Green." *New England Quarterly* 23, no. 2 (June 1950): 147–171.

Wymard, Ellie. *Conversations with Uncommon Women.* New York: AMACOM, 1999.

Yost, Edna. *Famous American Pioneering Women.* New York: Dodd, Mead, 1961.

———. *Frank and Lillian Gilbreth, Partners for Life.* New Brunswick, NJ: Rutgers University Press, 1949.

Zachary, Mary-Kathryn. "FMLA Poses Many Issues for Companies." *Supervision* 60, no. 7 (July 1999): 23–27.

Zamora, Dulce. "Gail Berman: TV Topper Choreographs Own Fox Trot." *Variety* (June 2, 2003): A10.

Zanjani, Sally. *A Mine of Her Own: Women Prospectors in the American West, 1850–1950.* Lincoln, NE: University of Nebraska Press, 1997.

Zawacki, Michael. "Aces not Faces." *Inside Business* (June 2000): 38–42.

Zellner, Wendy. "Holding Steady." *Business Week* (February 2, 2003): 66.

Zia, Helen. *Notable Asian Americans.* Detroit: Gale Press, 1995.

Zierdt-Warshaw, Linda, Alan Winkler, and Leonard Bernstein. *American Women in Technology.* Santa Barbara, CA: ABC-CLIO, 2000.

Zilboorg, Caroline, ed. *Women's Firsts.* Detroit: Gale Research, 1997.

Zinn, Maxine Baca, and Bonnie Thornton Dill. *Women of Color in U.S. Society.* Philadelphia: Temple University Press, 1994.

Zuber, Amy. "Time Inc.'s *People* Person." *Folio: The Magazine for Magazine Management* 23, no. 21 (December 15, 1994): 70–72.

Index

About the Author

CAROL H. KRISMANN is head of the William M. White Business Library at the University of Colorado, Boulder. She is the author of *Quality Control in Business and Industry: A Bibliography* (1990), and her work has appeared in such journals as *College & Research Libraries* and *Journal of Academic Librarianship*.